The Guinness Encyclopedia of
Signs & Symbols

John Foley

GUINNESS PUBLISHING

Editor Beatrice Frei
Design and Layout Michael Morey
Illustrations Victoria Kropacsy and Paul Finn

First published in 1993 by Guinness Publishing Ltd.
33 London Road, Enfield, Middlesex.

Typeset in Meridien by Ace Filmsetting Ltd, Frome, Somerset
Printed and bound in Great Britain by The Bath Press, Bath

A catalogue record for this book is available from the British Library.

ISBN 0–85112–945–5

Contents

Preface

Or so the Chinese philosopher Confucius is reputed to have said. Exactly what he meant of course, in the context of his own times (c. 551–479 BC), is open to debate. Well, whatever... there is no doubt that throughout man's history, signs and symbols have been used to engage our powers of recognition, assimilation, and understanding, to guide, warn, direct, and inform us.

Signs and symbols rule the world – not words nor laws...

This book is about some of these signs and symbols, and about the origins and derivations of many other kinds: from the letter symbols you are now reading and the number symbols with which the book is paginated, to the signs and symbols, for example in religion, art and science, which convey a deeper meaning.

The information is drawn from a wide variety of sources: in addition to dictionaries and encyclopaedias, many specialist reference books, literary and pictorial works, both ancient and modern, have been consulted. The anecdotes and quotations have been chosen as illustrative and entertaining supplements to the text. I would welcome suggestions for any other anecdotes, quotes or, indeed, sources which may seem apposite. Equally, I would be pleased to hear of alternative origins of the many kinds of signs and symbols within these pages, and of additional interpretations (of which, doubtless, there will still be a few).

I am indebted to the many friends and colleagues who have advised and encouraged me in the preparation of this book, and to the companies and organisations who have generously supplied information and given permission to reproduce their badges, logos and trademarks.

Very special thanks are due to Leslie Dunkling, without whose encouragement and enthusiasm for the initial serendipitous and later detailed research, this book would not have been possible; to Victoria Kropacsy, for her excellent work on the illustrations; to Clare Howse, Ruth Graham, Ken Johnson, and Hilary Neville; to Honor Head, who first proposed the subject; and most importantly to Béatrice Frei for her unfailingly good-humoured patience and guidance, both practical and symbolic!

John Foley

Cross-referencing In the text an asterisk (*) after a word denotes that additional information relating to the word may be found by referring to the index; the note 'see p.xx' after a word indicates specific or more detailed information regarding the subject.

Acknowledgements

The following have been reproduced by kind permission: The Royal Arms: Her Majesty the Queen; the Kitemark and Safety Mark: British Standards Institution; His Master's Voice Trade Mark: EMI Records Ltd; the badge of the 'Desert Rats' and the Pegasus badge of the Airborne Forces, © British Crown copyright 1988/MOD: Controller of Her Britannic Majesty's Stationery Office.

The majority of the signs and symbols in the book have been specially drawn by Victoria Kropacsy. In addition, the author and publishers are grateful to the following individuals and organisations for providing information and/or artwork: Alfa Romeo (GB), Slough; Anthony Bowles (for music: key signatures); Apple Computer UK Ltd, Uxbridge; Deputy Warden, Assay Office, Goldsmiths' Hall, London; Aston Martin Lagonda Ltd, Newport Pagnell; Gillian Wright (International Affairs), The Automobile Association, Basingstoke; Bank of England; BMW (GB) Ltd, Bracknell; The British Egg Industry Council, London; British Petroleum Company, London; Cadillac, General Motors Corporation, Detroit, Michigan; Canadian High Commission, London; Citroën UK Ltd, Slough; The Company of Cutlers in Hallamshire; Department of Transport, London; Embassy of Israel, London; Fiat Auto (UK) Ltd, Slough; Paul Finn (for hand signs pp.60, 62, 65); William G. Crampton, The Flag Institute, Chester; Sally Bates Goodroe, Houston Public Library; The Harris Tweed Association Ltd, Stornoway, Isle of Lewis; ICI, London; International Phonetic Association, University of Leeds; International Wool Secretariat, Ilkley, Yorkshire; Jaguar Cars Ltd, Coventry; Toyota (GB) Ltd, Redhill; Lancia, Slough; Liberal Democrats, London; London Borough of Enfield; London Business College (for speedwriting); Lord Chamberlain's Office, Buckingham Palace; Maranello Concessionaires Ltd, Egham (for Ferrari); Mercedes-Benz (United Kingdom) Ltd, Milton Keynes; Michelin Tyre Public Limited Company, Harrow; Midland Bank plc, London; Ministry of Defence, London; Mitsubishi Motors, The Colt Car Company, Cirencester; National & Provincial Building Society, Bradford; National Deaf-Blind League, Peterborough; Nissan Europe N.V., London; Ordnance Survey, Southampton; Page Hargrave, Chartered Patent Attorneys, London; Patent and Trademark Office, United States Department of Commerce, Washington DC; The Patent Office, Newport, Gwent; Penguin Books Ltd, London; Peugeot Talbot Motor Company Ltd, Coventry; Pewterers' Hall, London; Lynn Turnbull, Pitman Education and Training Ltd; Porsche Cars Great Britain Ltd, Reading; The Procter & Gamble Distributing Company, Atlanta, Georgia; Procter & Gamble Ltd, Newcastle upon Tyne; Renault UK Ltd, London; Republicans Abroad (US Republican Party), London; Rolls-Royce Motor Cars Limited, Crewe; Rover Group Ltd, Coventry; Royal Astronomical Society, London; Royal Mint, Llantrisant, Wales; Royal National Institute for the Blind, London (Braille, Moon alphabets); Royal National Institute for the Deaf (now renamed The Royal National Institute for Deaf People), London; Royal Naval Museum, Portsmouth; Royal Society for the Prevention of Accidents, Birmingham; Royal Society for the Protection of Birds, Sandy, Bedfordshire; Saab-Scania AB, Linköping, Sweden; Shell UK Ltd, London; Skoda (Great Britain) Ltd, London; Subaru UK Ltd, London; Tate & Lyle Sugars, Bromley; Thorn EMI Patents Ltd, Hayes; United Kingdom Atomic Energy Authority, Harwell; V. A. G (United Kingdom) Ltd, Milton Keynes (for Audi, Volkswagen); Vauxhall Motors Ltd, Luton; Victoria Cross and George Cross Association, London; Volvo Car UK Ltd, Marlow; World Council of Churches, Geneva.

Sign

derives from Old French *signe* from Latin *signum*, mark, i.e. something which is seen and represents a known meaning. It first appeared in English in this sense in the 14th century, slowly supplanting the native 'token'*. The earliest sense as a verb (15th century) was to mark with the cross*, and according to Professor Weekley 'most of our ancestors "signed" their letters in the same way, instead of subscribing their names' (see p.211). Today, 'sign' is applied principally to any conventional graphic mark or 'symbol' used to convey a specific meaning (as for example in mathematics*), or to any gesture* intended to convey an idea or command. The word also describes a board, placard, or other notice displayed for information, advertising, etc, or to warn or direct.

&

Symbol

comes via Latin from Greek *sumbolon*, meaning sign, mark, token, sign of recognition, and ultimately from Greek *sumballein*, literally 'to throw together'. Originally, the word described one half of an object such as a ring broken in two, which, when joined with its other half, confirmed the identity or authenticity of the person or persons presenting it. Today, 'symbol' is commonly defined in two ways: first, as 'something that stands for, represents, or denotes something else', particularly some tangible object representing something intangible or abstract, such as an idea or concept (as for example the owl*, or its depiction, as wisdom). This meaning is first recorded in Spenser's *The Faerie Queene* (1590). Secondly, and often interchangeable with 'sign', 'symbol' describes a written character or mark used conventionally to stand for some object, quantity, value, or process. Obvious examples are the letters of our alphabet*, punctuation* marks, numerals*, and such graphic signs as are employed in music*, mathematics*, and so on. Usage of the word in this latter sense is first found in English in the early 17th century.

Chapter 1

From the beginning

Early writing and numerals

The single most important function of signs and symbols is communication, particularly communication by writing. The invention of writing, by which thoughts and speech could be accurately recorded in visible form, has been described as one of man's greatest imaginative feats. It enabled the preservation and transmission of accumulated experience and knowledge through space and time, which is itself a prerequisite of complex civilisation.

Although it may be said that the most primitive stage in the evolution of writing dates back to marks and drawings made by our cave-dwelling ancestors (beginning *c.* 25 000 BC), archaeological evidence suggests that it was not until around 5400 years ago that the earliest attempts to portray language systematically started to appear.

The first scripts were predominantly pictorial. Simplified pictures were used to represent only the things depicted. A drawing of a leg or foot, for example, meant 'leg' or 'foot'; a drawing of the Sun meant 'sun', and no more. From these **pictograms**, developed what are referred to as **ideograms**: pictures that stand not only for the things they show, but also for ideas associated with those things. Thus the sun-pictogram was able to represent related concepts such as 'day', 'time', 'heat', 'light', 'power'; similarly, the drawing of a leg or foot could signify ideas associated with those parts of the body, e.g. 'to stand', 'walk', or 'go'.

In time, pictographic writing was succeeded by scripts in which symbols were used to signify the words themselves, rather than the things the words represented (just as Arabic numerals* commonly take the place of words, e.g. '7' for 'seven'; other modern examples of the **logogram**, as this type of symbol is sometimes called, are the ampersand* '&' for 'and', '$' for 'dollar'*, and mathematical signs such as '+' for 'plus'*). Chinese writing, which derives from an ideographic script, is now highly logographic.

A minor revolution in writing types occurred in the Middle East *c.* 2000 BC, with the appearance of **phonograms**: symbols representing sounds. The first systems to use phonograms were **syllabaries**: sets of symbols in which each corresponds to the sound of a syllable (usually

Missing the point

When the Persian king Darius I (ruled 521–486 BC) invaded Scythia to the north of the Black Sea in the year 512, he received from the enemy a message depicting a mouse, a frog, a bird, and seven arrows. After studying these symbols, Darius proudly announced his interpretation to his generals: 'Thus the enemy writes, "Persians, we surrender our land and our water [the mouse and the frog]. We fly [the bird] from the might of your forces. We lay down our arms [the arrows]". Behold, the cowardly Scythians want to surrender to us even before they have felt our swords.' That night the Scythians attacked and defeated the Persians. After the battle, Darius learned the true meaning of the message: 'Persians, unless you can turn yourselves into birds and fly away, become as field mice and burrow under the ground, or be as frogs and take refuge in the swamps, you will perish by our arrows.'

a consonant plus vowel). Two examples of modern syllabic scripts are Cherokee, whose set of 86 symbols was perfected in 1823 by the American Indian teacher and scholar, Sequoyah (1773–1843), and Japanese, which has two types of *kana* or syllabic 'characters': the angular *katakana*, used mainly in the transcription of foreign words, and the cursive *hiragana*, for general usage.

Syllabaries, which broke language down into simpler units, reduced the number of symbols needed to record a language from at least several thousand to between 50 to 200. The final stage in the evolution of writing carried the process of simplification even further, and led ultimately to the creation in Greece in the 9th century BC of the most efficient system yet devised: the **first true alphabet**, in which each symbol represents a consonant or vowel (and from which all other alphabets are derived; see Chapter 2).

Ancient scripts

Three of the earliest and most-thoroughly studied writing systems: those of Egypt, Mesopotamia, and China, all originated as pictograms and evolved into highly distinctive forms. Only Chinese survives today.

Mesopotamian cuneiform

The **first true writing system** was invented by the Sumerians, a people with a highly developed culture (they are also credited with the invention of the plough and wheeled vehicles), who lived in the lower Tigris and Euphrates valley in the 'cradle of civilisation' Mesopotamia (modern southern Iraq). Their earliest written records (in pictograms), found at Nippur, the region's chief religious and political centre, on numerous clay tablets from one of the lowest excavation levels, have been dated to *c.* 3400 BC.

It is thought that Sumerian priests devised the writing initially for accounting purposes: to record inventories, contributions to the temple granaries, and transactions such as the sale of land and slaves. In its early form, the writing was composed of vertical columns of picture-signs (pictograms and ideograms) of animate and inanimate objects such as human and animal heads, other parts of the body, birds, oxen, sheaves of barley. The signs were made by scratching a pointed reed stylus over tablets of damp clay. However, this stylus was not best suited to drawing on clay: it raised bumps and ridges, and smudging occurred frequently. Later, the scribes found they could avoid the smudging by turning their tablets 90 degrees and drawing horizontally from left to right in such a way that the picture-signs appeared sideways. Thereafter, they were always so inscribed.

A more radical change occurred when scribes discarded the pointed stylus, and began instead to impress their signs with one with a blunt triangular tip. The wedge-shaped writing this stylus produced is called cuneiform (from Latin *cuneus*, 'wedge'). Clusters of these wedge-shapes became increasingly abstract, till eventually they lost any resemblance to the thing signified.

Most cuneiform signs were logograms* (i.e. stood for words). Around 100 to 150 signs were also used to represent syllables, or to stand for another word that sounded similar but had a different meaning; for instance, as the Sumerian word for 'fish' (*ha*) also meant 'may', scribes used the same sign to write both words. Sometimes signs were combined to stand for one word: e.g. the sign for 'man' combined with 'great' made 'king'. In the same way, combining the sign for 'mouth'

Early Sumerian pictograms

with that for 'food' (initially represented by a pictogram of a food bowl) produced the logogram for 'to eat'.

Additionally, to eliminate ambiguity, about 25 logograms were employed as determinatives*. Placed before other signs, these determinatives (unpronounced) indicated the class of object or being to which the spoken signs belonged. For instance, the sign for 'wood' denoted words associated with trees and objects of wood. During the development of cuneiform, the former 2000 or so picture-signs were reduced to around 600 symbols (not counting combinations).

Although cuneiform looks complicated, it proved to be highly successful. It was adopted by the Akkadians, who pronounced the symbols as corresponding Akkadian words; similarly by the Babylonians, and later by the Assyrians, who simplified cuneiform and (as may be seen in the chart of examples) made it more square in appearance. The system was also adapted outside Mesopotamia, notably in Elam (southwestern Iran), and by the Hittites in Anatolia (the Asian part of Turkey). Thus cuneiform became the most widely used medium of written communication in the ancient Middle East.

Because of the imperishable nature of baked clay, numerous examples of cuneiform have survived: historical inscriptions, business, technical, and religious documents, dictionaries, law codes, mathematical and other scientific texts, astronomical tables, and literary

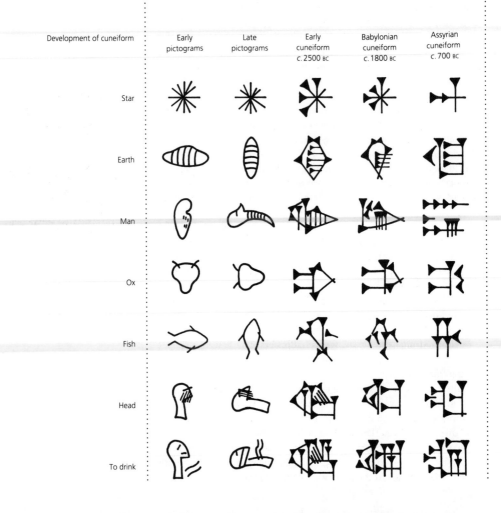

Development of cuneiform	Early pictograms	Late pictograms	Early cuneiform c. 2500 BC	Babylonian cuneiform c. 1800 BC	Assyrian cuneiform c. 700 BC
Star					
Earth					
Man					
Ox					
Fish					
Head					
To drink					

works such as the 3500-line 'Epic of Gilgamesh' (*c.* 2000 BC). Examples have also been found on stone, pottery, bronze, copper, silver, gold, and ivory, and on amulets (to ward off evil).

Following the Persian conquest of Babylonia in 539 BC, the use of cuneiform in Mesopotamia began to decline, to be superseded ultimately by the more accessible and efficient alphabetic systems. Nevertheless, kept alive by priests and scholars, the script continued to reappear sporadically over the next seven centuries. The latest surviving record for cuneiform is a tablet of AD 75.

Egyptian hieroglyphs

The ancient Egyptians called their writing 'speech of the god', because they believed that Thoth, their ibis-headed god of wisdom and learning, had given them both their language and the symbols to record it. When the Greeks invaded Egypt in 332 BC, they named these symbols *hieroglyphikà grámmata* ('sacred carved letters'). Hieroglyphs were carved on the walls of temples and tombs, and on statues and coffins. They were also painted on vessels and implements, and inscribed on historical, legal, and scientific documents.

Where and how this second most ancient writing originated is not known. One theory suggests that the system, which appeared in an already advanced stage in the First Dynasty (3110–2884 BC), may have evolved from early Sumerian writing. During the initial period, around 700 hieroglyphs were in use; many of them are of human or animal forms, and of natural and man-made objects. New symbols, however, were constantly being invented, and by about 500 BC numbered several thousand. They were written and read from right to left, or less frequently from left to right, or up and down; the direction of the writing was indicated by the animate beings, which always face the beginning of the inscription.

Traditionally, the symbols are classified into three groups: ideograms*; phonograms*; and determinatives*. An example of the first group is the hieroglyph for 'scribe', which depicts his equipment (a container for brushes, a bag for powdered pigments, and a palette for inks). By extension, it also represents the word 'write'. The majority of phonograms were either bi-consonantal (some 50 were in regular usage), or tri-consonantal. By 1500 BC, scribes had developed around 24 signs to represent a single sound. The third group, determinatives (unpronounced), were placed after words to indicate the class of meaning to which they belonged. In the example shown, the first sign of a hoe stands for mr (pronounced mer), the second sign of a mouth is the phonogram for r. Followed by the determinative of the man with his hand to his face, the combination means 'love'; followed by the 'cloth' determinative, it means 'to bind'. Because some signs could function in all three ways (i.e. as ideogram, phonogram, or determinative), the hieroglyphic system was, to say the least, highly complex. It need not have been: the 24 or so single-consonant signs could have been used as an alphabet and thus have made the writing much simpler. But this was a direction the Egyptians chose not to take, possibly for elitist reasons. Writing was a highly-prized art possessed only by royalty, high officials, priests, doctors, and of course the scribes themselves (who, as this quotation from a papyrus in the British Museum in London shows, enjoyed an exalted status: 'the scribe directs every work in the land . . . for him there are no taxes . . . he payeth tribute in writing').

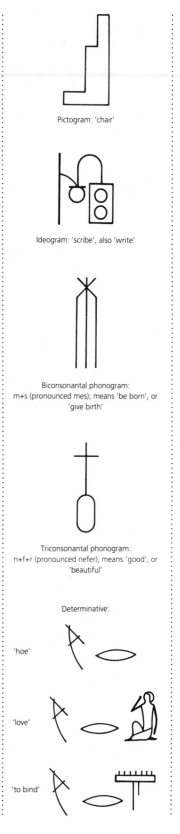

Pictogram: 'chair'

Ideogram: 'scribe', also 'write'

Biconsonantal phonogram: m+s (pronounced mes); means 'be born', or 'give birth'

Triconsonantal phonogram: n+f+r (pronounced nefer); means 'good', or 'beautiful'

Determinative:

'hoe'

'love'

'to bind'

Almost an alphabet

The 24 Egyptian hieroglyphs representing single sounds and their approximate sound value

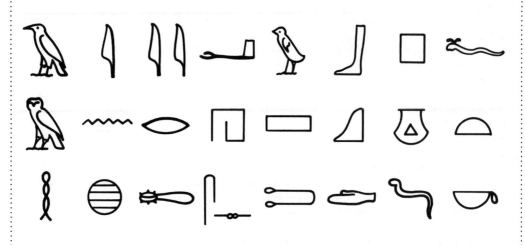

First row: vulture (glottal a as in ah), flowering reed (i as in it), two flowering reeds (y as in baby, also y as in yes), arm and hand (ar as in bark), quail chick (oo as in too; also w as in water), foot (b as in bat), mat (p as in pup), horned snake (f as in fat).

Second row: owl (m as in mother), water (n as in no), mouth (r as in rat), reed shelter (h as in hut), pool (sh as in shoe), hillside (qw as in quick), stand for jar (g as in good), loaf of bread (t as in tool).

Third row: twisted flax (h as in ha), placenta (ch as in loch), animal belly with teats (ch as in German ich), folded cloth; or door bolt (s as in sit), rope (ch as in chair), hand (d as in dirt), snake (dj as in journey), basket with handle (k as in kitten)

As well as being one of the most complex systems ever devised, Egyptian writing has also been judged the most beautiful. As in all Egyptian art, great care was taken to achieve maximum harmony, and this consideration played an important role in dictating the signs' order and proportions. In addition to their aesthetic and linguistic value, hieroglyphs had the magical power to 'make to live' the things depicted. Egyptians believed that if their names were written down, both they and their names would survive in the afterlife. Especially important

Hieroglyphic amulets

Certain hieroglyphs were made into amulets* of wood, metal and semi-precious stones such as turquoise or lapis-lazuli and worn round the neck, waist, wrist or ankle as protection against evil, bad luck, reptiles, storms, disease or hunger. Such amulets were also placed with the dead to protect them on their journey to the next life:
1. an amulet against injury, the udjat, 'Eye of Horus', represents the eye of the falcon-headed god Horus. According to myth, the storm god Seth once ripped it from Horus' head; it was later restored to him by Thoth, the god of wisdom and learning.
2. the fish was an amulet against drowning; the good luck charm of boatmen, sometimes also worn by children on the end of a plait.
3. the djed, which originally stood for a column of trimmed papyrus stalks, but later identified with the backbone of the god Osiris; the sign of endurance and stability.
4. the sign meaning horizon and representing the sun rising over the mountain allowed the dead to witness the sun's rebirth each day, and be reborn themselves.
5. the most powerful of all hieroglyphs: the ankh*. Though it represents merely a sandal tie with a loop, it also means 'eternal life'.

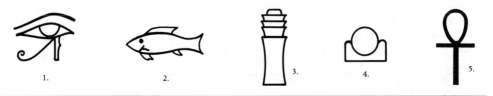

1.　　　　2.　　　　3.　　　　4.　　　　5.

were royal names, which were enclosed in an oval ring or cartouche. This had a dual purpose: it symbolised that the name-bearer ruled over everything the Sun encircled, and it protected the enclosed name (and thus the person) from injury or evil. On the other hand, it was feared that certain signs (those representing humans, or creatures such as scorpions*) might devour the offerings of food and drink left in the tomb to sustain the deceased in the next life, or even attack the dead person's body. Where such signs could not be avoided, they were rendered harmless by being depicted nailed down, without heads or legs, or in a disjointed form.

In addition to hieroglyphs, the Egyptians developed two cursive scripts. **Hieratic** (named *hieratikos*, 'priestly', by the Greeks *c.* 300 BC, since by that time the script was used solely by priests), which was adapted from hieroglyphic *c.* 2900 BC, became Egypt's administrative and business script for more than 2000 years. The signs, much simplified and often joined up (and thus to hieroglyphs what modern handwriting is to printed type), were written from right to left with a reed pen on papyrus, a paper-like surface made from papyrus reeds. This enabled faster, easier writing, with characters requiring only one or two pen-strokes. Faster still was the highly cursive **demotic** script (from Greek *demotikà grámmata*, 'popular letters'). Developed in the early 7th century BC from hieratic (which it soon supplanted), demotic was widely used for legal, administrative, and commercial documents, for literary and scientific texts, and later for commemorative inscriptions on stone or wood.

Egypt's conversion to Christianity in the 3rd century eclipsed not only the ancient pagan religion, but also its writing system, which was ultimately supplanted by the new Greek-based Coptic* alphabet adopted by Egyptian Christians. By the end of the 5th century, all knowledge of the old ways had disappeared. The latest hieroglyphic text, dating from 24 August 394 AD, is a temple inscription on the island of Philae; the latest hieratic appeared in the 2nd century AD. The latest demotic inscription, also found on Philae, has been dated to AD 450.

The seat of life

In the temple of Osiris at Karnak the sun god Amen-Ra is depicted holding the ankh*, the sign of life, to the nose of King Psammetichus III. Egyptians believed the nose was the 'seat of life'. Therefore, an enemy could be destroyed simply by smashing the nose on a statue or on any other representation of the person. To hold the ankh to the king's nose guaranteed his eternal life.

Breaking the code

For nearly 1400 years after its virtual extinction in the 5th century AD, knowledge of the writing of ancient Egypt, particularly of hieroglyphs, remained a complete mystery, even to the Egyptians themselves. The beginning of the breakthrough to their decipherment came in July 1799, when soldiers of Napoleon's invading army, digging foundations for a fort near Rosetta (Arabic Rashid) near the mouth of the Nile, unearthed a thick broken slab of black basalt 46 in (118 cm) by 30 in (77 cm). This 'Rosetta Stone' (in the British Museum since 1802), incised with a decree drawn up by the priests of Memphis on a date corresponding to 27 March 196 BC in honour of the Egyptian king Ptolemy V Epiphanes (205–181 BC),

was in two languages: Egyptian and Greek (the official language of Egypt after its conquest by Alexander the Great in 332 BC) and three scripts: 14 lines of hieroglyphs at the top, a middle section of 32 lines in the very cursive demotic script, and at the bottom, 54 lines in Greek alphabetic script. Working with this last section, which could of course be translated, scholars throughout Europe attempted decipherment of the Egyptian. Though some came close over the next 20 years, the final solution always eluded them, mainly because they believed the signs were ideograms. The prize fell ultimately to a young Frenchman, Jean-François Champollion (1790–1832) who found the key to the mystery in the ovals or cartouches

Ptolemaios

Cleopatra

containing the name Ptolemy. By comparing the hieroglyphs in these cartouches with those first on another inscription containing Cleopatra's name, and later on others, Champollion was able to prove that they were not ideographic as previously believed, but phonetic. His eventual decipherment of the Stone in 1822 paved the way to the development of Egyptology.

continued on p.16

Breaking the code (*continued*)

The decipherment of **cuneiform** was due largely to the efforts of two men: a German schoolmaster Georg Grotefend (1775–1853) in 1802, and more importantly Major Henry Creswicke Rawlinson (1810–95) who first copied, and later translated a trilingual inscription some 500 ft (150 m) above ground level on an almost sheer rock face at Behistun near Kermanshah in western Iran. This substantial inscription, which records the victory in 520 BC of the Persian king Darius the Great (ruled 521–486 BC) over a usurper named Gaumata, is

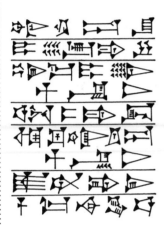

Babylonian cuneiform, c. 1750 BC

written in three languages of the Achaemenid Empire – Old Persian, Babylonian, and Elamite. Rawlinson's decipherment of the Old Persian in 1846, and later of the Babylonian, provided the key to more obscure cuneiform texts, including man's earliest identified writing system, Sumerian, of which the first translation was produced in 1905 by François Thureau-Dangin (1872–1944).

In 1900, Sir Arthur Evans discovered three scripts from different periods on clay tablets in the ruins of the palace at Knossos in Crete. The latest of these (*c.*1300 BC), which Evans named **Linear B**, was finally deciphered in 1953 by

Linear B, c. 1250 BC

the architect and amateur archaeologist Michael Ventris (1922–56) using techniques learned while code-breaking during World War II. It consists of around 90 signs used to spell words phonetically, a number of 'commodity signs', ideograms of animals, vessels, weapons, etc, used to signify the object being counted, and a decimal numerical system. However, the two earlier Cretan scripts Evans discovered, one highly pictorial (dated to between 2000 and 1650 BC), and the other (thought to be a simpler version and dated to between 1750 and 1450 BC), which he named Linear A, have so far defied all efforts.

Equally mystifying is the **Phaistos Disc**, discovered in 1908 in a Minoan palace at Phaistos in southern Crete, and dated to about 1600 BC. The disc, of baked clay 6 in (160 mm) in diameter, is covered on both faces with 45 signs of animals and everyday objects impressed with a specially cut punch or stamp. It is thought that the signs, which run in a spiral, are intended to be read from the edge of the disc. No similar examples have ever been found.

No translation has yet been offered for the pictographic script of

From the Phaistos disc, c. 1600 BC

more than 500 different signs on the wooden tablets discovered on **Easter Island** in the South Pacific in the early 18th century. The direction of the writing on the tablets is in the style known as boustrophedon*, but the alternate rows are inverted so that the reader has to turn the tablet upside down at the end of each line.

Another writing system that has steadfastly resisted decipherment is that of the **Maya** civilisation which survived in Central America until the Spanish invasions of the early 16th century. The Mayas left a number of monolithic pillars carved with 'glyphs' and figures, some standing for ideas, other for sounds

Mayan glyphs

(the earliest dating from the first centuries AD), and three books or codices written on bark paper (the oldest dated to the 12th century, the latest to the middle of the 15th century). Though progress has been made since the 1950s, the greater part of this elaborate system which used pictograms, ideograms, and the principle of rebus* writing, remains a secret.

Easter Island script

Chinese characters

Chinese has been described as the **world's oldest written language**. The **earliest known signs** are those found on pottery of the Yangshao culture at Pan-p'o near Sian in Shensi, north China in 1962. The pottery, which has been dated by the radiocarbon method to 5000–4000 BC, bears proto-characters for the numbers 5, 7, and 8. Pictograms for 'sun' and 'mountain' have been found on pottery vessels at Ch'ü-hsien in Shantung belonging to the Ta-wen-k'ou culture (c. 4000–3000 BC). The pictograms are regarded as the ancestors of the so-called Archaic Characters from which modern Chinese characters are descended.

The **earliest writings** (in the sense of representing language) in Archaic Characters have been found inscribed on thousands of fragments of bone and shell excavated since 1899 at Yin, the ancient capital of the Shang dynasty (c. 1766–1123 BC) by the Huan River near present-day Anyang in Henan province, northeast China. The inscriptions are connected with a form of divination known as scapulimancy, in which a flaming torch was inserted into a hole cut in a shoulder bone (scapula). The resulting cracks, visible and audible, would be interpreted positively or negatively, and an account of this interpretation recorded on the bone. Turtle shells were also used (as the longest-living creature, turtles were believed to be endowed with magical properties, and to be the repository of eternal truths). About 2000 characters from these inscriptions have been identified so far.

The characters which evolved from the early signs are composed of a number of strokes. While most characters have fewer than 15 strokes, others have many more. The **most complex character** is that representing *xiè*, meaning 'talkative': it consists of 64 strokes. The most complex in current use is *nang*, 'a blocked-up nose', with 36 strokes.

Traditionally, characters are classified into six categories known as *liu-shu*, 'six types of writing'. Introduced by Hsü Shen (AD 58?–147?), who compiled the first dictionary *Shuo-wen chieh-tzu* ('Simple and compound characters explained') of 9353 characters in AD 121, the categories include pictograms (for example, 'mu', tree, and 'shan', hill or mountain), and simple and compound ideograms: signs denoting abstract concepts. The words 'clear' or 'bright' (in Chinese, *ming*, hence the Ming dynasty which ruled from 1368 to 1644, a period of great enlightenment) are formed by the combined characters representing 'Sun' and 'Moon'. By the same process, 'field' + 'strength' gives 'man' or 'male' (the logic here being that a man is one who uses his strength in the fields), while 'man' + 'tree' gives 'rest'. Ideograms are also formed by repetition of the same sign: two trees, for example, means grove, and three trees forest; similarly, 'fire' + 'fire' makes 'very hot', and 'child' + 'child' means 'twins'. In addition, turning a character in a different direction gives another word: 'child' written upside down means childbirth.

The most important of the six categories, phonograms, comprises more than 90 per cent of all characters. Phonograms are composed of a **radical** and a phonetic element. In much the same way as determinatives* were used in Egyptian hieroglyphic* writing, radicals provide the key to the character's overall meaning. Thus for instance, all words relating to wood such as a tree or table contain the 'wood' radical; words connected with emotions contain the 'heart' radical. Hsü Shen's 2nd-century dictionary defined 540 radicals; in the late Ming dynasty these were reduced to their current 214. These simple symbols

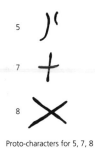

Proto-characters for 5, 7, 8

	Ancient	Modern
Sun		
Moon		
Rain		
Water		
Fish		
Tree		
Mountain		
Man		
Child		
Horse		

are written below, above, around, or within the **phonetic** element which gives a clue to the sound of the word. The character for 'to hear' (*wén*), for example, is composed of the radical for 'ear' and the phonetic element 'door' (*mén*), thus indicating that the sound should rhyme with *mén*. Similarly, 'ocean' contains the radical 'water' plus the phonetic 'sheep'; the same radical combined with the phonetic 'tree' gives 'to wash the hair'.

The exact number of characters is unknown. During the Shang dynasty, 2500 were listed; by AD 100 the number had increased to 9000, and by AD 1000 to 27 000. The *Kang-hsi tzu-tien* dictionary completed in 1716 contains 49 174. The eight-volume *Dictionary of Chinese Characters* completed in 1991 contains more than 56 000 characters; a standard dictionary, around 40 000 characters. One type of Chinese typewriter has 5400 characters. Some 4000 to 7000 characters are used in contemporary Chinese (a modern newspaper uses up to 7000 characters). To read a simple novel in Chinese demands knowledge of at least 3500, while to read classical Chinese with ease a person would need to recognise about 10 000. Even the most basic list in the first four grades at school contains 1200.

The complexity of Chinese characters, which have been likened to onions comprising layer upon layer of meaning, partially accounts for the 180 million Chinese (more than one-sixth of the 1.1 billion population) who are *wenmang*, 'character blind' or illiterate. In 1956, work began on the graphic simplification of the most commonly used characters; by 1992 about 2500 had been simplified or abbreviated, and in some cases the number of strokes has been greatly reduced.

There is a practical advantage to this complexity. Putong'hua (meaning 'ordinary speech') is the 'national language' of the People's Republic. Officially adopted in 1949, and spoken by an estimated 770 million people (which makes it the **world's most widely-spoken language**), it is very different from Cantonese (50 million speakers), or Wu or Min (around 40 million speakers each); additionally, there are many other 'dialects' which are not mutually intelligible. The system makes the writing of these identical so that, though he may not understand a dialect, a literate person may yet decipher any text.

(Japanese writing, which developed about AD 800 from Chinese, uses some Chinese characters; this makes both written languages partially intelligible, even though the two spoken languages are completely different. Korea and Vietnam also borrowed the Chinese system, though today the characters are used only in South Korea in combination with the Korean* alphabet.)

In an attempt to standardise Chinese spelling, more than 50 phonetic alphabets have been devised since the 17th century; there are 21 international and European systems currently in use. The most important is Pinyin (*Hanyü P'inyin Fang'an*, 'Chinese language spelling scheme'), which was officially approved by the First National People's Congress on 11 February 1958. Initially intended to make the learning of characters easier, and for special purposes such as telegraphy*, Braille*, and fingerspelling* for the deaf, the use of this Roman-based 25-letter system has been greatly extended since 1979, particularly to the transliteration of personal and place names into all languages with a Roman-based alphabet (thus it replaces the previous internationally-accepted 'Wade-Giles', devised by Thomas Francis Wade in 1859 and revised in 1892 by Herbert Allen Giles). In Pinyin, Peking, for instance, becomes Beijing, and Teng Hsiao-ping becomes Deng Xiaoping.

Two other changes are worth noting. Traditionally, Chinese was written in vertical columns from right to left: since 1956, the Western left-right direction has been encouraged. Secondly, Arabic numerals* rather than Chinese are being used in official documents.

Numerical notation

Symbols to represent quantities or numerical values began to evolve at around the same time as symbols to represent language. The earliest numerical information was kept by means of single notches scored on wood, horn, bone, or stone. Pebbles placed in a row or counted into a bag, or even knots tied in pieces of string were also used. As people commonly counted on their fingers, and sometimes toes, so they began to group numbers of notches in fives, tens, and twenties. To record larger numbers, such as taxes due, wages paid, areas of fields, head of cattle, volume of granaries, or the number of bricks needed to build a tomb, more condensed systems were needed.

The **oldest known numeral system** (*c.* 3200 BC), was devised by the **Egyptians**. Numbers, expressed by hieroglyphs*, were formed by addition, with each hieroglyph being repeated the required number of times. A single vertical stroke represented numbers up to nine, and thereafter a different collective hieroglyph for each power of ten up to a million: a picture of a hobble (for fettering horses) represented 10, a coil of rope 100 (10^2), a lotus plant 1000 (10^3), a forefinger 10 000 (10^4), a tadpole 100 000 (10^5), and for a million (10^6) a man with arms raised:

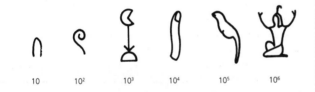

| 1 | 10 | 10^2 | 10^3 | 10^4 | 10^5 | 10^6 |

These hieroglyphs could be combined, with the higher number always appearing before the lower number. As with all Egyptian hieroglyphs, numbers were written to be read from left to right, from right to left, or from top to bottom. In the more common right-left direction, for example, the year 1993 would appear as:

$$(3 \times 1 + 9 \times 10 + 9 \times 10^2 + 1 \times 10^3)$$

For the same group of numerals in other systems, see p.23. Later, new hieratic* number symbols were used, which in turn gave way to the even more cursive demotic* numerals.

Sumerian numeration, which began before 3000 BC, is the **first known positional notation**, i.e. notation in which a symbol's numerical value depends on its position in the number group (this positional or 'place-value' principle is best exemplified by a number from our own Arabic numeration such as 555, where the symbol 5 represents three different values: 5 hundreds, 5 tens, and 5 units). Initially, the Sumerians used circular and triangular marks of varying sizes. Later, they recorded their numbers in the same way as they wrote their language: with wedge-shaped (cuneiform*) symbols impressed with a stylus in damp clay tablets, which were then baked in the sun or in kilns. The system (also used by the Babylonians and others who

Tens   Units

adopted cuneiform), which was based on the number 60, required only two symbols: a small wedge to designate units, and a broader wedge for tens. With these, all numbers up to 59 could be written by the additive principle. To express the number 60 and beyond, the small wedge was used again in a new position to represent a unit of a higher order.

The ancient **Chinese*** (c. 1000 BC) made manual computations with groups of sticks or rods. One to five rods placed vertically represented the numbers from one to five; one, two, three, four rods surmounted by a single horizontal stick gave the next four numbers six, seven, eight, nine. For the first five multiples of ten, one to five rods were placed horizontally; a single vertical rod surmounting one, two, three, four, indicated the numbers 60, 70, 80, 90. Such figures were also recorded in writing.

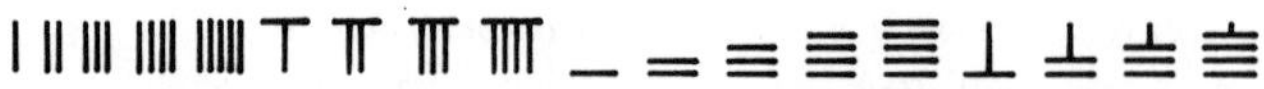

1 2 3   4   5   6   7   8   9   10   20   30   40   50   60   70   80   90

Chinese rod numerals

Numbers above 99 were indicated by a positional principle in which the symbol's value depended on its position in the group. Around 200 BC, a second system emerged in which nine distinctive symbols represented the first nine numbers, and another 11 symbols the first 11 powers of ten:

1   2   3   4   5   6   7   8   9   10 10^2 10^3 10^4

Traditional Chinese numerals

The modern and commercial systems now employed in China are positional, and use a circle O for zero.

Two systems developed in ancient **Greece**, the Attic (so-named after the region of Attica, whose capital was Athens), and the Ionian. **Attic numerals**, sometimes also called Herodianic numerals after the 2nd-century AD grammarian Herodianus who described them in his writings, appeared sometime around the 6th century BC. They were formed from the initial letters of the Greek numeral names ΠΕΝΤΕ (*pente*, written either as Π or Γ) for 5, ΔΕΚΑ (*deka*) for 10, ΗΕΚΑΤΟΝ (*hekaton*) for 100, ΧΙΛΙΟΙ (*chilioi*, from which comes our kilo, symbol k) for 1000, and ΜΥΡΙΟΙ (*myrioi*) for 10 000. Single strokes I, II, III, IIII, represented the numbers one to four. All other numerals were made up of aggregates of these symbols, or combined with the symbol for 5: for example ⊓ *pente-hekaton* = 5 × 100 = 500.

From the 3rd century BC Attic numeration was gradually supplanted by the more compact **Ionian** or Alexandrian system, in which the numbers one to nine, the first nine multiples of 10, and the first nine multiples of 100, were represented by the 24 letters of the alphabet plus three symbols discarded as letters in classical Greek: *digamma* (Ϝ) for 6, *qoph* or *koppa* (ϙ) for 90, and *sampi* (ϡ) for 900.

Originally these numeral letters were capitals; to distinguish them from word letters a line was sometimes drawn above. To represent the thousands, the 27 numeral letters were reused, usually with a distinguishing stroke to the left of the numeral (thus /A represented 1000, /Π 80 000). When small or lower-case letters were later introduced, a similar distinguishing principle was applied with a comma-like mark placed to the lower left of the letter (for example ,α for 1000).

By the 2nd century BC, the **Hebrews** had developed a similar alphabetic numeral system. Each of the first nine multiples of 100 were represented by certain final forms of letters; as with Ionian notation, the first nine letters were repeated for multiples of 1000 up to 9000. A deviation emerged with the representation of 15: because 10 + 5 would have appeared as the first two letters of the Hebrew word for Jahveh (God), it was written instead as 9 and 6.

The **Aztecs** of Mexico recorded their numbers principally by means of a dot for one, a flag-like symbol for 20, a tree for 400, and a purse for 8000. To avoid cumbersome repetition, they also adopted intermediate collective symbols such as fragments of a tree to denote 100, 200, or 300. For their accounts, the ancient **Peruvians** used a 'quipu': a length of cord about 2 ft long (60 cm) made of different coloured threads and tied with knots to represent numerical combinations. The most efficient and sophisticated of the numerical systems in the New World was devised by the **Maya Indians** of the Yucatán Peninsula in Central America, whose civilisation reached its height in about AD 300–900. Mayan notation used just three symbols: a dot for one, a bar for five, and for what is thought to be the **oldest zero** in the New World, the form of a shell.

In this system, positional notation began with the number 20. Numerals were written in vertical columns in descending order of value: the lowest position represented the number of units, the next multiples of 20, and the position above that multiples of 360 (the number of days in the Mayan year).

Mayan numerals

Roman numerals

The best known of the ancient systems is the notation used by the **Romans**. It consists of seven symbols: I, V, X, L, C, D, and M. The most plausible and widely accepted theory for their origin, proposed by the 19th-century German historian Theodor Mommsen, is that V (for 5) was a graphic representation of an open hand with the fingers held together and the thumb apart, and that X (for 10) was two V's for two hands back to back. L (50) may have evolved from the Greek letter *chi*, usually written as X, but also as ⊥. To write 100, the Romans adapted the Greek letter *theta* Θ; this finally evolved into C, the initial letter of the Latin word for 'hundred', *centum* (though which came first, the numerical symbol or the word, is not known). By a similar process, Mommsen suggests, the Greek letter *phi* Φ, adopted to represent 1000, became written as CIↃ and finally as I, or the favoured form M (perhaps to correspond with *mille*, the Latin word for 'thousand'; again, which came first is not known). Another form of 1000, (Ɩ), often appeared as ∞, now the mathematical symbol for infinity. D, the symbol for 500, is thought to derive from one half of CIↃ.

The Romans employed an additive principle: thus 160 (100+50+10) was written as CLX. Occasionally they also used a subtractive principle: nine, for instance, was expressed as IX (i.e. one less than 10) rather than VIIII, 40 as XL rather than XXXX, and 90 as XC rather than LXXXX. The now common use of IV for IIII, however, is of comparatively late occurrence. One suggestion for this is that, like the Hebrew example of 15 mentioned above, the Romans avoided the IV form as it was the same as the first two letters of the old Latin spelling of their principal god Jupiter.

For large numbers, the Romans used a variety of alternatives. 800, for instance, was sometimes expressed as IↃↃↃ, while numbers such as 10 000 and 1 000 000 were written respectively as CCIↃↃ and CCCCIↃↃↃ. In medieval Europe, a bar, called a titulus or vinculum,

> *The nine Indian figures are: 9 8 7 6 5 4 3 2 1. With these nine figures and with the sign 0... any number may be written.*
>
> Leonardo of Pisa *Liber abaci*

placed above a figure denoted multiplication by 1000: thus Ī for 1000, X̄ for 10 000, and C̄ for 100 000. In the same way, when other Roman capitals were introduced for certain numbers, such as N for 90, P for 400, T for 160, a bar surmounting the letter implied multiplication by 1000, thus N̄ represented 90 000, P̄ 400 000, and T̄ 160 000.

International Arabic

The most commonly used numerical symbols throughout the modern world, the so-called **Arabic numerals** 1 2 3 4 5 6 7 8 9, derive ultimately from a system developed by the Hindus in India sometime between the 3rd century BC and the 6th century AD. The Hindus are also credited with the invention at some unknown date of the symbol for zero, which was first written as a small circle and later reduced to a large dot.

In the early 9th century, the Indian or Hindu positional system reached the Islamic empire, where it quickly proved far superior in mathematical and astronomical calculations to the Roman and Greek systems. Incidentally, from the title of the most famous of the Arabic manuscripts in which it was presented, *Al jabr w'al muqabalah*, published in AD 830 by Muhammad ibn Musa al-Khwarizmi (*c.*780-850), comes the term algebra; the term algorism (also algorithm), for the process or rules for calculation in the decimal system, derives from the first sentence of the Latin translation of that book: *Algorismi dicit* – 'Al Khwarizmi says'.

Adopted for commercial use by Arabic merchants, the Hindu numerals evolved into an Eastern and a Western version. Eastern Arabic numerals, together with the dot for zero, are similar to those now used in the Middle East. Interestingly, though Arabic script is written from right to left, Arabic numerals run from left to right, like ours. The more rounded Western Arabic numerals were introduced into Spain by the Moors in the 10th century. The first European to take serious note of the new numeration was the French scholar Gerbert of Aurillac (Pope Sylvester II from 999 to 1003) who had studied the system in Spain. His enthusiasm for it, however, seems to have been largely ignored. The

Numerals: eastern variants	1	2	3	4	5	6	7	8	9	0
Bengali	১	২	৩	৪	৫	৬	৭	৮	৯	০
Burmese	၁	၂	၃	၄	၅	၆	၇	၈	၉	၀
Gujarati	૧	૨	૩	૪	૫	૬	૭	૮	૯	૦
Lao	໑	໒	໓	໔	໕	໖	໗	໘	໙	໐
Malayalam	൧	൨	൩	൪	൫	൬	൭	൮	൯	൦
Oriya	୧	୨	୩	୪	୫	୬	୭	୮	୯	୦
Teluga	౧	౨	౩	౪	౫	౬	౭	౮	౯	౦
Tibetan	༡	༢	༣	༤	༥	༦	༧	༨	༩	༠

Comparing dates: '1993' in other systems

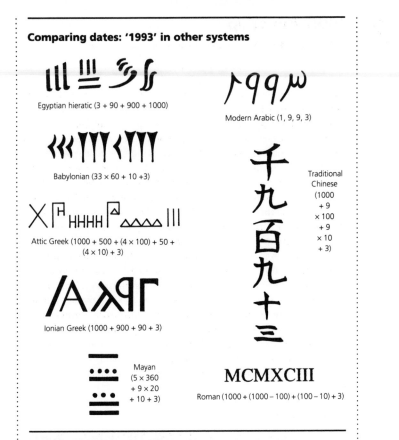

Egyptian hieratic (3 + 90 + 900 + 1000)

Modern Arabic (1, 9, 9, 3)

Babylonian (33 × 60 + 10 +3)

Traditional Chinese (1000 + 9 × 100 + 9 × 10 + 3)

Attic Greek (1000 + 500 + (4 × 100) + 50 + (4 × 10) + 3)

Ionian Greek (1000 + 900 + 90 + 3)

Mayan (5 × 360 + 9 × 20 + 10 + 3)

MCMXCIII

Roman (1000 + (1000 – 100) + (100 – 10) + 3)

adoption of the numerals is attributed to the Italian mathematician Leonardo of Pisa, also called Fibonacci (*c.* 1170-1240) who advocated their use in the first European work on Hindu-Arabic mathematics *Liber abaci* (*Book of the Abacus*) published 1202. Even so, despite their obvious advantages in greatly simplifying calculations, Arabic numerals were regarded with suspicion in the Christian world (in 1299, for instance, the Italian city of Florence banned the use of them or zero in accounts), and it was not until the late 16th century that Arabic began to replace Roman numerals in science and daily life.

Roman numerals are still very much in use: in their original capital forms on watch and clock faces, and for dates on old books and buildings. In lower case (i, ii, v, vii, ix, etc.), they are often employed to distinguish the introductory pages of books from the main text which is always paginated with Arabic numerals. Roman numerals have also been retained for other specialised uses, such as the numbering of monarchs and popes, for example Henry V, or John XXIII. According to *The Guinness Book of Numbers*, the record for the highest numbering of this kind belongs to Count Heinrich LXXV of Reuss, who ruled in Germany from 1799 to 1801. Additionally, some families in the US differentiate sons bearing the same name with a Roman numeral, for example John Z. Doe VI. BBC Television uses Roman numerals after the © (copyright) symbol at the end of a programme's closing titles to denote the year it was made. While cynics ascribe this idiosyncrasy to a desire to disguise the true antiquity of their programmes, the BBC insists it is merely continuing a tradition begun by the early film industry.

Alphabet soup
Alphabets and punctuation marks

Of all symbols, the most valuable and the most flexible are those of the **alphabet**. The syllabaries that began to develop from the cumbersome pictographic scripts broke language down into simple units which required far fewer symbols. The invention of the alphabet took this process even further, reducing language to a much smaller and fixed number of distinctive speech sounds, or **phonemes**, of which each could be represented by one distinctive and easily memorable letter-symbol, or **grapheme**. This concept, which to us now seems elementary, marked a revolutionary advance in cultural development. It provided the basis for the simplest and most efficient writing system yet devised, and the means, in theory at least, for a universal literacy.

No one knows exactly where, when, or even how this breakthrough to the alphabet occurred. Was it a momentary flash of inspiration on the part of one or several scribes, or merely the inevitable development of the systems already in use? Theories come and go, but there is still no definitive answer. Although the alphabet's origins puzzle and divide the experts, on one point at least they are virtually united. The invention happened only once, and from that first alphabet all the others past and present throughout the world – more than 200 of them – can be traced. That, of course, includes our own of 26 symbols in which this book is printed.

The first alphabets
It is generally agreed that the **first alphabet** appeared some time between 2000 and 1500 BC at the eastern end of the Mediterranean, possibly in what is now Syria. Called North Semitic, it consisted of 22 symbols which represented consonants only. As some of these bear a resemblance to Egyptian hieroglyphs, it is thought that there may be a link between the two systems. Interestingly, some of the oldest examples of alphabetic writing are not in North Semitic but in the wedge-shaped marks called cuneiform*. The earliest examples on clay tablets, dated to around 1400 BC, were found in 1929 on the site of the ancient city of Ugarit (modern Ras Shamra in Syria). The alphabetic nature of this previously unknown script was confirmed by the discovery in 1948 of the oldest cuneiform abecedary (i.e. the symbols in their traditional order) of 30 letters. Again, no clear link has yet been established.

Cuneiform abecedary

From North Semitic, three branches evolved. One, called South Semitic, gave rise to a number of alphabets, of which the main survivor is Ethiopic*. The second branch was Aramaic*, from which developed the alphabets of Asia, the Near East, and North Africa. These include modern Arabic*, Hebrew*, and the principal script of India, Devanagari*. From the third branch, sometimes called Canaanite, came the ancestor of all Western alphabets, Phoenician. Similar in many ways to other North Semitic offshoots, it was written from right to left and consisted of 22 symbols. These represented consonants only, the reader being left to decide which vowel should go where.

𐤊𐤒𐤂𐤃𐤄𐤉𐤇 ⊗𐤆 𐤊𐤋𐤌𐤍𐤎𐤏𐤐 𐤓𐤘𐤒𐤅𐤔𐤕𐤆

Phoenician alphabet

The best-known example of Phoenician occurs on a slab of black basalt called the Moabite Stone. Dated to the 9th century BC, it records the victory of Mesha, king of Moab, against the Israelites. Shortly after its discovery near the Dead Sea in 1868, the stone was very nearly lost when local tribesmen, to whom it had become a sort of talisman, broke it up and carried away the fragments as charms. Fortunately, a success-ful price was negotiated, and most of the pieces were retrieved. The restored stone is now in the Louvre in Paris.

The way to the west
The Phoenicians, who inhabited what is now Lebanon, were principally seafaring merchants. At some time during the 9th century BC, they introduced their alphabet to the Greeks who, whilst retaining the order of symbols, modified the Phoenician forms and, in many cases, their names. Thus aleph (meaning ox), beth (house), gimel (camel), for example, became in Greek alpha, beta, gamma. Unlike their Phoenician

A	B	Γ	Δ	E	Z
alpha	beta	gamma	delta	epsilon	zeta
α	β	γ	δ	ε	ζ
H	Θ	I	K	Λ	M
eta	theta	iota	kappa	lambda	mu
η	θ	ι	κ	λ	μ
N	Ξ	O	Π	P	Σ
nu	xi	omicron	pi	rho	sigma
ν	ξ	o	π	ρ	σ
T	Y	Φ	X	Ψ	Ω
tau	upsilon	phi	chi	psi	omega
τ	υ	φ	χ	ψ	ω

Greek alphabet

The straight and narrow

Until the 19th century, the letter Y was known sometimes as the Samian letter, or the letter of Pythagoras. This was a reference to the Greek mathematician and philosopher Pythagoras (born 580 BC on the Aegean island of Samos) who used *upsilon* (Y) as the symbol of human life: the foot being the innocence of the infant and the forked arms the choice of the ways of vice and virtue.

counterparts, however, the Greek letter-names have no meaning.

More importantly, the Greeks had no equivalent sound for some of the Phoenician consonantal symbols. However, instead of discarding them they adopted them for vowels, thus creating, in effect, the **first true alphabet**. They also added five new symbols: omega Ω, upsilon Y, phi Φ, chi X, and psi Ψ.

The earliest Greek writing followed the Phoenician direction from right to left. The Greeks also experimented with vertical writing, with a left–right direction, and with an alternate right–left, left–right system called **boustrophedon**. Around 500 BC, the left–right direction became the standard form.

Numerous local alphabets developed. In 403 BC, an eastern variant, Ionian, was adopted as the official Athenian alphabet; during the next century it spread throughout Greece. From this Ionian (now usually referred to as Classical Greek) the capitals of the modern 24 letter alphabet of 7 vowels and 17 consonants have descended virtually unchanged; the minuscules or lower-case letters developed around the 8th century AD.

From Tuscany to Rome

Around 800 BC, the West Greek alphabet began to be adapted for writing the languages of northern and central Italy, in particular Etruscan. Written either right to left or boustrophedon style, the alphabet for this mysterious language (spoken in the region which approximates to modern Tuscany) contains all 22 of the original Phoenician symbols plus four added by the Greeks. By 400 BC this number was reduced to 20, including four vowels.

The most important offshoot of Etruscan is the Latin or Roman alphabet which was formed during the 7th century BC from 21 of the Etruscan symbols. The earliest known specimen of Roman writing appears on a gold brooch dating back to the 6th century BC. Known as the *Praeneste Fibula*, the brooch, discovered in 1886, has the inscription MANIOS MED FHEFHAKED NVMASIOI, Manius made me for Numasius.

Following the conquest of Greece in the 1st century BC, two more letters were added, and by AD 100 the 23 letters were firmly established in much the same form as those in use today. During the rise of the Roman Empire, the alphabet was carried throughout Europe. When the empire collapsed in the 5th century AD, the alphabet's survival was ensured by the spread of Christianity, for which Latin was the international tongue. Adapted for writing most European languages, the Roman alphabet was subsequently introduced into many other areas that had extensive contact with Europeans. The majority of writing systems in Africa, for instance, are Roman-based. In India, where English is widely spoken, Roman is the second alphabet. For centuries, Turkish was written in Arabic* script, but in 1928 the Turkish president Kemal Atatürk ordered the conversion to Roman to facilitate literacy. The change proved successful: within six years illiteracy fell from 91.8 per cent to 55.1 per cent. In 1958, a Roman-based system called Pinyin* was officially adopted in the People's Republic of China to transliterate Chinese* characters.

The English 26

There are an estimated 400 000 000 speakers of English in the world today. Many of them use the English alphabet, which, since the 17th century, has consisted of 26 letters. The development of both form and phonetic value of each of these is described below; the accompanying illustrations show the principal graphic changes during their evolution from the North Semitic alphabet, through Greek, Etruscan, and Roman to the present day. Some alphabetologists believe that the first Semitic letters were adapted from Egyptian hieroglyphs*. This has been disputed, but where there is a possible correspondence, the Egyptian symbol is shown first.

In some cases, the minuscule or small letter is merely a smaller version of the majuscule or capital. In other cases, the form comes from the cursive or flowing handwriting that developed as scribes attempted to write faster and without lifting pen from paper, sometimes by rounding the letter (for example, e and n), by eliminating part of it (b, h), by adding a downward or upward stroke (p, d), or, in the case of q, by moving the existing vertical stroke to the right to distinguish it from the small p.

Aa has occupied the number one position in the majority of alphabets since it headed the North Semitic nearly 3500 years ago. Originally called *aleph*, possibly after the Semitic word for 'ox', it first served as a consonant with a glottal stop sound, similar to the a in the word 'about'. As *alpha* in the Greek alphabet, it became the first vowel, representing, as in the Etruscan and Roman alphabets, a long a as in 'father'. This, incidentally, is regarded as the most primitive sound, and also the simplest and purest. In English, the symbol represents at least nine quite different sounds. It is the third most frequently used letter in English, and on its own the fifth commonest word.

EGYPTIAN HIEROGLYPH	NORTH SEMITIC	PHOENICIAN	GREEK		ETRUSCAN		ROMAN	
			EARLY	CLASSICAL	EARLY	CLASSICAL	EARLY	CLASSICAL
𓃾	K	⟨	◁	A	A	A	A	A

Bb the 20th most frequently used letter derives from the Phoenician *beth*, which was also the Semitic word for 'house'. The Greek version, renamed *beta*, passed via the Etruscans, who named it bee, into the Roman alphabet where its present form was fixed around AD 100.

EGYPTIAN HIEROGLYPH	NORTH SEMITIC	PHOENICIAN	GREEK		ETRUSCAN	ROMAN	
			EARLY	CLASSICAL		EARLY	CLASSICAL
▢	9	⟨	◁	B	8	B	B

Cc the 13th most common letter, derives from the third of the Phoenician alphabet called *gimel*, which also means 'camel'. As *gamma* in Greek, it represented a hard g sound as in 'go'. Via the Etruscans, who used it for the sound k, it passed into the Roman alphabet where it functioned both as k and g. In 312 BC, to distinguish between the two sounds, the Romans redesignated C for the k sound, and by adding a downward stroke created G.

NORTH SEMITIC	PHOENICIAN	GREEK		ETRUSCAN		ROMAN	
		EARLY	CLASSICAL	EARLY	CLASSICAL	EARLY	CLASSICAL
⟨	⟨	⟨	Γ	⟨	⟩	⟨	C

Dd the 10th most common letter, evolved from the fourth of the North Semitic alphabet where, called *daleth*, meaning 'door', it was written as

A is for adultery

In Nathaniel Hawthorne's *The Scarlet Letter* (1850) the heroine, Hester Prynne, is convicted of adultery and condemned to wear forever the letter A embroidered on her gown. 'She turned her eyes downwards at the scarlet letter, and even touched it with her finger, to assure herself that the infant and the shame was real.' This punishment, inflicted equally on adulterer and adulteress, was one of many alphabetical stigmata in 17th- and 18th-century New England. (For a selection of other brandmarks, see Chapter 7.)

Alphabetical order

Thou must learn the alphabet, to wit, the order of the letters as they stand, perfectly without book, and where every letter standeth: as (b) near the beginning, (n) about the middest, and (t) toward the end.

Robert Cawdrey *Table Alphabeticall,* 1604

an irregular triangle. The Greeks modified the shape and named it *delta*. Via the Etruscans, who rounded two sides of the triangle, it passed into the Roman alphabet where it later received its new name dee, and present capital form.

NORTH SEMITIC	PHOENICIAN	GREEK		ETRUSCAN EARLY	ROMAN	
		EARLY	CLASSICAL		EARLY	CLASSICAL
◁	△	△	△	(	(	D

Ee is the **commonest letter in English**, reckoned to be used about 200 times more frequently than the least common z. In North Semitic, the symbol, *he*, was a consonant with an h-sound. The Greeks transformed it into a short e vowel, which was later named *epsilon*, literally 'bare e'. In the Etruscan and Roman alphabets, the vowel was sounded long and short.

EGYPTIAN HIEROGLYPH	NORTH SEMITIC	PHOENICIAN	GREEK		ETRUSCAN		ROMAN	
			EARLY	CLASSICAL	EARLY	CLASSICAL	EARLY	CLASSICAL
𝍏	⊒	⅄	⅄	E	⅂	⅂	⅂	E

Ff the first letter of *Futhark*, the Runic* alphabet, is sixth in the English and other Roman-based alphabets. It derives ultimately from the North Semitic *waw*, which was sounded as v or w. One form of *waw* became the Greek *digamma* (so-called by Byzantine grammarians because it resembled one *gamma*, Γ, superimposed on another). Later discarding *digamma* from their alphabet (using it instead as a numeral), the Greeks modified another form of *waw* for their w sound; this form eventually became known as *upsilon*. Meantime, the Etruscans took up *digamma* (F), which they used in combination with H to express the f sound (for which they also used, but later abandoned, a figure-eight symbol). When the Romans adopted the Etruscan alphabet they dropped the h from the FH combination, retaining only the *digamma* for their f sound.

NORTH SEMITIC	PHOENICIAN	GREEK		ETRUSCAN		ROMAN	
		EARLY	CLASSICAL	EARLY	CLASSICAL	EARLY	CLASSICAL
Y	Y	⅄⅄	Y	⅂	⅂	⅂	F

Gg in the early Roman alphabet, C, a rounded form of *gamma*, expressed both g and k. In 312 BC, to distinguish the two sounds, the Romans added a vertical bar to C to form G. This new symbol was placed seventh in line when z or *zeta*, which formerly occupied that position, was discarded.

NORTH SEMITIC	PHOENICIAN	GREEK		ETRUSCAN		ROMAN	
		EARLY	CLASSICAL	EARLY	CLASSICAL	EARLY	CLASSICAL
⌐	⋀	⌐	Γ	⌐	⟩	⟨	G

Hh called aitch, derives from the North Semitic *heth*, which signified the guttural sound kh. Simplified by the Phoenicians, the symbol passed into early Greek as *eta*. In the Greek alphabet used in Ionia (on the west coast of Turkey), which was adopted as the Athenian alphabet in 403 BC, this signified a long e. The aspirate value used for a time in mainland Greek later passed via Etruscan to the Roman alphabet, where the letter acquired its present capital form.

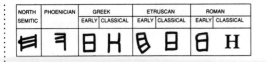

NORTH SEMITIC	PHOENICIAN	GREEK		ETRUSCAN		ROMAN	
		EARLY	CLASSICAL	EARLY	CLASSICAL	EARLY	CLASSICAL

Ii the third vowel and about the seventh most common letter in the 26, comes originally from a Semitic symbol named *yodh*. Renamed *iota* in the Greek alphabet, and with the vowel sound *ee*, it was eventually simplified into a single stroke. When the Romans adopted I, they used it both as the i vowel and the y consonant.

Until the 11th century, the minuscule was merely a smaller version of the capital but, as such, could be mistaken for part of another letter. To distinguish it, a mark like an acute accent (í) was added. This was later reduced to a tittle, the familiar round dot.

NORTH SEMITIC	PHOENICIAN	GREEK		ETRUSCAN		ROMAN	
		EARLY	CLASSICAL	EARLY	CLASSICAL	EARLY	CLASSICAL

Jj is the newest letter of the 26. Although introduced in the Middle Ages as a variant of i, it did not become generally accepted in England until the mid-17th century. Its form is merely a development of the medieval custom of elongating i with a curved tail when written at the beginning of words. This origin is reflected by the dot over the small j, and also by the symbol's Italian name *i lunga*, long i.

NORTH SEMITIC	PHOENICIAN	GREEK		ETRUSCAN		ROMAN	
		EARLY	CLASSICAL	EARLY	CLASSICAL	EARLY	MODERN

Kk may have started as an Egyptian hieroglyph of a cupped hand. In the early North Semitic and Phoenician alphabets it was a three-pronged symbol called *kaph,* meaning palm of the hand. The Greeks modified this, and named it *kappa*. The symbol passed virtually unchanged through Etruscan into the Roman alphabet, where it was later discarded, except for use in some official or common words. K did not appear in the English alphabet until after the Norman Conquest in the 11th century, when it began to be used instead of c in words such as *cyng*, 'king'.

EGYPTIAN HIEROGLYPH	NORTH SEMITIC	PHOENICIAN	GREEK		ETRUSCAN		ROMAN	
			EARLY	CLASSICAL	EARLY	CLASSICAL	EARLY	CLASSICAL

Ll the 11th most common letter evolved from *lamed*, the Semitic word-sign for 'ox-goad', the crooked staff used for driving cattle. The Greeks made this an inverted V and called it *lambda*. Adopting a variant from the Etruscan alphabet, the Romans gave 'ell' its present right-angled capital form.

NORTH SEMITIC	PHOENICIAN	GREEK		ETRUSCAN		ROMAN	
		EARLY	CLASSICAL	EARLY	CLASSICAL	EARLY	CLASSICAL

Mm the halfway letter of the English 26 began as the Egyptian hieroglyph for 'water'. Adapting this, the Phoenicians named it *mem*, their word for 'water'. The Greeks renamed it *mu*, and gave it the form which eventually passed via Etruscan into the Roman alphabet.

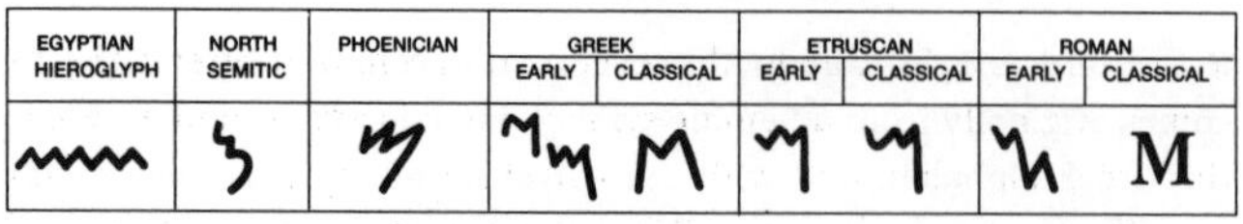

EGYPTIAN HIEROGLYPH	NORTH SEMITIC	PHOENICIAN	GREEK		ETRUSCAN		ROMAN	
			EARLY	CLASSICAL	EARLY	CLASSICAL	EARLY	CLASSICAL
ᴟᴟᴟ	ろ	ᙁ	ᙏᙏ	Μ	ᙏ	ᙏ	ᙖ	M

Nn the sixth most common letter in English is believed by some alphabetologists to derive ultimately from the Egyptian hieroglyph for a serpent. Simplified in form by the Phoenicians, who called it *nun*, their word for 'serpent', it was adapted by the early Greeks and renamed *nu*. After the direction of Greek writing was fixed as left to right in the late 5th century, the symbol was made more symmetrical. The Romans perfected its present form by AD 100.

EGYPTIAN HIEROGLYPH	NORTH SEMITIC	PHOENICIAN	GREEK		ETRUSCAN		ROMAN	
			EARLY	CLASSICAL	EARLY	CLASSICAL	EARLY	CLASSICAL
ᔕ	�	ᒼ	ᒻ	N	ᒼ	ᒻ	ᙀ	N

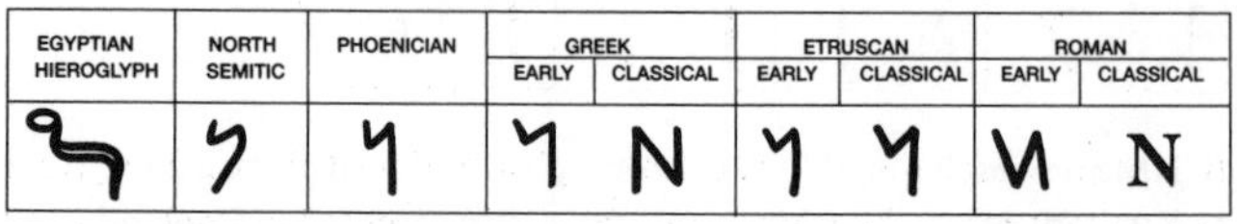

Oo is the **oldest alphabetic letter**, unchanged in shape since the Phoenicians adapted a symbol named *'ayin*, the Semitic word for 'eye', more than 3000 years ago. In the early Greek alphabet, the symbol served as both a long and short o. Later, to distinguish the long open o, the Greeks introduced a new symbol Ω (now called *o mega*, 'great o') which they placed at the end of the alphabet; the original o (now called *o micron*, 'little o') was then used only as short o. About the fourth most commonly used letter in English, o is the only graphic shape resembling its sound-forming lip movement.

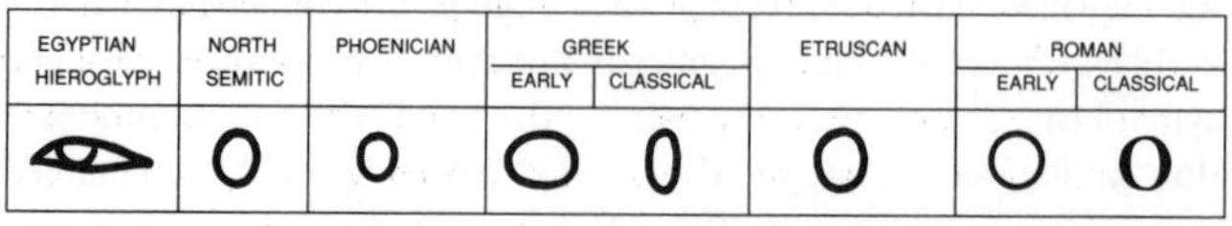

EGYPTIAN HIEROGLYPH	NORTH SEMITIC	PHOENICIAN	GREEK		ETRUSCAN	ROMAN	
			EARLY	CLASSICAL		EARLY	CLASSICAL
⬬	O	O	O	0	O	O	O

Pp is thought to derive from an Egyptian hieroglyph for 'mouth'. The Semites modified the symbol and called it *pe*, meaning 'mouth'. With the same name the symbol, changed to a round-hook shape, passed into the Phoenician alphabet. In Greek, as *pei*, it was written in a variety of forms, among them a squared hook which the Romans later rounded to its present form.

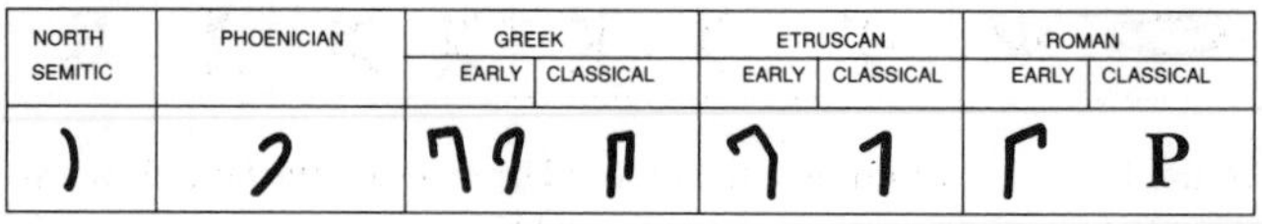

NORTH SEMITIC	PHOENICIAN	GREEK		ETRUSCAN		ROMAN	
		EARLY	CLASSICAL	EARLY	CLASSICAL	EARLY	CLASSICAL
)	?	ᒷᖅ	ᒎ	ᒋ	ᒍ	ᒥ	P

Qq the first letter of QWERTY, the typewriter and computer keyboard system used in English-speaking countries (so-called from the first row of letters; as opposed to the French system AZERTY, or the German QWERTZ) ranks 24th in frequency of use. For their k sound, the ancient Greeks modified a Semitic symbol named *qoph*. Renamed *qoppa* or *koppa*, it was eventually displaced by *kappa* but retained as the numeral* for 90. In the Etruscan alphabet, *koppa* represented the k sound only when followed by u. The Romans gave Q its present capital form, and also established the qu combination now pronounced in many European languages as k or kw. In his *Dictionary of the English Language* (1755), Dr Johnson suggests that the letter's English name, cue, derives from the French *queue*, 'tail', 'its form being that of an O with a tail'. Apparently not; the word 'cue', however, as used in performing arts terminology to mean the signal for some action, originates with the notation Q or q (an abbreviation of the Latin *quando*, 'when') in 16th-century playscripts.

NORTH SEMITIC	PHOENICIAN	GREEK		ETRUSCAN		ROMAN	
		EARLY	CLASSICAL	EARLY	CLASSICAL	EARLY	CLASSICAL
φ	φ	φ	φ	P	Q	Q	Q

Rr dubbed the dog's letter by the Roman satirist Persius because its *rrr* sound suggests a snarl. The sixth most frequently used letter comes from a Semitic symbol called *resh*, a word meaning 'head'. Through Phoenician, it passed into Greek as *rho*, where it was commonly P-shaped. The Romans took another form that had a short diagonal tail, and lengthened it.

EGYPTIAN HIEROGLYPH	NORTH SEMITIC	PHOENICIAN	GREEK		ETRUSCAN		ROMAN	
			EARLY	CLASSICAL	EARLY	CLASSICAL	EARLY	CLASSICAL
◓	◁	◁	◁◁	P	◁	◁	◁	R

Nurse *Doth not rosemary and Romeo begin both with a letter?*
Romeo *Ay, nurse: what of that? both with an R.*
Nurse *Ah! mocker; that's the dog's name.*

Shakespeare *Romeo and Juliet* Act 2 Scene 4

Ss is the **most common initial letter**, occupying about one seventh of the dictionary; and the eighth most frequently used. It derives ultimately from the North Semitic *shin*, meaning 'tooth'. Via the Phoenicians, it passed into the Greek alphabet where it was used in both an angular and slightly rounded form. Eventually, turned on its side, it became the Classical Greek letter *sigma*. The Romans may have borrowed their rounded form from a Greek alphabet in use in southern Italy. In English printing, the rounded small s first appeared in Joseph Ames' *Typographical Antiquities* in 1749. Prior to that, and occasionally even as late as the 19th century, the small letter in English manuscripts and printing, was similar to the modern f.

EGYPTIAN HIEROGLYPH	NORTH SEMITIC	PHOENICIAN	GREEK		ETRUSCAN		ROMAN	
			EARLY	CLASSICAL	EARLY	CLASSICAL	EARLY	CLASSICAL
𝍖	⌇	W	Ϟ	Ϩ	Ϟ	Ϟ	Ϟ	S

Tt the second most common letter and the **most frequently used consonant** is descended from the final letter of the ancient Semitic alphabet called *taw*, a word meaning simply 'mark' or 'sign'. When the Greeks borrowed this for their last letter, they renamed it *tau*. Gradually, the crossbar moved to the top of the vertical, and in this form it passed via Etruscan into the Roman alphabet.

NORTH SEMITIC	PHOENICIAN	GREEK		ETRUSCAN		ROMAN	
		EARLY	CLASSICAL	EARLY	CLASSICAL	EARLY	CLASSICAL
+	+ ×	T	T	T	↑	T	T

Uu is a variant of V, with which it was interchangeable throughout the Middle Ages. It did not begin to function exclusively as the fifth vowel symbol until after 1700. It is now about the 12th commonest letter.

NORTH SEMITIC	PHOENICIAN	GREEK CLASSICAL	ETRUSCAN EARLY	ETRUSCAN CLASSICAL	ROMAN EARLY	ROMAN MODERN
Y	Y	Y	Y	V	V	U

Vv called vee, derives ultimately, like U, W, and Y, from the North Semitic *waw*, one form of which became known in the Greek alphabet as *upsilon*. Passing from the Etruscan alphabet, where it acquired its present form, into the Roman, V represented both the vowel sound u and the consonantal w. In Roman handwriting, V became U-shaped. Although scribes of the Middle Ages began to write V as the initial letter and U elsewhere in a word, there was no fixed differentiation. Even as late as the 18th century, the two forms remained interchangeable as consonant and vowel.

NORTH SEMITIC	PHOENICIAN	GREEK CLASSICAL	ETRUSCAN EARLY	ETRUSCAN CLASSICAL	ROMAN EARLY	ROMAN CLASSICAL
Y	Y	Y	Y	V	V	V

Ww the 19th most common letter in English is descended ultimately from *waw*, a North Semitic symbol used to express the w sound. In the Greek alphabet, where it was later named *upsilon*, 'slender u', *waw* came to signify a sound halfway between e and u. To express the w sound, the Greeks modified another form of *waw* (this form, later called *digamma*, was eventually abandoned; see F). In the Roman alphabet, a form of *upsilon* was adopted to express the w sound in early Latin. Gradually, this sound disappeared; in the Romance languages (i.e. French, Italian, Portuguese, Romanian, Castilian Spanish) the sound and symbol occur only in borrowed words. In Old English, the w sound was represented by a Runic* symbol named *wen* or *wyn*. Following the Norman Conquest of England in the 11th century, scribes gradually replaced the rune with two 'V's. This VV form (later called *double-vé* in French) was also written UU, hence the letter's English name *double-u*. In the Welsh alphabet, w represents a vowel, pronounced u as in put.

NORTH SEMITIC	PHOENICIAN	GREEK EARLY	ETRUSCAN EARLY	ETRUSCAN CLASSICAL	ROMAN EARLY	ROMAN CLASSICAL
Y	Y	⅂	⅂	⅂	⅂	W

Xx Among the 19 Phoenician symbols the Greeks inherited was one for s named *samekh*. Adapting this for their ks sound, they renamed it *xei*. Later, they introduced a new symbol, *chi*. In the alphabet of the Greek settlement in Ionia (western Turkey) this took on the sound kh. The x form and ks value were adopted by the Romans, who called it ix and placed it at the end of their early alphabet. Although in the English 26 the letter x ranks only about 25th in frequency of use, it has numerous abstract and symbolic functions: for instance, it represents a kiss*. X is also the only letter in English to stand on its own as a verb, meaning to obliterate a typewritten character by typing x over it.

NORTH SEMITIC	PHOENICIAN	GREEK EARLY	GREEK CLASSICAL	ROMAN EARLY	ROMAN CLASSICAL
ꓵ	ꓵ	X	X	x	X

Yy acts as both vowel and consonant. Unlike its English name *wy*, both the modern German name *Ypsilon* and the French *i grec* or 'Greek i' give a clue to its origin in *upsilon*. The Romans introduced Y into their alphabet after the conquest of Greece in the 1st century BC solely to write words borrowed from Greek.

In English manuscripts of the early Middle Ages, one form of y closely resembled the Runic symbol, *thorn* **Þ**, which expressed the *th* sound. Y became a substitute for th, and long after 'thorn' was discarded, words like the, that, and them, were commonly abbreviated to y^e, y^t, y^m. One relic of this practice may still be seen in some pseudo-archaic signs, such as *Ye Olde Teashoppe*.

NORTH SEMITIC	PHOENICIAN	GREEK		ETRUSCAN		ROMAN	
		EARLY	CLASSICAL	EARLY	CLASSICAL	EARLY	CLASSICAL
Y	Ч	ı	ı	ı	ı	Y	Y

Zz called *zee* in the US, and *zed* or even *izzard* in Britain, this is the last and the **least used letter**. It derives from a Semitic and Phoenician symbol *zayin*, which also meant 'weapon'. The Greeks changed *zayin* to *zeta*, its form to Z, and placed it sixth. Because it had no value in the early Roman alphabet, z was discarded and its position taken by the newly introduced letter G. Later reinstated to write words borrowed from Greek, it was relegated to 23rd place at the very end of the alphabet. Because of this final position in the English 26, z is often used to denote the last of anything, as in the phrase 'from A to Z'.

NORTH SEMITIC	PHOENICIAN	GREEK		ROMAN
		EARLY	CLASSICAL	CLASSICAL
I	I	I	Z	Z

The write sound

In the best of all possible worlds, the symbols in an alphabet will do all the work asked of them, i.e. represent each significant speech sound of the language, and at the same time be distinct and easy to remember, to read, and to write. That, of course, is in the best of all possible worlds.

Some alphabets have come close to perfection with very few symbols. The Roman-based Hawaiian alphabet, for instance, has only 13 to represent its five vowels and eight consonants, including one like a question mark* without the dot. But the title for the world's **shortest** and simplest alphabet belongs to the Rotokas language of Bougainville, North Solomons Province of Papua New Guinea, which contains only 11. At the other extreme, the world's **longest** alphabet is the Cambodian with 72.

A Roman-based alphabet is generally thought to be the most 'user-friendly'. It is also the most compact. Many languages using it get by with an average of 20 to 30 symbols. Even so, because the alphabet is second-hand rather than tailor-made, there is usually a lack of correspondence between the symbols and the native sounds they represent.

Spelling trouble

English is notoriously unphonetic. It was once estimated that our alphabet of 26 letters is capable of more than twenty-nine thousand quatrillion combinations, or to put it numerically: 29 000 000 000 000 000 000 000 000 000 combinations.

Abstract friends

You feel obliged to ask the X's, the Y's, and the Z's from duty, and so you do . . . This is the kind of assortment that arrives: Papa X, Mamma X, and two girl X'es; Papa Y, Mamma Y, and Master and Miss Y; Papa Z, Mamma Z, Aunt Z . . . such a party!

Elinor Glyn *The Visits of Elizabeth*

Thou whoreson zed! thou unnecessary letter!

Shakespeare Kent to Oswald *King Lear* Act 2

& is for ampersand

In the Middle Ages, scribes began to write the symbol & for 'and'. In the course of time, this ampersand, as it is called, was added to the end of the alphabet, where it became, in effect, the 27th letter.

The symbol's origin is straightforward: formerly known as the 'tironian sign', after its inventor, Marcus Tullius Tiro*, '&' is merely a shorthand contraction of *et*, the Latin word for 'and'. But why 'ampersand'?

Long ago, single letters that could stand as words in their own right were given names. So, for example, 'a' as in 'a table' was described verbally as 'a *per se* a', *per se* being the Latin for 'by itself'. In the same way, when children in the 18th and 19th centuries were learning their alphabet, they chanted '...x, y, z, and per se and', meaning 'the symbol & by itself represents and'. Gradually, this 'and per se and' was garbled into 'ampassy-and', 'ampussy', or 'amsiam', but most generally 'ampersand'.

Mnemonic alphabets

In days of old, children of many countries learned the alphabet by rhyming verses and songs. The earliest known example in England was quoted in 1671 in John Eachard's 'Some Observations'. It remained a favourite for more than two centuries, often appearing under the imposing title 'The tragical Death of A, APPLE PYE Who was Cut in Pieces and Eat by Twenty-Five Gentlemen with whom All Little People Ought to be Very well acquainted'. The 'Gentlemen' to whom the original title refers included the ampersand, but excluded the letter U (in earlier versions, the letters I and J were not differentiated). This illustrated version, published around 1860 as *The History of an Apple Pie*, 'eaten by 26 gentlemen', comes from *The Oxford Nursery Rhyme Book* assembled by Iona and Peter Opie.

A was an Apple pie	B Bit it	C Cut it	D Dealt it
E Eat it	F Fought for it	G Got it	H Had it
I Inspected it	J Joined for it	K Kept it	L Longed for it
M Mourned for it	N Nodded at it	O Opened it	P Peeped in it
Q Quartered it	R Ran for it	S Stole it	T Took it
U Upset it	V Viewed it	W Wanted it	XYZ and & All wished for a piece in hand

Symbols for all sounds

Some unlikely symbols have been pressed into service in Roman-based alphabets. You might suppose, for instance, that '&' in written Marshallese, the language of the Marshall Islands in the Pacific, was the ubiquitous ampersand*, meaning 'and'. In fact, it represents a vowel sound somewhere between e and i.

Equally unconventional are some of the symbols used to represent the unique consonants in the southern African 'click' languages, so-called because the sounds are made by sucking air through the lips and clicking the tongue. Among this group of languages is Hottentot, which includes the additional symbols #, /, //, ≠, and !.

An impressive figure, and yet, we have no means of differentiating the various vowel sounds. For example, the letter a can be pronounced at least nine different ways in words like: any, cat, mate, war, orange, fare, want, about, farm. The letter e is equally indefinite, and the other three vowels also have a number of variations. The consonant symbols are more stable; but there is still room for confusion, as any foreign student of English will readily agree when it comes to spelling.

One of the problems is that our alphabet is inadequate: there are too few symbols to cope with too many sounds. For example, there are none specifically to write the sounds ch, sh, th, ng. On the other hand, three of the 26, c, q, and x, are redundant and could be discarded, though this would probably lead to new confusion.

Since the 17th century, there have been many attempts in Britain and the US to reform the alphabet. In the late 18th century, the statesman and inventor Benjamin Franklin (1706–90), lamented: 'If we go on as we have done a few Centuries longer, our words will gradually cease to express Sounds, they will only stand for things, as the written words do in the Chinese language'. Franklin published his own reformed alphabet in 1768; it was not adopted.

In the late 19th century, phonetic alphabets were introduced in the US to simplify spelling for the thousands of immigrants from Eastern Europe. The American Spelling Reform Association, founded 1876, produced a modified Roman alphabet of 32 letters. In 1906, with a similar goal, Andrew Carnegie donated a quarter of a million dollars to help found the Simplified Spelling Board.

Among recent proposals are Bernard Shaw's British alphabet*, and UNIFON which was invented in 1959 by John Malone, an economist from Chicago. Like i.t.a.*, a British invention of the same year, UNIFON is intended to help the learning of English in the earliest stages.

International phonetics

One alphabet that has achieved considerable and lasting success is **IPA**, the International Phonetic Alphabet. This was devised by the International Phonetic Association, which began in Paris in 1886 – originally under the title *Dhi Fonètik Tîtcerz' Asóciécon* – to reform modern language teaching by introducing phonetic notation into school class-rooms. Within a year membership of the association had spread to 11 other countries, including the US. Incidentally, among the early members were the English philologist Henry Sweet (said to be the model for Professor Higgins in Bernard Shaw's *Pygmalion*), and Melville Bell (father of the inventor of the telephone Alexander Graham Bell), who some twenty years earlier had devised his own system of phonetic notation called *Visible Speech*.

ᘊᖇᘋᘓᗯᘋᘝᖇᗯᖇᘓ ᘓᘐᘋᖇᗯᗉᘓᖇᘌᘋᘝᗷ ᘌᘐᘖᘝᖇᗷᖇᘓᘓᗷᗷ ᘓᗯᘋᘐᘋᗯ

From a text transliterated into Bell's 'Visible Speech'

IPA is regularly reviewed to symbolise, on phonetic principles, every sound in human speech. The last review was in 1989. Currently the system comprises a basic set of 115 independent vowel, consonant, and miscellaneous symbols, to which diacritics and other marks may be added to make an almost unlimited number of combinations.

Now widely accepted throughout the world, IPA symbols are used in the creation of new alphabets for previously unwritten languages, and in the teaching of foreign languages, or dialects containing unfamiliar sounds.

The heart of our trouble is with our foolish alphabet. It doesn't know how to spell, and can't be taught. In this it is like all other alphabets except one – the phonographic. That is the only competent alphabet in the world.

Mark Twain *Essays: A Simplified Alphabet*

In Europe and the United States, the most common application of IPA is as a pronunciation key in dictionaries. Many use around 40 to 45 symbols. The 2nd edition (1989) of the 20-volume *Oxford English Dictionary* lists 79.

| ɸ β | f v | θ ð | s z | ʃ ʒ | ʂ ʐ | ç ʝ | x ɣ | χ ʁ | ħ ʕ | h ɦ |

Fricative consonants from The International Phonetic Alphabet (IPA)

The most commonly used IPA symbol is the upside down e, known as the **schwa**. The name derives via German from the Hebrew *sheva*, a sign used in Hebrew grammar under a consonant to signify the absence of a vowel. In IPA it denotes the neutral vowel sound. It first appeared in a work for general readers in the *American College Dictionary* in 1947. The editor, Clarence L. Barnhart, felt it recorded the unstressed vowel sound better than any of the previously used phonetic symbols. Some years earlier, Shaw had included the symbol in the dialogue for his 1941 film edition of *Pygmalion*, for the 'indefinite vowel sometimes called obscure or neutral, for which though it is one of the commonest sounds in English speech, our wretched alphabet has no letter'.

Diacritics

The most common way of bringing the alphabet up to phonetic strength is by adding special marks called **diacritics** (from the Greek, 'to distinguish'). Such marks have been used since ancient times as vowel symbols in writing systems like Arabic and Hebrew. In others, particularly Roman-based systems, the marks, placed above, below, beside, or even through a letter, serve mainly to denote the difference between a symbol and a specific national sound that would otherwise have no symbol, or to change the vowel sound. Although English is one of the few systems without diacritics, they may still be found in borrowed foreign words.

The **most common diacritic** is the **acute accent** (´). Invented in the 3rd century BC by Aristophanes of Byzantium to indicate tone or pitch in Greek verse-speaking, it was introduced with its opposite sign, the **grave** (`), into French during the reign of Louis XIII (1601–43) to differentiate pronunciation of certain vowels, or to distinguish certain homonyms – words that have the same sound and often the same spelling but different meanings: for example *ou* (or) and *où* (where).

The acute is also used in Czech, Gaelic, Icelandic, Italian, Polish, Portuguese, Spanish, and Hungarian which holds the record for the **most accented word**: újjáépítésére, meaning 'for its reconstruction'. In Italian, the grave marks the stress point of a normally unstressed syllable. A similar use occurred formerly in English poetry as, for example, in 'time's wingèd chariot'.

Aristophanes also invented the **circumflex** (ˆ). This mark, whose name means literally 'bent round', served originally in classical Greek to indicate a rising–falling tone in verse-speaking. In the 16th century, French printers adopted the mark to indicate where a consonant had been dropped, as in *île* (formerly *isle*, island). A government proposal in 1990 to abandon the circumflex was withdrawn after a public outcry. Sometimes referred to as the bowed or umbrella accent, the sign is also affectionately known as the little hat. The Portuguese, Romanian, and Turkish alphabets also use the circumflex.

Although not a diacritic, a variant of the circumflex worth noting is the caret (∧) used by proofreaders to denote where something is to be inserted in written or printed matter. From this evolved the more general omission sign ⋏ . The name caret (first recorded in English in 1710) is derived from Latin meaning 'there is lacking'.

In Czech, an **inverted circumflex** is used. Also called the wedge, check, or hacek, the sign (ˇ) was introduced in about 1410 by the Czech religious writer and reformer Jan Hus (1371–1415).

Another common mark is the **cedilla** (¸). Derived from the Spanish *zedilla*, 'little z', and originally written in that form, it was introduced into French in 1529 by the printer Geoffroy Tory (*c*.1480–1533). Its most common function is best illustrated in the word 'façade' where the sign indicates the c is sounded not as k as usual but as s.

When placed over the second of two adjoining vowels, the **diaeresis** (¨), from Greek 'taking apart', indicates they are pronounced separately, as in naïve, or Noël. The sign also denotes pronunciation of a vowel which might otherwise have been interpreted as mute, as for example the name Brontë. Known in German as **Umlaut**, a name invented by the writer and philologist Jacob Grimm (1785–1863), the same sign replaces the older ae, oe, ue to make ä, ö, ü. In Hungarian a modified diaeresis, in effect a double acute accent (˝), lengthens the vowels o and u.

The **tilde** (~), from Latin *titulus*, 'superscription', was first used in medieval manuscripts to denote the abbreviation of double consonants, for example *año* for *anno*. Subsequently and almost exclusively, it was adopted in Spanish to indicate the nasal n, like ny in canyon. In Portuguese, the same sign called **til** nasalises the vowels a and o. The tilde is commonly used in dictionary articles as a symbol to represent the word, or part of the word, being defined.

Among other diacritics in European systems are the **breve** (˘), and the **macron** (ˉ), both also used in dictionaries as **quantity marks** to indicate short and long vowels respectively, the **hook** as in Polish ą, the **ring** or **bolle** (from Danish 'ball') as in Danish and Swedish å, and the **solidus** or **virgule** as in Danish ø.

Nue speling

Among the proposals for a simpler alphabet is the Initial Teaching Alphabet, or i.t.a. It comprises all the symbols of the English alphabet minus q and x, and an additional 20 modified conventional symbols, making a total of 44 in all.

Published in 1959, i.t.a. was devised by Sir James Pitman (grandson of the inventor of Pitman Shorthand*) to teach children and illiterate adults elementary reading and writing. As its name implies, the Initial Teaching Alphabet was intended as a stepping stone to the conventional alphabet, the theory being that the resemblance of its 44 symbols to those of the traditional 26 would enable students to acquire the basic skills of English before having to struggle with the irregularities of its spelling.

First introduced in 19 English infant schools in 1961, the system divided opinions. Some teachers viewed i.t.a. with suspicion and condemned it for being hastily conceived and developed. They argued that having to learn an extra 20 symbols that did not exist in the real world was ultimately confusing, and that this *nue speling* would lead students into bad habits which would later take time and effort to correct. One critic went so far as to describe it as 'one of the cruellest deceptions ever practised on children'. Nevertheless, other teachers welcomed i.t.a., and in some schools, both in Britain and the US, the system proved very successful.

Ghoti & chips?

Over the years numerous phonetic systems have been devised to eliminate inconsistencies in English spelling. In their *Dictionary of Word & Phrase Origins*, William and Mary Morris cite a few examples of the strange hybrids proposed. One of the most delightfully absurd is ghoti. This, believe it or not, is a phonetic spelling of 'fish', derived from the *gh* sound in rough, the *o* in women, and the *ti* as in nation. Quite simple, really!

Initial Teaching Alphabet (i.t.a.)

A Shavian solution

George Bernard Shaw (1856–1950) took a typically unique approach to the inadequacies of the English alphabet: he left them till after his death.

In his will, he bequeathed £10 000 for the development of a new and aesthetically pleasing alphabet which would be easy to learn, read, and write; be more efficient in time and effort and, to save printing costs, be more economical in space. Above all, Shaw wanted each distinct sound to be spelt with its own distinct symbol, without diacritics, assuming, as he put it, 'pronunciation to resemble that recorded of His Majesty our late King George V'.

A competition was announced for the design of this new British alphabet, and from more than 400 entries worldwide the £500 prize was divided among four winners. Finally, a design by the English typographer Kingsley Read was adopted. It contains 48 symbols, comprising 24 vowels and 24 consonants. Four 'word-signs' for the common words were also included: the (using the th symbol), and (n), of (v), to (t). Similar contractions were suggested for a number of other frequently used words such as have (hv) from (fm), etc.

Kingsley Read's design for the British alphabet first appeared in print in 1962 with this transliteration of Shaw's play *Androcles and the Lion*

Although it fulfills Shaw's criteria for a more efficient system, the new symbols were so totally different from those of the traditional alphabet, that beyond its original novelty value his legacy won few disciples and achieved only limited acceptance.

Symbols for speed

Since the earliest days, the quest for speed in writing has produced numerous methods known variously as bachygraphy (short writing), phonography (sound writing), stenography (narrow writing), or tachygraphy (swift writing). The generic term for these is shorthand. Specially devised for transcribing the spoken word, shorthand is used whenever the conventional alphabet cannot keep pace with normal speech, from taking a memo in the office to recording debates in Parliament.

Early shorthand

The ancient Egyptians, Hebrews, and Persians used shorthand systems in which words or even phrases were represented by arbitrary or hieroglyphic signs such as a small circle within a larger circle to signify 'around the world'. The early Greeks developed an abbreviated form of ordinary spelling. While this omitted all letters not essential to the meaning, it also required a large number of arbitrary symbols for the sake of brevity. This 'short hand' was used mainly by official chroniclers to record events and speeches. In the 4th century BC, the historian Xenophon used a similar system to write the memoirs of Socrates.

The **earliest known complete shorthand**, *Notæ Tironionæ* (Tironian Notes), was invented by a Roman slave Marcus Tullius Tiro in 63 BC to transcribe the speeches of his master, the statesman and orator Cicero (106–43 BC). Tiro's system, based on longhand script, gained widespread currency in Rome. It was taught in schools, and celebrated users included Julius Caesar and the emperor Titus. The system outlived the Roman empire and was widely used in Europe for more than a thousand years, only declining in the Middle Ages when it became associated with the dark mysteries of sorcery. During Elizabethan times the 'Notes' were successfully revived and expanded to several thousand symbols.

Although Tiro's shorthand is now forgotten, one survivor is **&**, the aptly-named Tironian Sign, more familiarly known as the ampersand*.

Tiro's shorthand

Elizabethan shorthand

In 1588, Elizabeth I granted a patent to Dr Timothy Bright for a 'shorte and new kynde of writing by character to the furtherance of good learning'. Bright's shorthand, published that year under the title *Characterie: an Arte of Shorte, Swifte and Secret Writing by Character*, used combinations of straight lines, circles, and half circles to denote particular groups of words. Bright claimed his system could be mastered in two months; a later critic complained it was as difficult to acquire as any foreign language.

The **first truly alphabetic shorthand** appeared in England in 1602 with *The Arte of Stenography*, by John Willis. This was followed by other orthographic systems, among them Thomas Shelton's *Tachygraphical Alphabet* (1626), which Samuel Pepys adopted for his diary. Twenty years later, Jeremiah Rich became the **first known teacher of shorthand**, instructing his pupils in his own system, and it seems with some success. His principal claim to lasting fame is the first shorthand transliteration of the Psalms and the New Testament.

In the 18th century, numerous other systems evolved, including one by Thomas Gurney, the official reporter at the Old Bailey Criminal Court. The young Charles Dickens used Gurney's shorthand in the early 1830s when he worked as parliamentary reporter for the *Morning Chronicle*.

The **first cursive shorthand**, grandly named 'speech-sign art', was developed by Franz Gabelsberger in Germany in 1834. Based on Roman longhand symbols, and relatively simple for adaptation to other languages, it became widely used during the 19th century in Austria, Switzerland, Scandinavia, and Russia. In 1928, it was adopted as the official system in Italy.

The **first important phonetic shorthand**, i.e. based entirely on the sound of words rather than on the spelling, appeared in England in 1783 with Samuel Taylor's *Universal Stenography*. Adapted by the English law courts, Taylor's phonetic system went on to world renown, providing the basis of the first systems to be published in several European countries and, in 1819, in the United States.

Phonographic forms

The two **most popular and enduring shorthand forms** since the 19th century were invented by Isaac Pitman (1813–97), and John Robert Gregg (1867–1948). In 1837 Pitman devised a phonetic system called *Stenographic Sound Hand*. Republished in 1840 under the title

Cutting the alphabet down to size

Concern about the illogicalities of the English alphabet has occupied professional writers for centuries. To aid reform, some advocated an increase in the number of symbols. Mark Twain proposed quite the reverse, and in *A Plan for the Improvement of English Spelling* he suggested how the necessary reduction could best be achieved:

'In Year 1 that useless letter "c" would be dropped to be replased either by "k" or "s", and likewise "x" would no longer be part of the alphabet.

'The only kase in which "c" would be retained would be the "ch" formation, which will be dealt with later. Year 2 might reform "w" spelling, so that "which" and "one" would take the same konsonant, wile Year 3 might well abolish "y" replasing it with "i" and iear 4 might fiks the "g/j" anomali wonse and for all.

'Jenerally, then, the improvement would kontinue iear bai iear with iear 5 doing awai with useless double konsonants, and iears 6–12 or so modifaiing vowlz and the rimeining voist and unvoist konsonants.

'Bai iear 15 or sou, it wud fainali bi posibl tu meik ius ov thi ridandant letez "c", "y" and "x" – bai now jast a memori in the maindz ov ould doderez – tu riplais "ch", "sh", and "th" rispektivli.

'Fainali, xen, aafte sam 20 iers ov orxogrefkl riform, wi wud hev a lojikl, kohirnt speling in ius xrewawt xe Ingliy-spiking werld.'

A phonographic record

In New York in December 1922, Nathan Behrin, using Pitman, set the world speed record for shorthand at 350 wpm for two minutes with 99.72 per cent accuracy. Behrin's record has probably stood unbroken through the years because it is almost impossible for anyone to talk any faster – at least, not coherently.

Phonography, it marked a breakthrough as the first truly practical shorthand in which all words are transcribed strictly according to sound. In 1852, Pitman's brother took the system to the US, and founded the Phonographic Institute in Cincinnati, Ohio. By 1889, 97 per cent of North American shorthand writers were using Pitman or a modified version.

Pitman shorthand

Pitman's name is almost universally synonymous with shorthand. It has been translated into more than 20 languages including Latin, Japanese and Tamil, and is currently used by around 30 million people worldwide. It is also the official shorthand for the reporters of Hansard, the offical verbatim record of the proceedings and debates of Parliament.

John Robert Gregg, who had taught himself an adaptation of Taylor's shorthand by the age of 10, rejected Pitman's intricate geometric forms in favour of a cursive script:

Gregg shorthand

In his *Light-Line Phonography* (1888), independent symbols for vowels and consonants, written with the same thickness on a single line, follow the slope and movement of ordinary handwriting. This makes it an altogether easier method to master. Being phonetic, Gregg can also be adapted to any spoken language, and is now, after Pitman, the world's second most successful system.

Speedwriting

Beyond Pitman and Gregg, the most successful rapid-writing system is Speedwriting. The invention of a Connecticut shorthand teacher, Emma Dearborn, it was introduced in the US in 1923, and in Britain in 1927.

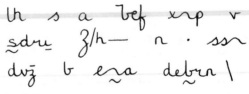

Speedwriting

Originally designed to be taken down on a typewriter, Speedwriting was modified in 1942 to be written with pen or pencil. As a form of abbreviated longhand, using only Roman letters and punctuation marks, it has the advantage over most other systems in that more than 20 000 words can be transcribed with a total of just 60 rules and around 100 brief forms and standard abbreviations.

Finger alphabets

A number of alphabetic systems have been devised for specific tasks or groups of people. Morse* and semaphore* are used for communicating over long distances, and for the deaf there are a variety of manual alphabets (see Chapter 3). Here it is worth recording two alphabets invented for the blind.

Until the mid-19th century, lessons in reading for the blind, if any, consisted of little more than feeling twigs in the shape of letters of the alphabet. In 1791, Valentin Haüy (1745–1822) founded the Institution for Blind Children in Paris. He also invented the means of producing large embossed Roman letters. Though this was a considerable step forward, the texts were heavy and unwieldy, and the letters themselves were difficult to read with accuracy. The breakthrough to something better occurred at the Institution in 1824 with Braille, a system of writing and printing in raised dots.

Braille's vision

Louis Braille (1809–52) the son of a saddler, was born in Coupvray near Paris. At the age of three, playing with an awl from his father's workbench, he damaged an eye. Blindness in both eyes followed shortly afterwards.

At the local school he learned his alphabet with the traditional twigs, and at the age of 10 was sent to the Institution in Paris. There, in addition to Haüy's embossed letters, he learned of a method devised by Charles Barbier, an artillery officer, for sending messages to his soldiers at night. Composed of holes punched in cardboard, the messages could be deciphered solely by touch. Barbier's invention was primitive and, for anything more than the simplest messages, impractical. Moreover, the symbols were too large for a child's fingertips. Nevertheless, the system sparked an idea in Braille. He began to experiment, and in 1824 at the age of 15, introduced his own system: a small 'cell' consisting of two vertical rows of three embossed dots arranged and numbered 1, 2, 3, down the left and 4, 5, 6, down the right.

1 • • 4
2 • • 5
3 • • 6

This gave 63 possible combinations. From these, Braille worked out the letters of the alphabet (originally excluding w which was rarely used in French), punctuation marks, numerals, mathematical signs, and a number of common words such as 'and', 'for', 'of', 'the', 'with'.

Braille alphabet

Braille looks complicated, but to a blind person with normal finger sensitivity, it is not so very different from deciphering the graphic symbols that form our written words. To read it, both hands are used: the right picks up the message as the left feels for the beginning of the next line. In this way, a skilled reader can understand up to 150 words a minute, about half the speed of a sighted person.

No less important was the fact that for the first time, by using a stylus (and later machines) to press out the raised dots on paper, blind people could also write. Like many a prophet in his own land, and in spite of his fellow students' enthusiasm, Braille's invention was not officially

Geometry and algebraille

If you have ever struggled with mathematical signs and symbols, imagine how much more difficult they are in Braille – especially if you have learnt one system and you suddenly find yourself about to be tested in another. Such was the case for the blind deaf-mute Helen Keller (1880–1968), as she prepared to sit the examinations for New England's prestigious Radcliffe College in 1899.

She was not unduly worried about the exams, which included Advanced Greek and Latin, until just before the algebra and geometry papers, when she found with dismay that the notation would be American. 'I was sorely perplexed', she wrote in *The Story of My Life*. 'I was familiar with all literary braille in common use in this country: English, American, and New York Point; but the various signs and symbols in geometry and algebra in the three systems are very different, and I had used only the English braille in my algebra.'

A table of the American notation was hurriedly provided, and she set to work to master it. Evidently her diligence paid off: she passed the exams and entered Radcliffe the following year.

---

accepted in France until 1853, a year after his death from tuberculosis. In 1869, it was adapted as the standard system in England, and in 1932 as the universal system for the English-speaking world.

The largest Braille publisher in Europe is the London-based Royal National Institute for the Blind. It regularly produces books, magazines, and many other items including sheet music, exam papers, even bank statements. However, while Braille is the most effective reading and writing system yet devised for the blind, the number of people learning it has declined. The RNIB estimate that of about one million people in Britain who are blind or seriously sight-impaired, only about 25 000 are now Braille users.

Moon type

A lesser known alphabet is Moon, so-called after its inventor William Moon (1818–94). Partially blind from the age of four, he lost his sight completely by the time he was 21. He began to teach blind children, but finding the conventional embossed letters unsatisfactory, and unaware of Braille, in 1847 he produced his own system of raised curves and lines, based on those of nine Roman capital letters.

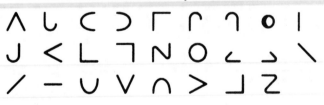

Moon alphabet

Over the years Moon has been expanded and now uses a full complement of letters, numerals, punctuation marks, and word signs. Originally devised to be read boustrophedon* style, the system was changed in the 1980s to the conventional left–right direction.

Larger than Braille and pressed only on one side of the page, Moon takes up more space and is consequently more expensive to produce and publish. However, because the symbols require less finger sensitivity, they are easier to read. This is a major advantage for people who lose their sight late in life. For the same reasons, Moon is sometimes used as a stepping stone to Braille.

Hands-on experience

Writer Aldous Huxley turned to Braille in his youth when he developed serious eye trouble. 'It is not without compensations,' he observed about his disability. 'Being able to read Braille, I can read in bed with the book beneath the blankets, so my hands are kept warm on even the coldest nights.'

A world of alphabets

Since the very first alphabet, around 3500 years ago, more than 200 scripts have evolved in an extraordinary variety of squiggles, dots, sharp angles and flowing curves. Here is a selection of just a few of them, past and present – in alphabetical order, of course.

Arabic third most widespread alphabet after Roman and Cyrillic. Evolved from Aramaic around the 4th century, and written right to left, Arabic consists of 28 consonant letters, with vowels indicated by marks above or below. With the exception of elementary school books and editions of the Koran, vowel marks are usually omitted. An unusual feature is that each letter is written differently according to its position: whether at the beginning, in the middle, at the end of a word, or even on its own.

Two forms developed. The first, dating from the 7th century, is **Kufic**, in which the Koran was originally written. This upright, decorative script for inscriptions on metal or stone is now rarely used.

ﺍﻟﻄﺎﺑﺎﺕ ﺑﺎﺑﻚ ﻣﺼﺪﻭﺍﻟﻤﺎ ﺳﺮ ﻧﺪﻩ ﻭﺑﺎﺑﺮﻙ ﺍﻟﻨﻮﺭﻩ،

From the second form, the 10th-century cursive **Naskhi**, come the numerous Arabic scripts in general use today, among them those adapted for writing Persian, Kurdish, Pashto, Sindhi, Urdu, some African languages such as Swahili, the languages of Indonesia and Malaysia, and in China the Turkic language Uigur.

فَوْتُ الغَنَى فِى لِعَزِمِثْلَ حَيَاتِهِ وَعِيشُهُ فِى الذُّلِ عَينَ مَمَاتِهِ

Aramaic alphabet of the lingua franca of the ancient Middle East, derived from Phoenician around the 10th century BC. The ancestor of Square Hebrew*, Arabic, and directly or indirectly, all the alphabets of the East.

Armenian early 5th-century invention by the missionary St Mesrop to translate the Bible into the Armenian language Hayaren. Originally 30 consonants and 6 vowels, the alphabet was enlarged to 38 symbols in the 12th century.

կուզեի հավատալ մեկին։

Batak 16 basic symbols, which can be modified with diacritics, record the language of the people of Sumatra. It is now being replaced by the Roman alphabet.

Brahmi derived from Aramaic in the 7th century BC. Now extinct, this earliest Indian alphabet is thought to be one of the most accurate and efficient ever devised. From Brahmi come more than 200 Indian and Southeast Asian scripts, including Gupta, Siddhamatrika, Devanagari.

Buginese alphabet for the language spoken on the Indonesian island of Celebes. It is believed to have originated in Java.

Burmese considered one of the most beautiful scripts. The alphabet, derived ultimately from Aramaic, has 32 consonants and 10 vowels. The distinctive circles and arcs evolved from the practice of writing with a stylus on palm leaves; straight lines would have split the leaf.

Coptic devised in the 2nd century to represent the Egyptian spoken by Egyptian Christians. The alphabet comprises 24 letters adapted from Greek, and seven from a simplified form of Egyptian hieroglyphs. Following the Islamic conquest of Egypt in the mid-7th century, both language and script were ousted by Arabic. It survives today only in the liturgy of the Coptic or Christian Church of Egypt.

ⲀⲨⲱ ⲈⲒⳜ ⲠⲔⲀⲢⲘⲎⲗⲟⳞ Ⲁⳡ

Cyrillic the second most important alphabet. Its invention is attributed to the Greek missionaries St Cyril (*c.* AD 827–869) and his brother St Methodius (*c.* AD 815–895). Originally of 43 letters adapted from Greek and Hebrew, the alphabet was reformed after the 1917 Russian revolution and reduced to 33. Cyrillic is used to write Russian (shown below), Bulgarian, Ukrainian, and many other languages. Some of these, such as Serbian, have introduced additional letters.

тельной, может быть, для всего

Devanagari means 'writing of the city of the gods'. The principal script of northern India (used for modern languages such as Hindi, Marathi, Kashmiri, and Gujarati) developed in the 7th century to write the ancient literary language Sanskrit. Distinctively, all the letters appear to be suspended from an overhead horizontal line.

प्रच्छाद्यारायसमीपे सस्यक्षेत्रे मोचितः ।

Ethiopic used to write Amharic, the national language of Ethiopia. This last surviving South Semitic script, dating back nearly 3000 years, was originally written right to left, but changed to left–right under Greek influence. Each word is separated from the next by two dots.

ተገነባኩ ። ወኦነኩ ። ከ ወ ። ዓፉ ። ነኩ ታ ዩ ። ወኩተ ። ናሐከ

Georgian invented by St Mesrop in the 5th century, the alphabet of Georgia is based in part on Pahlavik, an early Persian script. The present script of 33 letters, written right to left and called Mkhedruli ('secular writing'), replaced the original Khutsuri ('church writing') in the 11th century.

ცივცხლსა, წყალსა და მიწასა, ჰაერითა

Glagolitic an early Slavonic alphabet of 40 letters, invented by St Cyril in the mid-9th century for his translation of the liturgy and much of the Bible. It survives today only in religious texts used by some communities along the Dalmatian coast of Croatia.

ⱈⱏⰵⱁⰼⰻⰳⱁⱁⱁⰼⱑⰲⱀ ⰻⱁⰼⱈⰰⱂ ⰾⱁⱁⰽⰵⱜⱄ ⰲⱁⱁⰴⱄⰰ

Gurmukhi literally 'from the mouth of the guru', was invented in the 16th-century to record the teachings of the 10 gurus, the founders of Sikhism*; now used by the bearded Sikhs of Punjab. General use is declining as most literate Punjabi speakers are tending to write in Hindi and Urdu.

ੜ੍ਹ।੦੨ ॥।।ੱਚੜ ੫੭ ੭੭ਰੇ ਪ੍ਰ੍ਹ

Hebrew derived from Phoenician, the script of ancient Israel (now called **Early Hebrew**) was used by the Hebrew kings and prophets of the Bible. It was replaced by Aramaic after about 500 BC.

𐤋𐤉𐤄𐤕·𐤕𐤅𐤕𐤋·𐤒𐤏𐤄𐤉𐤉𐤍·𐤗𐤅𐤉

Many of the Dead Sea Scrolls are written in **Square Hebrew**, which developed from Aramaic in the 3rd century BC. Standardised around the beginning of the Christian era, it has remained virtually unchanged ever since. Like all Semitic alphabets, Hebrew is written right to left. There are no vowels, but four of the 22 letters are used to indicate long vowels. Since the 8th century, 16 signs placed above, below, and to the left of a consonant, denote the sound of the following vowel. The signs are used only for special purposes such as textbooks.

המעממסה על זכרונך קלה והנך

Javanese used to write both Sundanese, one of the major languages of Indonesia, and Javanese, the language spoken in parts of Java. Introduced from southern India more than 1000 years ago, the script is gradually passing out of use in favour of the now official Roman alphabet.

ꦮꦫꦶꦤ꧀ꦲꦶꦁꦏꦸꦭꦮꦃ ꦮꦫꦸꦩꦏꦼꦭꦸꦮꦫꦥꦤꦶꦭꦱꦫꦗꦤꦶꦁ

Korean the only true alphabet of the Far East. Invented about 1443, and probably based on Tibetan, this Chinese-looking script has 25 symbols of 14 consonants and 11 vowels which are grouped in clusters of syllables. After World War II, the alphabet was abolished in North Korea, and is gradually being phased out in South Korea.

쳐욷 갖이고 공부하는 동안에는

Laotian used for the Thai-related language of Laos. Adapted from the script written by the Mons, the earliest civilised people of Burma, Laotian consists of 45 consonants roughly divided into pure consonants and tonal indications.

ຄຸ້ຄຸງເຮັ້ານາ   ແຕ່ບານບ້ອບເອີບ

His father had been so proud of him when he'd learned the Hebrew alphabet in two lessons, faster than any of the others, and so disappointed when he lost interest in the language almost immediately.

'What's the use, Papa?' he asked. 'It goes in one ear and out the other... what good is saying words if you don't know what they mean?'

There was a hurt look in his father's eyes. 'It is our language,' the man who read and spoke six languages said. 'You may not know each word but you can feel what it means.'

His father felt the meaning and the beauty of the symbols, but he did not. It could have been Greek. He stopped going to Hebrew school.

Art Cohn *The Nine Lives of Michael Todd*

Nabataean extinct alphabet of Petra, an important early trading centre in North Arabia. Derived from Aramaic*.

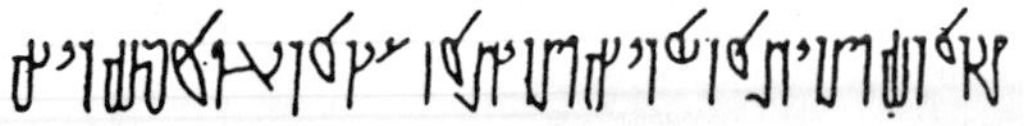

ぴ゛ヿ゚ヷゔ゚ヿゔ゚ヷ゚ゔ゚ヿゕ゚ヷ゚ゔ゚ヷ゚ゔ゚

Oriya records the language of the same name spoken in eastern India. Most of the symbols contain a large semi-circle at the top.

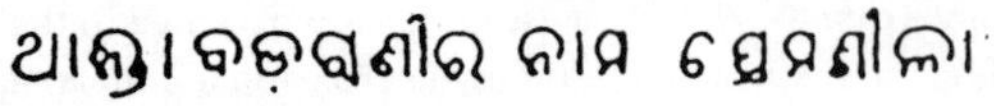

ଥାଲ୍ଯ।ବଚଗଣୀର ନାମ ୟେମଣୀଲା।

Pahlavi invented in the 2nd century BC, survived as the principal Persian alphabet until the 9th century, when it was ousted by a modified Arabic script following the Islamic conquest of Persia. Now extinct.

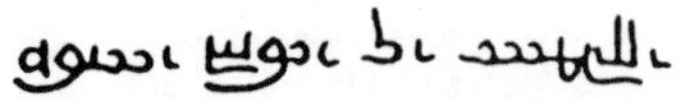

[Pahlavi script]

Runic the earliest north European alphabet (also known as **futhark** after the first six of 24 letters) may have derived from Etruscan* around the 3rd century BC. Originally written right to left, and later left to right and also boustrophedon style, runes were used mainly for mystical inscriptions on stone, wood, metal, and bones. A 6th-century Anglo-Saxon variant of 28 symbols, later extended to 33 to accommodate the sounds of Old English, was used till early medieval times. Another variant in Scandinavia with a reduced alphabet of 16 letters remained in use in Sweden till as late as the 17th century.

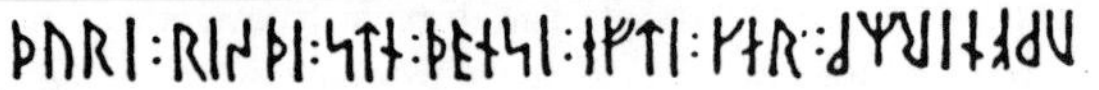

[Runic script]

Sabaean principal early alphabet of South Arabia, once associated with the kingdom of Sheba. Sabaean is the ancestor of Ethiopic*. Like all Semitic alphabets, it is written from right to left.

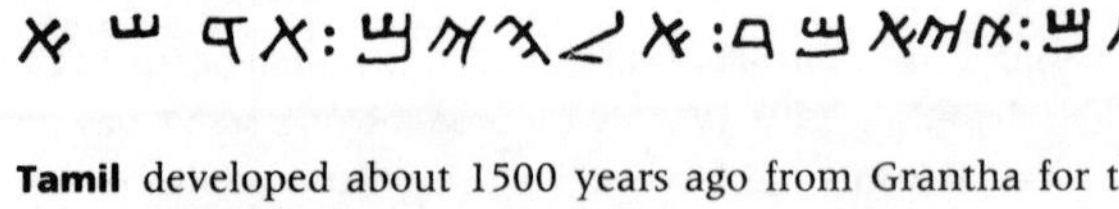

[Sabaean script]

Samaritan the only surviving descendant of Early Hebrew*. Now almost extinct, except for its use by a few hundred people in Jordan. Written right to left.

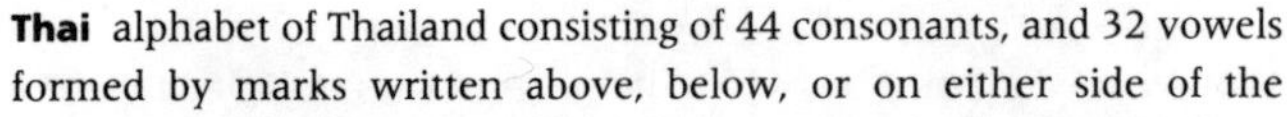

[Samaritan script]

Tamil developed about 1500 years ago from Grantha for the oldest Dravidian language of south India.

அவ ஜ்கடய முதத்கு மாரன் ஷயலிலிருந்தான்.

Thai alphabet of Thailand consisting of 44 consonants, and 32 vowels formed by marks written above, below, or on either side of the consonant. In speech, five different intonations distinguish words; in writing, signs over the consonants indicate four tones, the fifth being denoted by the absence of a sign. Words are not separated, but flow uninterrupted until a change of idea.

างประเทศมากมาย จนถึงกับสามารถบอกกับ

Tibetan possibly based on Gupta, the ancestor of Devanagari*. Tibetan script was adapted in the 7th century by a minister sent to Kashmir to study Sanskrit.

ཞེགས་ ཅུ་ གཉིས་ ཡོད་པ་རེད། དེ་དག་ ལས་

Pointing the way

After the invention of the alphabet, the next important development in the history of writing was a set of signs for **punctuation**. These small and rather unassuming signs vary in form and function from one writing system to another, and even within countries using the same system. Nevertheless, within each, be it Arabic* or Cyrillic*, Braille* or shorthand*, their function is basically the same: to separate clusters of alphabetic symbols into manageable pieces, and to bring order to such pieces and help clarify the meaning, or at least prevent the wrong meaning being deduced. Like the directing, warning, or informing signs along a road, punctuation marks tell us where we are and what to expect ahead.

Starting points

Punctuation was a long time coming. Even the word itself, derived from Latin *punctus*, 'point', did not appear in the sense we know today until the mid-17th century. Before then, it was called **pointing**, while punctuation referred instead to the insertion in Hebrew texts of points near consonants to indicate vowels. At some time around 1650, the two words exchanged meaning.

Some 2000 years earlier, the use of marks to divide text did not exist. Even the concept of using a blank space as a sign or boundary mark to separate words was unknown. In the earliest Greek inscriptions, all letters were written in majuscules or capitals, and they ran continuously, ONEAFTERANOTHERAFTERANOTHER.

Evidence suggests that some Greek writers were already using individual marks by the 5th century BC. The playwright Euripides (*c.* 480–406), for example, marked changes of speaker with a wedge, possibly a sideways *lambda* (<); the philosopher Plato (*c.* 428–*c.* 348 BC) sometimes ended a section with a double point (:).

The first important sign appeared in the 4th century BC. Invented by the philosopher Aristotle (384–322 BC) to denote a break of sense, and called *paragraphos*, from Greek, 'side writing', the sign was merely a short horizontal stroke under the beginning of a line. That of course has long since disappeared, but the essential idea of indicating a new topic, section, or subdivision in a text, survives in our word **paragraph**. In the 1st century AD, the Romans, who for a while separated words by points, introduced a more definite form of paragraphing by projecting the first few letters of each new section into the margin. In late medieval times, a mark representing c for *capitulum*, 'chapter', began to appear in some books and manuscripts. The modern practice of indicating paragraphs by indentation, again using space as a sign, was adopted in the 17th century.

So much for signposting longer sections. But what about signs for the lesser parts? Their history really begins around 194 BC, with the grammarian and lexicographer Aristophanes of Byzantium, head of the library at Alexandria. He devised a three-point system that divided text into short, medium, and long sections according to rhetorical theory. The end of the long section, called *periodos*, was marked after the final

Legal points

The concept of punctuation to help the sense is not shared by lawyers. Ever since the 15th century, when some legal documents appeared with no 'pointing' at all, lawyers have preferred to keep the signs to a bare minimum. This, they maintain, is to avoid possible ambiguities. In *Miscellaneous Thoughts*, the satirist Samuel Butler (1612–80), gives a more cynical reason for the practice:

> Old laws have not been suffered
>   to be pointed,
> To leave the sense at large the
>   more disjointed,
> And furnish lawyers, with the
>   greater ease,
> To turn and wind them any way
>   they please.

letter by a high point (˙), the end of the shorter section, *kolon,* was marked by a middle point (·), and the end of the shortest section, *komma,* by a point on the base line (.).

Aristophanes is also believed to have invented a number of other signs. They include the hyphen, used to denote compound words; and the virgule (/), which was inserted between words where the meaning might appear ambiguous.

Athough never widely adopted, Aristophanes' system lingered on in theory and rather sketchy practice until the 8th century AD. In the intervening years, two important changes took place. Scribes began to separate words on a regular basis, and to write with minuscule letters (similar to modern small letters). With their ascending or descending strokes, these were harder to read without punctuation.

The first person to bring some order to the subject was the English scholar Alcuin (AD 735–804), who was employed by Charlemagne (742–814), King of the Franks and later Holy Roman Emperor, to direct his palace school at Aachen (Germany). During this time Alcuin reformed Aristophanes' system and made a few additions.

Some of Alcuin's reforms spread to England. By the 10th century marks were appearing in Anglo-Saxon manuscripts to indicate a pause and a change of inflection. Among them were *punctum* (.), *punctus elevatus* (⸵), *punctus versus* (;), and *punctus interrogativus* (⸮). These were later joined by *punctus circumflexus* (⸴) to indicate a rising inflection.

Despite these improvements, the system was often muddled and haphazard. Throughout the Middle Ages numerous local variations crept in, more on the whim of a scribe than for any specific reason.

Credit for the **first punctuation signs as we know them** goes to the innovative Venetian printer, Aldus Manutius (1450–1515). Founder of the Aldine Press and the first publisher of popular editions of books, Manutius recognised the need for a more uniform system. His work paved the way for much of the punctuation used today, and for the comma, semi-colon, and colon signs. Some 60 years later, his grandson, also named Aldus, was the first person to define the role of punctuation signs as aids to sentence structure. Until this time, the signs had been used mainly to indicate breath points, pauses, and changes of expression when reading aloud.

The first person in England to recommend this syntactical role was the dramatist Ben Jonson (1572–1637) in his *English Grammar.* Even so, the signs continued to play an important part in reading aloud, particularly in church.

By the early 17th century most modern signs were already established. Shakespeare's first Folio (1623) includes . , ; : ? and !. By 1700, quotation marks were beginning to appear in English punctuation.

Punctuation today

The signs that evolved from the 16th century have since spread to many other writing systems. They are now the most widely-used in the world. The section that follows describes their principal functions in British and American English, and some of their alternative names. The signs fall into four main groups: separating, omission, expression, and repetition. A fifth group is included for reference marks.

Separating signs

The most important mark, the full point, is also the simplest of all graphic signs. More familiarly known in Britain as the **full stop** and in the US as the **period**, it was once used to indicate a minor pause in reading aloud. From the mid-15th century, it gained strength and came to indicate a full pause, and the end of a complete sentence.

In Britain, the full stop serves to divide hours and minutes in expressions of time; it also acts as the decimal point. In the US, the decimal point is placed above the base line, and called a **center dot**, **center point**, or **space dot**. This center dot is used in dictionaries to separate syl·la·bles.

The **comma** (from the Greek *komma*, meaning 'piece cut off') evolved from the *virgule* (see below). It first appeared in English printing in 1534 in *A Devout Treatyse called the tree and XII frutes of the holy goost*. Neatly described by the scholar G. V. Carey as 'the most ubiquitous and flexible, not to say slippery of all stops', the comma has more applications than any other sign, and consequently causes more problems. As well as marking minor divisions of a sentence, it is used to separate numbers, and in many European systems acts as the decimal point.

The **semi-colon** (;) is used principally as a sentence divider halfway between a full point and comma. Unusual is its use in Greek punctuation where, since the 9th century, the sign has acted as the question mark, while the role of the semi-colon is taken by the high point (·).

The word **colon** derives from the Greek *kolon*, meaning 'limb'. The sign (:) appeared in its present form in the late 15th century. Formerly applied like a full point and followed by a capital, the colon was used frequently during the 17th and 18th centuries. In the Authorized Version of the Bible, *King James's Bible* (1611), it indicated a pause in reading aloud only slightly shorter than a full stop. It still divides verses of the Psalms.

The colon is now used in sentence structure chiefly to separate cause from effect, a general statement from an explanation, example, or series, or to introduce a quotation. In the US, it takes the place of a comma after the salutation in a formal letter (e.g. Dear Mr Smith:).

The colon is also used with numbers, as in ratios (1:10), to separate chapter from verse numbers in biblical references (Genesis 2:25), and in the US to divide hours from minutes (10:30).

The word **parentheses** has come to us via Latin from Greek, meaning 'place in besides'. Originally applied to any incidental matter inserted into a text with which it had no grammatical connection, parentheses became the name of the signs that began to appear in the early 17th century. There are two principal kinds: the round ( ), familiarly called **brackets** in Britain, and most commonly used to enclose optional words, explanations, figures, references, and anything that could be omitted; and **square brackets [ ]**, which generally isolate comments, corrections, or other matter added subsequently to the original text. A third kind of parentheses, sometimes called **braces**, or **curly** or **hooked brackets { }**, are used principally in mathematics and expressions in symbolic logic.

The name **hyphen** (-), from Greek, 'together in one', originally applied to the curved mark Greek grammarians placed under a compound to indicate it was to be spoken as one word. That linking function continues today. The sign first appeared in its present form in England in the 10th century to mark words broken into two at the end of lines. From the 14th to 18th centuries this **division hyphen** was sometimes doubled.

Because these signs are troublesome, some computer software includes a special programme to aid hyphenation and prevent inconsis-

POINTING THE WAY

Slapdash

There is in the dash something rough, ready and haphazard that goes against my grain. I have seldom read a sentence in which it could not be well replaced by the elegant semi-colon or the discreet bracket.

Somerset Maugham *The Gentleman in the Parlour*

Dashed wit

In modern wit all printed trash is set off with num'rous breaks – and dashes – – – –

Jonathan Swift, 1733

tent, ugly, or even misleading division. 'If you take hyphens seriously you will surely go mad', states *The Oxford University Press* 'style book' in New York. On the other hand, as one guide warns, there is a world of difference between therapist and the-rapist.

The newest sign, the **dash**, has many functions. Taking its name from the idea of a sudden movement, as in a hasty stroke of the pen, it first appeared sometime in the late 17th century to denote a sudden pause. In the 18th and 19th centuries, and even until quite recently it was often combined with the comma (,–) or the colon (:–) to precede a list or explanation.

The dash is still used to mark a break in thought or change of construction. But increasingly it is replacing parentheses or commas to isolate an insertion. In addition, new printing technology prefers the dash to the slightness of a comma or full stop. Both the name and the sign also represent the long sound or signal in Morse Code*.

The least used of the separating signs, the **oblique** (/), also has a linking function. Originally called the **virgule** (diminutive of the Latin *virga*, 'rod' or 'twig'), it began to appear regularly in the 14th century as a minor pause. With this function, but later written with a curved tail, it sank to the base line to become the modern comma.

Known also as **solidus**, **slash**, **slant**, **stroke**, the oblique has a number of other applications: to indicate the end of lines of verse printed continuously; to join alternatives such as and/or; to represent the word *per* as in feet/second. As **scratch** it separates the numerator from the denominator in fractions (e.g. $^7/_8$).

An older and more technical name for oblique is **separatrix**. Formerly used to divide integers or whole numbers from decimal figures, but originally written **L** and later l, separatrix has been superseded by the decimal point. Today the name applies to the diagonal between several items listed in a book heading, and in proofreading to mark and separate alterations.

Yet another name, **shilling mark**, stems from the practice in Britain before decimalisation in 1971 of using it to denote the division between pounds, shillings and pence, for example: 10/6 (10 shillings and sixpence).

Omission signs

In medieval times, scribes used a full point to abbreviate long Latin word endings. A similar practice continues in initials such as I.P.A.* or T. S. Eliot, and forms like m.p.h. Incidentally, a notable exception in the case of names is that of Harry S Truman (US President 1945–53), in which the S takes no **abbreviation dot** since it is not an initial but a Christian name in its own right.

One of the most problematical signs is the **apostrophe**. Derived from the Greek *apostrophos*, 'turning away', the word referred originally to an orator digressing or turning aside during a speech to address a dead or absent individual, a thing, place, or even an idea. Possibly another of Aristophanes' inventions and first written as a curve, a straight mark or a point, the sign was used in Greek verse to indicate part of a word to be omitted for the sake of rhythm. It was also inserted after foreign names to denote their status.

Introduced into French by the typographer Geoffroy Tory in the early 16th century to mark elision, the apostrophe as a high comma sign (’), passed into English, and was in common use by the beginning of the 17th century. It first denoted the omission or elision of the final vowel

Power points

The commonest punctuation marks, sharing between them about 90 per cent of the workload, are the full stop and the comma. They are also the smallest signs of any kind in everyday use. But in spite of their size they wield considerable power in the battle between clarity and confusion, and in some cases even between life and death.

Consider the case of the warrior who consulted an ancient oracle and received the answer: *'Ibis redibis nunquam per bella peribis'*. This translates as 'Thou shalt go thou shalt return never by war shalt thou perish'. An ambiguous pronouncement to say the least. A full stop, of course, or even a comma, would have made all the difference, but such niceties did not exist then. On this occasion, the warrior believed the prediction to be in his favour, and went to war. He perished.

A happier example concerns the philanthropic wife of Czar Alexander III, Maria Fëdorovna (1847–1928). Intercepting an Imperial warrant for a prisoner which read 'Pardon impossible, to be sent to Siberia', the Czarina deftly transposed the comma, and returned the warrant. It now read: 'Pardon, impossible to be sent to Siberia.' The prisoner was saved.

---

of a word in poetry, as in *belov'd,* again for the sake of rhythm. Later it was used to show where any letter or letters had been dropped, such as in *can't, isn't.* The sign also came to indicate the omission of e in the English possessive or genitive case, as for example in *King James's Bible.* (Perhaps something of the sign's connection with this dropped e remains in the subconscious: even today it is not unusual to see potato's or tomato's on cafe menus in England.) From the early 18th century, this use was extended to all possessives.

The apostrophe may also denote omission of a number or numbers from dates, such as 'the year '93'. Another function is to separate the prefix O in an Irish surname derived from that of a father or ancestor, for example, O'Reilly. In the same context, but rarer, is the **inverted** or **turned comma** (') which abbreviates Mac, the Gaelic word for son, in Scottish surnames such as M'Gregor or M'Clure.

The other signs in this group are the **ellipsis** marks such as the **dash** (–), or a series of **asterisks** (*). They were frequently employed in the 18th and 19th centuries to show where letters had been dropped from an individual's name, perhaps for reasons of tact or diplomacy. More commonly, the marks indicated the omission of letters from 'strong language'. In this function the dash was especially useful, both in speech and print as a convenient euphemism for damn (dash!), and as a sign: 'Well, I'm d— '. This usage, it seems, is unique to English-language punctuation. Writing in *Maledicta* ('The International Journal of Verbal Aggression'), Reinhold Aman queries the lack of symbolic euphemisms in other countries. 'Are such dingbats used in foreign-language publications to represent offensive words? And if not, how do other languages defuse maledicta other than by d–mb dashes or a*inine asterisks?' (The Canadian humorist Stephen Leacock suggested the sign names themselves as handy substitutes for swearwords, for example: '"Asterisk!" shouted the pirate. "I'll make it two asterisks," snarled the other, "and throw in a dash".'.')

In general, such marks have lately been superseded by the three **suspension dots** or points (...). These also serve to express an incomplete thought or a break in a quotation.

Supermarks

flabbergasterix stupendapoint

In his entertaining *Words*, the American word collector Paul Dickson includes a number of names for useful, but as yet unadopted, printers' symbols. Take, for instance, the flabbergasterisk, and the super flabbergasterisk or stupendapoint, suggested by Fred Flanagan and Stan Merritt in an article in *Printer's Ink* for advertising copywriters in place of the worn out exclamation mark. Another handy symbol is the interrobang ‽ for colloquialisms such as 'What's your problem?' or 'Where's the fire?' which are both question and exclamation. According to Dickson, both the symbol and name (from *inter*rogation and *bang*, printer's slang for the exclamation mark) were invented in the late 1960s by Martin K. Spector.

An exclamation mark is like laughing at your own joke.

F. Scott Fitzgerald, quoted in *Beloved Infidel* by Sheila Graham and Gerald Frank

Expression signs

The **question mark** or **interrogation point** (?) derives from the Latin *quaestio* (a seeking), which later took on the meaning of inquiry, and came to be written at the end of a sentence whenever a query was intended. In time, *quaestio* was shortened to Qo. Later, scribes placed the Q above the o, and over the years the one became a squiggle and the other a dot.

Similarly, that much-overworked **exclamation mark** (!) derives from the Latin *Io*, an interjection of joy, with the I placed over the o. Known also as the **note of admiration**, and the **gasp-mark** (or sometimes by the slang names **bang**, **shriek**, **screamer** or even **squealer**), it is by far the most expressive sign. It may denote a wide range of states and emotions, including absurdity, admiration, command, contempt, disgust, enthusiasm, pain, regret, sorrow, surprise, warning, and wonder. The mark first appeared in print in England in the *Catechism of Edward VI* in 1553. Today it is used extensively in advertisements, tabloid newspapers and strip cartoons, but otherwise is seldom seen in print, apart from dialogue in plays and stories.

Both ? and ! occur now in punctuation systems throughout the world. They first began to appear in Japan shortly after regular contact with Europeans was established in 1868. In China, the two signs were adopted in 1912.

In Spanish, questions and exclamations are helpfully signposted at the beginning of the sentence with the inverted marks ¿ and ¡.

Repetition signs

The most common repetition signs are **quotation marks**. In factual texts, they signify that the words they enclose are those actually used by a real speaker, or are being quoted from another written text. In fiction, they denote dialogue. Increasingly, the marks highlight unusual or specialised words and expressions, or slang.

Quotation marks first appeared in French manuscripts of the early Middle Ages in the form of a sideways *lambda* symbol: <>. In French, the signs (now written «») are known as *guillemets*, possibly after the inventor of the practice, a scholar named Guillaume. Dashes are also used. In German, quotations are signed either by reversed guillemets (» «) or by pairs of commas („ ").

In English, quotation marks are often called **inverted commas**, or just **quotes**. Until recently double marks (" ") were always used. The modern convention is to open a quotation with a **semiquote** – a single inverted or turned comma ('), close with an apostrophe ('), and reserve

Ditto days

When Mr Eisman is in New York we always seem to do the same thing and if I wrote down one day in my diary, all I would have to do would be to put quotation marks for all other days.

Anita Loos *Gentlemen Prefer Blondes*

doubles for a quote within a quote. In the US, the convention is the opposite.

There are occasions, of course, when you want to avoid repetition of a word or phrase, for example in a list. For that, too, there is a sign. It started life as **ditto** which, derived via the Italian *detto* (from Latin *dictum*), meant that 'which has been said'. It began to appear in early 17th-century accounts or lists under a word or words that would otherwise need to be repeated. Ditto was later contracted to **d°**. The idea is now expressed by quotation marks, or more specifically two middle commas. Another name for ditto marks is **digits**.

Reference signs

The first reference signs or marks were invented by the Greeks. In the 3rd century BC, the scholar Zenodatus introduced the **obelus** (– or ÷) to indicate a doubtful word or passage. Although the original signs have long been obsolete in this context, the name survives for the sign †. Also known as the **obelisk**, or informally **dagger**, this may serve to indicate that the word or form marked is of obscure origin, or to call attention to a footnote. In obituaries, the mark may denote 'deceased'. Also found in reference books is the double obelus, double dagger, or **diesis** (‡).

From the Greek *aster* meaning star, comes the name for the **oldest and most commonly used reference mark**, the **asterisk** (*). This was introduced in the 2nd century BC in texts in the library at Alexandria, again by Aristophanes, to mark ambiguity.

Like the dash and ellipsis, the asterisk was sometimes employed in 19th-century printing to denote the omission of letters in a word or person's name for reasons of decency or diplomacy. Today, the asterisk is used much less dramatically to direct the reader to a note in the margin, at the foot of the page, or (as in this book) to consult the index for an entry or reference elsewhere in the text.

Known in US printshop slang as a **bug**, the asterisk is commonly used on racing programmes there as a rather different kind of reference mark: placed beside the names of some jockeys, it informs punters that the jockey is a *bug boy*, 'an apprentice'.

In the mid-17th century another 'star-sign' appeared to direct attention to a particular passage. Called an **asterism**, the cluster of three asterisks, printed *₊* or ₊*₊, became a favourite with 19th-century typographers. Such a sign is rarely seen today.

Two other signs are also used in printing as marks of reference to notes in the margin or at the foot of the page. The **paragraph mark** or **blind** or **pilcrow** (¶) – sometimes reversed – first recorded in 1538, originally signified the beginning of a new section, and later, an incidental note by an editor. The **section mark** (§) appeared in the early 18th century to introduce the number of a section.

In cases where a number of reference marks are needed on the same page the order of precedence runs as follows: *, †, ‡, §, ¶. Another sign, the **parallel mark** (‖), first recorded 1771, may also be used.

The asterisk

A writer owned an asterisk
And kept it in his den,
Where he wrote tales (which
*   had large sales)*
Of frail and erring men;
And always when he reached
*   the point*
Where carping censors lurk,
He called upon the asterisk
To do his dirty work.

Anon

Pointed correspondence

Victor Hugo (1802–85), prolific French novelist, poet and dramatist, was a man of many words. In his epic *Les Misérables* (1862) he set the record for the longest sentence in modern classic literature: 823 words, punctuated by 93 commas, 51 semi-colons, and 4 dashes.

But when necessary, Hugo could be concise to the point of bluntness. Shortly after the mighty *Misérables* was launched, anxious to know how the book was selling, he sent a note to his publishers on which he wrote simply '?'. Back came the equally short and cryptic reply '!'.

Chapter 3

Speaking with hands
Gestures and sign languages

As the tongue speaketh to the ear, so the gesture speaketh to the eye.

Francis Bacon *The Advancement of Learning*

The Greek philosopher Aristotle called the human hand 'the tool of tools'. An apt description. With 27 bones and almost as many muscles, it can perform the most savage and the most sensitive tasks. It can also be a highly expressive tool, capable of communicating both simple and complex information by a vast number of conventional gestures.

Codes of such gestures are known as sign languages. They may be classified broadly into four groups. The most common of these, the ordinary or, for want of a better term, **demotic** sign language, includes the stock of gestures available to us all. There are numerous **occupational** sign languages, those used for instance by auctioneers and divers, crane drivers and croupiers in their various work situations. More elaborate are the **alternate** sign languages, which have developed as substitutes for speech among the Aborigines of Australia, and the Indians of North America. Lastly, what are termed **primary** sign languages: the highly structured sign systems used by deaf people.

Demotic signs

In the course of an average day, we may call upon a wide variety of gestures. Most are what are called illustrators: spontaneous actions, usually made unconsciously, that supplement our speech and serve to illustrate what we are saying (e.g. stabbing the air to emphasise a point). To a second basic category belong many other gestures sometimes referred to as emblems, which can act as a replacement or substitute for speech. Emblems may themselves be divided into categories. The two most distinctive are mimic or iconic gestures, those which imitate a particular object or action and trigger an association in the mind of the onlooker (e.g. raising an imaginary glass to the mouth or making a scissoring motion with the first two fingers), and those hand movements, such as the 'thumbs up' or crossing the fingers, which are symbolic.

The following are some of the most distinctive symbolic gestures in Europe and the US. It is no accident that the majority of them are insulting: we are, it seems, especially adept at hurling manual abuse (probably because actions really do speak louder than words). They are drawn from a number of sources, in particular *Gestures*, the results of a survey by a team headed by Desmond Morris of 20 key gestures in 40 locations throughout Europe in the late 1970s; Theodore Brun's *International Dictionary of Sign Language*; and Roger E. Axtell's *Gestures: The Do's and Taboos of Body Language Around the World*. Incidentally, focusing as it does on the 'rights and rudes' of the subject, Axtell's book is invaluable for anyone planning to live or work in the Middle and Far East where 'western' gestures may be interpreted very differently. (The numbers in brackets beside the sign names refer to illustrations on p.60.)

V for victory

Probably the best-known gesture in the UK is the **V-sign**. As most people are aware, this has two sides and two very different meanings: one optimistic and triumphant, the other insulting and obscene. While the origins of the second sign are obscure, the first (made with the palm

Handpower

The hands may almost be said to speak. Do we not use them to demand, promise, summon, dismiss, threaten, supplicate, express aversion or fear, question or deny? Do we not use them to indicate joy, sorrow, hesitation, confession, penitence, measure, quantity, number and time? Have they not the power to excite and prohibit, to express approval, wonder, shame?

from *Institutio Oratoria*, a treatise on public speaking by the Roman rhetorician Quintilian (*c.* AD 35–95)

facing outward) sometimes called the **peace sign** or **victory salute** (1), is unusually well-documented (Charles J. Rolo, for instance, in his entertaining *Radio Goes to War*, devotes an entire chapter to it). It was invented during World War II. Casting around for some emblem of European solidarity which could be written on walls in the dark, Victor de Laveleye, programme organiser of the BBC's Belgian Service at Bush House in London, hit upon the initial 'V' for Victory, which would stand not only for *Vrijheid* in Flemish, but also for *Victoire* in French. 'Let the occupier,' de Laveleye said when first proposing his 'perfect symbol of Anglo-Belgian understanding' in a broadcast to Belgium on 14 January 1941, 'by seeing this sign, always the same, infinitely repeated, understand that he is surrounded, encircled, by an immense crowd of citizens eagerly awaiting his first moment of weakness, watching for his first failure.' Following its successful introduction in Belgium, the 'V Campaign' was extended to France. According to Rolo, the morning after one radio feature, the walls of Marseilles were covered with V's. Elsewhere, a French listener described the sign in his town as 'growing like mushrooms on the best sites, for which advertising firms in peacetime would have paid huge rents'. On 2 April, Radio Paris announced that the owner or tenant of any building on which the sign appeared would be prosecuted. Teachers were ordered to see that no children left school with any chalk.

Two months later, a bright spark at the BBC had the idea of transcribing the visual sign into sound, and incorporating into broadcasts the Morse* code symbol for V (dot-dot-dot-dash) which, by happy coincidence, had the same rhythm as the opening bars of Beethoven's Fifth Symphony. From then on, V became the BBC's call sign in Europe, as both the Fifth Symphony motif (known prophetically as 'Fate knocking at the door') and the Morse signal were broadcast relentlessly. Now in addition to being chalked, daubed in paint or lipstick, even cut with glaziers' diamonds on the windshields of German cars, the sign was also whistled in the streets. With mounting exasperation, the Nazi Minister of Propaganda, Dr Goebbels, hit back. 'V', he insisted lamely, being the initial of the old German victory cry *Viktoria*, was a rallying sign for all Europeans 'united in the struggle against Bolshevism'. He even had a huge 'V' placed on the Eiffel Tower in Paris. But, if anything, Goebbels' counter-offensive only served to spread the 'V' even further into occupied Europe. What had started as a means of undermining German morale became, as one American radio commentator described it, 'the most amazing piece of propaganda devised in this war'.

In Britain, the sign became indelibly fixed in the public consciousness when the Prime Minister, Winston Churchill, began using it as a victory salute. 'The V sign', he affirmed in a broadcast on 18 July, 'is the symbol of the unconquerable will of the people of the occupied territories and of Britain; of the fate awaiting Nazi tyranny.'

The vulgar V

Turned around and made with an upward jerking motion, the 'V' is an insulting and even phallic gesture. (In parts of Europe, and even in the UK, it is still mistaken for the victory sign: Desmond Morris' *Gestures* includes a photograph of an exuberant Margaret Thatcher giving the wrong V. Churchill, incidentally, used both versions.) The earliest mention of the gesture occurs in a piece by the 16th-century satirist François Rabelais, in which a character thrust towards his opponent 'the forefinger and middle finger, or medical, of his right hand, holding

She raised her hand in a peace sign. . . . He realized it was not the peace sign at all. To those of the old woman's generation it was V for Victory.

David Westheimer *Going Public*

V for Victory:

in Morse

and music:

being the opening bars of Beethoven's Symphony no 5, C minor, opus 67. (Coincidentally, the Roman numeral for 5 is V)

From the horseman's mouth

On 15 August 1971, the V-sign acquired a new name. It came during a horse show at Hickstead, Sussex, after British international show-jumper Harvey Smith completed his winning round on the favourite Mattie Brown and, in a gesture of triumph, raised two fingers at the judges. For his action, Smith was disqualified and his £2000 prize-money forfeited (the decision was later reversed). To many people today, the V-sign is known as the 'Harvey Smith'. But as Smith explains in his autobiography, *V is for Victory*, his gesture was misinterpreted: 'It was meant to show how delighted I was that Mattie Brown had become the only horse ever to win the British Jumping Derby in successive years. If it was also interpreted as an 'up you' to those on that balcony who had made it plain that they wanted Mattie Brown to lose, then all well and good . . . But above all, the gesture was meant to be light-hearted and the crowd received it as such.'

them asunder as much as he could'. But it may be much older. No doubt apocryphal, but nonetheless entertaining, is one tale dating back to the Battle of Agincourt (St Crispin's Day, 25 October 1415), and an eve of battle confrontation between French soldiers with their cross-bows and English archers with their superior longbows. Hoping to intimidate their enemy, the French taunted them across the lines that they would cut off the first two fingers (those used to draw back the bowstring) of every English archer they captured. At dawn the next morning, the archers assembled in full view of the French, proudly displaying their two fingers in what is now the most popular British gesture of defiance.

Finger and forearm

Two close relatives of the vulgar V, are the **forearm jerk** (2) and the more basic **obscene finger** (3). Made by holding up the fist, palm inward, and extending the middle finger, the latter is one of the most phallic signs. It is also one of the oldest recorded insults, dating back at least 2000 years. According to Desmond Morris, the Roman emperor Caligula (AD 12–41) is believed to have used the *digitus impudicus* (impudent digit) 'when offering his hand to be kissed, as a deliberately scandalous act'. In recent years it has become increasingly popular in the US. In his *Do's and Taboos*, Roger Axtell notes that due to frequent usage among frustrated drivers in California, the sign has acquired the name the 'expressway digit'. In some parts of the Middle East, the same insult is signalled by extending the hand palm down, with the middle finger pointing down and the other fingers splayed (not an easy gesture to make unwittingly, which is probably just as well!).

A greatly exaggerated version of the phallic 'finger' is the forearm jerk, which is performed by jerking the bent arm and clenched fist upwards, and simultaneously slapping the other hand on to the upper arm. There are varying degrees of intensity to this action, which may also be made forwards, sideways, or diagonally. However it is made, the message is unmistakeably, to put it at its mildest, 'up yours'. While this gesture is common in southern Europe as an offensive insult, it exists in the UK more as a vulgar comment on someone's sexual qualities: a sort of wishful thinking compliment.

Thumbing the nose

Somewhat surprisingly, the gesture most commonly known as **thumbing the nose** (4), in which the thumb touches the tip of the nose with the splayed fingers pointing upwards, proved to be the best-known and least ambiguous of all the signs in the Morris survey (recognised by 88 per cent of the 1200 people interviewed). However, this particular sign has its variations: sometimes the fingers are waggled, sometimes the other hand is added, either side by side, or in tandem, to double the insult (in some cases the ears are similarly 'thumbed'). It is known by a number of names: in Italy, for instance, as 'palming a nose', and in France *pied de nez*, 'a fool's nose' (from the slang meaning of *pied*, 'foot' as 'fool'). In Britain, more than 15 names have been recorded, among them: to cock a snook (a word related to snout or nose), to cut a snooks, the five-finger salute, to make a long nose, to take a sight, the Shanghai gesture, Queen Anne's fan, the Japanese fan, the Spanish fan, to pull bacon, coffee-milling, and taking a grinder. For these last two names, Farmer and Henley's *Slang Dictionary* (1909) offers this explanation: 'by putting the thumb of one hand to the nose and grinding the little finger with the other, as if you worked an imaginary coffee mill'.

Taking a grinder

Here Mr Jackson smiled once more upon the company; and, applying his left thumb to the tip of his nose, worked a visionary coffee-mill with his right hand, thereby performing a very graceful piece of pantomime (then much in vogue, but now, unhappily, almost obsolete) which was familiarly denominated taking a grinder.

Charles Dickens *Pickwick Papers*

The origin of the gesture is unknown, though it may once have represented the hostile erect comb of a fighting cock. An alternative explanation, Morris suggests, relates to the ancient practice of imitating grotesque, long-nosed effigies. Supplanted in the UK by the more aggressive V-sign in the past 50 years, the gesture is now regarded as more comical and childish than overtly insulting. But while the power of the physical sign itself may have diminished, the contemptuous message behind it is deemed literally to be as strong as ever: in the lead story in *The Independent* (18 August 1992) about Allied plans to enforce Gulf War ceasefire terms, President Bush was quoted as saying that Iraq's Saddam Hussein was 'trying to thumb his nose at the rest of the world'; in the same paragraph, a Downing Street spokesman accused the Iraqi authorities of 'cocking a snook at the UN'.

The badge of cuckoldry

Two fingers come into play for the **horns** (5), an ancient gesture made by extending the first and fourth fingers while retaining the second and third in the palm. The gesture can be performed horizontally, or vertically. Though both positions predominantly signal sexual betrayal or cuckoldry, the horns may also be used in Italy as a protective gesture against the evil eye (Morris notes that the wearing of amulets depicting the horned hand has been commonplace for at least 2000 years), or sarcastically as a taunting gesture about the power of that age-old symbol of male virility, the bull*. Thus Bulwer (1644) records that it is 'used in our nimble-fingered times to call one cuckold, and to present the badge of cuckoldry, that mental and imaginary horn . . . common use hath made it the known signal of disparagement, so naturally apt are the fingers to speak scoffs'.

An entirely different meaning occurs in the US, where, known as **'hook 'em horns'**, and used both as a gesture and rallying call, it signals support for the Texas Longhorns, the football team of the University of Texas at Austin.

Giving the fig

The gesture known as the **fig** (6), which is made by thrusting the thumb between the first and second fingers, is another which may be employed to avert the evil eye (this time, mainly in Portugal). More commonly, it is used in a number of places in Europe either as a sexual insult, or as a sexual comment. The reason for this is unknown. So too is its origin, although the following legend from 12th-century Milan suggests one possible source. In a bold expression of proclaiming independence from the rule of the Holy Roman Emperor Frederick I, Barbarossa (*c.* 1123–90), the Milanese expelled the Empress from the city mounted backwards on a mule. When Barbarossa retook Milan in 1162, he assembled the people and under threat of instant death if they refused, ordered each of them to remove with his teeth a fig stuck in the rear end of a mule.

In 16th-century England, the fig also served as a verbal insult. Thus Shakespeare's irascible Pistol says to Fluellen in *Henry V*, 'Die and be damn'd! and figo for thy friendship! . . . The fig of Spain'. Today the gesture lives on in the UK only in the colloquial phrase 'not to give a fig' for someone.

Another expression of contempt is the **teeth flick** (7), which is made by biting the thumb nail and then jerking it forwards. One variant of this, biting the thumb, was obviously in use in Shakespeare's day, as

'I have few facts,' he reached up a big index finger and laid it alongside his nose, 'but I have this.' He tapped the side of his nose as if he was patting a dog. 'But this is a good friend of mine and I trust him.'

Ian Fleming *From Russia, With Love*

Neapolitan nuances

One area that has for centuries been rich in gesture is southern Italy, and in particular, Naples. Visiting the opera there one evening in the mid-19th century, the author of *The Three Musketeers*, Alexandre Dumas (1802–70), witnessed a lively conversation in Neapolitan sign language between a musician in the orchestra and one of the audience some distance away in a box.

Intrigued by their gesturing, Dumas approached the musician and asked him what it was all about. The musician explained he was questioning an old friend whom he had not seen for three years. The friend told him that in the intervening time he had married and then left the city with his wife to travel in Austria and France. They had, in fact, arrived back in Naples by steamboat just the previous day, but he had come to the opera alone that night as his wife was still suffering from sea-sickness.

Surprised and not a little sceptical that such details could be conveyed in gestures, Dumas arranged to meet the musician's friend after the performance. The subsequent conversation confirmed the exchange between the two Neapolitans to be true in every respect.

Talking art

In *Charmed Lives*, an affectionate biography of the film director Alexander Korda and his brothers, Michael Korda relates a story told to him by Brendan Bracken about the time Alexander visited the painter Marc Chagall in his Paris studio. Finding a painting he wanted to buy, Korda asked Chagall if it was for sale. The painter, embarrassed by money talk, said he never thought about such things, and withdrew from the room to let his wife negotiate for him. Bracken continues:

'Just as Alex was leaning forward to talk to Madame, he realized that she could see Chagall in a mirror – he was standing just outside the room in the hallway. Chagall drew a dollar sign in the air, then held up the five fingers of his left hand so that she could see it in the mirror, then dropped it and held up both hands with all the fingers spread wide, indicating ten. Then he crossed both fingers to indicate that she should multiply.

'Alex was delighted by the charade. Before she could say anything, he offered her $50 000, and she looked at him with some surprise.

'"Why that was just the sum I had in mind, monsieur," she said. "How did you know?"

'"Ah, madame," he said, "the painting speaks for itself!"'

---

evidenced by the opening scene of *Romeo and Juliet* (1595) in which Capulet's servants Sampson and Gregory attempt to provoke their rivals from the house of Montague. 'I will frown as I pass by, and let them take it as they list', says Gregory, to which Sampson replies: 'Nay, as they dare. I will bite my thumb at them; which is a disgrace to them, if they bear it.' (In time-honoured tradition, Montague's servants rise to the bait, and fighting ensues.)

On approval

The **ring** (8) has been linked with the colloquial 'okay' (which, according to *The Oxford English Dictionary*, first appeared in the US with the meaning 'all correct' in an article in the *Boston Morning Post* on 23 March 1839). Certainly, the dominant message of this sign with its round shape implying 'wholeness' is approval of varying degrees from okay to excellent in the UK, and more particularly in the US: hence it is sometimes referred to as the 'OK gesture' or the 'American OK'. But it is not as modern as one might expect. John Bulwer's *Chirologia* (1644) records: 'The top of the fore-finger moved to joyne with the naile of the Thumbe that's next to it . . . is opportune for those who relate, distinguish, or approve'. Even further in the past, the Roman teacher Quintilian (AD c. 35–95) notes in his *Institutio Oratoria* : 'If the first finger touch the middle of the right-hand edge of the thumb-nail with its extremity, the other fingers being relaxed, we shall have a graceful gesture well suited to express approval'. This positive message, however, is by no means universal, as Axtell demonstrates in an anecdote about an American and a German working together for the first time on a new machine in a factory. Intending to praise his colleague's work, the American gave him the ring sign. The German promptly downed tools and refused to have anything further to do with him. Only later was the situation defused, when it transpired that in Germany the gesture means 'asshole'. (For some other interpretations, see pp.61–62.)

Thumbs up

Better known in the UK as a gesture of approval is the **thumbs up** (9), so-called even though it is usually performed with one thumb. Con-

---

Survival signs

In Arthur Hailey's bestseller *The Evening News*, Crawford Sloane is a highly-respected newscaster for an American network television company. Fearing that he may soon be kidnapped by terrorists, he arranges a series of signals with his wife Jessica, so that if he is forced to make a videotape recording she will know what he is really saying. In the event, it is Jessica who is kidnapped. Some days into her captivity, when the time does indeed come to make a video-recording, she struggles to remember her husband's signals:

'The conversation at Larchmont was coming back . . . Crawf had said, "*Licking my lips with my tongue would mean, 'I am doing this against my will. Do not believe anything I am saying.'*' . . . *Scratching or touching my right earlobe - 'My captors are well organized and strongly armed.'* . . . *Left earlobe - 'Security here is sometimes lax. An attack from outside might succeed.'*' ... There were other signals, Crawf had said, though he hadn't described them. So the three – or rather two, since she could only use one of the earlobe messages – would have to do.'

SPEAKING WITH HANDS

58

versely, giving the **thumbs down** is a popular gesture of disapproval. Folklore has it that both signs originated during the days of gladiatorial combat in ancient Rome, when the crowd, eager to advise their emperor of the fate of the defeated, recommended either mercy by displaying up-turned thumbs, or by pointing their thumbs down, death. However, according to Morris there are no references to thumbs 'going either up or down in the Colosseum at the vital moment of decision'. And as the Roman historian Pliny, writing about everyday life in the 1st century AD in his *Historie of the World* (translated by Philemon Holland, 1601) notes: 'to bend or bow down the thumbs when we give assent unto a thing, or do favour any person, is so usuall, that it is growne into a proverbial speech, to bid a man put down his thumb in token of approbation'. Apparently the misconception arose from a mistranslation of the term *pollice verso*, which does not mean down-turned thumbs, but turned thumbs, with no particular movement specified. Thus, if spectators wanted the fallen gladiator slain, they stabbed the air with their thumbs extended. The accepted position of thumbs to indicate acquittal was *pollice compresso* – compressed thumbs, i.e. the thumb hidden away in the fist.

A variant of the thumbs up is used for 'thumbing' a lift, but like the ring this is not recognised or accepted everywhere. Try it when hitch-hiking in Nigeria, for instance, and you are liable to receive more than a verbal or gestural insult in return.

Fingers crossed and kissed

While the verbal 'keep your **fingers crossed**' (10), meaning 'wish me luck' or 'here's hoping', is comparatively recent (UK, 1920s; US, 1930s), the gesture from which it derives, dates back to the first centuries AD and the early Christians, who devised it as a secret version of making the sign of the Cross*. Whether the original usage was primarily as an identification sign between fellow Christians during times of persecution, or as a protection against evil, is not known, but it is this latter meaning which has survived through the ages. By extension, it has become the most popular gestural expression of good luck, either for the person making it or for someone else. Additionally, children cross their fingers to protect themselves against the consequences of lying, i.e. in the belief that the sign will cancel the sin of lying.

There may be a distant religious connection, too, in **kissing the fingertips** and gently throwing the 'kiss' into the air. Morris reports that this gesture, once common in ancient Greece and Rome as a long-distance version of the mouth kiss, was performed as a 'solemn act of greeting towards a powerful dominant figure'. Early Christians may have made the fingertips kiss towards the crucifix*. Today, in a more lighthearted role, the gesture is sometimes used in parts of Europe as a salutation; more commonly in countries like France and Italy, it signifies approval or praise about someone or something. In *A Year in Provence*, Peter Mayle describes the patron of a restaurant enthusing over the food on offer . . . 'it was a gastronomic aria which he performed at each table, kissing the tips of his fingers so often that he must have blistered his lips'.

If only meanwhile he could just sit here in the cool, with his fingers crossed against all dangers.

Angus Wilson *The Wrong Set*

Conversation à la provençale

For any serious and satisfactory discussion both hands must be free to provide visual punctuation, to terminate dangling sentences, to add emphasis or simply to decorate speech . . . it is often possible to follow the gist of a Provençal conversation from a distance, without hearing the words, just by watching expressions and the movements of bodies and hands.

Peter Mayle *A Year in Provence*

Demotic signs

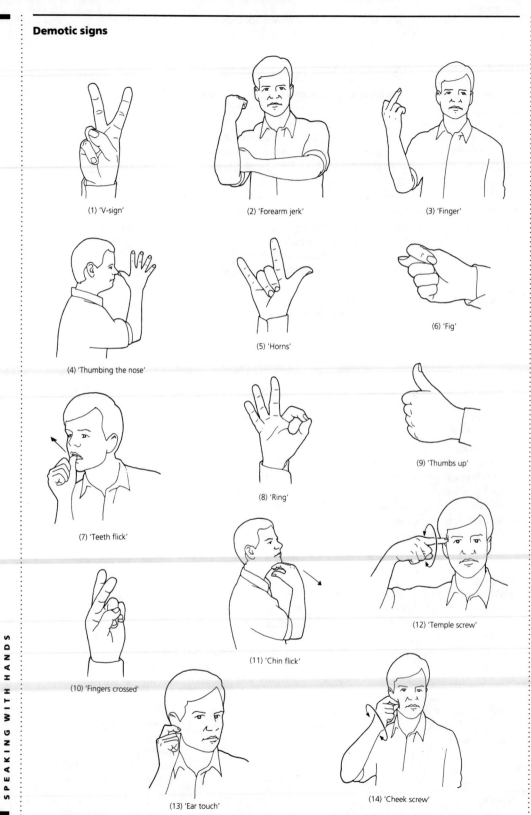

(1) 'V-sign'

(2) 'Forearm jerk'

(3) 'Finger'

(4) 'Thumbing the nose'

(5) 'Horns'

(6) 'Fig'

(7) 'Teeth flick'

(8) 'Ring'

(9) 'Thumbs up'

(10) 'Fingers crossed'

(11) 'Chin flick'

(12) 'Temple screw'

(13) 'Ear touch'

(14) 'Cheek screw'

Articulate gesticulations

A selection of silent but meaningful signals from around the world. (The numbers in brackets refer to illustrations opposite.)

Argentina The 'chin flick' (11) signifies 'I don't care', or 'I don't know'; similarly in Brazil and Paraguay. Rotating the forefinger near the temple means 'you have a phone call'.

Australia The 'thumbs up' (9), especially with an upward jerking motion, is considered offensive.

Austria Stroking an imaginary beard means that someone's comment is 'old news'. Austrians signal 'good luck' by pounding clenched fists on an imaginary table.

Brazil The 'ring ' (8) is offensive; however, the 'fig' (6), a rude sign in many countries, signals 'good luck'. To express appreciation, a Brazilian pinches his earlobe.

Bulgaria Confusingly, Bulgarians say 'no' by nodding, and 'yes' by shaking the head from side to side.

China According to Wolfram Eberhard's *Dictionary of Chinese Symbols*, children express fear by sticking their tongues out. If a Chinese sticks out his lower lip, wrinkles his nose, and frowns, he is expressing dislike; if he holds his right hand with outstretched fingers across his body then jerks it forwards, he is telling you to 'get lost'. Stroking the cheek downwards with the forefinger indicates 'shame on you'. Rubbing two open hands together signifies bankruptcy.

Colombia Colombians express disbelief in a statement or story by cupping the hand about 6in (15 cm) below the chin; the gesture is thought to have originated as a visual description of a goitre, a symbol of stupidity. Making the 'ring' (8) and twisting it over the nose indicates that some other person is homosexual.

Egypt Tapping two forefingers together side by side is a non-verbal way of saying 'do you want to sleep with me?'

France In some parts of the country, the 'ring' (8) means 'zero' or 'worthless'; however, the same sign twisted over the nose indicates

someone is drunk. Thumbing the nose (in French *pied de nez* or *le nez long*) is a gesture of mockery; the 'fig' (6) is a sexual insult. The forearm jerk is known as *le bras d'honneur*, the arm of honour. If someone plays an imaginary flute while you are talking, he may be telling you that you are boring.

Germany The 'temple screw' (12) made by one driver to or about another, means, to put it mildly, 'you're mad'; the gesture is considered highly offensive, and people can be arrested and prosecuted for it. To signal 'good luck', Germans tuck the thumb into the fist, or sometimes pound an imaginary table with clenched fists.

Greece Instead of the customary raised middle finger to signal 'up yours!' Greeks extend the hand, palm down with the middle finger pointing downward; not the easiest gesture to make, so it is unlikely to be accidental. The 'teeth flick' (7) is made in anger; the 'ear touch' (13) is a warning; the 'thumbs up' (9) may be a sexual insult. 'Fingers crossed' (10) means 'I am no longer your friend'.

Holland The 'cheek stroke' with thumb and forefinger down each cheek means that someone is thin and ill. Sucking the thumb signifies that someone is lying, or at the least being too liberal with the truth; tapping the side of the nose with the forefinger means 'I'm drunk' or 'you're drunk'; rubbing the bridge of the nose with the forefinger indicates someone is cheap or stingy; to indicate that someone is crazy, the Dutch tap the centre of the forehead.

India Grasping one or both ears with the fingers is a sign of apology or remorse; it is sometimes made by children or servants. Pointing is done with the open hand, or the thumb; another way is with the chin, but not to superiors.

Iran People in Iran toss the head back sharply to signal 'no'; and 'yes' by dipping the head downwards with a slight twist.

Israel If an Israeli points to his palm while someone is speaking, he is saying that it will sprout grass

before what he is hearing comes true.

Italy A 'cheek screw' (14), where the thumb and forefinger are pressed into the centre of the cheek and rotated as if screwing something into it, is used to express praise, especially of food. Desmond Morris suggests this may be a relic of the days when Italian men twiddled the tips of an imaginary moustache at the sight of a beautiful woman. Tossing the head back is a negative sign; the 'ear touch' (13) signals that someone is effeminate. Italians wave with the back of the hand; they beckon with the palm down and fingers wagging.

Japan The 'ring' (8) signifies money, due to the shape which resembles a coin. Japanese beckon someone by extending the hand with the palm down, and making a scratching motion with the fingers.

Malaysia Indians in Malaysia signify agreement by shaking the head quickly from side to side.

Malta The 'horizontal horns' (5) is commonly used as protection against evil (Desmond Morris found that cars and boats are often adorned with it). The 'forearm jerk' (2) is highly offensive, and illegal.

Mexico The V-sign with the palm inward over the nose is an obscene gesture.

New Zealand Maoris greet each other by rubbing noses.

Nigeria The 'thumbs up' (9) as a hitch-hiking sign is considered offensive. The Yoruba of southwestern Nigeria wink at their children when they want them to leave the room.

Paraguay Crossing the fingers, a 'good luck' or protective sign elsewhere, is offensive, as is the 'ring' (8).

Peru Tapping the underside of the elbow with the fingers indicates that someone is cheap or stingy; tapping the middle of the forehead signals that someone is stupid.

Poland If a Pole flicks his finger against his neck, he is inviting someone, usually a close friend, to

(continued)

have a drink; in some cases, however, the gesture may also be considered rude.

Portugal The 'fig' (6) is used for protection; the 'ear touch' signifies praise.

Sardinia Using the 'thumbs up' (9) when hitch-hiking will most certainly be interpreted as 'get stuffed'; similarly in Greece.

Serbia The 'victory V' salute (1) is made using the thumb and the first two fingers. Also in Serbia, and in other parts of what was formerly Yugoslavia, if a waiter or taxidriver signals to a colleague by pulling down his lower eyelid with a forefinger he is saying 'I got no tip'.

Sicily The 'ring' (8) signifies 'nothing'; pinching the cheek denotes 'excellent'.

Spain Giving the 'thumbs up' (9) in northern Spain may imply support for the Basque separatist movement. Pulling down the eyelid with a forefinger signifies a warning to someone to be alert; similarly in Italy.

Syria Nose-picking is a signal to indicate 'Go to the Devil!'

Thailand Because the foot is considered the lowliest and dirtiest part of the body, pointing any part of it or showing the sole of the shoe at someone is an insult. The same is true in many parts of Asia, and the Middle East.

Tunisia Flicking an imaginary beard with the backs of the fingers under the chin signals disbelief (also in Italy, and France, where the gesture is called *la barbe*, the beard). The 'teeth flick' (7) means 'zero'; the 'ring' (8) can be 'zero', and a threat.

Turkey To signal 'good', Turks hold up the hand with the palm outward and bring the fingers into the thumb in a grasping motion. If a Turk pulls down the lower eyelid with the forefinger he is saying he is alert, and not likely to be fooled (also in Greece). Crossing the fingers denotes that a relationship is about to be broken.

United States In southern states, people sometimes cross their fingers when passing a graveyard as a protection against any evil influence. Wetting the little finger and stroking it over the eyebrow may signal that some other person is homosexual. In Hollywood, holding the nose with thumb and forefinger in reference to a film signifies a flop.

Occupational signing

Just as trades and professions have their own vocabulary or jargon, so a number of groups have developed a code of specialised gestures for occasions when speech is undesirable, difficult, or impossible. In many cases, for example the tick-tack language used by 'bookies' on English racecourses, these gestures have evolved naturally; in some others they have been specifically structured and defined for use internationally.

Taking a gamble

Croupiers sometimes use hand signs for a quick but silent interchange with a supervisor. If a croupier wants to be relieved from his position, for example, he signals the fact by crossing his fingers. If he suspects a player of cheating, he may discreetly call for help by pointing to his ear or temple and then signalling his suspicion by placing the fingers of his left hand on the table. After observing the situation, his supervisor will then point to his left thumb to signal that the player may continue (or take some other appropriate action). These and other signs were noted by Theodore Brun in his *International Dictionary of Sign Language* from those used in casinos in Monte Carlo; other casinos may well have their own special variants.

To signal that a player may continue to play, a croupier points to his thumb

Odds and evens

Far less discreet is **tick-tack**, the code of signals bookmakers and their agents use to communicate odds to each other at English race meetings. If the odds on horse number 15, for instance, are 9 to 4, the tick-tack man, usually wearing white gloves, first signals 10 (by moving both clenched hands together and apart at chest height) and 5 (by touching his right shoulder with his right hand) for the horse's number, then follows with the signal for 9/4 (by touching the top of his head).

A man on top of the half-crown stand tic-tacked to Bob Tavell of Clapton, and a tiny man who was studying the ten-shilling enclosure through binoculars suddenly began to saw the air. . . . 'There,' the Boy said, 'what did I tell you? Black Boy's going out again.'

Graham Greene *Brighton Rock*

Tick-tack code (after Brun)

1

2 or 2/1

3 or 3/1

4 or 4/1

5 or 5/1

6 or 6/1

7 or 7/1

8 or 8/1

9 or 9/1

10 or 10/1

Evens

11/10

6/5

5/4

11/8

6/4

13/8

7/4

15/8

9/4

5/2

7/2

9/2

11/2

11/4

100/30

Odds on

Handy tips

Writing in the *Daily Express* in July 1991, columnist Peter Tory lamented 'can there ever, ever have been a time in our parliament's history when there was such a lack of performing talent? A lack, to put it crudely, of showbiz?' Tory was referring to the fact that so few modern politicians know the value of gesture in public speaking, of 'the grandeur of the shrug, the sudden slump of despair, the stunning application of the raised index finger'. He did, however, have a word of praise for the former Prime Minister Margaret Thatcher, whom he described as a master of the carefully chosen gesture. 'Maggie's technique is unequalled. One only has to look at her use of her spectacles . . . She snatches them off with a fierce sense of sudden interest, gazes at her tormentor as if he or she was slightly mad and then replaces them slowly with a gesture of quiet regret'.

Similar tricks were stock in trade for the politicians of yesteryear, who seem to have been as naturally well-versed in gesture as in speechifying. Perhaps, before entering Parliament, every fledgling MP should study the works of the 17th-century English essayist John Bulwer. Bulwer had no time for 'naked narration', as he called rhetoric without gestures, and in *Chirologia* (1644), a detailed treatise in praise of the power of the hand, he urged public speakers to tailor their movements to 'the requirements of art'. Here are some examples of his more general 'Cautionary Notions' for 'the better regulating the important gestures of the Hand and Fingers':

● To use no action at all in speaking, or a heavy and slow motion of the hand, is the property of one stupid and sluggish.

● The incomposure of the hands is to be avoided, for to begin abruptly with the hand is a sin against the laws of speech.

● When the oration begins to wax hot and prevalent, the hand may put forth with a sentence but must withdraw again with the same.

● No gesture that respects the rule of art directs itself to the hinder parts . . . whereas there are seven parts of motion: to the right hand, to the left, upwards, downwards, forward, backward, and circular; the first five are only allowed a rhetorician.

● Shun similitude of gesture; for as a monotone in the voice, so a continued similitude of gesture and a hand always playing upon one string is absurd, it being better sometimes to use a licentious and unwarrantable motion . . .

● The gestures of the hand must be prepared in the mind, together with the inward speech that precedes the outward expression.

Bulwer concludes with the warning: 'Use no uncomely or irregular excess of gesturing with your fingers in speaking, nor draw them to any childish and trifling actions . . . lest you diminish the glory of fair speech and rhetorical persuasion, and offer a great indignity to Minerva [the Roman goddess of wisdom and the arts] to whom these organical parts of elocution were sacred'.

In February 1957, twelve men from Lake Wobegon Lutheran were going to come to Honolulu for the National Church Ushers Convention, including the finals of the Ushers Team Competition. The guys had raised thousands of dollars for the trip and had been drilling for two nights a week for six months, practising their silent usher signals, a complicated set of hand and eyebrow signals like this: cupped hands (it means 'need additional hymnal in this pew'), or crossed arms and kicking motion ('remove this child'), or fluttering fingers with arms akimbo ('need a new collection plate, this one is too full'), a signal seldom used in church but popular at contests.

Garrison Keillor *Leaving Home*

Where and when this once secret code originated is not known, though it is certainly more than a century old. As to the origin of the word tick-tack or tic-tac, there are a number of theories. One is that it derives from ticker, a nickname for the telegraphic recording instruments or stock indicator machines that first appeared in banks and stock exchanges on both sides of the Atlantic in the late 19th century. More plausible is Julian Franklyn's suggestion in his *Dictionary of Rhyming Slang*, that it comes from a slurring of 'tin-tacks', a variation of 'brass tacks', which is Cockney rhyming slang for facts. Thus to tick-tack is to signal the facts. According to *The Oxford English Dictionary*, the word first appeared in print in 1899. An early example of its use occurred in a report in the *Daily Chronicle* on 1 February 1905 of the proceedings of the Magistrate's Court in Kingston, Surrey, when 'a prisoner puzzled the Kingston Bench by describing himself as a "racecourse telegraphist". A detective explained the man practised what is known as "tick-tack telegraphy" – signalling by means of the arms to outside bookmakers'.

Interestingly, tick-tack has spawned its own vocabulary. For example, the numbers from two to ten (with the exception for some reason of nine) have their own codewords, as do some of the odds: 6/4 is 'ear 'ole', 11/8 is 'up the arm', and 100/30 'Burlington Bertie'.

Buying and selling

Hand signals are also used in the process of buying and selling at sales and auctions, whether it be a ton of coffee or a Ming vase. In some salerooms or commodity exchanges, the signals are pre-arranged between the auctioneer and dealer: a raised hand, palm held outwards or inwards, may mean an offer either to sell or to buy. In other places, signs follow a standard code. In the grain exchanges of the American mid-West, each finger raised by a buyer denotes 5000 bushels, while each finger held horizontally will signify a fraction of a cent above the full cent price at the start of bidding.

In the more rarefied atmosphere of fine art salerooms, bidders sometimes avoid attracting the attention of other dealers by means of a private code, in which case only the vigilant auctioneer will know if the bid has been raised and by whom. Commonly-used signals include raising an eyebrow, stroking the nose, holding a jacket lapel (in Robert Graves' 1936 novel *Antigua, Penny, Puce*, which has as its theme a family feud over a rare postage stamp, there is a fine description of a stamp auction in which one character bids with 'a modified Fascist salute'). Confusingly, a buyer may look away from the auctioneer to signal that he is bidding, and only establish eye contact again to indicate that he has ceased to bid.

Such signs belong increasingly to the past as the major auction houses turn to less idiosyncratic methods. The world's largest and oldest, Sotheby's, recently introduced a system of making a bid by raising a numbered 'paddle'. Their brief guide, *How to buy and sell at Sotheby's*, comfortingly assures the prospective buyer that with the paddle 'there is no longer any danger (never very real in any case) that a wave to a friend or a scratch on the nose will land you with a Rembrandt at £6 million'.

More mysterious, and certainly more secretive, is an ancient method of saleroom sign language believed to have originated in China. Buyers stand in a semi-circle and, one by one and under cover of a piece of cloth, squeeze the hand of the auctioneer at the same time as verbally indicating the units in which they will bid (e.g. in units of ten). The multiple of this spoken figure is signalled by the number of fingers squeezed and sometimes the number of squeezes. When all bidders have had their say and squeeze, only the auctioneer knows who has bid highest. Auctioneers who use the 'hand-shake auction', as Brian Learmount describes this method in *A History of the Auction*, 'may be identified by their bruised hands and swollen fingers'!

Studio talk

Radio and television production personnel throughout the world use a variety of hand and arm signals in the studio, particularly during newscasts, interviews and other 'live' productions where verbal communication is not possible.

In television, signs are used to cue a presenter (or any other performer), to tell him to speed up or slow down, to move closer to the camera or microphone, to speak louder or more softly, to wind up or 'wrap up' what he is doing, and of course to stop (which the floor manager indicates by a cutting motion of his hand across his throat).

Two distinctive American signs worth noting are pulling an imaginary beard to signify a blunder, and tapping the tip of the nose to indicate that a programme is running to schedule. From this last, incidentally, derives the now colloquial expression 'on the nose'.

Safety signs

One area in which some form of coded signs is not merely useful but essential is where matters of safety are concerned, particularly when

Circling the ear with the finger signals 'speak up'

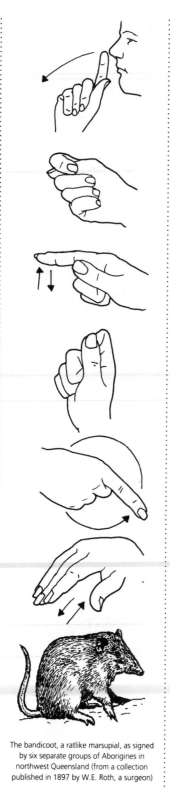

verbal communication is impossible, perhaps because noise levels are too high, or because of the distance separating the sender and receiver. Obvious examples are the manual signals made by policemen on traffic duty, by crane-drivers, and by firemen. These may vary from country to country.

A more universal code of signals has been developed by the International Civil Aviation Organisation to guide pilots of fixed-wing aircraft manoeuvring on the tarmac. By day, these may be given by hand or with circular bats, by night by torches or illuminated wands. Marshalling signalmen use another set of signals to give instructions to helicopter pilots.

Skin-divers, who often operate in pairs, use a system known as **buddy signals**. These originated in the US and have since become widespread. They include signals for simple messages such as yes, no, up, down, good, bad, and okay. Danger is signified by one hand across the throat, cramp by rhythmically opening and closing one hand. There are also signs for numbers from zero to nine, and for other important information such as the depth, time, and compass course. So for instance to signal 4.30 p.m., the diver gives the time sign by tapping his wrist followed by signs for the numbers 1, 6, 3, 0, holding each sign until his partner returns it. The end of a number is signified by a clenched fist.

Alternate languages

Gesture codes, as alternatives to speech, were occasionally forced on people. In his *Chirologia: or the Natural Language of the Hand* (1644), the English physician John Bulwer cites one such instance concerning the 4th-century BC 'Tyrant of Syracuse' Dionysius, who 'prohibited the Syracusians all commerce of speech and the vocal liberty of communication, commanding them to call for their necessaries by nods and significant motions of their hands, eyes, and feet'. Apparently, his long-suffering subjects did this with some success. The 'motions' they invented developed into a flourishing gesture language which spread to southern Italy. Similarly, when some 2000 years later in 17th-century Constantinople (modern Istanbul), the Sultan indulged in the practice of cutting out the tongues of his harem attendants to ensure their discretion, they too compensated with an effective language of signs (realising he could do no more – short of cutting off hands as well – the Sultan desisted from the practice).

Aboriginal sign

Non-verbal communication also developed amongst so-called primitive peoples. In southwestern Africa, the **Bushmen** use signs when hunting to let each other know what animal they have sighted without scaring it away. Similarly, in Australia, **Aborigines** have invented numerous signs for animals and birds; the Worora in the far northwest often have a different sign for both the male and female of a species.

The earliest mention of Aboriginal sign language is given in 1874 by Samuel Gason, a police trooper of Coopers Creek, South Australia, who reported on a 'copious' language of signs used by the local tribe: 'all animals, native man or woman, the heavens, earth, walking, riding, jumping, flying, swimming, eating, drinking, and hundreds of other objects or actions have each their particular sign, so that a conversation may be sustained without the utterance of a single word'.

Some Aboriginal sign languages are relatively basic, and their use is confined mostly to the necessities of survival. Others are more elabo-

The bandicoot, a ratlike marsupial, as signed by six separate groups of Aborigines in northwest Queensland (from a collection published in 1897 by W.E. Roth, a surgeon)

rate. In his detailed study *Sign Languages of Aboriginal Australia*, Adam Kendon notes that the latter are structurally dependent on the spoken language: signs match words, and signed sentences are often manual translations of spoken sentences. Though commonly used as an addition to speech, signs may serve as a total substitute: when referring to sacred matters, for instance, or in male initiation rites. Kendon notes that such rites are regarded as a form of death (in which the boy dies and the man is born), and of course someone who is dead cannot speak. The dead, however, can hear. Thus sign language has become the safest means of communication among women during long periods of mourning, when silence is essential between female relatives and friends of the deceased to ensure that its spirit will not be drawn back by the voices of those to whom it was close in life.

Indian sign

Until quite recently, the best studied sign languages among hearing people were those used by the **North American Indians** in hunting, war, formal addresses, religious ceremonies, storytelling, and trade. The use of signs was first noted by European explorers of the mid-16th century among the tribes of northern Mexico and what is now Texas. With the new mobility afforded by the introduction of the horse into the New World by the Spanish in the 17th century, some of these tribes extended their territory northwards to hunt buffalo on the Great Plains. Within this vast area of more than a million square miles, they came into contact with other tribes. In the absence of a dominant spoken language, a common 'hand talk' developed.

Used both intertribally, and to a lesser extent by white settlers and traders (who often found it easier to negotiate directly by signs than through an interpreter), Plains hand talk expressed simple ideas or allusions. 'Man' (the erect one, the one alone), was signed by an extended forefinger held at chin-height; 'woman' by a sweeping downward movement of the hand with fingers extended by the side of the head to denote long flowing hair. Miming gestures commonly depicted some detail readily associated with a subject: thus the Sioux were signified by drawing the right forefinger across the throat, an allusion to that tribe's custom of cutting their enemies' throats or decapitating them. Compounds were also used: 'drought', for instance, was expressed by the signs LONG TIME+RAIN+NO. But compounding could be a lengthy business: a word such as skunk required eight signs: SMALL ANIMAL+PLUMED TAIL+STRIPED+BACK+ODOUR+BAD+EGG+SMASH.

By the late 19th century, hand talk was widely established among more than 30 tribes speaking 22 separate languages. Since the beginning of the 20th century, the use of English has gradually eroded the need for sign language, and in many areas it has disappeared altogether. In recent years, however, there have been attempts to revive it, mainly in connection with programmes of cultural re-education.

Monastic sign

Monastic orders such as the Cluniacs (founded AD 910 at Cluny in Burgundy, France) and the Cistercians (founded 1098 at Cîteaux, near Dijon, France) also communicate with signs. These developed in response to the 'Rule' of St Benedict (AD 480–547), which prescribed a life devoted to prayer, contemplation, and manual labour – in silence. Some orders adhered to this silence more strictly than others: Trappists

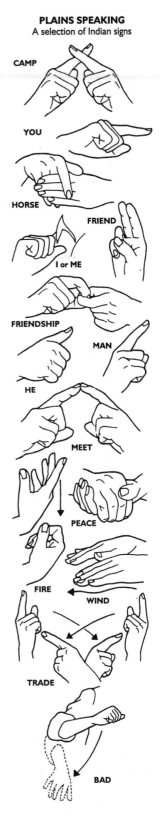

PLAINS SPEAKING
A selection of Indian signs

CAMP

YOU

HORSE

FRIEND

I or ME

FRIENDSHIP

MAN

HE

MEET

PEACE

FIRE

WIND

TRADE

BAD

(a branch of the Cistercians, established 1664 at La Trappe, Normandy), for instance, spent their lives in perpetual silence until as recently as the mid-1960s when the 2nd Vatican Council, which introduced changes in religious orders, relaxed the rule (though it is still observed in certain places, and at certain times).

As communication was regarded as a distraction, Benedict's rule discouraged all forms of it; a minimal amount, however, was permitted through signs. In the 10th century, a list was drawn up of 296 signs sanctioned mainly for the religious side: daily offices, prayers, objects used for rites and ceremonies. This authorised list is occasionally updated. New orders have also established their own systems. Inevitably, like dialects in speech, many other signs have evolved or been invented over the years both officially within the orders themselves, and within individual houses to meet everyday needs, so that today there may be little sign correspondence between one isolated monastery and another.

The natural development of a monastic sign vocabulary is demonstrated in Robert Barakat's comprehensive *The Cistercian Sign Language*, which contains more than 1400 signs in use at St Joseph's Abbey in Spencer, Massachusetts, a community which may be traced back to Cistercians who emigrated to America at the time of the French Revolution. In addition to those of the original list, plus 199 derived compounds, Barakat describes signs from St Joseph's own basic list and more than 600 originals. The study reveals some interesting compounds. While some are comprised of only one, two, or three signs (for example WHITE+RAIN makes snow, Christmas is signed by BABY+GOD+DAY, and Easter by GOD+UP+DAY, or just EGG+ DAY), others are more complex. In some cases, such as the compounds invented to express personal names, these encapsulate a complete story. Noah, for instance, is composed of the signs for OLD+SAINT+ARRANGE+BIG+BOAT+TIME+BIG+WATER+FILL+ COME; Judas is SECULAR+TAKE+3+0+MONEY+KILL+CROSS+GOD. Equally telling are some place name compounds: BAD+SECULAR+ COURTYARD+BURN+TIME+LADY+CHANGE+TWO+SALT signifies the wicked city of Sodom; since 1964 Dallas has become SECULAR+ COURTYARD+PRESIDENT+K+SHOOT.

In a silent world

Cistercian monks have accepted silence, where prescribed, as a part of their vows. Deaf people have no choice. **Deaf sign language**, therefore, is necessarily more complex, its visual vocabulary richer and more sophisticated than any other. Before looking at that, it is worth noting here two other methods of communication amongst deaf people, and between deaf and hearing people: **lip-reading** and **fingerspelling**.

Lip service

As a means of communication, **lip-reading** is rarely practicable on its own. Most deaf children nowadays learn to lip-read as a matter of course. But the skill to do so accurately is very much instinctive rather than one which can be learned. While some people – deaf or hearing – may become reasonably adept, others attain only minimal proficiency, often resorting to guesswork. Letters which sound different to a hearing person, for example F and V, or T, D, and N, look indistinguishable on the lips, while some sounds cannot be seen at all. Added to that, people mumble or speak in an accent which changes the shape of their words,

Strange to behold what dialogue of gestures exists between deaf and dumb who are able by this means alone to answer and reply to one another without the benefit of speech.

Bishop John Wilkins *Mercury – The Secret and Silent Messenger*, 1697

or they over-compensate and speak so slowly and distinctly that all natural rhythm is lost. Bearded men, smokers, and gum-chewers compound the problem.

Finger talk

Fingerspelling, otherwise known as **dactylology**, involves a manual alphabet of specific hand and finger positions to spell words letter by letter. Currently, there are more than 40 such alphabets and even some syllabaries* worldwide. While some national systems (that in use in the UK, for example) are two-handed, the great majority require only one hand. This is said to be 'more comfortable'; it also leaves one hand free for other actions.

The number of configurations in each country's manual alphabet depends on the size of the spoken language alphabet, though not always exactly to the letter. In Russia, for example, 30 fingerspelling signs correspond roughly to the 33 letters of the Cyrillic* alphabet. In China, 30 signs reproduce the symbols of Pinyin*, the roman-based phonetic alphabet now in use there. In 1963 an International Fingerspelling Alphabet was devised for multi-language situations, such as the Deaf Olympics, or congresses of the World Federation of the Deaf.

Although finger-spelling can serve as a self-contained means of communication, neither the one-handed nor two-handed systems have signs for capital letters, punctuation*, or breaks between words and, compared to speech or signing, both are slow. Among deaf people today, the use of manual alphabets is limited mainly to the spelling of place or proper names, foreign words, and any other words or expressions where no sign exists, assuming of course that both the sender and receiver have a good working knowledge of that language.

The **one-handed alphabet** used in the US (which is similar to that in France and some other European countries), derives from the early 17th century. In 1620, a Spanish Benedictine monk, Juan Pablo Bonet, published *Reducción de las Letras y Arte para Enseñar a hablar los Mudos* (simplification of the letters and the art of teaching mutes to speak). The manual alphabet he devised for this, was, he claimed modestly: 'so well adapted to nature that it would seem as if this artificial language had been derived from the language of nature'. Whether this alphabet was his own invention or an adaptation of an existing monastic alphabet is not known.

As easy as ABC

I had better explain our use of the manual alphabet, which seems to puzzle people who do not know us. One who reads or talks to me spells with his hand, using the single-hand manual alphabet generally employed by the deaf. I place my hand on the hand of the speaker so lightly as not to impede its movements. The position of the hand is as easy to feel as it is to see. I do not feel each letter any more than you see each letter separately when you read. Constant practice makes the fingers very flexible, and some of my friends spell rapidly – about as fast as an expert writes on a typewriter. The mere spelling is, of course, no more a conscious act than it is in writing.

Helen Keller *The Story of My Life*

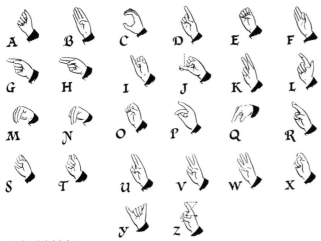

One-handed alphabet

In the 18th century, a Spanish Jew named Jacob Pereire used Bonet's signs to teach his deaf sister. When Pereire and his family fled from persecution in Spain to France, he took the alphabet with him and adapted it to the French language. A modified version of this, taught in the first school for the deaf in Paris in 1760, was introduced into the US in 1816.

The earliest record of a **two-handed alphabet** is found in *Didascalocophus, or the Deaf and Dumb Man's Tutor* (1680), by George Dalgarno, a teacher from Aberdeen, Scotland. Among other two-handed systems which followed soon after was *Digiti-Lingua* (1698), a 30-page treatise described as 'the most compendious, copious, facile

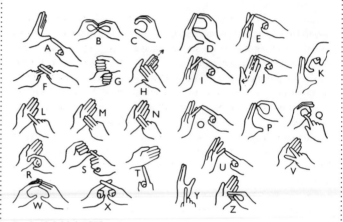

Two-handed alphabet (UK)

and secret way of silent converse ever'. Claiming to have 'conversed no otherwise in nine years', the anonymous author thoughtfully offered a choice of two alphabets so that 'every person is left to his liberty to make one for himself and friend out of the two, that will be private from all the world'. The modern UK two-handed alphabet is thought to have

The deaf–blind manual alphabet

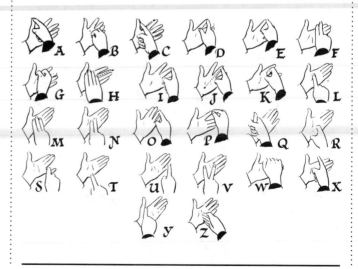

Sharing signs

For communicating with people who are blind as well as deaf, there are two alphabets. The first, called **block**, depends on the accurate tracing of ordinary capital letters on the receiver's palm. Much faster is the **deaf-blind manual** (specially adapted from the modern two-handed), in which the 'speaker' converses by 'imprinting' letters with the right hand on the receiver's left hand.

The earliest report of such signing in England appears in John Bulwer's *Philocophus, or the Deafe and Dumbe Man's Friend* (1648). It tells of a Mistress Babington of Burntwood, Essex, who could converse with her deaf husband on his fingers in the dark. Unfortunately, Bulwer does not mention whether this form of communication was used only at night, or if the man was also blind.

evolved from one of the Digiti-Lingua versions. The same alphabet is also used in Commonwealth countries such as Australia, where it was introduced in 1860.

True sign

Hearing people sometimes confuse fingerspelling with **deaf sign language**, or **Sign** as it may be called. The two, however, are worlds apart. While manual alphabets are directly related to the spoken or written word (i.e. spelt out letter by letter), true sign uses naturally-evolved signs that have no connection with any word-based language.

Deaf signs date back to antiquity. Writing in the 4th century BC, the Greek philosopher Plato refers to movements of the head, hand and body used by the 'speechless'. The *Mishnah*, a compilation of Jewish oral law of the late 2nd century AD, accepts that 'a deaf-mute may communicate by signs and be communicated with by signs', and that such means of expression may be used in law. Some 200 years later, St Augustine mentions a deaf man who could converse in gestures. But as to the shape of these early signs, or the ways in which they were developed and used, we know next to nothing.

Deafness has been called the least understood and most misunderstood of all disabilities. The same could be said about deaf sign language. Until the late 1950s very little was known about the subject, and the mystery that surrounded it in the hearing world gave rise to misconceptions: that it was, for example, merely broken speech on the hands. Nothing could be further from the truth. Linguistic studies have revealed that it is as much a real and living language as English, Arabic, or any other spoken language, with its own vocabulary, syntax and grammar. And though the most visible movements to a hearing person are those of the hands, to a deaf person the eyes, face, head and arms may play an equally important part.

Another popular misconception is that deaf sign language is international. Again, far from it. Each country has its own indigenous and naturally developed form. In the US, there is **American Sign Language**, also known as **Ameslan** or **ASL**. Used by more than half a million people, it is now (after Spanish and Italian) the third most widely used non-English 'language'. In the UK, more than 50 000 deaf people communicate with **British Sign Language** or **BSL**. But while the common spoken language of the two nations is basically the same, the two sign languages are very different. Similarly, deaf sign language in China is not the same as that in Taiwan. Nor do national frontiers always correspond to those of sign language. In Belgium, one sign language is used by both Flemish and Walloon signers. Ireland, on the other hand, has two deaf sign languages, one used by Catholics and one by Protestants.

Just as in spoken languages there are many variations and dialects within each country, so too in deaf sign language there may be numerous regional and local differences. Ed Shroyer demonstrates this in his book *Signs Across America*, a collection of 1200 signs from 25 states of 130 basic words, of which each had at least three different variations (quite apart from the standard ASL sign). There were, for instance, 16 ways of signing 'hot dog'. Shroyer also gives some interesting sign derivations. 'Christmas' in Maine is signed by picking pine needles off clothing: the implication being that if you walk in a forest in Maine (famous for its pine trees) you are likely to find some of the needles sticking to your clothes.

A selection of 'work survival' signs designed by James Gibson for the Royal National Institute for the Deaf

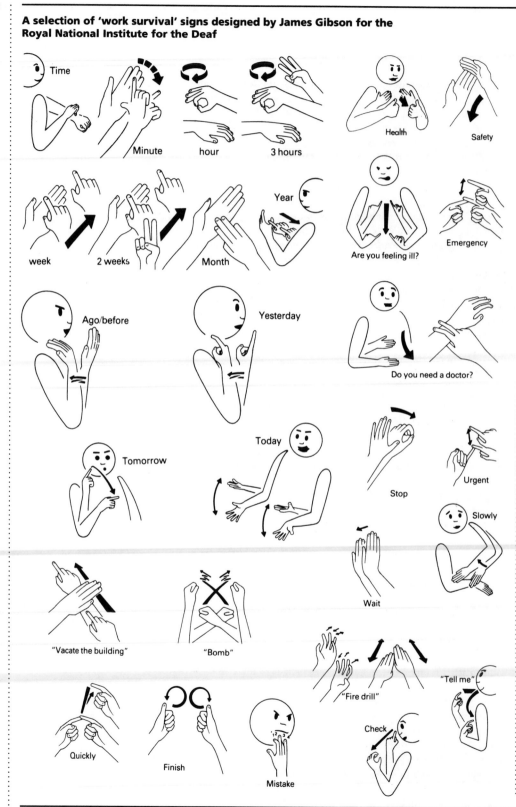

Time

Minute

hour

3 hours

Health

Safety

week

2 weeks

Month

Year

Are you feeling ill?

Emergency

Ago/before

Yesterday

Do you need a doctor?

Tomorrow

Today

Stop

Urgent

Slowly

Wait

"Vacate the building"

"Bomb"

"Fire drill"

"Tell me"

Quickly

Finish

Mistake

Check

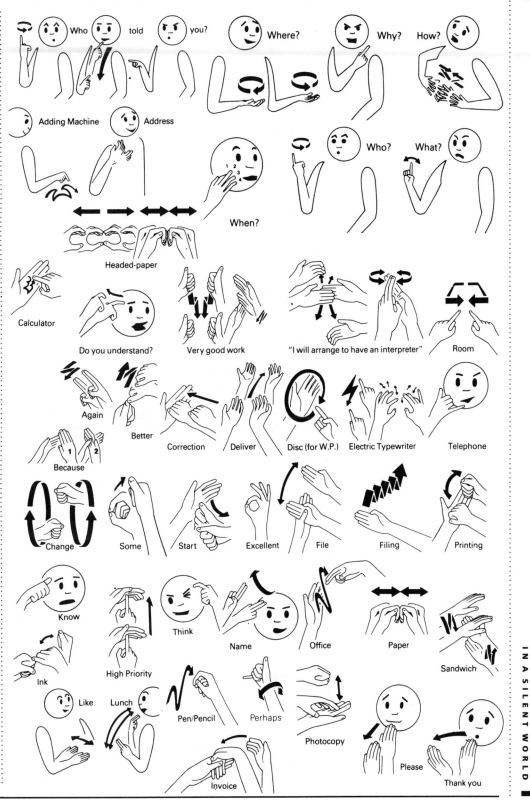

Who told you? Where? Why? How?

Adding Machine Address

Who? What?

When?

Headed-paper

Calculator

Do you understand? Very good work "I will arrange to have an interpreter" Room

Again

Better

Correction Deliver Disc (for W.P.) Electric Typewriter Telephone

Because

Change Some Start Excellent File Filing Printing

Know

Think

Name Office Paper

High Priority Sandwich

Ink

Like Lunch

Pen/Pencil Perhaps

Photocopy

Please

Invoice

Thank you

Despite their differences, deaf sign languages bear common linguistic features. Two deaf people from different countries – Japan and Italy, for example – will find it easier to communicate informally with each other than their speaking counterparts. For formal occasions, the World Federation of the Deaf introduced an international deaf vocabulary in 1975. Called **Gestuno**, and comprising nearly 1500 of the most readily understood signs from numerous systems, it has been developed to help deaf people converse more freely at international conferences and events – much as its speech equivalent Esperanto was intended to act in the hearing world.

Ideas, not words

Deaf sign is based on concepts – abstract ideas. As far as the hands are concerned, these concepts are expressed through two principal types of signs. **Iconic** signs mean what you think they should mean: 'house', for example, may be signed by outlining a pitched roof and two walls with both hands. Other **arbitrary** signs have no obvious connection with anything: 'sister' is made by curling the right index finger around the end of the nose.

Many signs derive from a bygone age. To take three random examples in BSL: the sign for 'milk' imitates milking a cow by hand; the sign for 'woman', made by stroking the cheek with the forefinger, refers to the days when women wore bonnets with ribbons; the sign for 'brother', made by rubbing two fists together, is said to represent the friction between Cain and Abel.

Nevertheless, changes occur in sign language in much the same way as they do in spoken languages. The earliest sign for 'telephone', for instance, required the use of both hands: one to imitate holding the stem and mouthpiece, the other the earpiece. When the all-in-one handset supplanted this two-piece model, the sign changed – to an extended thumb and little finger held close to the ear and mouth respectively. In recent years, that sign has again changed to a cupped hand to reflect the new designs of cordless and mobile phones. Similarly, the index finger's circular motion to imitate dialling is now changing to a pushbutton action.

Another example of changing with the times may be seen in signs that represent nations. Entertainment at the British Deaf Association's 100th anniversary congress in Brighton in August 1990 included mime by a troupe from the former USSR, who requested the audience to note that the outward palm clenched fist sign for 'Russia' was not a suitable symbol for *glasnost*. Consequently a new sign has replaced it: brushing the right forefinger across the chin. (Seemingly irrational too, is the recent sign change for 'Ireland'. While the old one represented flicking a shamrock from the lapel, the new derives from that of pricking a potato with a fork!)

Teaching signs

The **first free school for the deaf** was the Institut des Sourds-Muets, which was founded in Paris in 1760 by a priest, Charles Michel de l'Epée (1712–89). De l'Epée became a teacher and champion of deaf people by accident. The story goes that he took refuge from the rain in the house of two deaf sisters, who had devised their own communication code of facial expressions and hand signs. Entranced by their silent conversation, de l'Epée set out to learn their signs. He also studied the language of the Parisian deaf, and from his observations began to formulate a vocabulary of signs to act as a bridge between natural signing and the spoken language. With these *signes methodiques* (methodic signs) and his adaptation of Bonet's manual alphabet, de l'Epée developed the first standardised sign system, and taught his pupils to read and write French. His pioneering work formed the basis of today's **Signe Langage Français** or **SLF**. It also influenced other systems in Europe, Russia, parts of Africa and India, and most notably in the United States.

The **first deaf school in the US** was founded by Thomas Hopkins Gallaudet of Hartford, Connecticut. In 1815, he had sailed to Europe to study the latest teaching methods. After some months' tuition under de l'Epée's successor at the Institut in Paris, Gallaudet returned to Connecticut, taking with him the one-handed alphabet and the school's star pupil, Laurent Clerc.

When Gallaudet founded the American School for the Deaf in Hartford in 1817, Clerc became the **first deaf teacher** there, combining de l'Epée's alphabet and methodic signs with the natural signs already in use within the local deaf community. The school's success prompted the foundation of similar establishments in New York (1818), Pennsylvania (1820), and elsewhere. By 1863 there were 22 schools for the deaf throughout the US.

In 1864, Gallaudet's youngest son helped found the **first US college for the deaf** in Washington. Today, as Gallaudet University, it is the world's only liberal arts university for deaf people. Every subject, from business management to physics and philosophy, is taught in sign. A student protest in 1988 culminated in another notable first: the appointment of a deaf person as University President.

The **first school for the deaf in Britain**, the Braidwood Academy (Edinburgh, 1765), was anti-sign. Spoken and written English was taught to the virtual exclusion of sign language (although fingerspelling was permitted). The Braidwoods considered speech essential: if not proof absolute of intelligence and gentility, it was certainly far superior to gesture. They were not alone in this opinion. Two centuries earlier in Spain, for example, a Benedictine monk Pedro Ponce de Leon (1520–84), is said to have used a combination of a manual alphabet and monastic signs to teach deaf children to speak, principally to conform to Spanish law which decreed that a person must have that noble human faculty of speech in order to inherit.

Speech versus sign

From the earliest days of deaf education there has been conflict between the manualists and the oralists. Samuel Heinicke, who founded the **first state-supported school for the deaf** in Leipzig in 1778, regarded de l'Epée's signs as 'utterly vain and fruitless'. In common with some educators even to this day, Heinicke believed that deaf people could be integrated into the hearing world only if they learned speech. Others dismissed sign language as 'monkey gestures', primitive, crude, incapable of conveying anything but the simplest messages; at best a poor substitute for lip-reading, at worst actually damaging to the deaf person's mind. It was even argued that without speech training, children's vocal organs would atrophy!

In 1880, sign suffered a major setback at the Milan Congress of Educators of the Deaf, when delegates voted to ban sign language in education throughout the world. In 1889 this decision was endorsed in Britain by a Royal Commission. From then on, sign was suppressed, sometimes forcibly, in favour of speech training.

Sign in drama

'She has to learn that everything has its name! That words can be her eyes, to everything in the world outside her, and inside too, what is she without words? With them she can think, have ideas, be reached, there's not a thought or fact in the world that can't be hers. You publish a newspaper, Captain Keller, do I have to tell you what words are? And she has them already . . . eighteen nouns and three verbs, they're in her fingers now, I need only time to push one of them into her mind! One, and everything under the sun will follow.'

Annie Sullivan, Helen Keller's teacher and mentor in William Gibson's *The Miracle Worker*

'My eyes are my ears; and my hands are my voice; and my language, my speech, my ability to communicate is as great as yours. Greater, maybe, because I can communicate to you in one image an idea more complex than you can speak to each other in fifty words.'

James translating Sarah's signing in ASL in Mark Medoff's *Children of a Lesser God* (Tony 'Best Play' Award, 1979/80 Broadway Season)

Partly to alleviate the conflict, the British Deaf Association was founded in 1890, and in 1911 Leo Bonn, a merchant banker, who was himself deaf, set up the National Bureau for Promoting the General Welfare of the Deaf. This became the National Institute for the Deaf in 1924, and the Royal National Institute for the Deaf in 1961.

In spite of the efforts of these and similar organisations elsewhere, sign remained, for the most part, underground. Much of the credit for its recent emergence is due to the American linguist William Stokoe, who was the first person to look at the subject from a linguistic viewpoint. In the late 1950s and early '60s his studies of ASL proved that it is a language in its own right, with its own structural richness.

In the past 30 years, and particularly in the past 10, public awareness and acceptance of sign language as an alternative means of communication has grown. Media coverage is gradually making the language more visible to the hearing public. There is increased coverage on television; some theatres, such as the Royal National in London, present at least one signed performance each season; and political parties often provide interpreters at their annual party conferences.

Signs in symbols

Because sign language is three dimensional, it has long been difficult to provide an accurate representation of the signs used by deaf people. Two-dimensional pictures convey little hint of the many subtle elements of motion that come into play. Equally, verbal or written descriptions, however detailed, can serve only as a rough guide.

To remedy this situation, there are a number of systems in which signs are notated by symbols. The first and best-known of these was invented by William Stokoe, and published in his *Sign Language Structure* in 1960. Many sign language writers have since adapted Stokoe's symbols to serve individual needs (for instance, to notate his *Sign Languages of Aboriginal Australia*, Adam Kendon* uses a stock of 181 symbols).

Within the Stokoe system, there are basically four sets of symbols for each sign. Almost all signs are made within an imaginary square enclosing the top of the head, the hips, and the width of the extended elbows. The first symbols signify the location – where the sign is being made within the square, for example in the space in front of the body, or above the head. This is followed by symbols to indicate the arm position and the exact shape of the hands used to make the sign, either of the active 'dominant' hand – usually the right hand – or the passive hand. The third set signifies the position of the hand or hands in relation to the signer, and the fourth the movement of the hand, wrist, and fingers, and how it is performed. Thus, for example, the sign equivalent of 'believe' (literally described: 'move index finger straight down from forehead towards open left palm, change right hand into vertical open hand, then bring vertical open hand smartly down at right angles on to open left palm') may be accurately and concisely notated as φD>ΓǁK^$\underline{K}$<ˣ.

Educational signs

In recent years, special 'manually-coded' systems have been developed for educational purposes. These usually combine signs adapted from existing languages with newly-invented signs to represent spoken language. In Britain, the traditional compromise between sign and speech is called **Signs Supporting English**. This form, in which BSL signs are matched to words of simplified English for lip-reading, is used mainly between deaf and hearing people, or where something originally in English is to be conveyed to deaf people (e.g. on television or in the theatre). It is also called 'sign English', 'pidgin sign English', or 'signed English'.

This last named is different from **Signed English**, a structured method of teaching deaf children developed in the US in the 1970s. Now used in some schools in England, the system provides a complete signed representation of simultaneous speech with signs from ASL or BSL, some fingerspelling, and special signs for words and elements such as verb endings which are not present in sign language.

Two other systems are **Cued Speech** (devised 1966), an aid to lip-reading consisting of hand movements or 'cues' to help lipreaders distinguish vowels and consonants which look similar on the lips; and **Total Communication** (1970), which combines body language, gesture, mime, and traditional signs, with amplified sound, lip-reading, fingerspelling and writing.

Remedial signs

Manually-coded systems have proved valuable in remedial work with the mentally handicapped, children with learning or language disabilities, or adults suffering communication problems – perhaps as the result of a stroke. One of the first and best-known systems was invented by Sir Richard Paget in 1934, originally for use with deaf children. Greatly extended, **Paget-Gorman Signed Speech** now has a stock of more than 4000 signs to provide a grammatical representation of spoken English in the same order as the words in the phrase or sentence being signed. Another remedial system, **Amerind** (devised in the US from North American Indian signs), is now also used in Britain with speechless and mentally retarded patients.

Chapter 4

Signs from afar
Signal codes

Signal failure

In Greek legend, the Minotaur, a half-bull half-man monster housed in the Labyrinth at Crete, demanded from the city of Athens an annual tribute of seven youths and seven maidens. Finally the long-suffering Athenians decided enough was enough, and the king's son, Theseus, was sent to slay the monster and so end the tribute once and for all. Before he sailed, Theseus promised his father, Aegeus, that as he returned home he would signal his survival (and thus his success), by hoisting white sails. Unfortunately, he forgot. Seeing black sails and fearing the worst, Aegeus drowned himself in the sea, which ever since has been named Aegean.

However expressive manual signs may be, they are effective only over relatively short distances. For communication further afield, other signs or, more specifically, **signals** were devised. Since earliest times, these have included the use of musical instruments such as whistles, bells, gongs, flutes, pipes, bugles, trumpets, and drums: via the so-called 'bush telegraph' of the Ashanti of Ghana and Yoruba of southwestern Nigeria, for instance, two drummers can talk to each other up to 20 miles (32 km) apart. The favoured visual method in ancient times seems to have been by fire. The 5th-century Greek playwright Aeschylus relates how Agamemnon relayed news of the fall of Troy (*c.* 1200 BC) via a chain of beacon fires to his wife Queen Clytemnestra at her palace at Argos, Greece some 500 miles (800km) away. Nearer our own time, beacons across England gave warning of the approach of the Spanish Armada in 1588. In North America, Indian tribes such as the Cheyenne and Sioux produced smoke signals by covering and uncovering the flames of a fire with a blanket or animal hide. Contrary to some legends of the American West, however, it is doubtful if such signals could transmit much more than the simplest pre-arranged messages. This was a problem common to most early signals: although effective up to a point, they were in general strictly limited in the amount of information they could convey.

To meet the increasing demand for more articulate signalling, particularly in time of war, when rapid, efficient, and sometimes secret communication between the line of command and the line of action was vital, new signal systems using codes were invented. Of these, the most important from a sign or symbol point of view are the flag codes used at sea, semaphore, and Morse.

Sea signals

The **earliest recorded instance of a naval signal** comes from the Greek historian Herodatus: at the Battle of Salamis in 480 BC the Athenian statesman Themistocles hoisted his red cloak as the signal for the Greek fleet of about 380 ships to attack the thousand-strong Persian fleet. The **earliest known example of a naval signal code** occurs, on paper at least, in the 9th century AD. In a treatise on tactics, the Byzantine emperor Leo VI (866–912), urged his naval commanders to carry a conspicuous standard, banner, or streamer on their ships to signal, for example, 'whether to fight or to withdraw, to open out to surround the enemy, to slow the rowing or increase speed, to make an ambush'. Such signals, Leo suggested, could be made by raising or lowering the standard, shaking it, inclining it to the left or right in an agreed number of moves, or 'by varying the appearance of the head by means of devices or colours'.

The **earliest record of signalling in the British Navy** by 'devices or colours' appears in 1338 in the *Black Book* of the Admiralty, with two instructions for the use of a banner: one to be raised aloft 'in case any ship or other vessel of the fleet perceive any enemy vessel upon the sea', and the other, a 'Banner of Council' (usually the Royal Standard*) to be carried high in the middle of the mast to summon the captains of the fleet to a council on board the admiral's ship.

The **first record of an official code** is found in the *Instructions for the better ordering of the fleet in fighting* (1653). These stipulated the use of a number of flags, including the Union Flag* of 1606 (the predecessor of the so-called 'Union Jack'), to convey to the rest of the fleet signals whose meaning depended on which mast the flag was hoisted. The red 'flag of defiance', for example, flown from one mast signified 'engage the enemy', from another mast it meant 'vice-admiral and ships of the starboard squadron to come to the starboard tack'.

Over the next 100 years additional flags, sometimes in conjunction with the firing of guns, and the raising and lowering of certain sails, provided an increasing number of signals. Even so, the variations in meaning were necessarily limited, and not always practical – particularly in the heat and confusion of battle.

The **first flexible system** appeared in 1780 with 10 flags numbered from zero to nine. For instance, signal number 53 in the code, 'prepare for battle', was made by the number 5 flag (quartered white and red), flown above the number 3 flag (vertically divided blue/white/blue).

The **first printed signal book**, comprising about 400 'numeral' signals, was issued by the Admiralty in 1799. This *Signal Book for the Ships of War* was supplemented the following year with a dictionary devised by Captain Sir Home Riggs Popham (1762–1820) entitled *Telegraphic Signals, or Marine Vocabulary*. It contained the 1000 most useful words for naval purposes. Popham expanded his vocabulary in 1803 with another 1000 words, plus 1000 sentences 'most applicable to military or general conversation'. Less usual words had to be spelled letter by letter using one flag for the letters A to I, and two each for the remaining letters. A 'preparative' or 'telegraph flag', divided diagonally into red and white, indicated decipherment from the numbered dictionary rather than the Signal Book. In 1812, Popham increased the number of instructions with alphabetical flags which, when combined with numeral flags, provided a vocabulary of over 30 000 words.

Nelson confides...

The most famous signal in British naval history is 'England expects that every man will do his duty'. It was sent by Admiral Horatio Nelson (1758–1805) from his command ship HMS *Victory* on 21 October 1805, shortly before the decisive Battle of Trafalgar which destroyed Napoleon's naval power.

In their biography *Nelson: The Immortal Victory*, David and Stephen Howarth write that Nelson had intended the rather more personal message: 'Nelson confides that every man will do his duty', but first someone suggested 'England' instead of 'Nelson', then his signal officer, Lieutenant John Pasco (1774–1853), pointed out that as the word 'confides' was not listed in the signal book – and would need to be spelt out with 11 flags in 8 hoists

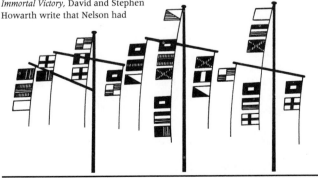

– it would be quicker to substitute 'expects', especially as 'duty', which surprisingly was absent from the vocabulary, would also have to be spelt.

No doubt the fleet would have preferred Nelson's confidence to England's expectations, but Nelson agreed to the changes, and at 11.35 a.m., with the English and French fleets a mile apart, the revised signal was hoisted to the *Victory*'s mizzen-mast.

According to the Royal Naval Museum at Portsmouth, the signal would have been flown from the mizzen-mast two words at a time. The order shown here, as hoisted each Trafalgar Day, 21 October, on HMS *Victory* (now in dry dock at Portsmouth), was devised many years later so that the whole signal could be seen at once.

Turning a blind eye

Fearing defeat at the Battle of Copenhagen on 2 April 1801, the British commander Sir Hyde Parker hoisted the signal to 'leave off action' and withdraw. Admiral Nelson, in the thick of the action, is reported to have exclaimed: 'Leave off action! Damn me if I do. I have only one eye, I have a right to be blind sometimes.' Clapping a telescope to this blind eye, he announced, 'I really do not see the signal!' then continued the battle, and soon after turned potential failure into a resounding victory.

Merchant signals

During the Napoleonic Wars (1803–15), the Royal Navy sometimes escorted merchant ships. But since no mercantile flag language existed with which ordinary ships could signal each other or their protectors, there were frequent difficulties.

To improve communication, a Royal Navy captain, Frederick Marryat*, who later achieved fame as the writer of adventure stories such as *Mr Midshipman Easy* (1836), compiled in 1817 a *Code of Signals for the Merchant Service*. Based on Popham's signals, and consisting of 15 multi-coloured flags and pennants, Marryat's code included words, sentences, names of ports and lighthouses, and a register of shipping. The code proved highly successful, and before Marryat's death in 1848, went through 10 greatly expanded editions.

In the mid-19th century, concern about an increasing number of rival codes, notably from France and the US, prompted the Board of Trade in London to propose a single international code. Published in 1857 as the *Commercial Code of Signals*, it comprised flags to denote all the letters of the alphabet apart from X, Y, Z, and the five vowels. With the remaining 18 (assuming none was used more than once in the same hoist), 78 642 permutations of hoists of one to four flags were possible. Incidentally, while X, Y, and Z were omitted as unnecessary, the vowels were excluded for a rather different reason: the Board of Trade claiming that their omission was 'forced' upon them 'from the circumstance, that by introducing them every objectionable word composed of four letters or less, not only in our own but in foreign languages, would appear in the Code in the course of the permutation of the letters of the Alphabet'.

International signals

In 1887, the code, renamed *The International Code of Signals*, was revised. X, Y, Z, were added to the system, as were the forbidden vowels (previous objections being by then judged 'sentimental rather than practical'). The full alphabet allowed 26 one-hoist signals, 650 with two, 15 600 with three, and 358 800 four-flag signals, making in all a possible 375 076 permutations. The revised code, adopted by all maritime nations, came into use on 1 January 1901.

Despite the improvements, misunderstandings between ships of different nations during World War I proved the signals were by no means foolproof. In December 1931, after lengthy revision, a new code drawn up by an eight-nation committee was published in English, French, German, Italian, Japanese, Norwegian, and Spanish. The 1931 code was published in two volumes, one for visual signals, the other for radiotelegraphy. Thirty years later, in a further revision to meet 'present day requirements of mariners', the two volumes were reduced to one, Greek and Russian were added to the languages, and each signal was given a complete meaning. No translation is necessary: with the code book, any captain can understand messages received.

This latest International Code came into operation on 1 April 1969. It is the most complete flag signalling system, and the most commonly used worldwide by merchant ships of all nations, and between merchant ships and warships. The code is made up of groups of signals of one to four letters.

Single-letter signals relate to phrases which are very urgent, important or of very common use. The meanings may vary according to the circumstances in which the flags are hoisted. For example, the flag

International Code of Signals

The phonetic alphabet and meaning of single-letter signals in the International Code (signalled by any means):

A ALFA
I have a diver down; keep well clear at slow speed

B BRAVO
I am taking in, or discharging, or carrying dangerous goods

C CHARLIE
Yes

D DELTA
Keep clear of me; I am manoeuvring with difficulty

E ECHO
I am altering my course to starboard

F FOXTROT
I am disabled; communicate with me

G GOLF
I require a pilot

H HOTEL
I have a pilot on board

I INDIA
I am altering my course to port

J JULIETT
I am on fire and have dangerous cargo on board; keep well clear

K KILO
I wish to communicate with you

L LIMA
You should stop your vessel immediately

M MIKE
My vessel is stopped and making no way through the water

N NOVEMBER
No

O OSCAR
Man overboard

P PAPA
(in harbour) All persons should report aboard as the vessel is about to proceed to sea

Q QUEBEC
My vessel is healthy, and I request free pratique

R ROMEO
(No meaning assigned in the International Code, but used by vessels at anchor to warn of danger of collision in fog)

S SIERRA
My engines are going astern

T TANGO
Keep clear of me: I am engaged in pair trawling

U UNIFORM
You are running into danger

V VICTOR
I require assistance

W WHISKEY
I require medical assistance

X X-RAY
Stop carrying out your intentions and watch for my signals

Y YANKEE
I am dragging my anchor

Z ZULU
I require a tug

All aboard!

The longest-running children's television show in Britain is the BBC's magazine programme *Blue Peter*, which began transmission in October 1958. It takes its title from the oldest signal code flag – the small blue and white rectangular flag of the same name. As well as the letter P in the International Code, the flag when hoisted singly by a ship in port signifies 'All persons report on board – vessel is about to proceed to sea', which meaning it has had since the mid-18th century. Hoisting this flag also served to notify any landlubbers having a money-claim on the ship's captain or crew to make it without delay.

Many theories explain the origin of 'Blue Peter' as a name: that it was nicknamed after Admiral Sir Peter Parker, who, as Chief of Command of the Royal Navy in the 1790s, used personally to give the signal for the fleet to sail; or that it is a corruption of the flag's technical description 'blue pierced with white', or of the French *partir*, to leave. Two most plausible explanations come from the 1750s when the initial signal for departure had to be repeated by all ships under sailing orders; or, that the flag having been used originally to mean that a signal had not been read and should therefore be repeated. Thus, Blue Repeater became Blue Peter.

But what has the name to do with a magazine programme for children? The producers felt it was like 'a ship setting out on a voyage having new adventures and discovering new things'.

nicknamed 'Blue Peter'* hoisted in harbour means all persons should report on board as the vessel is about to put to sea; hoisted at sea on fishing vessels, 'Blue Peter' signifies 'my nets have come fast upon an obstruction'.

Two-letter hoists apply to the General Section. This deals with signals for a wide range of messages, including those to do with distress, emergency, casualties, aids to navigation, weather, and international health regulations. For instance, NC means 'I am in distress and require immediate assistance'; SN means 'You should stop immediately. Do not scuttle. Do not lower boats. Do not use the wireless. If you disobey I shall open fire on you.'

Three-letter signals begin with M for the Medical Section, which covers almost every possible medical contingency. MGS, for example, signifies 'Patient is suffering from snake bite'.

Four-letter hoists relate to the Signal letters and radio call signs of ships. The first letter or first two letters indicate the ship's nationality. For British ships the initial letter is G or M.

Navy codes

National navies still retain flag codes of their own. Before and during World War II, some of these were more elaborate and flagbound than others: the Royal Navy's, for example, comprised 126 flags. After the War this number was greatly reduced. Today, when warships use the International Code, they fly the red-and-white striped 'code and answering pennant' to inform other ships that they are not speaking in secret code.

Following the formation of the North Atlantic Treaty Organisation in 1949, a separate NATO code was adopted.

Alternative signals

In addition to flag signalling, the 1969 International Code defined the other methods which could be used for communication. These are by flashing light using **Morse** code; by sound signalling using Morse; by voice through a loud hailer; by radiotelegraphy or radiotelephony; and by signalling with hand flags or arms, either by **semaphore,** or by Morse.

Telescopic telegraphy

The invention of the telescope in Holland in 1608 greatly increased the possibilities of signalling from afar, and throughout the 17th and 18th centuries, numerous optical systems were devised to take advantage of it. Among the most ambitious was one proposed by the English physicist Robert Hooke in 1684. It involved a chain of stations manned by three operators, two of them using telescopes to view boards of different shapes – round, square, triangular, octagonal – answering to letters of the alphabet. When displayed in a large square frame divided into four compartments and shown in the required order from behind a screen, these shapes could, Hooke optimistically predicted, be varied 10 000 ways and read in Paris only minutes after display in London. Although theoretically feasible, due to factors such as the unstable English weather, the invention was not a success in practice, and after brief trials it was abandoned.

Some 90 years later, during the War of Independence in America, a more modest signalling was achieved with a portable mast and a barrel, basket, and flag which, when hoisted in certain combinations, could convey pre-arranged messages.

Chappe's talking arms

The first person to exploit the telescope's potential as an aid for long-distance communication on land was the French inventor Claude Chappe (1763–1805). The second of five sons of prosperous parents, Chappe had trained originally for the church, but in the late 1780s turned his attention to signalling.

His first system, to be mounted on a series of towers within telescopic sight of each other, used dials on which rotating pointers (similar to the hands of a clock) indicated letters. This was destroyed by the Paris mob who suspected the device of signalling to the enemies of the State. His second apparatus, a rectangular board which could show six colours, suffered a similar fate.

Undismayed, Chappe continued his experiments, this time with moving arms. In 1793, with the help of his brother, a member of the Legislative Assembly, Chappe secured permission – and protection – for three watchtowers on an experimental 22-mile (35 km) line outside Paris. On top of each tower, a vertical post supported a crosspiece or regulator with a hinged wooden arm or indicator at either end. By ropes and pulleys both the regulator and indicators could be tilted clockwise or anticlockwise to create distinct positions in a pre–arranged code. The signals transmitted from the first tower or station were viewed by telescope by an operator in the next watchtower, who then relayed the same positions to the third tower.

Chappe named his invention the *tachygraphe*, from the Greek, 'swift writing', but later adopted **télégraphe** (Greek 'far writing'), a word coined in April 1793 by Miot de Mélito, a departmental chief in the Ministry of War.

Following successful trials in July 1793, Chappe was authorised to build a chain of 16 stations between Paris and Lille on the northern border with Belgium, a distance of 150 miles (240 km). On 15 August 1794, the first important message on the line carried news of Napoleon's recapture of Le Quesnoy in northern France from the Austrian forces. Relaying the news within an hour of the victory took just 20 minutes, some 10 hours faster than the usual couriers on horseback.

The *télégraphe* had its disadvantages – it could not be used at night or when visibility was poor, and the mechanism and towers were expensive to build and maintain. But these minor matters were far outweighed by the speed, the possibility of secrecy – only the sender and the final receiver needed to know the meaning of the signals – and in particular by the number of signals that could be transmitted. These went far beyond the basic alphabet and numeral code of 36 signs.

Each of the two indicators could assume seven positions, making 49 in all. When multiplied by the four regulator positions – vertical, horizontal, inclined to the right or left – 196 configurations could be achieved. In 1795, Chappe reduced these to 92 positions or 'working signals' for use in three codes. In the first, the positions, numbered from 1 to 92, were assigned to a vocabulary of 92 pages, each containing 92 words. The initial signal indicated the page of the vocabulary, the second indicated a word on that page. In this way, by just two signals, 8464 words could be expressed.

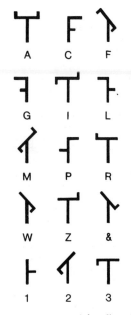

Sample letters and numerals from Chappe's first telegraph code, 1793

Hanky panky

Before he turned his pen to thrillers, and incidentally to becoming one of the most prolific and successful writers of all time, Edgar Wallace (1875–1932) served as a war correspondent for the *Daily Mail* during the Boer War in South Africa. His methods were frequently unorthodox, and he enjoyed an enviable reputation, both for the stories and for getting them past the censor. His most notable scoop came in May 1902 during negotiations for a peace treaty. Security at the camp where the peace talks were being held was especially tight; no one was allowed in, and no news came out. But, as he explained in his 1926 autobiography *People*, Wallace was undeterred:

'There was a good pal of mine in the camp, a Tommy with whom I had soldiered, and meeting him, I arranged a code of signals. He was to have three handkerchiefs – one red, one white, one blue. The railway ran within sight of the camp, and every morning I journeyed down to the Vaal River by train, took the next back, keeping my eye on the camp for the signal. Red meant 'nothing doing', blue 'making progress', and the white handkerchief was to signify that the peace treaty had actually been signed. I don't know how many journeys I made on that infernal railway, but never once was the red handkerchief displayed. Then one morning, when rumour was rife that the negotiations had fallen through, I saw my friend standing on the end of the tent lines, and he was displaying a white handkerchief conspicuously.'

Wallace immediately cabled London: 'Contract signed'. And the *Daily Mail* published the news of the War's end a full 24 hours before anyone else. Incidentally, this was the last time Wallace fooled the censor, who banned him forever as a frontline correspondent.

Similarly, the second vocabulary of 92 pages gave a total of 8464 phrases specially applicable to the army and navy. For this vocabulary three signs were required: the first to indicate the 'phrase code', the second and third to indicate the page, and the number on that page. The third code, devised in the same way, listed 8464 place names and geographical words and phrases.

Equally remarkable was the speed of transmission. On a clear day it was possible to start receiving a message in Paris three minutes after it was sent via 33 stations from Calais 148 miles (238 km) away; or from Toulon, 667 miles (837 km) and 100 stations away in the south, in 20 minutes.

Other lines were built during the years of the First Republic in France, and Napoleon's 'revolutionary wars' against Britain, Austria, Holland, Prussia, and Spain, when the new administration urgently needed a way to communicate quickly and secretly with the armies in the field. By the end of the Napoleonic era in 1815, a nationwide network crisscrossed France. Lines also extended into Germany, and over the Alps to Milan, Venice, and the Adriatic coast. When the electric telegraph and Morse code replaced Chappe's in the 1850s, more than 2485 miles (4000 km) in France were linked by 556 stations on eight mainlines and 11 branchlines.

International imitations

Chappe's *télégraphe* was widely imitated throughout Europe, in Russia, and as far away as Egypt and India. In 1801, a Massachusetts lawyer, Jonathan Grout Jr, patented his version for the first optical telegraph in the US, to relay shipping news from Martha's Vineyard (an island off Cape Cod) to merchants in Boston, and Salem, North Carolina. Over the next 40 years many other optical telegraphs, either home-grown or imitations of European systems, evolved. In 1837, for example, the year that Samuel Morse first applied for government funding for his new electric telegraph and dot-dash code, Congress was debating a petition to authorise a Chappe line between New York and New Orleans.

Poor Chappe, incidentally, never lived to enjoy the widespread success of his moving arms. Deeply depressed about his health and, it is said, by rivals claiming the invention of this first telegraph as their own, he committed suicide in 1805 – throwing himself off one of his own towers at the telegraph headquarters in Paris.

Channel vision

The **first optical telegraph in England** was installed by the Admiralty in 1795. Developed by a bishop, the Reverend Lord George Murray (1761–1803), the **shutter telegraph**, as it was known, worked on much the same principles as Chappe's telegraph, except that instead of movable arms, the apparatus consisted of six square or octagonal shutters in a three-by-two pattern in a boxed frame. By opening or closing one or more of the shutters, 63 combinations were possible. These represented the letters of the alphabet, numerals, frequently-used words such as fog, fleet, convoy, admiral, French, Russia; and complete phrases, among them 'to sail, the first fair wind, to the southward', and 'court-martial to sit'.

The first line of stations between the Admiralty in London and Deal, some 70 miles (113 km) away on the Kent coast, was opened on 27 January 1796. Although transmission was initially slow, eventually a message could be sent and an acknowledgement received in two minutes. Later that year, the second and most famous line of 10 stations was built to join London and the naval base at Portsmouth. By 1806, 22 stations linked London to Plymouth, and the daily signal transmitted at 1 p.m. could be acknowledged within three minutes. A fourth line connected Yarmouth on the Norfolk coast.

Semaphorically speaking

In 1801, a former French artillery officer named Depillon devised a means of ship-to-shore communication using the movement of three arms pivoted on a mast. Depillon's invention, which he called *sémaphore*, from Greek, 'sign bearing', was quickly adopted for coastal signalling, in particular to report English fleet movements.

Fifteen years later in England, Sir Home Popham modified Depillon's *sémaphore* to two movable arms for mounting on British ships. That same year, 1816, the Admiralty chose the Popham apparatus to replace the now defunct shutter telegraph. Compared to Murray's 63 combinations, Popham's were limited: only 48 were available to represent letters of the alphabet, numerals, and a few words and expressions, such as 'and', 'fog', 'closing down'. Nevertheless, the signals were clearer to read, the overall system was easier to operate, and it needed fewer relay stations.

The first line of only eight stations between the Admiralty and the naval yard at Chatham in Kent was opened on 3 July 1816. By 1823, 15 stations linked the Admiralty and Portsmouth dockyard. An extension to Plymouth was abandoned before completion when Admiralty funds for the project ran out. The existing land stations continued to function until the electric telegraph was installed, with the last in use – the London–Portsmouth line – closing on 31 December 1847.

HMS Semaphore

In 1826, ten years after Popham's system replaced Murray's telegraph on land, his seaborne mechanism was itself replaced by a simpler semaphore devised by Charles William Pasley, an officer in the Royal Engineers. By the 1870s such devices were widely-used for short-distance communication from ship-to-ship or ship-to-shore station. In later years, larger semaphore machines, sometimes with arms as long as 12 ft (3.7 m), were installed to increase the range.

To the casual observer on the shore, such masthead contraptions must have appeared comically ungainly as they waved their arms out at sea. When W. S. Gilbert sat down to write a naval parody in 1878, he

Railway semaphore

Semaphore was modified for signalling use on the London and Croydon Railway by Charles Hatton Gregory, a telegraph engineer, in 1841. His apparatus consisted of a single movable arm mounted on a vertical post. When the arm was moved by a handle at the foot of the post to a horizontal position, it signified 'stop, danger'; at a downward angle of 45 degrees, 'caution'; and when hanging vertically (in which position the arm disappeared into a slot in the post), 'clear'. That same year, a second arm was added to the other side of the post for trains in either direction on the newly-built London and Brighton Railway. More advanced signals, with additional semaphore markers to indicate which way the points are set, and with lamps for night signalling, developed later on railway systems worldwide. In many cases, these are still in use today.

Enthusiastic eyewitness

If we take up our station on the esplanade in St James's Park, the eye is caught by a huge upright beam erected on the roof of the Admiralty, with straight arms extending from it laterally at different angles. They may be seen altering their positions, remaining a few moments at rest, and then changing again. The giant upon whom the stranger gazes with uncomprehending curiosity is whispering to his huge brother on Putney Heath who will repeat the intelligence to his neighbour behind Richmond, and he to the next in order, so that by their unconscious agency the heads of the Navy in London give and receive intelligence to and from the great naval stations hundreds of miles off as quickly as they can communicate with a storehouse at the other end of the metropolis. The semaphore is, as any man may see, but a block of wood, and, heaven knows, no beauty, yet in the hands of man it becomes instinct with wondrous power . . .

Charles Knight *London* (1843)

TELESCOPIC TELEGRAPHY

first titled it HMS Semaphore. Before he finished it he had second thoughts, and 'Semaphore' became 'Pinafore'.

Handy flags

From 1880, a simpler and more reliable semaphore, using two small hand-held flags, was introduced to supplement the semaphore machine. In this method of signalling, based on the circular movement of the two hands of a clock, the operator moves his arms through various positions to represent letters, numbers and special signs. Although suitable for messages because of its speed – an average of eight words a minute – it is not readable much further than 2 miles (3 km) even on a clear day.

Early this century, two flags divided diagonally red and yellow (similar in design to Oscar, the International Code flag for the letter O) became standard for semaphore signalling. In the International Code, semaphore signals are always in plain language, and when numbers occur they are spelt out. A numeral sign indicates that the numerals that follow are to be recorded as digits.

Semaphore code

In the US Navy, the first 10 letters – A to J – preceded by the numeral sign, denote the numerals 1–0. Two additional signals indicate 'error', and the end of a word.

Although no longer used in the Royal Navy, semaphore remains a recognised method of visual signalling. To a limited extent, it is still in use in the Merchant Navy.

Wigwagging

In 1856, a US Army surgeon Albert J. Myer (1829–80) invented a single-flag semaphore. He called it flag telegraphy, but as the motions involved something of a cross between wiggle-waggle and zig-zag, it soon acquired the more descriptive nickname **wigwagging**.

As detailed in Myer's *Manual of Signals* (1879), letters of the alphabet are signalled by three motions with a large flag on a long pole. To sign the first motion (1), the signaller swings the flag from a vertical position to the ground on the right; for the second (2), he swings it to the ground on the left; and to sign the third (3), he lowers it to the front (separating each motion by returning the flag to the vertical). In this way, all 26 letters are signalled thus:

A–112	H–312	O–223	V–222
B–121	I–213	P–313	W–311
C–211	J–232	Q–131	X–321
D–212	K–323	R–331	Y–111
E–221	L–231	S–332	Z–113
F–122	M–132	T–133	
G–123	N–322	U–233	

Myer's code also included a number of signal directions: 3 on its own denoted the end of a word; 33, the end of a sentence; 333, the end of a message. Among the other directions 121.121.121.3 meant 'repeat', and 22.22.22.333 'cease signalling'.

Adopted by the US Department of War in 1859, wigwagging was used effectively during the Civil War (1861–65) by both sides. In 1864 Myer, by now the army's first chief signal officer, adapted the same principles for wooden canvas-covered discs by day, and for torches and lanterns by night.

Slower and more laborious than ordinary semaphore, Myer's system is rarely used now. The term wigwagging, however, is often applied to manual semaphore in the US, particularly to a method used by Boy Scouts there, in which the dots and dashes of Morse Code are signalled by a dark flag against a light background, or a light flag against a dark background.

Annihilating space by dot and dash

The fastest means of long distance communication in the mid- to late-19th century was the electric telegraph, using the code named after its American inventor Samuel Finley Breese Morse (1791–1872). Originally a portrait painter, Morse had studied art in London, and exhibited with some success at the Royal Academy. But in 1832 on his voyage back to America after a study trip in France and Italy, a conversation with a fellow passenger about electromagnets changed his future. By the time he reached New York, he was obsessed with the idea of transmitting information along an electric wire.

He first exhibited his 'telegraph machine' five years later in 1837, demonstrated it with the **first message in Morse**: 'Attention, the

Message understood

William Tecumseh Sherman (1820–91), the US general who captured Atlanta in the Civil War and forced the Confederate army northwards, had little patience with the latest signal codes. Sending a division to attack the enemy's left during one prolonged engagement in Georgia in 1864 – a move which necessitated a circuitous march – Sherman ordered the officer to signal his progress by burning a few barns as he advanced. 'I can't understand those signal flags', he claimed, 'but I know what smoke means.'

Shade secrets

'You know all the real things, don't you? Like the signals that spies use. Are you allowed to tell me one?'

Robert said seriously, 'Well, I really shouldn't, but I suppose one would be all right.' What can I tell her that she'll believe? *'There's the old window shade trick.'*

She was wide-eyed. 'The old window shade trick?'

'Yes.' Robert pointed to a window in the bedroom. 'If everything is under control, you leave the shades up. But if there's trouble, you pull one shade down. That's the signal to warn your fellow agent away.'

Pier said excitedly, 'That's wonderful! I've never read that in a book.'

'You won't,' Robert said. 'It's very secret.'

Sidney Sheldon *The Doomsday Conspiracy*

Universe, by Kingdom's Right Wheel', at the Speedwell Iron Works in Morristown, New Jersey on 6 January 1838, and was granted a patent in New York on 20 June 1841. During these years, Morse applied several times to Congress for finance to construct an experimental line; finally in 1843, he was granted $30 000.

On 24 May 1844, with a wire strung from the United States Supreme Court in Washington to Mount Clare Station in Baltimore, a distance of 37 miles (60 km), Morse inaugurated the line with a quotation from the biblical book of Numbers – 'What hath God wrought!' At 2 p.m. the following afternoon, the system was put to its **first commercial use** when a Congress reporter in Washington telegraphed to the editor of the *Baltimore Patriot:* 'There has just been a motion in the House to go into Committee of the whole of the Oregon question. Rejected. Ayes, 79; Noes, 86.'

Following this success, which the New York *Daily Sun* dubbed 'the annihilation of space', Morse offered his system to the nation for a mere $100 000. The federal government decided the revenues would never justify such expenditure. Undeterred, Morse founded his own company, establishing the first line between New York, Baltimore and Washington. By 1851 lines linked all the major cities; by 1861 the network had been extended to California, eight years before the first railroad link.

Meanwhile, the system was widely adopted elsewhere. The first cross-Channel telegraph cable was laid between Dover and Cap Gris Nez in France on 28 August 1850. A transatlantic cable, was laid in 1858 by USS *Niagara* and HMS *Agamemnon*, with the first message being sent from Newfoundland to Valentia in Ireland on 12 August. Four days later, the service was opened to the public – the average cost per telegram: £20.

Morse alphabet

Morse was by no means the first to invent an electric telegraph. During the 1820s and early '30s there had been a number of successful experiments in England and Germany. What distinguished Morse, however, was the 'alphabet' code he invented around 1835.

Originally, this consisted of dots, short and long dashes, and a pattern of dots and spaces to represent the letters C, O, R, Y and Z. Morse chose his signs after noting the number of each letter of the alphabet in a local printer's type cases, assigning the shortest signs to the most frequently used letters such as E and T, and the longest to the least common. Morse alphabet also included numerals, some punctuation*, the ampersand*, and even a combination to represent the dollar* sign.

Signalling Morse by handflags, or arms

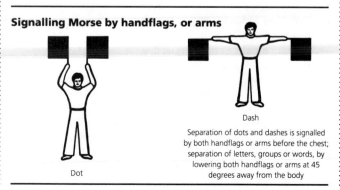

Dot

Dash

Separation of dots and dashes is signalled by both handflags or arms before the chest; separation of letters, groups or words, by lowering both handflags or arms at 45 degrees away from the body

Initially, these signs were cut or marked on a hand-turned roll of paper tape; eventually the tape was discarded as operators, becoming more familiar with the code, found it easier to listen to the clicks of the marking bar or 'sounder'.

International Morse

To make American Morse, as the original code is known, more adaptable for other languages, a variation was devised in 1851 by a special conference of European nations. This International Morse (or sometimes Continental Code), differs in 11 letters and all numerals except four. Diacritics*, more punctuation including the apostrophe* and brackets*, and even underlining were also added. The symbols are expressed purely by combinations of two signs: the dot (verbally represented by *di* and *dit*), and the dash of one length (verbally represented by *dah*). A dash equals three times the length of a dot, and different intervals separate letters and words; so while the pause between each dot and dash is one dot or one unit, between letters it is three, and between words seven.

What further distinguished Morse code was the number of ways that its dot/dash symbols could be conveyed, particularly at sea. Following trials in 1865, the Royal Navy adopted Morse for a flashing system in which two hand-held flags were used by day and lamps by night. In 1897, a slatted shutter fixed to a searchlight extended the range even further. Another shutter device, the heliograph, which reflects the sun's rays, was also used, as was signalling by sound with a siren or foghorn. The fastest and most effective long-range method, wireless telegraphy, was introduced in 1905.

Although Morse has to some extent been superseded by other methods, it is still widely used and, greatly improved by technological innovations, remains one of the most reliable and far-reaching methods of communication. The traditional sending device or 'key' still functions, but often a keyboard is used. Coding and decoding is done automatically with a computer screen to spell out the messages.

INTERNATIONAL MORSE CODE

A	● —
B	— ● ● ●
C	— ● — ●
D	— ● ●
E	●
F	● ● — ●
G	— — ●
H	● ● ● ●
I	● ●
J	● — — —
K	— ● —
L	● — ● ●
M	— —
N	— ●
O	— — —
P	● — — ●
Q	— — ● —
R	● — ●
S	● ● ●
T	—
U	● ● —
V	● ● ● —
W	● — —
X	— ● ● —
Y	— ● — —
Z	— — ● ●
1	● — — — —
2	● ● — — —
3	● ● ● — —
4	● ● ● ● —
5	● ● ● ● ●
6	— ● ● ● ●
7	— — ● ● ●
8	— — — ● ●
9	— — — — ●
0	— — — — —

SOS

The first official distress signal using Morse code was CQD. Devised by the Marconi International Marine Communication Company in 1904, it was made up of CQ – the general call for all stations – and D for distress. This combination soon acquired the meaning Come Quick Danger.

In 1908, CQD was replaced by SOS. Contrary to popular belief, SOS does not mean Save Our Souls or Save Our Ship or even, as sometimes interpreted, Stop Other Signals. In fact, the letters have no meaning. They were chosen by the International Radio Telegraph Convention to signify extreme distress by ships at sea simply because their equivalent in Morse of 3 dots, 3 dashes, 3 dots, is the

easiest and most distinctive combination to transmit and receive. During World War II, a new signal, SSS, was devised specifically for use when the vessel in distress was a submarine.

The first transmission of SOS in a major disaster was shortly after 11.46 p.m. ship's time on 14 April 1912, when the supposedly unsinkable White Star liner *Titanic* struck an iceberg on the fifth day of her maiden voyage from Cherbourg, France to New York. More than 1500 passengers and crew were lost. Both SOS and CQD were sent, but neither proved immediately effective. Ironically, the signal operator on the *Californian*, the closest ship to the accident, less than

20 miles (32 km) away, was off duty at the time.

The days of SOS are numbered. Officially, a new signal, the Global Maritime Distress and Safety System (GMDSS), comes into effect on 1 February 1999 for all ships carrying passengers or weighing more than 300 tons. Introduced by the International Maritime Organisation, and already in use on some ships, GMDSS sends digitally-encoded messages by Emergency Position Indicating Radio Beacon (EPIRB). Even if a ship sinks before the alarm has been raised, EPIRB is capable of activating itself and sending a signal to a satellite which then relays the location, time, nationality, and name of the ship, to a land terminal.

ANNIHILATING SPACE BY DOT AND DASH

Chapter 5

Divine designs
Religious signs and symbols

The Cross

. . . preceded the resurrection; but the resurrection has not abolished the cross. Suffering, sin, betrayal, cruelty of every kind, continued to exist after the crucifixion and they continue still. This is the failure of the cross. God made failure an instrument of victory.

Una Kroll *Lawsuit for a Lost Enemy*

. . . is where history and life, legend and reality, time and eternity, intersect. There, Jesus is nailed forever to show us how God would become a man and a man become God.

Malcolm Muggeridge *Jesus Discovered*

. . . is a picture of violence, yet the key to peace, a picture of suffering, yet the key to healing, a picture of death, yet the key to life.

David Watson *Is Anyone There?*

The signs and symbols mentioned so far have been predominantly of a direct communicative nature, either by writing, or by gestures and signals. But signs, and especially symbols, can of course go much further and deeper, and in no other subject is their multi-layered role more evident than religion, where symbols and symbolic images, both natural and invented, have long been encouraged to give visible and tangible form to what is in essence totally invisible and intangible. This is certainly true in Christianity, which has been the guiding force behind much of Western thinking for more than 1000 years. Even in our modern, largely non-religious society its symbolism continues to play an important, if not always obvious, part in our everyday lives. Inevitably, therefore, the greater part of this chapter is devoted to Christian symbols.

The sign of signs

The cross has been described as the sign of signs. It is, however, by no means, specifically Christian. Formed by the intersection of two lines, this most basic of shapes, has since prehistoric times been employed as a sacred, protective, or decorative emblem in almost every culture throughout the world. The early Scandinavians, for instance, depicted the hammer of Thor, their god of thunder and war, as a T-shaped cross; it symbolised thunder, lightning, storm and rain. It has also been an attribute of the deities of Assyria, Persia and India. For American Indians the cross represented both the human form, and the four cardinal points and the four winds. According to J. C. Cooper's *Illustrated Encyclopaedia of Traditional Symbols*, the north arm represents the north wind, the most powerful, the all-conquering giant, the head and intelligence; the south arm is the south wind, the seat of fire and passion, and of melting and burning; the east arm is the east wind, the heart and the source of life and love, and the west the gentle wind from the spirit land, the dying breath and the subsequent journey into the unknown. To the alchemists, the cross was a symbol of the four elements: air, earth, fire, water. Elsewhere, the cross variously symbolised health, fertility, life, immortality, the union of heaven and earth, spirit and matter, the sun, and the stars.

But it is as the prime symbol of Christ, of his crucifixion and glory, and thus of the Christian faith and Church, that the cross has achieved the most widespread and enduring significance. Wherever Christianity has been established, the sign has been adopted not only as an integral part of the ritual of worship, but also as a principal device in art, architecture, and many other areas including flags, and heraldry (where nearly 400 separate and sometimes bizarre forms have been recorded).

Here is a selection of some familiar and not so familiar crosses from the past and present, together with their origins and applications:

Anchor cross a disguised form of the cross among the earliest Christian inscriptions in the catacombs, sometimes drawn with a dolphin or two fishes suspended from the crossbar. In Christian symbolism generally, the anchor is the sign of security, steadfastness, and hope. St Paul writes in his Epistle to the Hebrews of the 'hope we have as an anchor of the

Anchor cross

soul'. The anchor cross – really a combination of two symbols, the cross and the crescent – also symbolised the birth of Christ from the body of Mary, whose emblem was a crescent moon.

Ankh the most valued symbol of the ancient Egyptians, also known as *crux ansata*, or the 'ansate' or 'handled cross'. It combines two symbols, the tau cross – 'life', and the circle – 'eternity', thus together – 'immortality', and also the male and female symbols of the two principal Egyptian deities Osiris and Isis, thus the union of heaven and earth. In hieroglyphic writing, it stands for 'life' or 'living', and forms part of words such as 'health' and 'happiness'. Egyptians wore the ankh as an amulet to prolong life on earth, and were buried with it to ensure their 'life to come' in the afterworld; belief in the ankh's power was reinforced by its resemblance to a key which would unlock the gates of death. This 'key' symbol was also carved on canal walls on the Nile, in the belief that its presence would control the flow of water and so avoid both floods and drought. The ankh was adopted by the early Coptic Christians of Egypt who also used it on their monuments to symbolise life after death. In more recent times, the ankh has been used by witches in spells and rituals involving divination, fertility and health. During the hippie movement of the late 1960s, it became a popular symbol of peace and truth.

Calvary cross a Latin cross known as a 'graded' or 'degraded cross' mounted on a plinth of three steps which symbolise the Christian Virtues: Faith (uppermost), Hope, Charity. One of the least decorated altar crosses.

Celtic cross sometimes also called Iona cross or Ring cross. The circle symbolises both the Sun and eternity. The design, which originated in Ireland before the 8th century, probably derived from the wreath-encircled form of the chi-rho (see Constantine's cross), the monogram of the first two letters of Christ's name in Greek which preceded the cross as a popular symbol of Christ. Often the cross was ornamented with carved figures, animals, and biblical scenes such as the fall of Man or sacrifice of Isaac.

Cloverleaf cross called in heraldry a cross bottonny. The cloverleaf* is a symbol of the Trinity. Expressing the same idea is the cross with lilies* or fleurs-de-lys* sprouting from its arms. Such flowering crosses may also symbolise Christ's resurrection.

Consecration cross a small Greek cross enclosed in a circle placed about 8 ft (2.5 m) above the ground on the inner and outer walls of medieval churches. Altogether there were 24 such crosses, carved outside or painted in red inside, three to each wall. Beside or above the 12 crosses inside, brackets held long candles to represent the 12 apostles who carried the light of Christianity. The crosses, symbols of Christ to ward off the Devil and his demons, were an important part of the consecration ceremony: the bishop had to climb a ladder to anoint each one by tracing it out with a thumb dipped in holy oil, after which burning incense was waved under it.

Constantine's cross the monogram known as the chi-rho, and formed from X *(chi)*, and P *(rho)*, the first two letters of the word Christ in Greek.

Ankh

Calvary cross

Celtic cross

Cloverleaf cross

We do not attach any intrinsic value to the Cross; this would be sinful and idolatrous. Our veneration is referred to Him who died upon it.

James, Cardinal Gibbons *The Faith of our Fathers*

Constantine's cross

To each his cross

No man ought to lay a cross upon himself, or to adopt tribulation, as is done in popedom; but if a cross or tribulation come upon him, then let him suffer it patiently, and know that it is good and profitable for him.

Martin Luther *Table Talk*

If you bear the cross unwillingly, you make it a burden, and load yourself more heavily; but you must needs bear it. If you cast away one cross you will certainly find another, and perhaps a heavier.

Thomas à Kempis

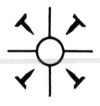

Coptic cross

Sorrows our portion are: ere hence we go
Crosses we must have; or hereafter, woe.

Robert Herrick *Sorrows*

Legend has it that marching to Rome to confront his rival and joint-emperor Maxentius, Constantine saw this luminous symbol in the sky inscribed with the words *In hoc vinces*, meaning 'by this conquer'. According to another legend, the sign appeared to him in a dream the night before the battle, accompanied by a voice saying *In hoc signo vinces* (by this sign, conquer). Either way, the omen is said to have converted Constantine to Christianity. He made the monogram his emblem, substituting it for the Roman eagle on the labarum, the Imperial standard. His subsequent victory at the Milvian Bridge outside Rome on 27 October 312 made him sole emperor of the West. The following year, by the Edict of Milan he formally recognised Christianity as a permitted religion within the Roman Empire; believers were no longer persecuted as a matter of policy, and the monogram, previously used only in secret, became the first public symbol of Christianity, and a widely adopted sign of victory and salvation.

The thing was the size and shape of a military standard. Its head formed a Latin cross, gold-plated. Above was a jewelled wreath of elaborate design and in the centre of the wreath a jewelled monogram, the sacred XP. From the crossbar hung a banner of purple satin richly embroidered and gemmed, bearing the motto TOYTΩI NIKA and a series of delicately stitched medallion portraits.

'What on earth have you got there?' asked Helena.

'Can't you see. It's It, my Labarum. . . . In this sign I conquered.'

'But, Constantine, the story as I always heard it was that you had a vision on the eve of the battle and that then and there you changed the markings on the troops' shields and had the armourer knock you up your own standard in the shape of the cross.'

'Certainly. This is it.'

Evelyn Waugh *Helena*

Coptic cross of the Coptic Church in Egypt; the four nails represent those used in the Crucifixion.

Criss cross originally Christ cross or Christ's cross, a small cross paty placed at the beginning, and often at the end, of the alphabet on a child's hornbook: a sheet of paper or vellum protected by a thin plate of transparent horn and mounted on a wooden tablet with a handle. Such 'books', which might also display numerals and the Lord's Prayer, were used as learning devices from Elizabethan times until the mid-18th century. Sometimes the alphabet was arranged in the form of a cross. The row of letters, known as 'Christ-cross-row', 'criss cross' or 'cross row' became synonymous with 'alphabet'. In Shakespeare's *Richard III*, George, Duke of Clarence, tells us his father Edward IV has banished him to the Tower (where he is soon liquidated in a butt of malmsey) because:

He hearkens after prophecies and dreams;
And from the cross-row plucks the letter G,
And says a wizard told him that by G
His issue disinherited should be;
And, for my name of George begins with G,
It follows in his thought that I am he.

Ultimately the term 'criss-cross' came to mean merely a series of crossing lines. It also survives as the formal name of the game otherwise known in England as noughts and crosses and in the US tick-tack-toe.

Incidentally, from another form of crossing lines derives the word 'cancel'. When scribes of the Middle Ages made a mistake in their manuscripts they marked out the error by drawing lines obliquely across it. As the resulting patterns resembled latticework they came to be called *cancelli,* from Latin for 'lattices', hence 'cancel' – to x, to mark out with crossed lines.

Cross crosslet also called Germanic cross. The four small crosses formed by crossed ends symbolise the Evangelists. When oblique, like the saltire, with crossed ends, it is called St Julian's cross.

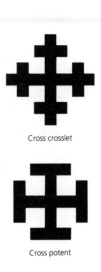

Cross crosslet

Cross potent

Cross potent one of the principal heraldic crosses, so-called not from potent in the sense of powerful, but from the French *potence,* meaning 'crutch' – in reference to the additional cross-piece on each limb resembling the head of an old-fashioned crutch. Also called Hammer cross.

Crucifix from the Latin *crucifixus,* 'the crucified', the Cross with the image of Christ nailed to it. When the image is depicted with closed eyes it is known as 'the Dead Christ' or 'Corpus Christi', with open eyes 'Christ in Agony'. When depicted crowned, robed and alive as the High Priest, the crucifix is called a Crucifix of Christus Rex. The earliest figures used in connection with the Cross were a youth holding a jewelled cross, symbolising victory, or a lamb above or below the Cross, symbolising 'He who takes away the sins of the world'. Christ on the Cross first began to be used after the Council of Constantinople in AD 692 prescribed it instead of the Lamb. Initially, the image was unattached to the Cross, clothed in a long tunic, with crowned head erect and with outstretched arms. The beard and loincloth appeared by the 11th century, and to symbolise suffering, the five wounds and the crown of thorns were added. A scroll bearing the letters INRI and standing for IESUS NAZARENUS REX IUDAEORUM (Jesus of Nazareth, King of the Jews) was also often attached to the upper limb. A crucifix is commonly displayed in Catholic homes, hospitals and institutions. Among some Protestants, the crucifix is regarded as a 'popish' symbol, and is generally absent from their churches and homes. Even so, some Protestant sailors were probably not averse to the 18th-century custom of having a crucifix tattooed on their backs in the belief that should the lash be prescribed for some misdemeanour, it would deter the flogger or even the lash itself from striking the face of Christ.

Overheard in a Chiswick jeweller's shop, assistant to customer examining a collection of crucifix pendants: 'Are you looking for a plain one, or one with a little man on it?'

The Times 'Diary', 3 February 1987

Crusader's cross five gold crosses on silver, the arms adopted by the Norman warrior Godfrey de Bouillon, who became Guardian of the Holy Sepulchre and first ruler of Jerusalem after its liberation from Mohammedans at the end of the First Crusade in 1099. The Crusader's cross (also called Jerusalem cross) is often used today on altar cloths: the large cross signifies Christ, the four small crosses represent the Evangelists spreading their gospels to the four corners of the globe. The five crosses together may also symbolise Christ's wounds.

The word crusader derives from the cross which the soldiers bore on their banners, shields, and surcoats, initially as symbols of their Christian faith and mission. During the eight Crusades, or 'Wars of the Cross'

Crusader's cross

Cross judgment

In days of old, when it came to determining innocence or guilt in a matter, or simply to settling disputes between accuser and accused, there were no half measures. Innocence was determined by survival – or not – of a physical 'ordeal', the outcome of which was regarded as God's judgment, hence the name *Judicium Dei*. Among the ordeals commonly prescribed in England until they were abolished in 1215 were walking nine steps carrying hot iron in bare hands, or walking barefoot and blindfold between nine red-hot ploughshares. Even though people of the time believed that God would protect the innocent, such methods invariably meant death, permanent disfigurement, or at the very least a great deal of pain for guilty and innocent alike.

Two equally irrational but less fatal ordeals were associated with the Holy Cross. In one, the accused and his accuser stood with their arms folded over their breasts in the shape of a cross. In the other, *Judicium Crucis* – Judgment of the Cross – both parties had to stand with arms outstretched before a cross. In either case the winner of the suit was whoever endured the position longest.

Gamma cross

which lasted until 1272, a wide variety of plain and highly decorative forms of cross evolved as distinguishing marks for men often obscured by armour. In addition, an early form of 'colour-coding' appeared, with each nation adopting its own colour. According to the 13th-century English chronicler Matthew Paris, these were white for England, red for France, green for Flanders, blue or azure for Italy, gules (heraldic red) for Spain; Scottish crusaders bore a St Andrew's cross; the Knights Templar adopted a cross of eight points red on white, and the Knights of St John a cross of eight points white on black (now known as a Maltese cross).

Eleanor crosses a series of monuments in memory of Edward I's wife Eleanor of Castile, who is said to have saved the King's life by sucking the poison from a poisoned arrow wound inflicted during the eighth and last Crusade in 1270. When the Queen died at Harby near Lincoln on 29 November 1290, her body – minus her bowels which were buried in Lincoln Cathedral – was carried to London's Westminster Abbey. At each place where the funeral cortège stopped for the night en route to its final destination, an elaborate stone cross was later erected. Of the original 12 crosses, only three survive, at Geddington, Northampton and Waltham. The most famous of the Eleanor crosses erected in the village of Charing, midway between the cities of London and Westminster, was destroyed by the Puritans in 1647. The present cross, a replica based on drawings of the original, was erected in the forecourt of Charing Cross railway station in 1863 by the London, Chatham and Dover Railway Company, at a cost of £1800.

Fiery cross a trademark* of the Ku Klux Klan or KKK, a secret society founded in 1866 at Pulaski, Tennessee. Officially disbanded in 1869, but revived in Georgia in 1915 as The Invisible Empire, Knights of the Ku Klux Klan, the society won support in the southern states from white Protestants for its anti-Black, anti-Catholic, anti-Jewish activities. Symbolic of the purging qualities of fire and sword, the fiery cross is said to derive from an ancient signal in the Scottish Highlands, where a flaming wooden cross, a 'crostarie', quenched in fresh goat's blood was carried from settlement to settlement to summon the clan, usually in an emergency. Anyone who disobeyed the summons of this Fiery cross (also called Cross of Shame), was branded a traitor and forever cursed. 'Woe to the wretch who fails to rear at this dread sign the ready spear!' wrote Sir Walter Scott in *The Lady of the Lake*, in which he describes the custom in vivid detail.

Gamma cross or Gammadion, so-called from its formation from the Greek letter gamma, whose shape in this context is said to signify Christ as the 'Cornerstone of the Church'; it is frequently seen on vestments in the Greek Orthodox Church. (See swastika.)

George Cross the highest symbol of bravery for civilians in Britain, ranking second only to the military Victoria Cross*. Created by King George VI on 23 September 1940 as 'a new mark of honour for men and women in all walks of life', the award is given for 'acts of the greatest heroism or the most conspicuous courage in circumstances of extreme danger'. The plain silver Greek cross bears a medallion in the centre depicting St George slaying the dragon and is inscribed simply 'For Gallantry'; the ribbon is dark blue, threaded through a bar adorned with laurel leaves. To date, 154 GCs have been awarded, including one to the people of the island of Malta in April 1942 for their heroism under constant air attack during World War II, hence Malta's soubriquet George Cross Island. The medal was added to the national flag in 1943.

Greek cross the cross in its simplest form. With arms of equal length forming four equal angles this mark – also called *crux quadrata* – has been used since prehistoric times by cultures worldwide, variously as a symbol of the rain god, the sun god, or of the elements of creation: air, earth, fire, and water. In early Christianity, the Greek cross supplanted the chi-rho as a symbol of Christ. On the national flag of Greece, the cross, white on a blue field, first appeared in the 1820s to symbolise the struggle against rule by the Moslem Turks. The first known use of the white Greek cross on a red field in Switzerland is as a military banner in Schwyz, one of the three cantons which united against the Holy Roman Empire in 1291. Although its use on the Swiss flag dates back to 1339, this 'sign of the Holy Cross' (otherwise known as the Geneva cross) was not officially adopted as the national flag of the Swiss Confederation till 1848.

Iron Cross Germany's first and highest military decoration: a cross of iron edged with silver, instituted by Frederick William III of Prussia in 1813 during the war with Napoleon. During World War II, Hitler added the Nazi swastika* emblem to the cross; this was officially removed in 1957. In heraldry, the shape is known as formée, or paty or pattée – the last two referring to the four 'paw-shaped' members.

Jewelled cross or *crux gemmata*. It first appeared as an emblem of victory after Constantine's Edict of Milan in 313 which granted religious tolerance to Christians and the restoration of their civil rights. Ornamented with flowers and leaves, the cross symbolised a living tree; sometimes, the Greek letters alpha and omega were suspended from either end of the crossbar.

Latin cross the most familiar religious symbol in the western world, and according to tradition the form of cross on which Christ was crucified, hence an alternative name, Crucifixion Cross; other names include cross of the West, cross of life, Passion Cross, *crux immissa*. It is usually left as natural wood, but sometimes may be coloured gold to signify glory, or stained red for Christ's blood or green to symbolise the tree of life. The shape, in which the proportions correspond to the outstretched human body, was a symbol of godhead in Greece and China long before the Christian era; rising out of a heart, it was the Egyptian hieroglyph* for goodness.

Long cross yet another name for the Latin cross. Used as a graphic mark in medieval church and prayer books, to remind the priest where to make the sign of the cross, it has since become one of the six reference marks, coming second in order after the asterisk. As such it is also called dagger* or obelisk*.

Lorraine cross or cross of Lorraine, with its double crosspiece is derived from the badge of the Guise family who ruled over the Duchy of Lorraine in NE France from the beginning of the 16th century. Joan of Arc, born in Domrémy near the Lorraine border on 6 January 1412, is

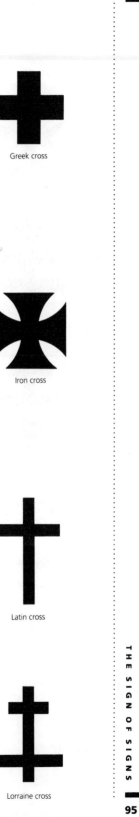

Greek cross

Iron cross

Latin cross

Lorraine cross

Maltese cross

Papal cross

Patriarchal cross

Peace cross

said to have adopted the two-barred design, which is often confused with the Patriarchal cross. A form of the latter was adopted by General Charles de Gaulle in June 1940 as a symbol of the liberation of France from Nazi occupation in general, and of the 'Free French' forces in particular.

Maltese cross otherwise known as the 'cross of eight points' each standing for one of the Beatitudes. Formed from four barbed spear or arrow-heads with their tips joined at the centre, this white cross on black was the original badge of the military and religious order of the Knights Hospitaller (or Knights of St John), who devoted themselves to the liberation of the Holy Land from the Mohammedans during the Crusades (1095–1272). Expelled in 1291, they moved their headquarters to Rhodes in 1310, and in 1529 to Malta – hence the name. Today, the Maltese cross is commonly seen in Britain as the insignia of the St John Ambulance Brigade; it also occurs in the insignia of certain Orders of Knighthood such as the Order of the Bath.

In philately, the name Maltese cross was applied to the design of the mark used to 'obliterate' the first adhesive postage stamps in Britain from May 1840 till 1844 (see postmark).

Papal cross also referred to as the Triple cross; used in Papal processions. The three crossbars symbolise power and the tree of life.

Patriarchal cross the symbol of the Greek Orthodox Church, also known in the Catholic Church as the Cardinal's, or Double-barred cross. The upper bar represents the *titulus* or inscription panel added to the cross at the time of the Crucifixion by order of Pontius Pilate. As the Archiepiscopal cross, it forms a part of the heraldic arms of an archbishop. This design, adopted as the emblem of the Free French in World War II, is frequently miscalled the cross of Lorraine, where technically the second bar or traverse is as near to the foot as the upper is to the head.

Peace cross sometime soubriquet of the symbol designed by Gerald Holtom in 1958 for the newly-formed Campaign for Nuclear Disarmament, CND. Holtom originally intended incorporating a more orthodox cross in his design, but decided that this carried too many other connotations, notably of war decorations. Ultimately finding inspiration in the semaphore alphabet, he composed his symbol from the semaphore N (for nuclear), and D (disarmament), combining both within a circle to symbolise global or total agreement. The symbol came to public attention during the first protest march from London to the Atomic Weapons Research Establishment near Aldermaston in Berkshire on Good Friday, 4 April 1958. It rapidly became one of the most widespread and successful of all signs of the '60s, often symbolising both peace and anarchy.

Pectoral cross from Latin *pectus*, breast – to describe a cross suspended from the neck by a chain or ribbon. Sometimes a personal possession for private devotion, it is principally a symbol of authority worn by cardinals and bishops. Usually of gold, the cross may be ornamented with precious stones, or incorporate emblems such as the heart or the rose. In medieval times it was sometimes made in the form of a small reliquary – to contain holy relics of the saints, or the True Cross.

Processional cross a cross or crucifix mounted on a long staff, carried at the head of the choir or an ecclesiastical procession of clergy.

Red Cross the symbol of the International Committee of the Red Cross founded in Geneva in 1863, and so-called from the red Greek cross on a white ground – also known as the Geneva Cross – formed from the reversed colours of the Swiss flag. The brainchild of a Swiss banker Henri Dunant (1828–1910), for which, incidentally, he shared the first Nobel Peace Prize in 1901, the organisation was originally set up to provide medical relief and a neutral status for ambulance and field-hospital staff wherever Christian armies were at war. The activities of the International Red Cross have since been greatly extended. In Muslim countries, the Islamic equivalent of the symbol – a red crescent – was adopted by the Red Crescent Society founded in Turkey 1877. The equivalent in Iran used to be the traditional Persian emblem of a lion and sun, also in red on white; following the 1979 revolution, this was replaced by the red crescent. In countries of the former USSR, the flag has the cross and crescent side by side; in Israel, relief workers fly the Red Shield of David or Magen David Adom. There are national Red Cross and Red Crescent societies in 149 countries with a membership of 250 million.

Rose cross originally the emblem of the Society of the Rose Cross, a religious sect reputedly founded by a German scholar, Christian Rosenkreuz ('rose cross'), in 1484. In the 17th century the emblem and the name 'Rosicrucian' were adopted by secret societies of philosophers interested in alchemy and mysticism who venerated emblems of the rose and cross as symbols of Christ's Resurrection and Redemption. Some of the societies founded in Vienna, Germany, Poland, Russia, were allied to masonic ideas and principles. Rosicrucian societies still exist in Europe, and in the US, where the most important, the Ancient and Mystical Order of the Rosy Cross has its headquarters in San José, California. According to J. Stafford Wright in the *New International Dictionary of the Christian Church*, the cross represents the human body, and 'in the rose at centre is a chaste and pure vital fluid to overcome the passion-filled blood of the human race'. In general, the rose and cross together are variously interpreted as the divine light of the universe with the cross as the earthly world of suffering and sacrifice, as the Virgin Mary and Christ, female and male, the material and the spiritual, or as sensual and spiritual love. In another sense, the rose growing on the cross or tree of life signifies regeneration and resurrection.

Russian cross also called the Eastern or St Lazarus cross, the symbol of the Orthodox Churches of the eastern Mediterranean, eastern Europe, and Russia. The upper of the three crossbars represents the *titulus* or inscription panel as in the Patriarchal cross, the oblique lower bar the support for the feet.

St Andrew's Cross a saltire named after the apostle and patron saint of Scotland, who by tradition was martyred on an X-shaped cross. Adopted as the national emblem of Scotland sometime before the 13th century and depicted white on a blue field, it was incorporated into the new Union Flag on 12 April 1606, three years after James VI of Scotland became James I of England. Andrew is also the patron saint of Russia, and when Peter the Great founded the Russian navy in the 1690s he

Red Cross

If you cannot have your dear husband for a comfort and a delight, for a breadwinner and a crosspatch, for a sofa, chair or hot water bottle, one can use him as a cross to be borne.

Stevie Smith

Rose cross

The cross of Christ, on which he was extended, points, in the length of it, to heaven and earth, reconciling them together; and in the breadth of it, to former and following ages, as being equally salvation to both.

Samuel Rutherford

Russian cross

THE SIGN OF SIGNS

The road began to curve among hills as I approached Starbridge, and soon I glimpsed the Cathedral in the distance. The road curved again, the spire vanished, but at the next twist it was once more visible, slim and ethereal, a symbol of man's inchoate yearning to reach upwards to the infinite.

Susan Howatch *Glittering Images*

adopted a blue saltire on white for the flag of his fleet. This was used until the revolution in 1917.

St Antony's cross T-shaped cross named after the 3rd-century Egyptian-born hermit regarded as the founder of monasticism. According to some sources he lived to the age of 105, spending his last 40 years in a cave on Mount Kolzim near the Red Sea. St Antony's cross is also known as the *crux commissa*, Egyptian or tau cross. Francis of Assisi adopted it as an emblem in the early 13th century.

St George's Cross a red cross on white, named after the 4th-century martyr who in legend rescued a princess from a dragon. It has appeared on English banners since at least 1277 – most probably as a result of its popularity and significance during the Crusades which ended in 1272 – although it seems George was not chosen as the patron saint of England till around 1348, when Edward III founded the Order of the Garter under his patronage. As well as the sole charge or design on the traditional flag of England, the cross of St George has formed the focal point of the Union Flag* or 'Jack' since its adoption in 1606, and on the flags of four of the Channel Islands: Alderney, Guernsey, Herm, and Sark. From 1953 to 1972 it was also the principal charge on the flag of

---

Power-baking

'Perhaps no cry – though it is only for one morning – is more familiar to the ears of a Londoner, than that of One-a-penny, two-a-penny, hot-cross buns on Good Friday'. So wrote the Victorian chronicler Henry Mayhew in 1851 in his *London Labour and the London Poor*. The days when you could be wooed by such street jingles, let alone buy a bun or two for a penny, are of course long gone. And though our national consumption of these special spicy currant buns marked with a cross and traditionally eaten hot on Good Friday grows each year – more than 170 million of them were sold during the 1990 Easter season – gone, too, is much of their associated symbolism.

It is a symbolism that predates Christianity. In ancient Greece and Rome, small cross-marked cakes were eaten at the festival of Diana, the Olympian goddess of the moon, which was celebrated at the vernal equinox – the quarters formed by the cross representing the quarters of the moon. Two petrified loaves incised with a cross, probably in connection with the same pagan festival, were excavated from the ruins of Herculaneum, the town near Naples buried by volcanic ash in AD 79. And at about the same time of the year, similar cakes were eaten by the early Saxons in honour of their goddess of spring, Eostre – from whose name our Easter derives. For them, the round shape represented the Sun, and the quarters the four seasons.

Nearer our time the cross on the bun, reinterpreted as the sign of the Holy Cross, was a timely reminder of the Crucifixion – tradition has it that something of the sort was first distributed among the poor at St Alban's Abbey, Hertfordshire, on Good Friday 1361. A further sacred significance derived from the custom of kneading the buns from the dough used for baking the consecrated Host. This also protected the buns from mould, as *Poor Robin's Almanack* of 1733 attests:

> Good Friday comes this month: the old woman runs,
> With one a penny, two a penny 'hot cross buns',
> Whose virtue is, if you believe what's said,
> They'll not grow mouldy like the common bread.

Armed with the cross, the power of the bun knew no bounds. People sometimes suspended one or two of them from the ceiling in their homes until the following Good Friday to confound the Devil and other evil spirits like witches, to protect the house from fire, and to cure ailments such as whooping-cough and dysentery; in *Letters From England* the poet Robert Southey recorded in 1807 that 'in the province of Herefordshire a pious woman annually makes two upon this day, the crumbs for which are a sovereign remedy for diarrhoea'. The bun's power extended even to the sea, where carrying a hot-cross bun or two on board was believed to protect sailors from shipwreck.

In spite of its popularity, the home-made variety is becoming increasingly rare. Could it be that would-be bun-bakers are put off by nothing more than the business of making the cross and getting it just right? The home-baker's baker Elizabeth David offers an excellent and simple recipe in her classic *English Bread and Yeast Cookery*, together with these words of wisdom: 'To emphasise the cross, some bakers superimpose strips of candied peel or little bands of ordinary pastry. Both these methods involve unnecessary fiddling work. Neither, in my experience, is successful. There is no need to worry overmuch about the exactitude of the cross. You have made the symbolic gesture. That is what counts.'

Northern Ireland; since 1972, when Britain imposed direct rule on the province, the Union Jack has been the official flag, and the St George's Cross is used only as a loyalist emblem.

St Patrick's Cross so-called after Ireland's patron saint who introduced Christianity there around AD 432. A saltire like St Andrew's Cross, but differing in colour – red on a white ground – it was originally the heraldic arms of the Fitzgeralds, who were sent by Henry II in 1169 to subdue the Irish. Although never used by the Irish as a national device, following the Act of Union with Ireland, the cross was incorporated into the flag of the United Kingdom on 1 January 1801. The union was dissolved in 1921, but the cross remains in the flag. It also features on the flag of the island of Jersey.

St Peter's cross since the 4th century one of the symbols of St Peter, who is believed to have been crucified head down at his own request in AD 65 during the reign of the Roman emperor Nero.

Saltire heraldic name of the cross resembling the letter X, Greek letter chi, the initial of Christ. Also called transverse cross or *crux decussata* (from the Roman numeral* for 10), the saltire represents different saints according to colour: gold, St Alban (the first British martyr); blue or white, St Andrew; black, St Osmund; red, St Patrick.

Scandinavian cross so-called because the upright limb is offset towards the hoist in the national flags of Denmark*, Norway, Sweden, and also Finland, Iceland and a number of Scandinavian islands.

Southern Cross also known as Crux Australis or the 'Pole-star of the South', a constellation of four principal stars in the shape of a cross in the southern hemisphere. The stars are depicted on the national flag of New Zealand, adopted 1896. The design of the Australian flag, adopted when Australia became a federal dominion in 1901, includes an extra smaller star within the cross. In the northern hemisphere, the constellation Cygnus or Swan is also called the Northern Cross.

Swastika predominantly associated with good luck and fortune – the word derives from Sanskrit, 'well-being' – this equilateral cross with arms bent at right angles, usually in a clockwise direction, is found on Navajo blankets, Greek pottery, Cretan coins, Roman mosaics, on relics excavated on the site of Troy, on Hindu temple walls, and in many other cultures throughout history. Frequently a symbol of the Sun's rotation through the heavens, turning darkness to light – and thus by extension a symbol of fertility and regeneration – it has also been interpreted as an emblem of the winds, the rain, and of fire and lightning. In Japan it is a symbol of long life and prosperity. In China too, as an ancient form of the sign *fang*, meaning 'the four regions of the world', it later became a symbol of immortality and of the number 10 000 – a Chinese way of representing infinity. It is also one of the sacred signs of both Buddhism* and Jainism*.

Early Christians inscribed the swastika on tombstones as a disguised form of the more orthodox cross, and in churches during the Middle Ages it was commonly used as a motif to 'fill the foot' or base of stained-glass windows – hence its English name, fylfot. Other names for this most distinctive symbol include the crooked cross, Thor's hammer,

St Peter's cross

Saltire

Swastika, or fylfot

Navajo swastika

Sumerian swastika

Tau cross

Grave errors

In *A Thing or Two about Music*, Nicholas Slonimsky includes this anecdote about the Italian composer Gioacchino Rossini (1792–1868), who occasionally supplemented his income by teaching. Commonly he marked mistakes in his pupil's compositions with crosses. One student, receiving his manuscript with scarcely a cross on it, crowed with pride that his work was obviously flawless till Rossini told him pointedly: 'If I had marked all the blunders in your score with crosses, it would have looked like a cemetery'.

gammadion or *crux gammata* – so-called because it is formed by joining four Greek gamma letters (see Gamma cross). In heraldry, the swastika is known as a cross *cramponnée*, from 'crampon', 'iron hook'.

There are exceptions, of course, to the swastika's positive image – most notably the German *Hakenkreuz** or 'hooked cross' which the Nazi party adopted as their symbol in 1919. In the East, too, the swastika may have negative associations. In India, for example, the reversed or counter-clockwise form, sometimes called *sauvastika*, may stand for night and black magic, or for the goddess Kali, the 'black one' who symbolises death and destruction.

Tau cross   named after the T-shaped letter of the Greek alphabet which derived from a Phoenician X-shaped symbol called 'taw', meaning 'mark' or 'sign'. The ancient Egyptians used the T-form as a symbol both of fertility and life; when combined with the circle – which signified eternity – it became the ankh, the symbol of everlasting life. In Biblical times, as the last letter of the Hebrew alphabet, the T-form was associated with the end of the world, and was traditionally the mark of Cain and salvation, and the sign the Israelites made in blood on their doorposts to protect them when the Angel of Death passed through Egypt to 'smite all the firstborn in the land', and in general the protective device with which the righteous would be marked in the last days. Alternative names are Egyptian cross, *crux commissa*, and in the Christian church St Antony's cross. Because of its similarity to an ancient gibbet it was once also called the gibbet cross. Some believe it was this form of cross on which Christ was crucified.

True Cross   the original Cross of the Crucifixion, whose discovery by Helena, mother of Emperor Constantine during her pilgrimage to Jerusalem in AD 326, is known as the Invention of the Cross, from the Latin *invenio*, 'to come upon' or 'find'. The story goes that after a long search, Helena discovered the three crosses of Calvary buried in a pit, and identified the 'True Cross' by restoring a dying woman to health with it. Parts of this Cross are preserved and revered in numerous places throughout the Christian world. In the Welsh Annals, an 11th-century document in the British Museum, there is a reference to the legendary King Arthur and the 'Battle of Badon' in AD 518, 'in which Arthur carried the cross of Our Lord Jesus Christ three days and three nights on his shoulder and the Britons were victorious'.

Victoria Cross   the highest symbol of valour, awarded for conspicuous bravery in the face of the enemy, was instituted by Queen Victoria on 29 January 1856. Technically known as a cross *pattée*, the bronze cross bears the royal crown surmounted by a lion with the inscription 'For Valour'. Worn on the left breast, the VC takes precedence over all other decorations. So far, 1354 VCs have been awarded; the first to Mate Charles Lucas on 26 June 1857 for action aboard HMS *Hecla* two years earlier. The medals were originally struck from the metal of cannons captured in 1855 from the Russians at Sebastopol in the Crimea, but since 1942, when that supply was exhausted, they have been made from gunmetal supplied by the Royal Mint.

Sacred monograms

Since the earliest days of Christian art, designs composed of two or more interwoven initial letters or abbreviations of Greek and Latin words

DIVINE DESIGNS

The Cross: a selection of other ecclesiastic and heraldic forms

Aiguisée

Barbée

Bezant

Branchée

Canterbury

Chain

Cramponnée

Croissantée

Easter

Entrailed

Fitchée

Flamant

Fleurée

Fleurette

Fourchée

Four pheons

Frettée

Fusily

Interlaced

Lambeau

Looped

Lothringian

Masclée

Milrine

Nebulée

Parted and frettée

Paternoster

Patonce pattée

Perronnée

Pommée

Quadrate

Ragulée

St Julian's

Sovereignty

Trononnée

Wavy

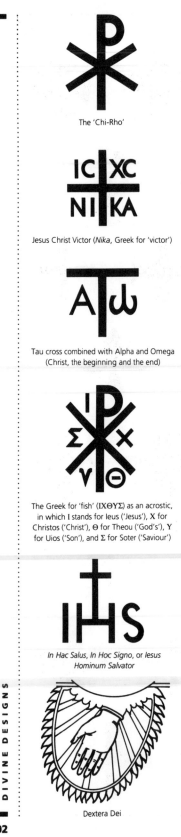

The 'Chi-Rho'

Jesus Christ Victor (*Nika*, Greek for 'victor')

Tau cross combined with Alpha and Omega
(Christ, the beginning and the end)

The Greek for 'fish' (ΙΧΘΥΣ) as an acrostic,
in which I stands for Ieus ('Jesus'), X for
Christos ('Christ'), Θ for Theou ('God's'), Y
for Uios ('Son'), and Σ for Soter ('Saviour')

*In Hac Salus, In Hoc Signo, or Iesus
Hominum Salvator*

Dextera Dei

have been used to form a monogram. The first and most famous of these, the chi-rho or Christogram, is composed of the first two letters of the Greek word ΧΡΙΣΤΟΣ, meaning Christ. Following the Roman emperor Constantine's adoption of it as the emblem on his standard in AD 312 (see Constantine's cross), it became the official and most widespread symbol of Christianity – and by extension of victory and triumph – until the cross began to supplant it after the fall of the Empire in the 5th century. Incidentally, James Hall in his *Dictionary of Subjects and Symbols in Art* points out that the 'chi-rho' mark had long existed as a symbol of good omen, being an abbreviation of the Greek *chrestos*, meaning 'auspicious'.

A favourite monogram was the combination of Alpha and Omega, the first and last letters of the Greek alphabet, which the early Christians used to symbolise the omnipotence and infinity of God, as expressed in the Book of Revelation: 'I am Alpha and Omega, the beginning and the ending'. One variation has the two letters on either side of the chi-rho enclosed in a circle – the symbol of eternity. The more usual form of omega was the minuscule ω, sometimes drawn as the letter w or depicted as a hand-sign of it. Alpha was also combined with tau, the final letter of the Hebrew alphabet and at one time of the Greek alphabet.

Another popular monogram is IHS, the first three letters of the Greek word for Jesus. With the decline of Greek during the Middle Ages, other meanings were taken from Latin letters, usually combined with the cross. Among these were *In Hac Salus* – 'In this (cross) is Salvation', and in reference to Constantine's vision *In Hoc Signo* – a shortened form of *In Hoc Signo Vinces*, meaning 'in this sign, conquer', and *Iesus Hominum Salvator* – 'Jesus Saviour of Men'.

Despite the modern use of monograms on the cover of Bibles and on altar cloths, hassocks, and other church embroidery, their significance often remains a mystery today, even to churchgoers. This is nothing new. As early as 1887, the *Daily News* noted that 'the monograms IHS and XP which are so often to be seen in our churches, sorely puzzle a portion of the congregation'. Some 25 years earlier, the novelist George Eliot commented on this puzzlement in *Silas Marner*, when a neighbour presents Silas with some fresh-baked cakes: ' "There's letters pricked on 'em," said Dolly. "I can't read 'em myself, and there's nobody, not Mr Macey himself, rightly knows what they mean; but they've a good meaning, for they're the same as is on the pulpit-cloth at church".' Silas, incidentally, identifies the letters as IHS, but even though a former churchman himself, he is as unable to interpret them as Dolly.

One in three in one

As it was considered blasphemous in medieval times to depict God in human form, symbolic representations developed. These included a ray of light, an 'all seeing eye', or the Right Hand of God – the *Dextera Dei* – coming down from heaven, usually emerging from a cloud in the act of blessing.

As well as being represented in human form or by a monogram, Christ was symbolised by the **lamb** and the **fish**. Christ is frequently the 'Agnus Dei', the sacrificial Lamb of God, which in St John's Gospel 'taketh away the sins of the world'. From the 4th century the lamb appeared in many forms, balancing a staff by its right forefoot, or with a wound in its chest pouring blood into a chalice – symbolising Christ's blood in the Passion. The lamb represents Christ as both suffering and triumphant – with a cross it depicts the crucifixion, with a pennant or banner of victory the resurrection. In art, where a lamb is flanked by sheep, the lamb is Christ, the sheep his disciples. The fish, perhaps the first Christian symbol, is found on the tombs and walls of the catacombs – the underground passages outside Rome where Christians buried their dead, and where during times of persecution they could meet in comparative safety. The fish was a powerful symbol, both in image and name. The letters of ICHTHUS, Greek for 'fish', provide the initial letters of the Greek words *Iesous Christos Theou Uios Soter*, meaning Jesus Christ, Son of God, Saviour, although this acronym may have been discovered later. Fish, one of the two foods which fed the five thousand, represented the mystical union with Christ. Additionally, this symbol of a faith that worked miracles is also an emblem of the fishermen Apostles – Andrew, Peter, James and John, whom Christ would make 'fishers of men' to spread their nets and gather in followers.

Agnus Dei

Descending Dove

Sanctus Spiritus

Triangle   3 triangles   3 circles

Triquetra   Trefoil   Fork

Pentalpha

The universal symbol of God the Holy Spirit is the **dove***. For long a symbol of peace and God's messenger of forgiveness, the dove became from the earliest days of Christianity a symbol of what no man can see. In the Gospels of Mark (1:10) and Matthew (3:16), the Spirit descends like a dove at Christ's Baptism; thus the dove is found on many font covers. Seven rays or tongues of fire proceeding from the dove signify the Seven Gifts of the Holy Spirit – Wisdom, Understanding, Counsel, Fortitude, Knowledge, Piety, and Fear of the Lord. The gifts may also be represented by seven doves. Twelve doves surrounding the cross in orderly array represent the Apostles. The dove bearing a ring is an attribute of St Agnes; among other saints who have this attribute are Ambrose, Augustine, Dunstan, and Gregory the Great. David, the patron saint of Wales, is sometimes represented with a dove on his shoulder.

To express the mystery of the Trinity – One God existing in Three Persons and One Substance – geometric shapes such as the equilateral **triangle, three triangles**, or **three circles**, or sometimes a combination of shapes interwoven with each other, were used. A frequent symbol on Celtic crosses was the **triquetra** – three interlaced arcs whose continuous form representing eternity encloses the triangle of the Trinity in the centre. Commonly found, too, in the Middle Ages were the **trefoil**, and the Y-shaped **fork** (which also stood for Christ's arms on the Cross or the 'lifting up of hands', as mentioned in Psalm 141: 'Let my prayer be set forth before thee as incense; and the lifting up of my hands as the evening sacrifice'). The trefoil is also similar to the shamrock* – the 'little clover' with three leaves on one stem, which St Patrick is said to have used to explain the concept of the Trinity to the Irish.

Also signifying the Trinity is the five-pointed star or **pentagram**, whose three overlapping triangles may be known as a pentacle, pentangle, or **pentalpha** – this last because the crossing of the lines suggests five As. This was long used as an amulet to guard against fever and other diseases, and to ward off the Evil Eye and other supernatural forces. According to Heather Child in *Christian Symbols, Ancient and Modern*, the pentagram is the sign of the five senses, and when the letters SALVS are found in the five points, a symbol of health. The pentagram is sometimes also called the **Endless Knot**, or **Seal of Solomon**. This symbol in green was added to the red national flag of Morocco* in 1915.

A popular abstract device in wood carvings and stained glass of the later Middle Ages was the *Scutum fidei* or **Arms of the Trinity**, which

Arms of the Trinity

Three fishes

Three hares

encapsulated the doctrine of the unity and individuality of the Trinity. The device reads 'the Father is not the Son, the Son is not the Holy Spirit, the Holy Spirit is not the Father; the Father is God, the Son is God, the Holy Spirit is God'. **Three fishes**, or sometimes **three hares** with three ears between them forming a triangle, were also used to express the Trinity.

Emblems of the Passion

With the development of religious symbolism in medieval times came the cult of honouring the **Instruments of Christ's Passion**. Emblems of these instruments were used alone or together in stained-glass, on ecclesiastical embroidery, wood and stone carvings, on fonts, tombs, and bench-ends, and generally in folk art. Although by the mid-15th century these implements had become independent and separate from depictions of the Crucifixion, they were still frequently arranged together around the Cross. Most commonly they included the small board with INRI – the abbreviation of Pilate's taunting title *Iesus Nazarenus Rex Iudaeorum* (Jesus of Nazareth, King of the Jews), the crown of thorns, the pincers and the hammer, four nails (sometimes only three), the pillar, cord and scourges with leaded thongs, the ladder, the reed and sponge, the jug of vinegar, the lance and sword, the seamless robe, and the sheet used to lower Christ's body from the Cross – which, when draped over the Cross, was also a universal emblem of the Crucifixion. Other emblems are the money-bags with Judas' payment of 30 pieces of silver, the lantern carried during Christ's arrest in the Garden of Gethsemane, the dice the soldiers used to cast lots for Christ's tunic, the cock that crowed thrice after Peter's denial, the wound touched by the doubting hand of Thomas, and the head-cloth or veil a woman used to wipe Christ's face as he carried the cross to Calvary. According to legend, as this cloth was found afterwards to be impressed with an image of Christ's face, it was named Vera-Icon, meaning 'true likeness', and some centuries later the woman became known as St Veronica. In later medieval art, Christ's five wounds were also included among the emblems.

Wrongly attributed

Among the many anecdotes and observations recorded by the Duc de Saint-Simon, gossip and diarist at the court of Louis XIV, and quoted by Lucy Norton in *Saint-Simon at Versailles,* is this revealing tale about a certain ill-informed aristocrat:

'In the king's apartments one day, he was holding forth in praise and criticism of the fine pictures there. Pointing to several Crucifixions by great masters, he maintained that they had all been painted by the same artist. People began to mock him, pointing out the various painters and how they might be recognized by their personal styles. "Nonsense," exclaimed the Marquis, "the painter of all of them was called 'INRI', cannot you read his signature?" '

The emblem of the World Council of Churches, which was founded in Amsterdam in 1948. The Greek word surmounting the ship, which loosely translates as the whole inhabited world, represents the Church's global mission. The ship has been both a graphic and literal symbol of Christianity since the earliest days. The 3rd-century Roman theologian and martyr Hippolytus, for example, described the Church as a 'boat beaten by the waves but never submerged', while others regarded the ship as a vessel of salvation, carrying the faithful under the sign of the Cross (either formed by the mast and yardarm, or with a cross on the sails) through the turbulent seas of life. In association with this symbolism, it is thought that the word nave – for the main body of the church where the congregation sit – derives from the Latin *navis* meaning 'ship'. In churches in Denmark, a sailing ship is often hung in the nave to symbolise mankind's journey through both calm and stormy weather.

Emblems of the Virgin Mary

During the Middle Ages, a cult of devotion to the Virgin Mary developed. Among the many emblems linked with her were the crowned M, the monogram formed from MR for Maria Regina – Mary, Queen of Heaven, and a wing-enclosed heart. Sometimes pierced with a sword and displayed on a shield, this last is known as *Arma Virginis*, the Arms of the Virgin. The crescent moon, the cypress and the olive tree, were also linked to her name, as were the lily (purity), and the white **rose** which, as the queen of all flowers, symbolised Mary as the Queen of All Saints. Often referred to as the Mystical Rose, she is also the 'rose of paradise', or the 'rose bringing salvation to all who call upon her'. The rose's five petals had an extra significance – they were regarded both as the five letters of her Latin name Maria, and the Five Joyful Mysteries (the Annunciation, the Visitation, the Nativity, the Presentation in the Temple, and the finding of the Christ Child in the Temple). From the title Mystical Rose also derives the word **rosary**, which in the Roman Catholic Church is both a devotion of repeated prayers commemorating the joys, sorrows, and glories relating to the life of Christ and Mary, and, by association, the string of beads (fifteen 'decades' of ten small beads and one larger bead) used to assist memory in recitation of the prayers. Founded in medieval times to perpetuate the rose symbol, the rosary established in addition to the use in art of a white rose for the Joyful Mysteries, a red rose to symbolise the Sorrowful Mysteries (the Prayer and Agony in the Garden, the Scourging at the Pillar, the Crowning with Thorns, the carrying of the Cross, the Crucifixion), and a yellow or gold rose for the Glorious Mysteries (the Resurrection, the Ascension, the Descent of the Holy Spirit to the Apostles, the Assumption, the Virgin Mary's Coronation in Heaven and the Glory of all the Saints).

Later medieval artists represented the traditional Seven Sorrows of Mary (the prophecy of Simeon, the flight into Egypt, the loss of the Holy Child, meeting Jesus on the road to Calvary, standing at the foot of the Cross, the taking down from the Cross, and the burial), by a figure of her with seven swords radiating from her heart like rays of light.

Signing the cross

Since as early as the 9th century the sign of the cross as a sacred gesture has been an integral part of religious services. The Western or Latin benediction is made outwardly with the extended thumb, index and middle fingers. This formation, called the *Mano Panten*, symbolises the

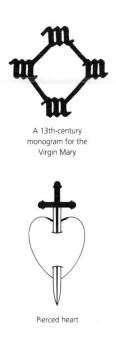

A 13th-century monogram for the Virgin Mary

Pierced heart

The right move

In his autobiography *Just Williams*, the actor Kenneth Williams recalls an incident in 1951 during a production in Cardiff in which he played the Welsh martyr John Penry:

'On the opening night, when we came to the execution scene, I mounted the scaffold, the rope was placed round my neck, and just before the lights dimmed, I made the sign of the cross with my hand. It wasn't rehearsed, I did it instinctively. Several newspaper critics mentioned it disapprovingly in their reviews, asking what on earth a Protestant was doing making such a Catholic gesture. However, on the following Sunday there was a broadcast by a distinguished Welsh scholar who said how interesting it was that the portrayal of Penry saw him return to the custom of his fathers at the moment of death and that the actor was to be congratulated on making such a subtle point.'

'Watch for surprises, I beg of you.' He made a cross with his finger over the centre of his coat. 'I do not cross my heart. That is being too serious. But I cross my stomach, which is an important oath for me.'

Ian Fleming *From Russia, With Love*

I always got into bed from the left side. I lay on my right side. I prayed the exact same prayer. And although I knew I shouldn't, in the dark I made the sign of the cross, on the odd chance that God was not Protestant.

Garrison Keillor *Leaving Home*

Benedictio latina

Benedictio graeca

Cross cures

Until quite recently, people
sometimes made the sign of the
cross as a cure for numerous
complaints such as a stitch, frostbite,
pins and needles. In his *Table Talk* of
1832 the poet and philosopher
Samuel Taylor Coleridge offers this
'Charm for Cramp':

'When I was a little boy at the
Blue-coat School, there was a
charm for one's foot when asleep;
and I believe it had been in the
school since its foundation, in the
time of Edward the Sixth. The
march of intellect has probably now
exploded it. It ran thus: "Foot! foot!
foot! is fast asleep! Thumb! thumb!
thumb! in spittle we steep: Crosses
three we make to ease us, Two for
the thieves, and one for Christ
Jesus!" And the same charm served
for a cramp in the leg, with the
following substitution: "The devil is
tying a knot in my leg! Mark, Luke,
and John, unloose it, I beg! Crosses
three, &c." And really, upon getting
out of bed . . . pressing the sole of
the foot on the cold floor, and then
repeating this charm with the acts
configurative thereupon prescribed
. . . I can safely affirm that I do not
remember an instance in which the
cramp did not go away in a few
seconds.'

Trinity. The closed fourth and little fingers are said by some believers to
signify Christ's two natures – the human and the divine. To make the
outward blessing in the Greek or Eastern Church the priest joins the
thumb with the fourth finger; together with the other upright fingers
the formation is thought to represent *chi* and *rho*, the initial letters of
Christ's name in Greek.

One of the earliest, if rather exaggerated, references to the gesture is
found at the end of the 2nd century in *De Corona* by the theologian
Tertullian: 'In all our actions, when we come in or go out, when we
dress, when we wash, at our meals, before retiring to sleep, we make on
our foreheads the sign of the cross'.

This forehead cross was initially a secret sign by which Christians
identified themselves to each other. Today, Roman Catholics and some
Anglicans make the sign during their prayers in two ways: as the 'Great
Sign' with five fingers – for Christ's five wounds – on the forehead,
breast, and from the left shoulder across to the right; or at the beginning
of the Gospel at Mass as the 'Lesser Sign', with only the thumb on the
forehead, the lips, and the heart.

Eastern Christians trace the sign of the cross on the forehead, stomach
and from right shoulder to left with the thumb, forefinger and middle
finger. Again this is symbolic of the Trinity. The fourth and fifth fingers
pointing into the palm signify Christ's two natures.

Angels and Archangels

Angels have appeared in Christian art since the late 8th century. During
the Middle Ages, nine orders of angels were identified: Seraphim,
Cherubim, Thrones, Dominions, Virtues, Powers, Principalities, Archangels and Angels. Seraphim and Cherubim are often depicted with six
wings which may be strewn with eyes. Thrones are represented as
scarlet wheels with wings and sometimes with eyes. All three principal
orders may also be depicted as warriors or judges. Angels usually have
a nimbus* and a pair of wings, and may hold scrolls, instruments of the
Passion or musical instruments.

The four principal archangels, God's messengers, also have emblems
to distinguish them. **Gabriel** (Hebrew for 'the strength of God'), who
announced to Mary that she was to conceive the Son of God, is
represented with lilies*, the symbol of purity in his hand, or handing a
lily to her. **Michael** (Hebrew, 'the likeness of God'), the guardian of
peoples, is usually depicted as a warrior with a shield and lance or
sword, in white or armour, sometimes with a dragon* at his feet, and
sometimes with the pair of scales (symbolic of justice) in which he
weighs the souls of the dead on Judgment Day. The prince of guardian
angels **Raphael** (Hebrew, 'the healer of God'), and guardian angel of
humanity, especially of pilgrims, is usually represented in the dress of
a traveller with a pilgrim's staff, scallop shell, and a gourd of water. **Uriel**
(Hebrew, 'the light of God'), the angel who reveals to man the light of
divine wisdom, is most often depicted with a scroll and book.

The Evangelists

Since the early 5th century, the four Evangelists, the authors of the New
Testament Gospels have been represented in ecclesiastical art as a
winged man, a **winged lion***, a **winged ox***, and an **eagle*** respectively. The symbols derive ultimately from two biblical passages. In the
Old Testament, the 6th-century BC Hebrew prophet Ezekiel records his
vision of four beasts around the throne of God: 'they four had the face

of a man, and the face of a lion, on the right side: and they four had the face of an ox on the left side; they four also had the face of an eagle'. And in Revelation, St John describes the four beasts, the Tetramorph, grouped around the throne of the Lamb: 'And the first beast was like a lion, and the second beast was like a calf, and the third beast had a face as a man, and the fourth beast was like a flying eagle'.

Early Christian writers interpreted these beasts variously as: man, king of the visible world, corresponding to Christ's humanity and Incarnation; the ox, king of domestic animals, stands for strength and sacrifice, and corresponds to the Passion; the lion as king of the beasts, for pride, royalty, the Resurrection; and the eagle as king of the birds, for dignity, grace, divinity, and the Ascension. Their use as symbols of the Evangelists was given by St Jerome, who wrote: 'The first face, that of a man, signifies Matthew, who begins to write, as of a man, the book of the generation of Jesus Christ, the son of David, the son of Abraham; the second, Mark, in which is heard the voice of the Lion roaring in the Desert, "Prepare ye the way of the Lord".' Similarly, Jerome assigns the ox to Luke because he begins his Gospel with the priest sacrificing in the temple and later emphasises the sacrificial aspects of Christ's life; and the eagle to John (traditionally believed to be the same as John the Apostle, brother of James the Great, and also the author of Revelation), because he begins like 'an eagle hastening to lofty things' with the Logos, the Divine Word: 'In the beginning was the Word . . .'

These symbols also appear as emblems beside or behind the Evangelists, who are often depicted with pen, ink, and scrolls or books. Occasionally, Luke is shown with a portrait of the Virgin Mary, since he is thought to have painted one. Matthew and John, as apostles, have additional emblems.

Emblems and symbols of the Apostles

In the earliest Christian works, the 12 Apostles were often represented as sheep standing on either side of Christ – the Good Shepherd, or *Agnus Dei* – the Lamb of God. By the Middle Ages they, too, were distinguished in paintings, sculpture, and stained glass by their emblems.

Here are the emblems and symbols of the 14 apostles (the original 12 disciples and Matthias and Paul):

Andrew is symbolised by the saltire* or X-shaped cross – usually silver or gold on a blue ground – on which he is thought to have been crucified. Like other saints who were fishermen, he sometimes has a fish as emblem. Andrew is the patron saint of Scotland.

Bartholomew is traditionally depicted with a butcher's knife in commemoration of his being flayed alive; he may also carry a piece of skin over his arm.

James the Great, the first of the apostles to be martyred, is sometimes depicted with the sword by which he was beheaded. More commonly, as the patron saint of pilgrims – in particular to the Holy Land – he appears with a staff and gourd bottle, and a scallop shell. Pilgrims often placed a shell in their hats as a good luck symbol, and more practically used it as a spoon, cup or dish. James is Spain's patron saint.

James the Less, James the Little, is depicted with a fuller's club, because he was killed by a blow on the head with one by Simeon, a fuller.

John, as a disciple, may be shown holding a chalice with the Devil in the form of a winged serpent fleeing from it – a reference to the legend that when challenged to drink a cup of poison, John rendered the potion harmless by making the sign of the cross on the cup.

Judas Iscariot may be shown with a money bag, in allusion to his criticism of Mary Magdalene and her costly ointment, as told in St John's Gospel: 'Why was not this ointment sold for three hundred pence, and given to the poor? This he said, not that he cared for the poor; but because he was a thief, and had the bag, and bare what was put therein'. In paintings and tapestries, Judas' beard is often yellow – the symbolic colour of both cowardice and treachery.

Jude has a club, the instrument of his martyrdom in Persia. He is also shown with a staff, a carpenter's square – in allusion to his trade – and an oar, boathook, or ship to symbolise his missionary journeys.

Matthew, as apostle, carries a purse or money-bags, in allusion to his former position as a tax collector for the Roman government at Capernaum (hence his adoption as the patron saint of accountants, bankers, and book-keepers). Sometimes he carries a carpenter's rule or square; or, as the instrument of his martyrdom, a spear, axe, or halberd – an axe-blade mounted on a spear in common use in the 15th–17th centuries.

Matthias, not one of the original twelve, was chosen by lot after the Ascension to take the place left vacant by Judas. His emblems are a battle-axe – the instrument of his martyrdom – and an open book.

Paul, often depicted as a short man with a balding forehead and a long pointed beard, may carry a book in reference to the new law he propagated as the apostle of the Gentiles. His principal emblem is a sword, because he was beheaded with one, and because he urged Christians to arm themselves with 'the helmet of salvation and the sword of the Spirit, which is the word of God'. Paul is the patron saint of preachers, and tentmakers.

Peter also carries a sword – in allusion to the sword with which he lopped the right ear of the high priest's servant Melchius in the Garden of Gethsemane. Among his other emblems are a fish, and a cock*, a reference to his denial, as Christ had prophesied at the Last Supper: 'Before the cock crow, thou shalt deny me thrice'. The cock is also a symbol of Peter's repentance, and his vigilance as the first Pope. His principal symbols are an inverted cross* and two crossed keys, because Christ entrusted him with 'the keys of the kingdom of heaven'.

Philip is often shown with a T-shaped cross, supposedly because he was hung by the neck from a tall pillar, and a basket containing loaves – a reference to the feeding of the 5000.

Simon is sometimes depicted carrying a fish in one hand, in allusion to his occupation, and in the other a saw – the instrument of his martyrdom in Persia.

Thomas carries a lance or spear, because he was pierced with one. As the patron saint of masons and architects, his symbol is a builder's square.

Divine light

Common to all saints is the **nimbus** or bright disc which encircles the head. This is more commonly known as a **halo**, a word derived from Greek *halos* – the round threshing floor on which oxen trod a circular path as they threshed sheaves of corn to make grain. The word was revived by astronomers in the 16th century to describe the luminous orb around the Sun, Moon, and other heavenly bodies caused by the refraction of light through mist. Theologians adopted the word to signify the 'crown of glory' above or behind the heads of angels, saints and martyrs.

The halo as a symbol of light shining from a divine personality was not exclusive to Christianity. In ancient times it was widely-used to represent power and majesty. In Indian art, for instance, Buddha is sometimes shown with a solid red halo. Greek and Roman deities were often represented with a halo; the sky god Zeus, and his Roman counterpart Jupiter, has a blue nimbus. Roman emperors, who considered themselves divine, were also depicted with a halo, particularly in sculpture in the open air: the solid halo served to protect the head from the elements, and more importantly from bird droppings. In Byzantine art, Satan was depicted with a halo as a radiation of power.

The Christian nimbus first began to appear during Constantine's reign in the 4th century. Until the 12th century it was like a plate of gold. Later, an ornamental border was added, and radiating beams of light. For simplicity, the form was reduced to the familiar band or ring of gold by the end of the 16th century.

There are four other principal kinds of nimbi: for a living saint or holy person such as the Pope, the form is square; for persons of the Trinity, particularly Christ, cruciform or three-rayed; and for God, triangular. A fourth kind is the pointed oval aureole enclosing the whole body and known as the **mandorla** (Italian, 'almond') or **vesica piscis**, which derives from the fish symbol. Originally this represented the cloud in which Christ ascended. In time it was also used to represent the light emanating from a divine being such as the Virgin Mary.

Mandorla

What, after all,
Is a halo? It's only one more
thing to keep clean.

Christopher Fry *The Lady's Not For Burning*

A selection of saints and their emblems
(asterisked emblems denote the instrument of martyrdom)

alms-box round neck – John of God
anchor* Clement; Nicholas
anvil Adrian; Eloi
apples three golden – Nicholas
armour in, and trampling the devil underfoot – Michael; in, and on a white horse spearing a dragon – George, patron saint of England
arrow* piercing breast or hand – Giles
arrows* piercing crown – Edmund; piercing bound naked body – Sebastian; two piercing heart – Augustine
ass kneeling to Blessed Sacrament – Anthony of Padua,

patron saint of Portugal
axe* Matthew; Mathias
bag of money – Matthew
balls three – Nicholas, patron saint of Russia, bankers and pawnbrokers
banner with red cross – Ursula
barge Bertulphas
barn Bridget of Kildare
barrel Antonia; cross in – Willibrord, patron saint of Luxembourg
basket of fruit and flowers – Dorothy; of loaves – Philip; of roses – Elizabeth of Hungary
bear Columba; Edmund
beard Uncumber; Paula Barbata

bedstead of iron – Faith

beehive Ambrose; Bernard of Clairvaux; John Chrysostom

beggar having feet washed by – Edith of Wilton; or cripple receiving half the cloak of Martin

bell and **pig** – Anthony; in fish's mouth – Paul de Leon

bellows held by devil – Genevieve

birds Francis of Assisi, patron saint of Italy

boar Emilion

boat or boathook – Jude

bodkin Leger; Simon of Trent

bones Ambrose

book common attribute of Apostles, Abbots, Abbesses, Bishops; with child Jesus standing on it – Anthony of Padua; with hunting horn or stag with crucifix between horns – Hubert; and crook – Chad; transfixed by a sword or stained with blood – Boniface, patron saint of Germany

bottle James the Great

box or **vase** of alabaster – Mary of Magdela

breasts on a dish – Agatha

broom Gisella, Petronilla

builder's square Thomas

bull Adolphus, Sylvester; tossed or gored by – Blandina, Saturninus

calves two at feet – Walstan, holding scythe

camel Aphrodicius; bound to – Julian of Cilicia

candle with devil blowing it out – Genevieve; two crossed – Beatrix

cardinal's hat Bonaventure

cauldron* of oil – Vitus

chafing dish Agatha

chains held by – Leonard

child Jesus on shoulders and crossing river – Christopher; on arm – Anthony of Padua; crucified – William of Norwich; two carried by – Eustace; three in a tub – Nicholas

club* Boniface; Valentine

cock Peter; Vitus

comb of iron – Blaise

cow Bridget

crocodile Helenus; Theodore

cross Helen; inverted – Peter; red on white – George, patron saint of England; saltire – Andrew, patron saint of Scotland; T cross – Philip;

carried on shoulder – Anthony

crow Vincent

cup and serpent symbolising poison – Benedict; John the Evangelist

dagger* Agnes; Canute, patron saint of Denmark; Edward; Irene

devil underfoot – Michael; with bellows – Genevieve; seized by the nose in pincers – Dunstan

distaff Genevieve; also a symbol of Eve's expulsion

dog Bernard; with wounded leg – Roch; with torch – Dominic

dolphin bearing corpse – Adrian

dove Ambrose; Basil; Catherine; Dunstan; Gregory the Great, Bridget, patron saint of Sweden; on sceptre – King Edmund; shoulder – David, patron saint of Wales; doves in cage – Joseph

dragon commonly in the West a symbol of Satan, evil, sin; slain by – George; underfoot – Archangel Michael; and cross – Margaret; led by chain – Juliana

eagle Augustine; Gregory the Great; on shield – Wenceslaus, patron saint of the Czechs; John the Evangelist

eyes two in a dish – Lucy

falcon or **hawk** Bavo, Edward, Julian Hospitator

firebrand Anthony the Great

fish Andrew; Raphael; Simon; Peter, patron saint of fishmongers

flail Varus

fleur-de-lys Virgin Mary

flowering rod Joseph, patron saint of Belgium

flowers Dorothy, patron saint of florists and gardeners

forceps gripping tooth – Apollonia, patron saint of dentists

frog Huvas

goose Martin, patron saint of France

gosling or **hen** Pharaildis

gridiron* Lawrence, patron saint of cooks and curriers

halberd* Jude

hammer Adrian; and chalice – Eloi

harp Cecilia; Dunstan

hatchet* Matthew; Matthias

head crowned and carried by – Cuthbert or Dennis; man's at feet of – Catherine of Alexandra; carried by herself before altar – Winifred

heart flaming or transfixed by sword – Augustine or Mary; with sacred monogram – Ignatius

hermit Anthony

hind Giles

hook* of iron – Agatha; Faith; Vincent

hops Arnold

horseshoe Eloi

hourglass . . . Hilarion, Theodosias

idols broken – Wilfred, baptising pilgrims

inkbottle Jerome; inkhorn and pen – John the Evangelist, patron saint of the Scriveners' Company

jar of ointment – Mary Magdalen

jug or **pitcher**...Agatha; Benedict; Vincent

key Hubert; two keys – Peter

knife* Agatha; and skin – Bartholomew

lamb Agnes; Francis of Assisi; John the Baptist

lamp Francis; Lucy

lance or **spear*** Barbara; Lambert; Matthias; Thomas

last or **shoe** Crispin and Crispinian – patron saints of shoemakers

leopard and **ox**, or **lions** – Marciana

lily Virgin Mary and Joseph; Antony of Padua; Sebastian

lion Adrian; Dorothea; Jerome; Mark; and raven – Vincent

loaves and **fishes** the disciples

loom Anastasia

manacles holding them – Leonard

mason's tools Marinus

musical instruments Cecilia

mule kneeling – Anthony of Padua

nails* held or piercing the body: Alexander; Denys; Quintin; William of Norwich

olive branch Agnes; Barnabas, patron saint of Cyprus

organ Cecilia, patron saint of musicians (according to tradition she invented the organ)

otter Cuthbert

ox Luke, patron saint of physicians

padlock on lips – John of Nepumuk

palm Agnes

pagans being baptised – Wilfred

partridge Jerome

pen, ink and **scroll** Bernard of Clairvaux; Mark; Matthew

pickaxe Leger

pig and **bell** Antony

pilgrim's staff Dominic, Louis

pincers Agatha, Dunstan, Lucy; and tooth – Apollonia

plough Exuperius, Richard

pot of water and **ladle** Martha

purse Nicholas

rats Gertrude of Nivelles

raven with a loaf in its beak, or with broken cup – Benedict, patron saint of Europe; bringing food – Paul the hermit

roses crown of – Cecilia; Dorothy; Teresa

saw* James the Less; Simon

scales weighing souls in – Michael

scallop shell Virgin Mary; Augustine; James the Great, patron saint of Spain

scourge Ambrose; Boniface

scythe and two calves – Walstan; and carrying head – Sidwell

shamrock Patrick, patron saint of Ireland

shears* Agatha

sheep Genevieve

ship Anselm; Bertin

shovel baker's – Aubert, Honorius

snakes Patrick

spade Fiacre, patron saint of taxi-drivers

spit Quentin

staff James the Great; James the Less

stag Aidan; Giles; Hubert; with crucifix between horns – Eustace; and dog with torch in mouth – Dominic

star on or over Bruno; Dominic; Thomas Aquinas

stigmata Francis of Assisi; Catherine of Siena

stones* the first martyr Stephen, patron saint of bricklayers

surgical instruments Cosmas and Damian, patron saints of

I am also inclosing Scetches of a very spacious and curious Peece of Painting to be placed at the West End of the Church – being the Figure of Time, with Wings display'd. Under the Feet of Time lyeth the Pourtrait of a Sceleton about 8 Foot in Length, under which is Glory in the form of an Equilateral Triangle within a spacious Circle. This being a most proper Emblemme for a Christian Church, and one that hath been imployed since the early days of Christianity. Your humble servant: Nich. Dyer.

Peter Ackroyd *Hawksmoor*

barbers and surgeons
swan Cuthbert; and three
flowers – Hugh of Lincoln
sword* Agnes; Barbara; James
the Great; Paul, patron saint of
preachers and tentmakers; and
hammer – Adrian; and stones –
Pancras; and wheel –
Catherine; piercing breast –
Euphemia; piercing neck –
Lucy
thistle Caroline, Narcissus
tongs Dunstan, patron saint of

blacksmiths and goldsmiths
torch Dorothea; Medard
tower Barbara, patron saint of
armourers and gunners
unicorn Virgin Mary
wheel Catherine of
Alexandria
windlass Erasmus
winged man Matthew
wolf guarding his head –
Edmund
woolcomb Blaise, patron saint
of woolcombers

Emblems of faith

A selection of the more frequently used graphic 'identifiers' for some other major religious and philosophical beliefs.

Buddhism is the doctrine attributed to Siddhartha Gotama (*c.* 563–483 BC), an Indian prince who came to be called 'Buddha' – a title meaning 'enlightened one'. The two principal and most ancient motifs of the faith are the founder himself in an attitude of calm repose, and the **Wheel of Law**, or *Dhamma Chakra*. This eight-spoked circle represents the essence of Buddhist discipline – the Noble Eightfold Path. Only by following this path – the right faith, right values, right speech, right conduct, right livelihood, right endeavour or effort, right awareness of one's feelings and actions, and the right concentration or meditation – may a believer attain the ultimate goal of enlightenment and the immortal state of Nirvana or blessedness, and so leave the otherwise endless circle of birth and rebirth.

Dhamma Chakra: The Wheel of Law

Another symbol is the flag adopted by the World Fellowship of Buddhists, and widely used in Buddhist buildings and during celebrations. Devised in Ceylon in 1885 by J. R. de Silva and Colonel Olcott, the founding President of the Theosophical Society, it was first displayed in 1888. The design consists of vertical bands of red, blue, yellow, white, and orange, with 'a tint compounded of them all together' represented by the same colours repeated horizontally in the fly. These colours are said to be those which radiated from the aura of the Buddha.

China's **Confucianism** is a philosophy or system of ethics based on the teachings of the sage and scholar K'ung Fu-Tzu (551–479 BC) whose name was Latinised by Jesuit missionaries in the 17th century to Confucius. Confucianism was the state religion until the Cultural Revolution of 1966–68. It is sometimes symbolised by the figure of the 'Supreme Saint' himself.

Confucius: The Supreme Saint

India's dominant religion, **Hinduism**, is sometimes symbolised by images of its two principal deities: the creator and destroyer Siva or Shiva, and the preserver Vishnu.

More familiar, worldwide, is the sign as shown here in Sanskrit calligraphy of the most sacred Hindu word '**Om**' or '**Aum**', with which all chanting begins. The word's three sounds – A, U, M – represent the 'fundamental sound of the universe', and the Trimurti, the triad formed by the divine forces of Brahma (once the supreme god in Hindu belief), Vishnu, and Shiva, who together impel the wheel of life endlessly from birth to rebirth.

'Om' or 'Aum': The Sacred Syllable

The principal emblem of the world's youngest major religion, **Islam**, founded by the prophet of Allah, Muhammad or Mohammed (570–632), is the **crescent**.

As a favoured symbol, the crescent has a long history. To the ancient Egyptians, for instance, the crescent was the waxing moon – a symbol of growth and prosperity. Artemis, the Olympian goddess of the moon in Greek mythology, Diana, her Roman counterpart, and Luna – Roman goddess worshipped as one and the same as Diana – all had the crescent as their attribute, with Diana in particular sometimes being depicted with a crescent on her brow.

In 339 BC, the crescent became especially associated with Byzantium (modern Istanbul). According to legend, Alexander the Great's father Philip of Macedon attempted to take the city by tunnelling under the walls, but a brilliant waxing moon betrayed his plan: the alarm was raised and the invaders routed. To commemorate their escape, the Byzantines adopted Diana as their patroness, and the crescent as the city's emblem.

In AD 330, Emperor Constantine made Byzantium his capital. He renamed it Constantinople, and rededicated it to the Virgin Mary, who as the 'Queen of Heaven' also had a crescent moon as an emblem.

Some thousand years after Constantine, the founder of the Turkish Moslem Empire, Sultan Osman or Othman, adopted the crescent as a symbol of his faith – the legend here being that shortly before he invaded what is now Turkey in 1299 he had a vision of the horns of the new moon extending from east to west over the entire world. Under Othman's successor, Sultan Orkhan (1326–60), the crescent began to appear first on the infantry standards of the Ottoman Turks, and in later years on other banners, and on top of religious monuments, often together with the traditional symbol of sovereignty and divinity, the star. When Mohammed II's forces captured Constantinople in 1453, the crescent assumed a double significance as the permanent symbol of both the Turkish Empire and of the Islamic faith.

A form of Turkey's present flag was established in 1793 under Sultan Selim III, when the navy's green flag was changed to red, and a multi-pointed star joined the white crescent. The familiar five-pointed star on today's national flag dates from around 1844.

In addition, the crescent and star as symbols of Islam now appear together on the flags of Algeria, Malaysia, Mauritania, Pakistan, Tunisia, and North Cyprus (a state recognised only by Turkey). The flag of the League of Arab States features an upturned crescent, encircled by a gold chain and olive* wreath. The crescent is also the symbol of the Islamic equivalent of the Red Cross*.

Jainism is a code of ethics based on compassion and belief in the reincarnation of the soul until it attains perfection and is liberated. This belief may be symbolised by a swastika-like **Jaina Cross**, whose arms are a reminder of the four possible worlds of existence – heavenly, human, animal, and hellish. A **brush** of peacock feathers or soft wool, and an **alms-bowl** also characterise Jainism. The bowl recalls the humility of the Jain's traditional founder Mahavira (599–527 BC), who is also known as the Jina or 'Victor'; the brush reflects the vow of non-violence: mindful that the reborn soul may return in any shape, the most devout Jains sweep the path before them as they walk to avoid harming even the smallest insect.

The world's oldest religion, **Judaism**, founded around 4000 years ago, is today most commonly identified by the six-pointed **Star of David**. Less common is the name **Creator's Star** – so-called because it represents the week, each point being one of the six days of Creation, and the central hexagon the Sabbath.

Islamic Crescent and Star

Brush and alms-bowl

Magen David, or Shield of David

'Frank passes an edict demanding that every Jew in the Government General wears a star. That edict's only a few weeks old. In Warsaw you've got a Jewish manufacturer churning them out in washable bakelite, at three zloty each. It's as if they've got no idea what sort of law it is. It's as if the thing were an insignia of a bicycle club.'

It was suggested then that since Schindler was in the enamel business, it might be possible to press a deluxe enamel badge at the Schindler works and retail it through the hardware outlet which his girlfriend Ingrid supervised. Someone remarked that the star was their *national insignia, the insignia of a state which had been destroyed by the Romans and which existed now only in the minds of Zionists. Perhaps people were proud to wear the star.*

Thomas Keneally *Schindler's Ark*

The origin of this distinctive form of two interlocked equilateral triangles as a Jewish emblem is obscure. Legend has it that David carried a hexagram-shaped shield when he slew Goliath, hence its Hebrew name **Magen David**, or **Shield of David**. Arnold Whittick in his *Symbols, Signs and their meaning* notes that according to a tradition of the medieval mystical philosophy of the rabbis known as the Kabbala, the form is a combination of the alchemical signs for fire △ and water ▽, and that the principal consonants of the Hebrew words for these 'elements' formed the word for heaven. Although the symbol is found occasionally among Jewish artefacts of early times – on a tombstone of the 3rd century AD, for instance – and as an emblem of the Jewish community in 17th-century Prague, it did not begin to acquire its now predominant association until comparatively recently.

When the newly formed World Zionist Organization met for their first Congress in Basel, Switzerland in 1897, they adopted a blue Magen David for their banner, together with the two blue horizontal stripes from the *tallit*, the prayer shawl. The blue symbolised heaven, the white backgound purity. At the 18th Congress in 1933, the banner was chosen as the flag of the Jewish people. The symbol gained further recognition in 1944 when, sanctioned by Winston Churchill, the banner became the flag of the Jewish Brigade Group, which was formed in Palestine as part of the British Army. Following Independence in May 1948, the newly created State of Israel officially adopted the blue and white colours with the Magen David as the national flag.

Far older as a specifically Jewish emblem is the seven-branched candlestick. Originally placed in the tabernacle in the Sinai Desert during the years of exile, this **Menorah** (Hebrew for candelabrum) later became the most prominent symbol in the Temple in Jerusalem, until it was removed by Titus when he destroyed the city in AD 70. The

Scorning the badge of shame

During World War II, Jews in Nazi-occupied Europe were forced to wear a six-pointed yellow cloth badge bearing the word *Jude*, 'Jew'. The badge, which resembled the 'magen David' or Shield of David*, the traditional emblem of Judaism, was first proposed in August 1941 by Hans Frank, the Governor-General of the 'Protectorate' of Bohemia and Moravia as a cheap and convenient means of identification for Jews within his territories. With Hitler's approval, a decree of 5 September 1941 ordered that the *Schandband* (German 'shame band') be worn by all Jews throughout the region, and later in other regions.

In occupied Denmark, however, the Nazis experienced defiance from an unexpected quarter, no less a person of rank than the king, Christian X. He is said to have warned the invaders that if they insisted on introducing the yellow

badge he and his family would also wear it, and wear it as a sign of the highest distinction. Faced with such an ultimatum, the Germans backed down and Danish Jews were spared the 'badge of shame'.

The accuracy of this heartwarming story, widely circulated at the time, is dubious. According to *Rescue in Denmark*, Harold Flenders' account of the secret evacuation of Danish Jews, the king never said he would wear the yellow star, because the situation probably did not arise. The people of Denmark were intensely opposed to anti-Semitism, and it is unlikely that the Germans ever seriously threatened to introduce the badge there. The Danish queen, Margrethe II, also denies the accuracy of this story, though she admits that her grandfather felt deeply for his Jewish subjects and such a defiant gesture would have been entirely in character.

branches symbolise the seven days of the Creation. According to the 1st-century Jewish historian Josephus, the branches also represent the Sun, Moon, and planets 'that lighten the darkness'. The Menorah was adopted as the official emblem of the State of Israel in 1949. On the President's flag it is framed by two olive branches symbolising peace; beneath the emblem is the inscription 'Israel' in Hebrew.

Japan's national religion, **Shinto**, whose name originated in the 6th century AD from the Chinese 'Shen-Tao', 'the sacred way' or 'way of the gods', is often identified in graphic form by the **torii**, the three-piece wooden arch through which the path leads to the shrine, or 'Jinja', where the gods reside.

Sikhism, founded in the Indian Punjab by Nanak (1469–1539), the first of the 10 'gurus' or teachers, may be characterised by the five 'Articles of Faith' a Sikh (a punjabi word meaning disciple) wears. These articles or symbols, prescribed by the 10th Guru Gobind Singh when he established the brotherhood of the Khalsa, 'the pure', in 1699, are known as the Five Ks – since each begins with the letter K. They are: *kesh*, long uncut hair, as a sign of devotion to God; *kangha*, a comb worn in the hair; *kacha*, knee-length shorts that represent chastity; *kara*, a steel bracelet, worn on the right wrist, denoting strength and commitment to God; and *kirpan*, the curved sword a Sikh wears to defend himself and his religion. More familiar as a graphic symbol is the **khanda** – the emblem in black on the Nishan Sahib, the small triangular yellow 'flag of respect' which Sikhs have flown outside their *gurdwaras* or places of worship (literally, 'doorway to the Guru') since the mid-17th century. This emblem is formed of the *khanda* itself, the double-edged sword surrounded by a *chakkar*, an ancient Indian symbol of the oneness of God, and flanked by two kirpans – one representing spiritual power, the other temporal power.

Next to Confucianism, China's second most important religious and philosophical system is **Taoism**. It is based on the Tao-te-ching, 'the classic of the way and its virtue', a collection of beliefs of Lao Tse, a philosopher of the 6th century BC, and on the theory that everything in the universe is composed of two forces – the active masculine positive Yang (literally, the 'light side' of a mountain), and the passive feminine negative Yin (the 'dark side'). Whoever follows the Tao – the way – and balances these two forces, which are at one and the same time both opposite and complementary, may achieve perfect harmony. Increasingly familiar in the West as a symbol of Taoism is the **Yin-Yang circle**, which is divided into two equal areas: one black representing Yin and the other white representing Yang. Each half contains a spot of its opposite colour to signify that there is always a germ of each in the other.

Once the faith of the mighty Persian Empire, **Zoroastrianism** is now the smallest major religion in the world, surviving mainly in India. It was founded more than 2500 years ago by the prophet Zoroaster or Zarathustra, whose teachings are centred on the perpetual conflict between good and evil, and in particular between the 'wise lord' Ahura Mazda or Ormuzd, creator and angel of Good, who will ultimately triumph over the 'hostile spirit' Angra Mainyu or Ahriman. **Fire**, a symbol of divine essence and the source of life present in all nature, and a principal feature of Zoroastrian ritual (for which reason followers are sometimes called 'fire-worshippers') is frequently used as an emblem. More specific as a symbol of this faith is the **head and torso of Ahura Mazda** joined to a winged disc.

Menorah ('candelabrum')

Shinto torii

Sikh khanda

Yin-Yang circle

Ahura Mazda

Chapter 6

Arms and the man
Flags and heraldry

Since the earliest days of organised society, man has employed a wide variety of symbolic devices for the purposes of identification: both on an individual level (himself and his rank or status), and on a collective level (his family, tribe, and ultimately his nation). One of the most colourful manifestations of this 'decorative name-tagging', has been the adoption and display of distinctive emblems on flags and coats of arms.

Flag beginnings

The **oldest known flag** is one dated to *c.* 3000 BC found in 1972 at Khabis, Iran. According to *The Guinness Book of Records*, it is made of metal, measures 9 × 9 in (23 × 23 cm) and depicts an eagle, two lions, a goddess, three women, and a bull.

Flags have their origins in standards known as **vexilloids,** staffs or poles topped with figures of objects or birds and beasts associated with speed, strength and courage, which first appeared in the ancient civilisations of the Middle East around 5000 years ago. The Egyptians used such standards on land (either carried manually or fixed to their chariots) and at sea, to distinguish various parts of the kingdom: the Ibis province, for instance, being identified by a carved ibis. Some of the figures represented gods or guardian spirits, whose presence on the standards was believed to imbue them with a power that would ensure both protection and victory. Early seals suggest that the favoured emblem on the standards of the Assyrians was their god of war Assur, who was depicted as a crowned and bearded winged archer drawing a bow. According to the Bible (Numbers 2), the tribes of Israel* assembled under standards, though their exact form is not known.

The earliest Roman standard was the *manipulus* (literally 'handful'), a bundle of straw held aloft on a spear, which may have served both as a rallying device for the soldiers of the maniple, a subdivision of the legion, and for signalling. Later, each maniple carried its own emblematic animal (e.g. the horse* or the wolf*) on a staff. The most important of such emblems, the eagle* (an attribute of the principal Roman god Jupiter) became the symbol for the whole legion, and eventually the symbol of the Roman Empire.

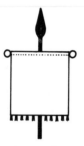

Roman vexillum

The **first true flag** in the western world, *c.* 100 BC, was the **vexillum** (Latin, 'standard'; from which 'vexillology', the term for the study of flags, was coined in 1959). Designed to be carried on horseback, the vexillum, a square of dark red cloth bearing an inscription, painted figure or symbol, was suspended from a cross-bar on a lance. Following his conversion to Christianity in AD 312, Constantine the Great combined spiritual and earthly authority in the **labarum.** Similar in form to the vexillum, the labarum displayed on the cloth Constantine's portrait, and on the staff, replacing the imperial eagle, the sacred 'chi-rho' monogram representing Christ (see Constantine's cross).

The **first fabric flags attached vertically along one side** appeared in China. In one of the earliest recorded instances, Emperor Zhou, the founder of the Zhou dynasty (*c.* 1122–256 BC), had a white flag carried before him to announce his presence (again, what form this took is not known). By extension, the flag came to symbolise his power and authority.

The power of emblems
See the power of national emblems. Some stars, lilies, leopards, a crescent, a lion, an eagle, or other figure which came into credit God knows how, on an old rag of bunting, blowing in the wind on a fort at the ends of the earth, shall make the blood tingle under the rudest or the most conventional exterior.

Ralph Waldo Emerson: Essays, *The Poet*

From China, the concept of laterally-attached flags, initially only of plain fabric, travelled via India to the Middle East. Although forms of such fabric flags appeared with designs in Europe before AD 1000 (the Vikings, for example, are believed to have flown a semi-lateral flag

Symbols of the tribes of Israel

One of the earliest references to the use of distinguishing symbols on flags appears in the Book of Numbers (2:1–2), which is thought to have been written by Moses c. 1450–1410 BC 'And the Lord spake unto Moses and unto Aaron, saying, ''The children of Israel shall pitch [camp] by their fathers' houses; every man with his own standard . . .'' ' According to the Midrash, ancient Hebrew commentaries on biblical texts, each of the tribes of Israel descended from Jacob's sons had its own prince and its standard or flag, whose colour corresponded to the colour of the 12 precious stones on Aaron's breastplate (although, as may be seen, there are discrepancies).

'**Reuben**'s stone was ruby, the colour of his flag was red, and embroidered thereon were mandrakes [plants whose forked roots resembled a human form]. **Simeon**'s was topaz and his flag was green, with the town of Shechem embroidered thereon. **Levi**'s was smaragd [emerald] and the colour of his flag was a third white, a third black, and a third red; embroidered thereon were the Urim and Thummin [sometimes translated as 'Curses and Perfections', Urim and Thummin are believed to have been two divinatory devices, possibly dice or coloured discs, used by the High Priest for sacred decisions and advice; Thummin signified 'yes', and Urim 'no'; an inconclusive casting signified 'no answer'. The sacred devices were kept in a pouch beneath the High Priest's 'breastplate of judgment']. **Judah**'s was a carbuncle [another source gives this as turquoise] and the colour of his flag resembled that of the heavens; embroidered on it was a lion. **Issachar**'s was a sapphire and the colour of his flag was black . . . embroidered thereon were the Sun and Moon. **Zebulun**'s was an emerald [alternatively a diamond] and the colour of his flag was white, with a ship embroidered thereon. **Dan**'s was jacinth and the colour of his flag was similar to sapphire; embroidered on it was a serpent. **Gad**'s was an agate [alternatively a crystal] and the colour of his flag was . . . a blend of black and white; on it was embroidered a camp. **Naphtali**'s was an amethyst and the colour of his flag was like clarified wine of a not very deep red; on it was embroidered a hind. **Asher**'s was a beryl and the colour of his flag was like the precious stone with which women adorn themselves; embroidered thereon was an olive tree. **Joseph**'s was an onyx and the colour of his flag was jet black; the embroidered design thereon for both princes, **Ephraim** and **Manasseh** [Joseph's sons] was Egypt because they were born there. A bullock was embroidered on the flag of Ephraim. A wild ox was embroidered on the flag of the tribe of Manasseh. **Benjamin**'s stone was a jasper and the colour of his flag was a combination of all the 12 colours; embroidered thereon was a wolf.'

charged with a raven* as early as the 9th century), it was not until the time of the Crusades* (1095–1272), that the use of symbols became widespread. In this, returning crusaders may have been influenced by their Saracen enemies, who carried flags on which religious inscriptions were incorporated into ornate abstract patterns.

The development of heraldry (see p.124) beginning in the 12th century led to the creation of new forms of flags to indicate a person's military or social status; among these were a long tapering standard showing the bearer's colours, badges, and motto; a swallow-tailed knight's pennon, also charged with badges; and a square or rectangular banner displaying the owner's coat of arms (a prime example of the latter today is the so-called Royal Standard, the official banner of the sovereign of the United Kingdom, which bears the quartered arms of England, Scotland, and Ireland). Later, with the emergence of true nation states, the elaborate heraldic flags of monarchs and leaders were gradually supplanted by simpler designs of geometric patterns such as crosses and stripes in the national colours. (The development of three distinctive flag designs, which have been an influence on others throughout the world, is described below.)

Today, flags on land and at sea play a more diverse role than ever before. Via a wide range of colours and devices, they are used to represent states, provinces, cities and towns; divisions of the armed forces; government departments; political parties; religious and ethnic groups; churches; academic institutions; clubs; youth groups such as the Boy Scouts; commercial organisations, shipping and air lines (known collectively as house flags; see housemark); regional groups (e.g. the European Community), and international organisations such

I can take no allegiance to a flag if I don't know who's holding it.

Peter Ustinov *Dear Me*

I crossed a high toll bridge and negotiated a no man's land and came to the place where the Stars & Stripes stood shoulder to shoulder with the Union Jack

John Steinbeck *Travels With Charley*

as the United Nations* and the Red Cross*. Flags are also used for signalling (see Chapter 4).

All these, of course, have their own special significance. But it is to flags which represent the nation-state (and thus, all its people), that we pay most attention. Probably the most universal identification devices today, national flags are also among the most potent of symbols, capable of inspiring emotions ranging from the contempt and hostility that provokes ritual acts of desecration (as during the build-up to the Gulf War in 1990, when Iraqi protesters burned the Stars and Stripes, the Union Jack, and the Israeli flag), to reverence and patriotic fervour.

The Union Jack

The first **Union Flag**, now commonly known as the Union Jack, was adopted on 12 April 1606, three years after the two kingdoms of England and Scotland were united under James I (formerly James VI of Scotland); it combined the red cross on white of St George, England's patron saint, with the white diagonal cross or saltire* on blue of Scotland's patron saint Andrew. The so-called cross of St Patrick*, a red saltire, was added 1 January 1801 after the union of Great Britain and Ireland. Both designs follow the heraldic rule that no two colours be placed on each other or side by side.

The Union Flag (pre-1801)

One derivation for the now universal Union Jack label dates back to James I: because he signed his name in the French form *Jacques*, his new flag was nicknamed the Union 'Jack'. The real derivation is probably more prosaic. The flag was originally designed as a naval flag, to be flown from the maintop of British ships. In time, a smaller version came to be flown from the *jack*-staff in the bows.

Incidentally, because Britain has no written constitution, the Union Jack has never been officially adopted; nor, unlike many other countries such as the US, does Britain have an official code of etiquette regarding its use on land. At sea, the rules are different. In 1624 it was reserved specifically for royal ships, and merchant vessels began to use red flags with the national cross in the canton, and later the Red Ensign, with the Union Flag in the canton. This practice was confirmed in 1864. At the same time, a White Ensign was reserved for the Royal Navy, and a Blue Ensign for government vessels. The choice of colours for the ensigns derives from an 18th-century naval custom of dividing the British fleet into three squadrons, each under the command of an Admiral, the White, Blue, and Red, in that order of seniority.

Both the Blue and Red ensigns were adopted for the design of flags of Commonwealth members. The Blue forms the basis of the flags of Australia (and the six state flags), New Zealand, and Fiji, and in those of crown colonies such as Bermuda, the Falkland Islands, and Hong Kong. Until replaced by the maple leaf* in 1965, the Red Ensign formed the basis of the Canadian flag; it still appears in the flags of the provinces of Manitoba and Ontario. An unusual variation occurs in the flag of the self-governing dependency of Niue in the Pacific: the Union Jack is in the canton on a bright yellow field to symbolise the country's warmth of friendship towards New Zealand and the Commonwealth. The Union Jack also appears on the flag of South Africa, and surprisingly, since it was never a British possession, on the State flag of Hawaii.

The Stars and Stripes

The Union Flag first appeared in North America in 1607 at the Jamestown colony in Virginia. Alongside a number of flags with local emblems such as the beaver* or the pine tree, it remained the principal flag of the British colonies until April 1775, when troops fighting Britain in the War of Independence began to hoist all-American flags. One depicted a coiled rattlesnake with 13 rattles, and the slogan 'Don't Tread On Me', a reference to the Scottish thistle* and motto *Nemo me impune lacessit*, 'Nobody provokes me with impunity'. Overall, the flag symbolised the revolutionary spirit of the colonies who were 'striking at Great Britain only with provocation and because they found that, like the snake's rattles, they could create a noise only in unison'. The rattlesnake and slogan were also depicted on a field of 13 alternating stripes for the first Navy Jack; another navy flag bearing the pine or 'Liberty Tree' device was flown by ships under George Washington's command.

The **first flag to represent all 13 colonies** was unfurled on Prospect Hill outside Boston on 1 January 1776, when the Continental Army came into formal existence. Known as the Congress Colors (also the Great Union, Grand Union, or Cambridge Flag), the flag had 13 alternating red and white stripes, but retained the Union Flag in the canton to symbolise the hope of remaining a part of Britain.

The flag of the new United States, now known as **The Stars and Stripes**, was created on 14 June 1777, when Congress formally abandoned the red ensign and resolved 'that the flag of the United States be thirteen stripes alternate red and white; that the union be thirteen stars white in a blue field, representing a new constellation'. It is thought that the star and stripe concept derives from George Washington's own arms. Washington himself explained it differently: 'We take the stars from heaven, the red from our mother country, separating it by white stripes, thus showing that we have separated from her, and the white stripes shall go down to posterity representing liberty.'

In 1792, when the Union expanded to 15 states, the design was updated with two more stars and stripes. As further states were admitted it became clear that the flag would become cluttered. Congress ordered that after 4 July 1818, when five new states were due for admission, the flag should have 20 stars but revert to the 13 original stripes, and that in future when a new state was admitted, a new star be added on the 4 July following admission. This practice has continued to the present flag of 50 stars. No star is specifically identified with any state.

As the first to make use of symbolic stars and/or stripes for each member state, and to popularise the combination of red/white/blue as colours of a free republican nation, the Stars and Stripes has greatly influenced the flag design of other countries. The most notable example is Liberia, which was founded in 1822 as an American colony for freed black slaves. The flag has 11 red and white stripes, and in the blue canton one white star.

The tricolour

Many of the world's national flags are based on tricolours, designs using three bands of colour. The **earliest known tricolour** is the Dutch *Prinsvlag*, with horizontal bands of orange, white, and blue. The colours derive from those of William I, Prince of Orange, who led the Dutch in rebellion against Spanish rule in the 16th century. Around 1630, the orange band was changed to red. The original colour combination, however, survives in South Africa's national flag, the 'Van Riebeeck Flag', which was chosen to commemorate the country's colonisation by Dutch settlers under Jan van Riebeeck in the 17th century.

Stripes of blood

When I think of the flag . . . I see alternate strips of parchment upon which are written the rights of liberty and justice, and stripes of blood to vindicate those rights, and then, in the corner, a prediction of the blue serene into which every nation may swim which stands for these great things. . . . God forbid that we should have to use the blood of America to freshen the color of the flag. But if it should ever be necessary, that flag will be colored once more, and in being colored will be glorified and purified.

President Woodrow Wilson: Address, New York, 17 May 1915

New stars: the 'Flag of the South' or 'Southern Cross', based on the Battle Flag of the Confederate States (1861–65)

Flag crime

Do you know you can go to jail for putting the American flag upside down on a government pole?

Jack Kerouac *On the Road*

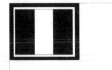

First version of the French *Tricolore*, 1790

The Dutch tricolour inspired a number of other flags, most notably that of Russia. During the late 1690s, the Czar, Peter the Great, worked in the Dutch shipyards. When he returned to Russia, he adapted the Dutch colours in reverse. Later, the blue and white bands were transposed. The Russian tricolour was used as a civil flag until supplanted by revolutionary flags in November 1917. On 26 December 1991, the tricolour officially returned when the red Hammer and Sickle flag of the Soviet Union was removed from the Kremlin by order of President Mikhail Gorbachev. The following day, 27 December, the tricolour was hoisted outside UN headquarters in New York between the flags of Romania and Rwanda.

The most famous and inspirational tricolour is the French *Tricolore* of blue, white, and red vertical bands. It first appeared in Paris during the Revolution. When Parisians stormed the prison fortress of the Bastille, itself a symbol of tyranny, on 14 July 1789, they wore cockades or rosettes of red and blue, the colours of the city's arms. Three days later, Louis XVI entered the city, wearing a cockade of these same colours next to the royal white, the colour of the ruling Bourbon dynasty. The three colours, in the order of red, white, blue, were adopted by the new republicans to symbolise the principles of 'Liberty, Equality, Fraternity'. This arrangement was first used at sea in 1790; the present arrangement was adopted in 1794.

Among the many tricolours worldwide inspired by the French flag, are those of Italy, and the Republic of Ireland. Italy's red, white, green tricolour has been in use since 1861. It derives ultimately from the standard of the Republican National Guard established by France in northern Italy after Napoleon's invasion in 1796. The Irish tricolour, which dates from 1848, was adopted by the first *Dáil Eireann* (Irish Parliament) in January 1919; green represents Catholics, orange Protestants (from William of Orange, who became William III of England), and white stands for the peace between them.

Singularities and superlatives

A selection of unique devices on the world's flags, and some other ways national flags have achieved distinction:

The **oldest** national flag in continuous use is that of **Denmark**; according to legend, the *Dannebrog* ('dyed red cloth'), a white cross on a red field, fell from heaven to the Danish Christian forces of King Valdemar II during the Battle of Lindanisa (modern Tallinn) on 15 June 1219; originally, the flag was square with an equal-armed cross, but in time the arm of the cross on the flying end was extended into the familiar form now known as a Scandinavian cross*.

The **most changed design** in modern history is the US **Stars and Stripes**, which since 1777 has been altered 26 times. The **shortest-lived** design was the flag of 49 stars (the 49th star was added when Alaska was admitted to the Union on 3 January 1959); the new flag had a minimum official life of one year, from 4 July 1959 to 4 July 1960. Unofficially, its existence was even shorter, less than eight months, for Hawaii was admitted the same year on 21 August. The **longest-lived** Stars and Stripes was that of 48 stars which preceded it, and lasted for 47 years from 4 July 1912. The **most recent** design of 50 stars was first raised at Fort McHenry National Monument in Baltimore, Maryland at 12.01 a.m. on 4 July 1960.

Red is the **most common colour** on two-thirds of the world's flags, closely followed by white, then blue, green, yellow, and black. **Libya**

Dying for the flag

Have not I myself known five hundred living soldiers sabred into crows' meat for a piece of glazed cotton which they called their flag; which, had you sold it in any market-cross, would not have brought above three groschen?

Thomas Carlyle *Sartor Resartus* 1836

has the **only single-colour** flag; adopted in 1977, the plain green field represents the 'Green Revolution' of Colonel Gaddafi. The **most colourful** flag is that of **Kiribati**, formerly the Gilbert Islands, in the West Pacific; taken from its coat of arms, the flag in gold, red, white, blue and black, displays a frigate bird (similar to the albatross*) flying above the sun as it rises over the waters of the Pacific.

Kiribati

The **only square** flag is that of **Switzerland**. The **most unusual shape** is the flag of **Nepal**, which originated in the 19th century when two separate triangular pennants were joined, one above the other: the upper, with a crescent moon* emblem, is the flag of the Royal House; the lower, with its emblem of the sun was the flag of the Ránás, the hereditary prime ministerial family which ruled Nepal until 1951.

Nepal

The **sun** appears on a number of other flags. The most famous is the 'Sun Disc' of **Japan**, which represents both the name of the country, *Nihon-Koku* 'Land of the Rising Sun', and the religious belief that the emperor is a direct descendant of the sun. The white sun on the flag of **Taiwan** is a political symbol of the Nationalist 'Kuo Min Tang' Party founded in China in the 1890s; in 1949, the party under Chiang Kai-shek was driven to the island of Formosa where it set up the Republic of China now called Taiwan; 12 points surrounding the sun represent the 12 hours of the day. In the **Philippines**' flag, the sun has eight rays for the eight provinces that rebelled against Spanish rule in 1898. The human-like face on the gold 'Sun of May' on the flag of **Uruguay** derives from that of Argentina, to which Uruguay once belonged.

Uruguay

The **most common device** is the **star**, which appears on more than a quarter of national flags. After the American flag of 50 stars, the **most-starred flag** is that of **Brazil**, which has 23 for the states and the Federal District; the scattered stars represent the night sky over Rio de Janeiro as it was on 15 November 1889 when the republic was created. The **most multi-pointed star** appears on the flag of **Malaysia**; its 14 points represent the 13 states and the capital Kuala Lumpur.

Brazil

The **largest animal emblem** is the lion* on the flag of **Sri Lanka** (formerly Ceylon) which derives from the flag of the island's former central kingdom of Kandy. The flag of the Himalayan kingdom of **Bhutan** (whose name *Druk Yul* means 'land of the Thunder Dragon') is charged with a large black and white dragon*. The device on the unofficial national flag of **Anguilla** (since 1980 a British dependency) is three interlocking dolphins*, which represent strength and endurance.

Sri Lanka

The **largest bird emblem** is the black double-headed eagle* of **Albania**, whose name *Shqipëria* means 'land of the eagle'; the emblem dates back to the Byzantine Empire. The eagle grasping a snake on the

Bhutan

Anguilla

Hungarian croissants

That symbol of the French breakfast, the croissant, may not be so French in origin. Legend has it that during the siege of the Hungarian capital Buda (now part of Budapest), in 1686, the Turks began to tunnel under the city walls. The sound of digging alerted bakers working through the night in the depths; they raised the alarm, and the invaders were routed. As saviours of the city, the bakers were invited to commemorate their vigilance with a new bread. This they did, taking their inspiration from the symbol on the Turkish flag, the crescent*. (Perhaps a part of this origin should be taken with a pinch of salt: the invention of the croissant is also linked to the Turks' siege of Vienna a few years earlier.)

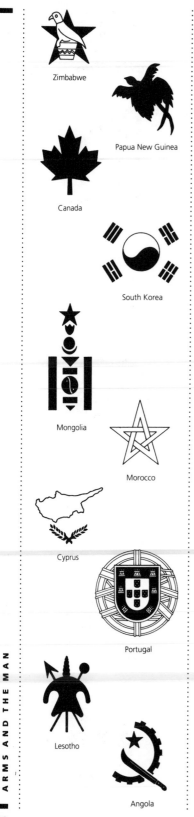

Zimbabwe

Papua New Guinea

Canada

South Korea

Mongolia

Morocco

Cyprus

Portugal

Lesotho

Angola

flag of **Mexico** is based on an ancient Aztec symbol; the emblem refers to a legend about the founding of Tenochtitlán (now Mexico City). On the flag of **Zambia** an eagle in flight, symbolising freedom, is taken from the national arms; also from the arms is the Zimbabwe bird on the flag of **Zimbabwe**. On the flag of **Uganda** is a crested crane*, a former colonial badge. The parrot on the flag of **Dominica** is taken from the supporters of the arms. A gold bird of paradise in flight appears on the flag of **Papua New Guinea**.

The **largest plant emblem** is the maple leaf on the flag of **Canada**; the design of the red 11-pointed leaf on a white field flanked by two broad vertical red stripes was officially adopted on 15 February 1965, after the longest parliamentary debate in Canadian history. Other singular plant emblems include the cedar tree of **Lebanon**, the nutmeg of the 'isle of spices' **Grenada**, and a rice plant on the flag of **Burma**.

Some flags are distinguished by symbols associated with **religion** or **philosophy**. **Israel** has the six-pointed Star of David*. A number of countries use a crescent*, or crescent and star, traditional symbols of Islam; the flag of **Turkey** is the most notable example. In the tricolour of **India**, adopted in 1947, the Wheel of Law or *Dharma Chakra*, represents both the 'dynamism of peaceful change', and Buddhism*. A blue and red *yin-yang** symbol, representing the union or balance of opposites, appears on the flag of **South Korea**; grouped around it are four black trigrams or *kwae* symbols from the I Ching, a system of divination widely used in the East; the trigrams represent the four winds, the four seasons, the four cardinal points, or the four elements of the universe: the sun, moon, earth, and heaven. Equally complex is the *soyonbo*, a combination of symbols, on the flag of **Mongolia**: a flame represents progress; the sun and moon, eternal life; the triangles are said to be a warning to enemies; the bars, honesty and strength; the *yin-yang* symbol, watchfulness; and the gold star, the Communist party. A green pentacle or Seal of Solomon was added to the plain red flag of **Morocco** in 1915; traditionally, the five points are spirit, air, fire, water, and earth.

The official flag of **Cyprus** is white charged with a map of the island, above two olive branches for peace and Greek and Turkish unity; the map is copper-coloured to express the name 'Isle of Copper'.

The flag of **Portugal** is charged with an armillary sphere, an early navigational instrument, as a symbol of Portugal's voyages of discovery and exploration in the early 16th century. **Barbados** recalls its links with Britain with a trident derived from the former colonial badge; to symbolise independence in 1966 and the nation's break with the past the trident is broken off from the shaft. **Kenya** has an emblem of a Masai warrior's shield with two crossed spears. The flag of **Swaziland** includes the traditional weapons of an Emasotsha warrior: an oxhide shield, two spears, and a staff; the staff and shield are ornamented with feather tassels of the lourie and the widowbird, an honour reserved for the king. In 1987, a traditional straw hat on the flag of **Lesotho** was replaced by a shield and spears from the national arms to represent defence. The central emblem on the flag of **Zaïre**, a hand grasping a blazing torch, represents the struggle for freedom; it was the symbol of the Popular Movement of the Revolution (MPR) formed in 1967 by Joseph Mobutu. The black and red flag of **Angola** is charged with a half gearwheel crossed with a machete, and a yellow five-pointed star; the flag is based on that of the liberation movement, the MPLA. **Mozambique** includes a modern automatic rifle among its symbols.

New World flags

Christopher Columbus 'officially' discovered the New World when he set foot on San Salvador in the Bahamas on 12 October 1492. Columbus took possession with the banner of Spain with quartered emblems of Castile (a gold castle on red) and León (a red lion on silver), and a standard with a cross flanked by the crowned initials of his Spanish patrons King Ferdinand (F) and Queen Isabella (Y). Columbus is remembered each year on 12 October on the 'Day of the Race', when a special **Flag of the Race** is flown by Spanish-speaking countries. Designed by a Uruguayan in 1932 to symbolise the cultural ties of people of Hispanic origin in both the Old and New World, the flag has three crosses for Columbus' ships (*Santa Maria*, *Pinta*, and *Santa Clara*, nicknamed *Niña*), and a gold sun for the Americas.

Although Columbus is credited with the discovery of America, he was not the first Westerner to set foot there (he never did in the North); the most likely of the earliest visitors to the North American continent was the Viking Leif Eriksson around the year 1000. Eriksson's banner depicted the raven*, a traditional Norse symbol of good luck.

The earliest English flag in North America was the **St George's Cross***, flown by the explorer John Cabot. Commissioned by Henry VII to discover 'lands unknown', Cabot landed on Cape Breton Island in the northern part of Nova Scotia in June 1497. The flag had a neat dual symbolism: like Columbus, Cabot was Genoese by birth, and the Cross of St George had been the flag of the city state of Genoa since the 12th century.

The **only flag with an inscription as principal feature** is that of **Saudi Arabia**. On a plain green field, above a white sword, the inscription in Arabic script means 'There is no God but Allah, and Mohammed is the Prophet of Allah'; the inscription reads from right to left on both sides; this is achieved by sewing two identical flags together. On the flag of **Iran** the inscription *Allah Akbar* (There is no God but Allah) is repeated 22 times as a reminder of the date, *22 Bahman 1357* (11 February 1979) when the Ayatollah Khomeini returned to Iran. On a central blue disc, the flag of **Brazil** bears the motto *Ordem E Progresso* (Order and Progress). On the flag of **Rwanda** a central yellow band is charged with a black capital 'R' to distinguish it from the flag of Guinea.

Paraguay has the **only flag with a different design on each side**: in the centre of the obverse, the state emblem of the May Star commemorates liberation from Spanish rule in 1811; the reverse of the same basic design has the Treasury Seal, which depicts a lion guarding a staff bearing a red liberty cap; the title *Republica del Paraguay* encircles both the emblem and the seal.

The **most 'convenient' flag** is that of **Liberia**, which is flown by foreign merchant ships registered there to avoid taxation or the more strict maritime regulations in their real country of origin, hence the label '**flag of convenience**'. Liberia has the largest merchant fleet in the world, followed by Panama and Honduras.

The **most international flag** is that of the **United Nations**, which, at the time of writing, represents 175 nations. The UN was founded on 24 October 1945; its flag was first hoisted over the interim headquarters at Lake Success, New York, at noon on 21 October 1947. The organisation's emblem, on a field of 'United Nations Blue', is a polar view of a map of the world within a wreath of crossed olive branches. In addition to its use by UN forces and observers in times of conflict, the flag is flown worldwide on United Nations Day, 24 October. At its headquarters in New York City, the UN flag flies above all others.

United Nations

The **first flag at the South Pole** was that of **Norway**, which was planted in the ice by Roald Amundsen on 14 December 1911. The **first at the North Pole** was the **Stars and Stripes**, planted two years earlier on 6 April 1909 by Commander Robert E. Peary of the US Navy. The American flag was also the **first on the Moon**; it was pitched there on 20 July 1969 by Neil A. Armstrong, commander of Apollo 11; to keep it permanently aloft on the windless lunar surface, the flag is stiffened by wire. The **first on the world's highest mountain** – Mount Everest, 29 002 ft (8840 m), was the **Union Jack** on 29 May 1953; with Tensing, the Sherpa who accompanied him, New Zealander Edmund Hillary also set up the flags of Nepal, and the United Nations.

The art of heraldry

Broadly defined, heraldry is the art and systematic use of hereditary identification symbols (i.e. inherited through the male line of descent in much the same way as surnames). It originated in the mid-12th century on the battlefield and in the 'mimic warfare' of the tournament as a means of distinguishing the medieval knight, who, clad in armour and with his face covered by a helmet, would otherwise have been unrecognisable to either friend or foe. Initially, bold and colourful symbols were painted on the shield; as these symbols were also repeated on the surcoat, the loose sleeveless tunic worn over the armour, they came to be known as 'coats of arms', or just 'arms'. The **oldest documented example of arms** in Europe is recorded in 1127, on the shield of Geoffrey, Count of Anjou (see 'Preferred charges', p.132). At a time when the majority of people were illiterate, knights and nobles found it convenient to have the same emblems on the personal seals they used to 'sign' their documents; the **earliest seal showing a heraldic shield** dates from 1136.

In its early stages of development, the art of 'armory', as the subject was first known, was popularised by the tournament. Said to have been invented in the mid-11th century by a French baron, Geoffroi de Pruelli, to give practice in mounted combat, the tournament became the great spectacle of the Middle Ages. As it flourished, so, too, did the fashion for emblematic decoration (not only on shields and surcoats, but also on helmets, banners, and horse trappings), which spread rapidly throughout Europe, and through all grades of feudal rank above squire.

It soon became clear that some form of control was needed to stem the proliferation and inevitable duplication of 'armorial bearings' chosen at will. This control was assumed by the messengers of royal and noble households, the heralds* (hence 'heraldry', which began to supplant 'armory' in the late 16th century). Becoming the official arbiters under the Crown, the heralds established a strict code to regulate and record the use of arms, and thus ensure that no knight displayed the same emblems as another.

Because arms granted by the heralds, initially only to knights and nobles, came ultimately from the 'fount of all honour', the Crown, they were regarded as the insignia of honour, and symbols of superior social status. From the early 15th century, the honour was extended to others in power and authority (e.g. to bishops, abbots, rich merchants), and to corporate bodies. In England, the **first corporate body to receive a coat of arms** was the Drapers' Company in London on 10 March 1439. In 1538, the City of Gloucester was granted the **first civic arms**. By the beginning of the 18th century, 90 towns and cities in England had acquired coats of arms.

Today, theoretically, anyone in the UK (including academic and religious institutions, hospitals, banks etc.) who can afford the fees involved may apply for a grant of arms. In many other European countries, arms may be freely assumed (though some governments require registration of certain arms). While this availability has to an extent diminished its traditional cachet, heraldry continues to play a colourful role in visual symbolism, particularly in the design of trade-marks and badges (see Cadillac, Porsche).

The section that follows pertains mainly to personal heraldry in the UK; many of the established conventions and devices described, how-ever, may be found in other parts of the world.

Naming of parts

The language of heraldry is known as blazon. Invented by the early heralds to enable them to provide a detailed and unambiguous verbal or written description of all the arms they needed to record (rather than having to draw them), this language consisted mainly of Anglo-Norman French. Many of the original terms are still used to describe coats of arms today.

Armorial tinctures

The term **tinctures** refers to the colours, metals, and furs used in heraldry. The principal **colours** are *Azure*, blue; *Gules*, red; *Sable*, black; *Vert*, green; and *Purpure*, purple (rarely used in British heraldry). Late medieval authors invented three 'stains': *tenné* (tawny or orange), *sanguine* (blood-red), and *murrey* (mulberry). A charge depicted in its natural colour is termed 'proper'.

Heraldic authorities

The world's foremost heraldic authority is the **College of Arms** in London, which was founded by Richard III in 1484. There are three ranks of permanent 'officers of arms': **Kings, Heralds,** and **Pursuivants** (originally apprentice heralds). There are three Kings of Arms: the principal is **Garter**; the title, created by Henry V in 1415, is so called from his duty to attend at the election, investiture, and installation of Knights of the Garter; **Clarenceux** is named after the Duke of Clarence, brother of Edward IV. Historically, his jurisdiction extends over England south of the River Trent. The third King of Arms, **Norroy and Ulster**, combines, since 1943, the office of the former Ulster King of Arms with that of Norroy to have jurisdiction over England north of the Trent and the six counties of Northern Ireland. (The 'Bath King of Arms' is not a member of the College, and is concerned only with the Order of the Bath.) The six Heralds are named **Chester, Windsor, Richmond, Somerset, York,** and **Lancaster**; the four Pursuivants, named after their ancient badges of office, are **Portcullis, Bluemantle, Rouge Croix,** and **Rouge Dragon**. All officers are part of the royal household, and are appointed by the Crown on the nomination of the Earl Marshal of England, a hereditary office held by the Dukes of Norfolk. The functions of these officers of arms are similar to those of their medieval predecessors; in addition to granting arms, and tracing and recording pedigrees, they deal with peerage law and other matters relating to official heraldry and insignia in England, Wales and Northern Ireland, and in all commonwealth countries of which the Queen is Head of State; they also officiate at important royal and state ceremonies, such as coronations and the State Opening of Parliament.

In Scotland, where heraldry is most strictly controlled, the principal officer of arms since 1377 is **Lord Lyon King of Arms** (so-named after the lion in the country's arms). He presides over the Court of the Lord Lyon, which is part of the Scottish legal system. The Heralds are named **Marchmont, Albany,** and **Rothesay**, and the Pursuivants **Dingwall, Kintyre, Carrick,** and **Unicorn**.

In the Republic of Ireland, all matters relating to heraldry and genealogy come under the jurisdiction of **Chief Herald of Ireland** at the Genealogical Office in Dublin Castle.

Though many of the equivalents of the British system have disappeared, some countries still maintain offices to deal with heraldic matters; these include Belgium, Denmark, Finland, Holland, Italy, Spain, Sweden, Switzerland, and South Africa. The Vatican maintains an office for assigning arms to prelates, sees and other corporate bodies of the Roman Catholic Church.

My mother always used to think that having been schooled at Tiverton, with thirty marks a year to pay, I was worthy of a coat of arms. And that is what she longs for.

R.D. Blackmore *Lorna Doone*

Ermine tail

The two **metals** are *Or*, gold (often painted in yellow); and *Argent*, silver (painted white). There is a fundamental rule in heraldry that no colour should ever be placed on colour, or metal on metal. For the most part these rules are strictly adhered to, though of course there are exceptions: for example, to give the ancient arms of Jerusalem (the Holy City) a unique status, five gold crosses were placed upon a silver field; similarly, the papal colours to honour the Head of the Church (hence yellow and white side by side on the flag of the Vatican City).

The two principal **furs** are ermine* and vair. Ermine, the winter coat of the stoat, may be represented by a variety of stylised black ermine tails on a white field; vair is represented by alternate blue and white skins of the grey squirrel. There are a number of variants of both furs; e.g. erminois, gold with black tails.

Arms may be recorded by a rough sketch in which abbreviations are substituted for tinctures with A argent, B azure, and so on. In the 17th century, the Jesuit writer Silvester Petra Sancta invented a system called **hatching** to represent tinctures in uncoloured illustrations. Thus gold is represented by dots, and silver by a plain field; blue is represented by horizontal lines, red by vertical lines, black by vertical and horizontal lines, green by diagonal lines running (from the observer's viewpoint) from left to right, and purple by diagonal lines from right to left. Widely used throughout Europe, hatching is invaluable in the identification of arms, for instance on silverware.

From the late 15th century till about the middle of the 17th century, various systems were devised to describe armorial bearings in words. But as Alexander Nisbet records in his *System of Heraldry* (1722), some of the more imaginative heraldic writers liked to attribute to the tinctures 'mystical significations, and to represent moral, politick, and military virtues, in the bearers of such colours: which fancies I design-edly omit as ridiculous: For Arms of whatsoever tinctures they be, are

The Royal Arms

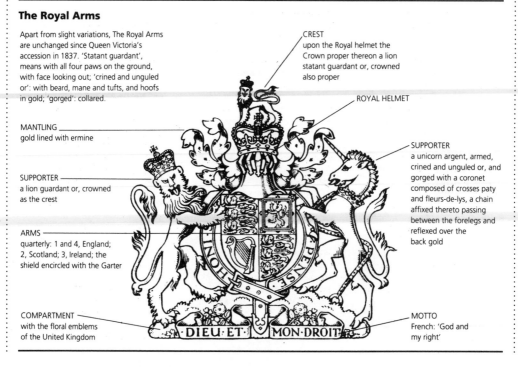

Apart from slight variations, The Royal Arms are unchanged since Queen Victoria's accession in 1837. 'Statant guardant', means with all four paws on the ground, with face looking out; 'crined and unguled or': with beard, mane and tufts, and hoofs in gold; 'gorged': collared.

MANTLING
gold lined with ermine

SUPPORTER
a lion guardant or, crowned as the crest

ARMS
quarterly: 1 and 4, England; 2, Scotland; 3, Ireland; the shield encircled with the Garter

COMPARTMENT
with the floral emblems of the United Kingdom

CREST
upon the Royal helmet the Crown proper thereon a lion statant guardant or, crowned also proper

ROYAL HELMET

SUPPORTER
a unicorn argent, armed, crined and unguled or, and gorged with a coronet composed of crosses paty and fleurs-de-lys, a chain affixed thereto passing between the forelegs and reflexed over the back gold

MOTTO
French: 'God and my right'

DIEU·ET· MON·DROIT

equally noble, if the bearers of them be of equal dignity'. Thus, for example, while normal blazon was for knights and gentlemen, descriptions using the names of precious stones were devised for the nobility, and planetary symbols for persons of royal blood. Among various other 'aberrations of intellect', as purists called them, was one which blazoned with parts of the body: the heart, liver, spleen, etc. The following is a modified version of a list of 'significations' reproduced in William Berry's *Encyclopaedia Heraldica* (1828). Berry, incidentally, assures the reader that he does not subscribe to such 'strange whims and fancies'.

Yellow (Or) planet: the Sun; precious stone: topaz; virtues: faith and constancy; celestial sign: Leo; month: July; day: Sunday; age: youth; flower: marigold; element: air; season: spring; complexion: sanguine; numbers: 1, 2, 3; metal: gold.

White (Argent) planet: the Moon; precious stone: pearl (or margarite); virtues: hope and innocence; celestial signs: Scorpio, Pisces; months: October, November; day: Monday; age: infancy; flowers: lily, white rose; element: water; season: autumn; complexion: sanguine; numbers: 10, 11; metal: silver.

Red (Gules) planet: Mars; precious stones: ruby (coral or carbuncle); virtues: charity, magnanimity; celestial signs: Aries, Cancer; months: March, June, July; day: Tuesday; ages: virility or man's age; flowers: gilliflower, red rose; element: fire; seasons: summer and harvest; complexion: choler; numbers: 3, 10; metal: latten (a metal resembling brass).

Blue (Azure) planet: Jupiter; precious stone: sapphire; virtues: justice, loyalty; celestial signs: Taurus, Libra; months: April, September; day: Thursday; age: puerility; flower: blue lily; element: air; season: spring; complexion: sanguine; numbers: 4, 9; metal: copper.

Black (Sable) planet: Saturn; precious stones: diamond or agate; virtues: prudence, constancy; celestial signs: Capricornus, Aquarius; months: December, January; day: Saturday; age: old age; flower: aubifane; element: earth; season: winter; complexion: melancholy; numbers: 5, 8; metals: iron, lead.

Green (Vert) planet: Venus; precious stones: emerald, smaragd; virtues: loyalty in love, courtesy, affability; celestial signs: Gemini, Virgo; months: May, August; day: Friday; age: lusty green youth; flower: all kinds of verdure; elements: water, earth; season: spring; complexion: phlegmatic; numbers: 6,12; metal: quicksilver.

Purple (Purpure) planet: Mercury; precious stones: opal, amethyst or hyacinth; virtues: temperance, prudence; celestial signs: Sagittarius, Pisces; months: November, February; day: Wednesday; age: cana senectus; flower: violet; elements: water, earth; season: winter; complexions: phlegmatic, with some choler; numbers: 6, 12; metal: tin.

Heraldic components

The basic components of an achievement of arms (the technical term for all the armorial devices to which the bearer or armiger is entitled), derive ultimately from the items a knight wore in battle or in tourna-

---

Petruchio *I swear I'll cuff you if you strike again*
Katharine *So may you lose your arms:*
If you strike me you are no gentleman;
And if no gentleman, why then no arms.
Petruchio *A herald, Kate? O! put me in thy books.*
Katharine *What is your crest, a coxcomb?*

Shakespeare *The Taming of the Shrew* Act 2 sc. 1

White, say they, denotes chastity; black constancy; blue loyalty, &c, &c. But as to such ridiculous fancies, the mere mention of them is fully sufficient.

Joseph Edmondson *Complete Body of Heraldry* 1780

Symbolic nonsense
The heralds tell us that certain scutcheons and bearings denote certain conditions, and that to put colours on colours, or metals on metals, is false blazonry. If all this were reversed, if every coat of arms in Europe were new-fashioned, if it were decreed that or should never be placed but on argent, or argent but on or, that illegitimacy should be denoted by a lozenge, and widowhood by a bend, the new science would be just as good as the old science, because both the new and old would be good for nothing.

T. B. Macaulay *Moore's Life of Lord Byron (Edinburgh Review*, 1831)

ments: a shield, helmet, mantling, wreath, and crest. The other principal components are the supporters, compartment, and motto.

The **shield** (also called escutcheon) is the most important component. Through the ages, shield shapes have varied both for utilitarian purposes and for the figures or symbols with which they were decorated. The most suitable for heraldic design is the 'heater' (so-called because of its flatiron shape), which became fashionable in the 14th century.

Next in importance to the shield is the **crest** (from Latin *crista*, 'cock's comb'). The word is often wrongly used instead of 'coat of arms', as in the 'family' or 'school crest'. In heraldry, it refers specifically to the device or emblem attached to the helmet; and while it is possible to have arms but no crest, a crest without arms is impossible.

Crests, which were made of painted metal and later of wood or boiled leather, originated in the late 13th century, as a reinforcement for the helmet, and to lessen the impact on the head from blows from battle-axe or sword. Frequently the device was derived from the charge on the shield. Animals, birds, parts of the human body such as a crooked arm, were common, as were inanimate objects (such as, in one case, a bucket and chain). As they became more fashionable, crests became elaborate and heavy, almost certainly losing any utilitarian value. It is unlikely that some of the more fantastic ever appeared in combat. The royal crest has been the lion ever since Edward III (1327–77) adopted it.

Below the crest is the **wreath** or torse. In heraldry, this is usually depicted as two bands of silk from the two principal tinctures of the shield, twisted together in six alternate sections to conceal where the crest is joined to the helmet.

Beneath the crest and wreath, comes the **helmet** or **helm**. Like the shield, helmet design in warfare changed considerably over the years, from a conical helmet with nose guard at the time of the Norman Conquest to an all-encasing type in the 15th century. Since the reign of James I (1603–25), stylised forms of different shapes and positions have been used to indicate the bearer's rank. The helmets of kings and royal princes are of gold, affrontée (facing the observer), with a number of bars across the front (the Queen's helm has five bars, that of the Prince of Wales seven); those of peers of the realm, are of silver and gold, with five bars in profile; those of baronets or knights, are of steel, with a visor open; and those of the humble 'esquires' or gentlemen, of steel, closed.

The figures which flank the shield and appear to hold it up, are called **supporters**. These too are symbols of rank, being granted only to the head of the family of royalty, to peers, to higher grades of knighthood such as Knights of the Garter, and other categories on which the College of Heralds has conferred the right to display; these include district and parish councils (if they have town status), and some corporate bodies.

Supporters may be natural figures such as humans, birds, beasts, or fish. Typically, the figures are allusive. The city of Glasgow, for example, has two salmon as supporters; the Cornish town Penzance has a pirate and a fisherman. Equally, they may be mythological figures: two golden unicorns* support the arms of the Society of Apothecaries, in allusion to the purifying qualities of the animal's horn. Inanimate objects include trees, lighted torches, and the pillars of Hercules. Although the two supporters on either side of the shield are often the same, they do not have to be: in the Royal Arms, the supporters are the Lion of England and the Unicorn of Scotland; the arms of the State of New York are supported by Liberty and Justice.

Helmet indicating Peer

Helmet indicating Esquire or Gentleman

Supporting cast

It is thought that supporters were introduced by the engravers of seals merely to fill the space between the shield and the edge of the seal. In his romantic novel *Ivanhoe* (1819), set in the reign of Richard I (1189–99), the formative years of heraldry, Sir Walter Scott records an alternative origin in the medieval tournament:

'On a platform beyond the southern entrance, formed by a natural elevation of the ground, were pitched five magnificent pavilions, adorned with pennons of russet and black, the chosen colours of the five knights challengers. The cords of the tents were of the same colour. Before each pavilion was suspended the shield of the knight by whom it was occupied, and beside it stood his squire, quaintly disguised as a savage or silvan man, or in some other fantastic dress, according to the taste of his master, and the character he was pleased to assume during the game.'

Mistaken identity

The use of badges and banners as identifying symbols was by no means foolproof in the heat of battle, and but for one mistake during the English 'Wars of the Roses', the course of English history might have been very different. On Easter Sunday, 14 April 1471, forces of the Yorkist king Edward IV, bearing the royal badge of the 'Sun in Splendour', a sun with rays, encountered the Lancastrian forces led by the Earl of Warwick, on a mist-shrouded battlefield at Barnet near London. On Warwick's side

Sun in splendour   Estoile

was De Vere, the Earl of Oxford, whose soldiers bore the 'Estoile', a star and rays. Mistaking this emblem for Edward's sun, Warwick led his troops in a fierce attack against those of Oxford. The resulting confusion, in which Warwick was killed, spurred Edward to a decisive victory which was to prove invaluable in the chain of events leading to the eventual Yorkist accession in 1485.

The earliest supporters often appeared to be suspended in mid-air or balancing on a scroll; later they were given a firm footing on which to rest. Called the **compartment** (from French *comporter*, 'to bear'), this is usually a stretch of green grass. From the compartment of the Royal Arms grow the floral emblems of England (rose*), Scotland (thistle*), Wales (leek*), and Ireland (shamrock*).

Attached to the helmet and artistically arranged round the shield, is the **mantling**, or **lambrequin**. This flowing drapery is thought to derive from the material some Crusaders used over their armour and helmets as a protection against the burning sun in the Holy Land. Since the reign of Elizabeth I (1558–1603) the royal mantling has been of gold lined with ermine; the mantling of peers is of red lined with ermine.

Inscribed on a scroll, beneath the shield in English heraldry, above in Continental (and usually also in Scottish) heraldry, comes the **motto**. Often a short pithy slogan expressing some noble sentiment or guiding principle, or alluding to the bearer's name, the motto is thought to derive originally from a war-cry.

Charging the shield

Any device placed on the surface of the shield, or field, is called a **charge**. So that the position of charges may be accurately described, or blazoned, parts of the field have been assigned specific names. The top, considered the most honourable position, is called the chief, the bottom is the base; the vertical centre is the pale, and the horizontal centre the fess. The right side from the bearer's viewpoint is termed the dexter, and the left side is the sinister.

The principal charges, shown here, are the **'ordinaries'** or 'honourable ordinaries'. These simple geometrical figures, which are among the earliest devices of heraldry, are thought to originate in the pieces fixed on the shield for reinforcement. Narrower forms are called **subordinaries**.

There are also a number of small circular charges or **roundels**. These are named according to colour; for instance, a green roundel is a *pomme*, a red one is a *torteau*, and a gold one a *bezant* (originally a gold coin from Byzantium). Another roundel, transversed by wavy bars of silver and blue, in heraldic terms *barry wavy azure and argent*, symbolises a spring of clear water (compare the housemark of ICI).

Some of the earliest heraldic shields bear no charges and consist solely of a field divided by a variety of plain or ornamental partition lines. Such

Bonus points

'This is the very warp and woof of history, my dear Commander Bond.' He reached for another volume that lay open on his desk and that he had obviously prepared for Bond's delectation. 'The coat of arms, for instance. Surely that must concern you, be at least of profound interest to your family, to your own children? Yes, here we are. "Argent on a chevron sable three bezants".' He held up the book so that Bond could see. 'A bezant is a golden ball, as I am sure you know. Three balls.' Bond commented drily, 'That is certainly a valuable bonus.'

Ian Fleming *On Her Majesty's Secret Service*

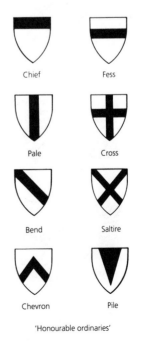

Chief   Fess

Pale   Cross

Bend   Saltire

Chevron   Pile

'Honourable ordinaries'

Fetterlock

Pheon

Clarion

Portcullis

Lion rampant

Lion passant

Double-headed eagle

lines may run in the direction of almost any ordinary, which in blazon will often be prefixed by the word *per*.

In addition to geometrical figures, literally anything under the sun, including the Sun itself and other celestial objects such as the Moon and stars can be, and has been, employed as a charge. Thus human and divine figures, animals, birds, fish, and insects (even flies and fleas) have all found their way onto shields; so, too, have all manner of inanimate objects, such as the fetterlock, the pheon, the clarion, and the portcullis.

Animate charges are commonly used to symbolise some characteristic of the armiger. They may also refer to an incident in a family's history, or to the occupation of the person to whom the arms were granted; thus the bee* (a symbol of thrift and industry) is sometimes used in the arms of a self-made man. More commonly, beasts were chosen for their implied qualities: for instance, the lion* for courage and nobleness, the bear* for strength and boldness, the eagle* for speed and keenness of vision.

Monsters of classical and medieval mythology were also adopted. As well as the familiar dragon*, unicorn*, griffin*, and wyvern*, hybrids of the imagination include such concoctions as the yale: an antelope with a boar's tusks and jaws, whose most important feature was two long horns, which could be rotated and used in either direction. The fabled enfield, which combines the head of a fox, chest of a greyhound, forelegs and talons of an eagle, hindlegs and tail of a wolf, and the body of a lion, is used both as a charge on the shield and as a supporter in the arms of the London Borough of Enfield, where the offices of Guinness Publishing are located.

More than 100 specific terms describe the posture or **attitude** of birds, beasts, and fish. Unless otherwise stated, a lion is usually rampant, i.e. standing upright, with face in profile; walking with its right paw in the air, and face in profile, it is described as passant; looking out at the observer, it is gardant. The most common attitude for the eagle and other birds of prey is displayed, i.e. with wings expanded; when flying horizontally, the term is volant.

A wide variety of plants are also used as charges. Among the most

---

Mark Twain on heraldry

The American humourist Mark Twain takes a swipe at heraldic symbolism and its jargon in at least two of his novels. In this example from *Huckleberry Finn*, Tom Sawyer and Huck devise a coat of arms for their friend, the runaway slave Jim:

'On the scutcheon we'll have a bend *or* in the dexter base, a saltire *murrey* in the fess, with a dog, couchant, for common charge, and under his foot a chain embattled, for slavery, with a chevron *vert* in a chief engrailed, and three invected lines on a field *azure*, with the nombril points rampant on a dencette indebted; crest, a runaway nigger, *sable*, with his bundle over his shoulder on a bar sinister: and a couple of gules for supporters,

which is you and me; motto, *Maggiore fretta, minore atto*. Got it out of a book – means, the more haste, the less speed.'

'Geewhillikins,' I says, 'but what does the rest of it mean?'

'We ain't got no time to bother over that,' he says....

'Shucks, Tom,' I says, 'think you might tell a person. What's a bar sinister?'

'Oh, *I* don't know. But he's got to have it. All the nobility does.' [Bar sinister: a misnomer once favoured by fiction writers for 'baton sinister', a narrow diagonal band on a heraldic shield, passing from the upper left corner to the lower right. It was used to signify bastardy.]

common are the trefoil*, thistle*, oak* leaves, grapes and vines*, the fleur-de-lys*, and the rose*.

Punning heraldry

Charges which play upon the bearer's name in the form of a pun or rebus are a popular feature in heraldry. One of the best known examples of this **canting** is the archers' bows and lions on the arms of Queen Elizabeth the Queen Mother, in allusion to her maiden name Bowes-Lyon. Less familiar perhaps is the tilting spear (used in tournaments) in the arms granted to John Shakespeare in 1596, and confirmed to his son William in 1606.

Pictorial puns in heraldry are used throughout Europe. The symbol of the Gruyère region in Switzerland where the cheese is made, is a crane*, from the French *grue*, 'crane'; the fabled basilisk*, appears as a supporter in the arms of Basel, Switzerland. Another notable example is the red shield (in German, *roth schild*) adopted by the Rothschild family of Frankfurt.

Sign into name

Sometimes this association with names worked the other way round. An obvious example may be found in a great number of English pub signs*. Following a decree by Richard II in 1393 that inns and taverns be identified by a sign, many keepers adopted his badge of a white hart. In time this sign became the name by which the pub was known. The same process occurred with a wide variety of heraldic arms and badges. Indeed, as Leslie Dunkling notes in *The Guinness Book of Names*, the word 'arms' became so closely linked with pub names that it became virtually synonymous with 'inn' or 'pub' (as many existing examples, such as Bricklayers' Arms or Railway Arms, bear witness).

Surnames, too, originate from heraldic devices. In *Heraldry of the World*, Carl Alexander von Volborth notes that when the Danish nobility were compelled to adopt surnames in 1526, some families chose their name from their coat of arms. Thus, for instance, the wreath of roses surmounting the helmet in one family's achievement made the name Rosenkrantz a natural choice; similarly the gold star on another family's shield suggested the name Gyldenstjerne (gold star).

From father to son

Although arms are hereditary, no two men can bear the same coat at the same time. The arms of sons, therefore, have to be 'differenced'. In

Quite armless

In her memoir of the clergyman and author Sydney Smith (1771–1845), his daughter, Lady Holland, tells of the time Smith was visited by a man who was compiling a history of the distinguished families of Somerset and wanted to identify his arms. To this the Reverend replied: 'The Smiths never had any arms, and have invariably sealed their letters with their thumbs.'

Shakespeare's shield

Arms of the London Borough of Enfield, granted 15 August 1966
Or, on a fesse wavy vert a bar wavy argent charged with a barrulet wavy azure; over all an enfield rampant gules. Crest: On a wreath Or and azure, a stag's head proper, wreathed about the neck a garland of roses gules, barbed, seeded, slipped and leaved proper. Supporters: On the dexter side a lion gules gorged with a collar engrailed with chain reflexed over the back and charged with a saltire couped Or, and on the sinister side an enfield gules. Motto: By industry ever stronger

Preferred charges

The **oldest and most common animate charge is the lion***. According to one medieval chronicler, when Henry I of England knighted his newly-wed 14-year-old son-in-law Geoffrey, Count of Anjou, in 1127, he hung around his neck a blue shield painted with gold lions. The first arms of England, *Gules three lions passant guardant or* (on a red shield three golden lions walking and looking outwards), appeared on the Great Seal struck for Richard I 'Coeur de Lion' around 1195. They have remained the favoured beasts of the English monarchy ever since. In Scotland, a lion rampant, red on gold, became the banner of the king of the Scots, William the Lion (1165–1214). Many other kings and princes of medieval Europe took one or more lions as their emblems; lions may still be seen in the arms of Denmark, Sweden, Norway, the Netherlands, Finland and Belgium, and in countless municipal arms.

The eagle* is the **most important heraldic bird**, and together with the lion, the most popular animate charge. A symbol of authority and power since ancient times, it became the **most common national and imperial symbol**. As the standard of the Roman legions, the eagle was adopted as the special emblem of Roman emperors, and later as the heraldic device of the Holy Roman Empire (962–1806). Imitating the Romans, Napoleon adopted an eagle for his imperial arms when he crowned himself Emperor of France in 1804. In the US, the indigenous Bald Eagle was chosen in 1782 as the principal device on the Great Seal*. (The eagle also appears in a number of American state seals.) A double-headed eagle, looking to the East and the West, was adopted as the device of the Byzantine or Eastern Roman Empire, which ended in 1453 when the Turks conquered Constantinople (modern Istanbul). By marriage to Sophia, the niece of Constantine XIV, the last emperor of Byzantium, Ivan III of Russia considered himself heir to the Byzantine Empire (for which he also assumed the title Czar, meaning Caesar, for the first time). The double-headed black eagle he took for his device in 1472 remained the principal charge on the arms of Imperial Russia until the revolution of 1917.

The **principal floral charge** is the **fleur-de-lys**, or fleur-de-lis (literally 'flower of the lily'), the traditional emblem of the kings of France. According to legend, when Clovis, King of the Franks, was converted to Christianity in AD 496, an angel presented him with a golden lily as an emblem of his purification. Centuries later, Louis VII (1137–80) adopted a shield strewn with gold fleurs-de-lys on blue (representing heaven). Charles V (1366–80) reduced the number to three for his coat of arms. To emphasise his claim to the French throne, the English king Edward III quartered the French arms with the lions of England in his Great Seal of 1340. The kings of England continued to emblazon at least one quarter of their shields with the arms of France until 1801, when George III finally relinquished the title 'King of France'. The fleur-de-lys is also the heraldic emblem of Florence, the 'City of Lilies'.

The **most important floral charge in British heraldry is the rose***. A golden rose was first introduced as a royal badge by Eleanor of Provence in 1236, when she married Henry III (reigned 1227–72). When Henry of the House of Lancaster came to the throne as Henry IV in 1399 he brought with him his badge of a red rose. After the dynastic 'Wars of the Roses' (1455–85; so dubbed by Sir Walter Scott in 1829 in his novel *Anne of Geierstein*) between the House of York (white rose) and Lancaster for possession of the English Crown, the two roses were united to form what is called the Tudor Rose.

English cadency marks

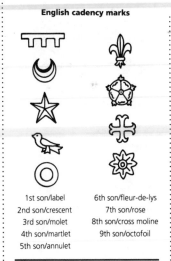

1st son/label	6th son/fleur-de-lys
2nd son/crescent	7th son/rose
3rd son/molet	8th son/cross moline
4th son/martlet	9th son/octofoil
5th son/annulet	

English heraldry, this is achieved with nine small charges known as **cadency marks**. Usually borne in the upper part of the shield, the marks serve not only to denote the seniority within a family, but also to distinguish one branch from another. The eldest son differences his arms with a three-pointed narrow bar or label (in the arms of the Prince of Wales, the label is silver of three points), the second son with a crescent, the third with a mullet, and so on. On his father's death, the eldest son inherits his coat and discards the label; the other cadency marks are permanent. In Scotland, a different and more strictly en-forced system applies, in which coloured borders, ornamental lines, and additional marks are used in a prescribed order.

Arms and the woman

A daughter may bear her father's arms on a diamond-shaped figure or lozenge, but without a helmet or crest. If her father has no male heirs, his daughter is his heraldic heiress. Consequently, when she marries she places her arms on a small shield known as an escutcheon of pretence at the centre of her husband's shield. When a daughter who is not an heiress marries, she 'impales' her arms, i.e. places them on a shield beside her husband's. A widow displays her marital arms on a lozenge.

Japanese heraldry

Outside Europe, the only comparable form of hereditary symbols occurs in Japan in the form of **mon**, highly stylised 'badges' (the nearest equivalent in English). Evolving around the same time as Western heraldry in the feudal society of 12th-century Japan, mon were originally used to identify members of noble houses. They displayed them on their robes, and on canopied bullock coaches. Samurai, or military retainers, and servants also wore the mon or some variant of their feudal lord, in much the same way as the retainers and domestic servants did their lord's livery in medieval Europe.

According to L. G. Pine's *International Heraldry*, the earliest recorded use of mon was in 1156, when two warring clans displayed them on their banners. By the end of the next century, the use of mon on shields and armour had become general among the warrior class. By the 16th century, the position of mon on warriors' ceremonial dress was regulated: it was displayed twice on the breast, on the sleeves, and on the back. Later the positions were restricted to three places: just below the collar at the back and on either sleeve.

In 1642 the military dictator, or Shogun, Iyemitsu ordered all aristocratic families to register at least two mon: a principal *jomon* for important or ceremonial functions, and for general use a lesser device or *kayemon*. The devices were also adopted by the merchant classes, scholars, priests, and even actors.

During the Meiji Restoration, the period of 'Enlightened Government' which began in 1868 and re-opened the country to Europeans, all Japanese were required to take a surname (until then this had been the prerogative of the nobles). In addition, many adopted a mon, which was passed on to the eldest son; sons also adopted symbols of their own. In this way, many variations of the same mon developed. Today, mon may be displayed on everything that belongs to the family including furniture, other everyday objects, and in particular clothing, though they are not worn on wedding or mourning robes, or on hara-kiri garments.

Initially irregular in form, the mon is now symmetrical, and most often circular, but semi-circular, square, rectangular, and fan- or lozenge-shaped forms are also used. As for the variety of subjects, there seems to be no limit. Highly stylised representations of botanical and geometric forms are the most popular, but Japanese fauna from the centipede and the lobster to the crane* and the phoenix*, and all manner of inanimate objects also appear. Other mon derive from Chinese or Japanese written characters. Often the choice of subject was arbitrary, other subjects have a military reference, or like canting arms* in Western heraldry, are an allusion to the bearer's name. Religious symbols were also adopted: the three hollyhock leaves of the Tokugawa dynasty, who held the Shogunate from 1615 to 1867, have a religious significance, the hollyhock being sacred to the Kamo-Zinsya shrine at Kyoto. Some Christian families based their mon on the cross.

Mon had a lasting effect on all Japanese flags. The red sun on the national flag, representing Nihon-Koku, the 'land of the rising sun', is a mon, so is the traditional symbol on the imperial standard, a 16-

Every coat tells a story

In civic and corporate heraldry the charges and accessories have always had, and continue to have, symbolic significance. A prime example of recent years is the armorial achievement of the United Kingdom Atomic Energy Authority (granted 12 April 1955). On the shield, the black represents the graphited core of an atomic pile; the superimposed silver dots represent uranium rods inserted into the pile. The triangular wedge in the centre of the shield (in heraldic terms a 'pile') is charged with alternate gold and scarlet zigzag lines: the lines (heraldic 'dancetty') symbolise the dancing heat and power of an atomic pile. The crest of the Sun, symbolising energy, is charged with a black martlet (a heraldic bird always shown without feet) from the arms of the 'father of nuclear science', Ernest Rutherford (1871–1937). The supporters are pantheons (a beast invented by Tudor heralds). Chained to the ground, the pantheons symbolise the destructive but firmly leashed potential of the atom; the points of the stars on the two beasts add up to 92 (the atomic number of uranium). The motto translates as 'the greatest from the least'.

Tokugawa

Imperial Mon

Paulownia

US 'Great Seal'

Obverse

Reverse

petalled chrysanthemum (for imperial brothers and sons the chrysanthemum has 14 petals). The other principal imperial, and more private, mon is the Paulownia, which derives from the trumpet-shaped bloom of the indigenous spring-flowering tree *paulownia imperialis*, (so-named after Anna Paulovna, daughter of Czar Paul I).

Until quite recently mon were rarely seen in the West, but with the continued expansion of Japanese trade abroad a number are beginning to make an appearance, either in their original form or as adaptations. A notable example is the three-diamond trademark of Mitsubishi*, which derives from the mon of the Iwasaki family.

Seals in the US

Although the United States frowned on heraldry because of its monarchical, and thus undemocratic associations, a form of it has been retained in the many federal and state seals in use.

The Great Seal

The **most important seal is the Great Seal**, which symbolises overall the federal government's power and authority. Unusually, the design consists of two faces, an obverse (front), and reverse (back). Only the obverse is used for authenticating certain documents such as treaties; it also serves as the national arms. The first Great Seal was cut in brass; the seal in use today, the seventh, is an engraved steel die of the original design.

Plans for the seal were initiated by the Continental Congress on 4 July 1776, the same day independence was declared. A committee consisting of John Adams, Benjamin Franklin, and Thomas Jefferson was set up to propose designs. These proved too allusive and allegorical, and were rejected. Jefferson, for example, suggested: 'Pharaoh sitting in an open chariot, a crown on his head and a sword in his hand passing thro' the divided waters of the Red Sea in pursuit of the Israelites: rays from a pillar of fire in the cloud, expressive of the Divine presence and command, reaching to Moses who stands on the shore and, extending his hand over the Sea, causes it to overwhelm Pharaoh. Motto: Rebellion to tyrants is obedience to God.' John Adams proposed Hercules resting on his club, with 'Virtue pointing to her rugged mountain on one hand, and pursuading him to ascend', and 'Sloth, glancing at her flowery paths of pleasure, wantonly reclining on the ground, displaying the charms both of her eloqunece and person to seduce him into vice'.

Eventually the seal was designed by William Barton of Philadelphia, and officially approved on 20 June 1782. It is highly symbolic. The obverse shows the American eagle*, symbol of strength, bearing on its breast a shield charged with 13 red and white stripes to signify the original 13 states; these are bound together by a blue band to signify 'unity of the whole in Congress'. The eagle holds the symbol of peace, an olive* branch, with 13 leaves in its right talon; the bundle of 13 arrows in its left talon symbolises readiness for war if necessary. Thirteen stars on a blue ground in the centre of the sun's rays breaking through a cloud are said to signify the 'new nation taking its place among the sovereign powers'. The streamer in the eagle's beak bears the national motto *E Pluribus Unum*, 'Out of many, one'.

This motto derives ultimately from Virgil. It is said to have been selected from the title page of *Gentleman's Journal*, January 1692, by Pierre Eugène du Simitière, a Swiss artist employed by the committee to contribute a design for the seal (his proposal, like the committee's, was rejected).

The reverse of the seal shows a pyramid, which represents strength and duration. The pyramid of 13 tiers is unfinished to signify that the new nation has room for development, that is, other states. The choice of pyramid is allusive: the founding fathers likened themselves to the children of Israel escaping from the Pharaohs' tyranny to build a new Jerusalem. Above the pyramid the eye of Providence is set in a triangle surrounded by a 'glory of light'. The two mottoes are also from Virgil: *Annuit Coeptis* translates as 'He has favored our undertakings', and *Novus Ordo Seclorum*, as 'A new order of the ages'. The date at the base of the pyramid is 1776.

The Great Seal was first used on 16 September 1782, on a document authorising George Washington to negotiate and sign an agreement with Britain for the exchange and better treatment of prisoners of war.

The reverse of the seal has never been used as a seal (there is no evidence that a die for it has ever been cut), but by an act of President Roosevelt, dated 2 July 1935, it was incorporated into, and remains on, the reverse of the $1 bill.

The Confederate Seal

During the Civil War, a seal of the Confederate States was authorised at the third session of their first Congress on 30 April 1863. The resolution reads 'that the seal of the Confederate States shall consist of a device representing an equestrian portrait of Washington, surrounded with a wreath composed of the principal agricultural products of the Confederacy, and having around its margin the words 'The Confederate States of America, twenty-second February, eighteen hundred and sixty-two' with the motto *Deo vindice*.

State seals

Each of the 50 states has its own seal. In some, the coat of arms forms the principal design; others employ a wide variety of traditional symbols and emblems; for example, the rising sun, symbol of life and regeneration, appears on 11 seals. Many seals record historical data, or depict landscape or fauna native to their state. Most include mottoes, some of which are in Latin; the motto on Oklahoma's seal is *Labor Omnia Vincit*, 'Labour conquers all'.

One of the oldest state seals, that of New Jersey (adopted 1776), is also the closest to European heraldry. It is composed of a shield charged with three ploughshares, a crest of a horse's head, and as supporters the figures of Liberty and the Roman goddess of agriculture Ceres. The youngest of the 50 states, Hawaii (admitted to the Union 21 August 1959), also combines some traditional elements, including a crest and quartered shield, beneath which as a symbol of eternal life, a phoenix* rises from flames. Its supporters are Liberty and the figure of Kamehameka, who united the islands in 1791. All the seals are circular, except that of Connecticut, which is an ellipse.

Fallen emblems

The **hammer and sickle**, synonymous with **communism**, was adopted in 1922, when Russia united with other communist states to form the Union of Soviet Socialist Republics (USSR). A simplification of the earlier emblem of the Russian Social-Democratic Labour Party (Bolsheviks) of a hammer crossed with the plough, the hammer and sickle

Franklin's turkey

Not everyone was happy about the eagle's suitability as the symbol of the new United States. In a letter to his daughter Sarah on 26 January 1784, the statesman Benjamin Franklin expressed his reservations: 'I wish the bald eagle had not been chosen as the representative of our country; he is a bird of bad moral character; he does not get his living honestly . . . like those among men who live by sharping and robbing, he is generally poor, and very often lousy. Besides, he is a rank coward . . .'

Franklin favoured the turkey, which 'is in comparison a much more respectable bird, and withal a true original native of America. Eagles have been found in all other countries, but the turkey was peculiar to ours; the first of the species seen in Europe, being brought to France by the Jesuits from Canada, and served up at the wedding table of Charles the Ninth. He is, besides (though a little vain and silly, it is true, but not the worse emblem for that) a bird of courage, and would not hesitate to attack a grenadier of the British Guards, who should presume to invade his farmyard with a red coat on'.

Hammer and sickle

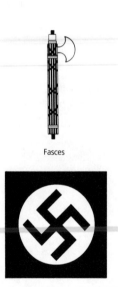

Fasces

Nazi *Hakenkreuz*

represented the industrial and agricultural workers, or the proletariat and the peasantry. More specifically, according to one official source, it symbolised 'the peaceful labour of Soviet people and the indestructible fraternal alliance of workers and peasant. It shows that all power in the land of the Soviet belongs to working people'. On the State Coat of Arms, approved on 6 July 1923, the emblem was depicted on a globe above the sun's rays, and framed by ears of grain with the inscription 'Workers of All Countries, Unite!' in the languages (from 1956 to 1991 in 15 languages) of the Union republics. It also appeared within a five-pointed red star on the earliest cap badges of the Red Army to symbolise the unity of the workers of five continents, and officially from 31 January 1924 on the Red Flag. Additionally, the emblem was used on stamps, official documents, treasury notes, medals and decorations, and buildings. Following the disintegration of the Soviet Union, the emblem was abandoned; the hammer and sickle flag was last flown above the Kremlin on 25 December 1991, and on 27 December it was replaced outside UN headquarters in New York by the former Russian tricolour. The emblem was also abandoned elsewhere. In the small European republic of San Marino, for instance, the Communist Party replaced it in favour of a dove* flying in front of three mountain peaks.

Fascism takes its name from the **fasces**, an ancient Roman symbol of authority and justice. The fasces (from Latin *fascis*, bundle) was a bundle of birch rods bound together with red thongs and enclosing an axe. It was carried in procession by the lictor, a functionary who attended the higher magistrates. The rods symbolised the authority to scourge, the axe the authority to behead. When Benito Mussolini (1883–1945) founded his Italian Nationalist Movement in March 1919, he chose for his badge a tricolour shield charged with the fasces to symbolise the unity of his organisation of war veterans, which he named the Fasci di Combattimento. This became known as the Fascist movement, and in 1922 the basis of the Fascist Party. The terms fascist and fascism have since been applied to similar right-wing or totalitarian movements in other countries.

The symbol of **nazism** is the **swastika*** or *Hakenkreuz* (German, 'hooked cross'). Adolf Hitler (1889–1945) is believed to have chosen it when he designed the banner for the German Workers' Party, which he renamed National Socialist German Workers' Party (NSDAP), in 1919. The most familiar form of the swastika in a white circle on a crimson background, used on the party's flag, badge, and armband, was de-signed under Hitler's instruction by a dentist, Dr Friedrich Krohn, in the summer of 1920. In the bible of Nazism *Mein Kampf* (My Struggle), which Hitler wrote in prison in 1923, he referred to the swastika as the symbol of 'the fight for the victory of Aryan man'. Some weeks after he was appointed Chancellor of Germany in January 1933, the swastika flag of his Third Reich was hoisted alongside the national colours. Officially adopted as the flag of Germany on 15 September 1935, it was the first political flag in the world to become a national flag. At the end of World War II in 1945, all forms of the swastika were banned by Allied occupation authorities. In recent years, however, the swastika has again returned to favour among some factions.

How Hitler came to choose the swastika – an ancient symbol of luck and fortune in many cultures (the word derives from Sanskrit *svasti*, 'good fortune') for the NSDAP is not known, although there have been numerous claims. According to one source, it was first proposed as a symbol for anti-Semitic organisations by the German nationalist poet

Guido von List in 1910. Von List mistakenly believed it to be uniquely Aryan and endowed with mystical significance. *Colombo's Canadian Quotations* cites an absurd claim, which appeared in the 'Golden Anniversary' edition (10 July 1969) of the *Northern Daily News*. This infers that Hitler embraced the idea of the swastika after his 'Nordic Goddess' Unity Mitford (1914–48) told him about it. Unity was the daughter of the eccentric Lord Redesdale, who lived in a log cabin near the gold-mining village of Swastika, five miles from Kirkland Lake, Ontario. The village had used the ancient swastika as a symbol of good luck at least since 1904. Unity did not meet Hitler until the late 1930s, by which time the Nazi swastika was well-established.

Echoing the swastika, is the three-armed device of the South African neo-Nazi Afrikaner Resistance Movement or Afrikaner Weerstandsbeweging (AWB), founded in 1973 by Eugene Terre Blanche. The AWB claims the device was adopted not for its resemblance to the swastika, but for its biblical origins.

The Jolly Roger

When pirates roamed the seas they displayed a variety of red, yellow, and black banners and flags to signal their presence and their intentions. During the 17th and 18th centuries especially, a few of the more enterprising 'gentlemen of fortune', as these freebooters preferred to call themselves, devised flags charged with emblems of mortality, such as a human skeleton, an hourglass, a skull and two crossed cutlasses, or Father Time wielding a scythe. More elaborate is the design quoted in *Flags at Sea* by Timothy Wilson: when a number of pirates were hanged at Newport, Rhode Island in 1723, their flag was fixed to the gallows. A contemporary account describes this as 'a Black Flag with the Pourtrature of Death having an Hour-Glass in one Hand, and a Dart in the other, at the end of which was the Form of a Heart with three Drops of Blood, falling from it'. The notorious Edward Teach, 'Blackbeard' (killed 1718) is said to have flown a similar flag.

How these flags acquired the ironic 'Jolly Roger' label is not known. The pirates hanged at Newport called their flag 'Old Roger', an early 18th-century nickname for the Devil; and in thieves' slang vagabonds and rogues were called 'rogers'. But whence the ironic 'jolly'? Two explanations derive the epithet from French: for his tailored red coat, the pirate Bartholomew Roberts was nicknamed 'Le Joli Rouge'; in English this came to mean the flag rather than the man. Equally plausible is the Jolly Roger as a corruption of *Jolie Rougère*, a red pennant flown by French buccaneers to show no quarter would be given.

Incidentally, although the design we associate most with the Jolly Roger, the skull and crossbones, has often been hoisted in romantic legend and literature, there is curiously little evidence of its use by pirates. Certainly it is an age-old symbol of death, and one which has been displayed on flags in more recent times. During World War II, submarines returning to base would sometimes fly the skull and crossbones to indicate 'a kill'; it was also flown occasionally during the Falklands War in 1982, and on some tanks during the Gulf War in 1991. Additionally, the symbol has been used as a military badge: in Nazi Germany it was the insignia of Himmler's *Schützstaffel*, or SS, and in the British army, together with the words 'Or Glory' it is the badge of the 17th/21st Lancers. Today it is most likely found on the helmets and jackets of Hell's Angels, and as a warning label on poisons.

Neo-Nazi symbol

Skull and crossbones

Flag of Edward Teach, 'Blackbeard' (killed 1718)

Flag of Bartholomew Roberts (1682–1722)

Death's flag

Flags are sometimes flown at half-mast, halfway up the flagstaff, as a signal of mourning. Traditionally, the reason for this custom, which began at sea during the early 17th century, is to leave space above for the invisible flag of Death. According to one source, the first time a flag was 'half-staffed' was on board the vessel *Heartsease* in July 1612, as a mark of respect to Captain James Hall, leader of an expedition in search of the North-West Passage, who was murdered by Eskimoes on the west coast of Greenland.

Chapter 7

Marksmanship
Marks of identity, origin, ownership

Ordnance Survey benchmark

Bishop mark, 12 July 1661

The word 'mark' encompasses a wide range of meanings. Almost as limitless in this respect as 'sign' or 'symbol', it is in many cases now commonly used instead of those labels. The following miscellany is predominantly a selection of marks past and present which indicate origin and ownership. It also includes a number of incidentals with which the word is linked.

Benchmark a surveyor's mark indicating a particular elevation, used as a point of reference in tidal observations and topographical surveys, or a point along a line of levels for determining the height above mean sea level. The mark, cut into rock, stone, or the face of a building such as a church, or as a brass plate fixed to a permanent object, is also found on maps, particularly those of the Ordnance Survey – so-named after the Board of Ordnance, which drew up the first official maps for the army in Britain in the late 18th century. The mark was devised sometime around 1840 by surmounting the King's Mark*, a broad arrowhead used to designate the property of the British sovereign, with a horizontal bar. When levelling or determining the height above sea-level, a surveyor fits an angle-iron into a notch in the bar to provide a temporary bracket or 'bench' upon which to support a levelling instrument. This bench is also a constant base on all subsequent occasions. In mining surveys, where the point is below sea-level, the mark is inverted.

The benchmark was first used by the Ordnance Survey in 1842 for levelling on the quay at Liverpool. This was the first constant, or Ordnance Datum (OD), from which all heights above sea level in Britain were measured. Since 1921, the constant has been the benchmark cut in 1914 on the quay at Newlyn in Cornwall.

By the end of the 19th century, the word 'benchmark', which first appeared at about the same time as the mark itself, was also being used figuratively as a reference point or standard against which some quality is measured. In *The Sunday Correspondent* in 1989, for example, Andy Gliniecki described the 'BBC microphone voice' as 'an important benchmark for spoken English'.

Bishop mark the **earliest postal datestamp** used by any Government Post. It was devised by Colonel Sir Henry Bishop, British Postmaster General (1660–63). Responding to complaints that letters were often delayed in the post, Bishop announced in *Mercurius Publicus* in April 1661: 'A stamp is invented that is putt upon every letter shewing the day of the moneth that every letter comes to the office, so that no Letter Carryer may dare detayne a letter from post to post . . .' The Bishop mark, forerunner of the modern postmark*, consisted of a small circle divided in two, one half bearing numerals for the day, the other a two letter abbreviation for the month. Initially used only in London (from 1661 to 1787), application of the Bishop mark spread to other cities, among them Dublin and Edinburgh, and in the late 18th century to Boston, New York, Philadelphia, Quebec, and Calcutta. Although all Bishop marks followed the same basic pattern, there were identifying variations in diameter, shape, layout of inscriptions, and sometimes colour.

Brandmark a mark burned on the hide of livestock with a hot iron to indicate identity and ownership, and thus aid recovery of strays or stock stolen by rustlers; derives from Old Norse *brandr*, 'to burn'. Evidence of branding dates back at least 4000 years to Egypt, where oxen belonging to a temple were sometimes branded with the symbol of a god. Spanish conquistadors introduced branding to the Americas in the 16th century. Their marks, usually very intricate, were gradually replaced with a wide variety of simpler designs. In *1001 Most-asked Questions About the American West*, Harry E. Chrisman gives an indication of brand designs with names such as the Scissors, Picket Pin, Rolling Swastika*, Two Up and Two Down, Crossed S, Gold Spectacles, Low Key, Crawfish, Pollywog Triangle, and the Ampersand*. Theodore Roosevelt used a Maltese Cross* design on his ranch in South Dakota; the Mexican revolutionary Pancho Villa had a brand resembling a human skull.

The first branding law in North America of February 1644 in Connecticut, ordered that all cattle and swine older than six months bear a brand or earmark*, and that such marks be registered by the first of May. A penalty for non-compliance was fixed at five shillings a head, two shillings of which were paid to informers. Today, in most US states brands are registered with a central agency. In the largest cattle state, Texas, where registration became law in 1838, each of the 254 counties maintains its own register. In some areas of the US, and everywhere in the UK, hot-iron branding has been supplanted by freezemarking*.

Any unbranded calf, cow or steer, is a 'maverick', named after a Texan lawyer of the 1840s, Samuel A. Maverick. In lieu of payment for legal services Maverick accepted 400 head of longhorn cattle; but he failed to brand them, and when he sold the herd some 11 years later, his buyer found less than he expected, as neighbouring ranchers had in the meantime branded Maverick's cattle with their own marks. By extension, the word maverick has since been applied to politicians, especially congressmen, who wear no party label.

Brands were not limited to livestock. In ancient times, slaves were sometimes branded with a mark of ownership; criminals too were branded as a punishment, often with a letter indicating the nature of the crime. In ancient Greece, such a mark or *stigma* (ultimately from the Greek 'puncture', and applied to either slave or criminal) was cut into the flesh or branded with a hot iron, and then fixed by rubbing colouring into the wound. False accusers were branded on the forehead with the letter κ, for *kalumnia*, whence the English 'calumny'; and recaptured slaves with φ, the initial of *pheutikos*, 'fugitive'. The Romans later adopted both the word, as *fugitivus*, and the practice. Interestingly, a person so marked in ancient Rome was said to be *litteratus*, 'lettered', a term used later to describe someone well-educated. In time, stigma came to mean any mark of shame.

In medieval Europe, such marks were widely used. In England, for example, blasphemers were branded on the forehead with B, rogues and renegades with R, vagabonds with a V on the breast, and brawlers or 'fraymakers' with F. Persons admitted in the Middle Ages to 'benefit of clergy' (trial in an ecclesiastical court, where punishments were less harsh than in a secular court) used to be branded with T for thief, and M for manslaughter. In both cases, the mark was branded on the brawn of the left thumb. Even as late as the Crimean War (1854–56), deserters in the British Army were branded with D, while soldiers who disgraced themselves and the regiment were marked with the letters B C, for bad character.

Ecuador, 1593

Texas, 1838

Montana, 1897

Wyoming, 1899

Essex Forest, 1908

Mark into name

Samuel Langhorne Clemens once said that he would never trust a man who knew only one way to spell a word. Perhaps he felt the same way about names. He derived his pseudonym Mark Twain from the call used by pilots on the Mississippi when taking soundings of the river's depth by a length of line marked at intervals. As the 'leadsman' threw the lead-weighted line, he called out the readings. One fathom (1 fathom: 6 ft/1.8 m) was 'mark one', two fathoms 'mark twain'. Twain, who had worked on the Mississippi, first used the name in 1862 in Nevada as city editor of the Virginia City *Enterprise*.

Irish Industrial Development Association. The lettering means 'Made in Ireland'

Harris Tweed 'Orb Mark'

In the American colonies, the Laws of Plymouth, Massachusetts, of 1645 state that 'Whosoever shall forge any deed shall be publickely whipt and burned in the face with a Roman F'. And in 1671, that burglars 'shall for the first offence be Branded on the right Hand with the letter B', for a second offence 'be branded on the other Hand and be severely whipped; and if either were committed on the Lord's day, his Brand to be set on his forehead'. During the same period, H was 'burnt in the Hand . . . for Heresie'.

In *The Man With the Branded Hand*, Frank Edward Kittredge writes of the first branding punishment imposed by a US federal court, at Pensacola, Florida in July 1844. Convicted of stealing seven slaves, ship's captain Jonathan Walker was sentenced to a year in jail for each of the seven, fined $600 for each, and branded with the initials SS for slave stealer on the palm of his right hand.

Broughton's mark in old boxing slang the pit of the stomach, so-named after the 'Father of Boxing' Jack Broughton, who was Champion of England from around 1734 to 1750. In addition to his skill in 'hitting his mark', Broughton invented boxing gloves and wrote the first code of rules governing the pugilistic art.

Cadency marks in English heraldry, a series of nine charges to differentiate or 'difference' the coats of arms of the sons in a family in order of birth (see Chapter 6).

Certification mark a registered device used in connection with certain goods to certify their origin – from a region rather than from one particular trader – or other particular characteristics such as quality, accuracy, material or mode of manufacture. Such marks are used in many countries throughout the world, by groups of peanut farmers in the US, for instance, or coffee producers in Colombia. Two notable examples of certification marks are the Kitemark* of the British Standards Institution, and the Woolmark*. In some countries, a certification mark may also be applied to certain services, such as the Good Housekeeping Seal of Approval in the US.

In Britain, the mark was introduced under the Trade Marks Act of 1905 as a **standardisation mark**. Under the 1938 Trade Marks Act, it was renamed **certification trade mark**. Occasionally, the mark is followed by the abbreviation ctm.

The first application for such a mark in Britain came from the Irish Industrial Development Association, which filed for registration in April and May 1906 in all 50 classes of goods. The second was the mark of the Union of Manufacturers of Cigars and Cigarettes of the Island of Cuba, in September 1907. Both marks have long since lapsed.

The **world's oldest surviving certification mark** in current use belongs to the Harris Tweed Association, which was formed for the promotion and protection of Harris Tweed. Registered in London in 1910, and subsequently in 40 other countries, the association's **Orb Mark** has since 1911 been stamped every three metres on the finished cloth, to guarantee its quality and authenticity as genuine Harris Tweed 'made from pure virgin wool produced in Scotland, spun, dyed and finished in the Outer Hebrides and handwoven by the Islanders at their own homes in the Islands of Lewis, Harris, Uist, Barra and their several purtenances and all known as the Outer Hebrides'. In addition, the mark features prominently on the association's garment labels. The orb device derives from the arms of the Earl of Dunmore in acknowledgement and appreciation of the role played by the Countess of Dunmore in promoting Harris Tweed for the benefit of the islanders in the 1850s.

Another British ctm familiar worldwide is the name SHEFFIELD. It was registered by The Master, Warden, Searchers, Assistants and Commonalty of the Company of Cutlers in Hallamshire in the County of York in 1924 to protect the goodwill in the city's name, which has been inextricably linked with metal goods for more than three centuries. (In a sense, the mark is also a rarity: except for food and drink, the registration of geographic names is not normally permitted.) Shown here is the new mark approved by the Department of Trade and Industry in 1992; the crossed daggers appear as a charge on the Company's coat of arms.

Chatter mark the riblike scar left by a chisel, drill, saw, screwdriver, or turning tool in a lathe, on the surface of the object being worked on. The term is also applied in geology to any of a series of such marks or grooves on a rock surface under glacier ice.

Earmark a distinctive mark on the ears of sheep or cattle for identification by owners or breeders. Sometimes used in conjunction with the animal's 'brand', an earmark may be a simple slit, or some more elaborate mark, cut or clipped on the ear. Such marks even have their own nomenclature. In his *1001 Most-Asked Questions About the American West*, Harry E. Chrisman gives as examples the overslope, underslope, overbit, crop, grub, swallow fork, and Jingle Bob – in which the ear was split and the lower cut left hanging loose.

Time was when humans also suffered earmarking. In the Laws for Menservants in Exodus 21, it is written: 'his master shall bore his ear through with an awl; and he shall serve him for ever'. And in 17th-century England, earmarking described the rather unsavoury practice – along with nose-slitting – of marking an offender in the pillory by cutting off his ears. In these more gentle times, the word is used mainly in connection with reserving something such as money or time for a specific purpose.

End mark or tailpiece, nondescript terms for an ornamental mark printed at the conclusion of an article, chapter, or book to indicate that it is finished. Rather more imaginative is the American term flubdub or dingbat for such typographical devices as the bullet point (●) used before itemised paragraphs, or the index or fist indicator (☞).

Firemark a distinctive metal plate issued by a fire insurance company and attached to the wall of an insured building for quick identification. The concept of fire insurance was born out of the devastation of the Great Fire of London in September 1666, in which more than 13 000 houses and churches – including St Paul's Cathedral – were destroyed.

To minimise losses, some of the new fire companies organised their own fire brigades, and to help them identify their policyholders' properties – which in those days were not numbered – they issued colourful plates bearing the company's name and symbol, and sometimes the policy number. Fixed to the walls of insured buildings, the plates or 'firemarks' also served as eyecatching advertisements. Initially, they were made of lead, but during the 19th century other materials were used, including copper, tin, iron, and porcelain.

⚔ SHEFFIELD ⚔ C.T.M.

Company of Cutlers

Ear, ear!

An unlikely sort of earmark cropped up in a story in the *Sunday Express* in April 1990. It concerned a burglar in Switzerland who specialised in raiding the homes of the rich in broad daylight. He would ring the doorbell, press his ear to the door, and then if no sound of movement came from within, set to work. By this simple method, he successfully relieved more than 30 absent owners of their valuables. Finally his technique caught up with him. What brought about his conviction were the ear prints he left on the doors which, in 11 cases, were positively identified.

© is for copyright

The symbol © has been used internationally since 1955 to signify that the material to which it is applied is protected by copyright. It was introduced by the Universal Copyright Convention (UCC), which was founded by UNESCO in Geneva in 1952. Unlike the ® symbol, © is not a registration mark in the UK, merely a warning signal against unauthorised reproduction. An interesting example of this appears on the front and back of currency notes issued by the Bank of England since 1990.

The **earliest known fire company in England** began operating in London's Threadneedle Street on 13 May 1680. It was established by Nicholas Barbon, whose baptismal name, incidentally, was 'If-Jesus-Christ-had-not-died-for-thee-thou-hadst-been-damned-Barebones'. Barbon's company, originally called simply the Fire Office, was renamed the Phenix in 1705. The company's policies were marked appropriately with an emblem of the mythical bird rising from the flames. The emblem may also have appeared on its firemarks, but the company ceased business by 1713, and no marks have been found. Such a symbolic figure was too good to disappear for long, and in 1782 a new company adopted both the name, with the more usual spelling for the Phoenix* Assurance Company, and the emblem for its policies and firemarks. Equally apt as a symbol on firemarks was the salamander* – a mythical creature which was reputed to eat fire. The creature appeared first on firemarks of the Salamander and Western Fire Assurance Society of 1803, and later on the arms of the Chartered Insurance Institute.

The **oldest existing mark**, issued by the Friendly Society of London (founded 1683), was a serpent. The Sun Fire Office (1710) was one of a number of companies to adopt the powerful 'Sun in his Splendour' emblem shown here, which was believed to avert the 'evil eye'. The British Fire Office used the lion* in different attitudes, Norwich Union showed the figure of Justice*, and the Yorkshire Insurance Company a view of York Minster. Britannia* and St George* were also popular figures. Other companies borrowed emblems from the civic arms of their place of origin. The Bristol Fire Office, for example, adopted a ship emerging from a castle gateway; the device of the Liverpool Fire Office was the liver bird. Hands clasped, a common symbol of union and friendship, was a popular device: the earliest such mark belonged to the Hand-in-Hand Fire Office which was established around 1696. Even more symbolic are the two pairs of hands on a cruciform plate shown here: one of a number of firemarks produced by the Union Assurance Society – alternatively known as the Double Hand-in-Hand (1714).

In the US, the earliest fire insurance companies also issued firemarks. These incorporated a variety of emblems, of which the most popular was the American eagle*. The Insurance Company of North America, founded in Philadelphia, for example, used the eagle from 1805 to 1815 in an attitude similar to the eagle on the military insignia of the period.

Once a common sight in many cities and towns, firemarks are now rarely seen outside museums and private collections.

'Sun in his Splendour': Sun Fire Office, 1710

Double 'Hand-in-Hand': Union Society, pre-1750

Flummux mark the term, according to Paul Dickson's *Words* for the old hobo mark of danger ☉; a house so-marked is a house to avoid. For a selection of other hobo marks see p.146.

Freezemark an identification mark on cattle made by a wire-faced copper iron, chilled in a mixture of solidified carbon dioxide (sometimes called 'dry ice') and an industrial alcohol, isopropanol, to a temperature of around −70° C (−94°F). On contact with the animal's clipped hide, the iron destroys the pigmentation cells in the hair, which then grows back white. This humane process, also known as cryobranding (from Greek *kryos*, 'cold'), was patented in 1966 by Dr R. K. Farrell of Pullman, Washington State. It has now largely replaced hot iron branding in many countries. Freezemarking was introduced into the UK in 1967. Cattle are marked with numbers or letters; occasionally symbols or the

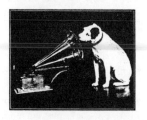

HMV past and present: the original 'dog picture', first used by His Master's Voice in 1909; and the outline version introduced in 1980 and for HMV shops

The **world's most famous musical trademark** of Nipper, a white fox terrier, with his ear cocked to a gramophone, originated as an affectionate portrait. The London artist, Francis Barraud, had inherited Nipper from his brother, who died unexpectedly in 1886. 'It suddenly occurred to me,' Barraud wrote some years later, 'that to have my dog listening to the Phonograph, with an intelligent and rather puzzled expression, and call it His Master's Voice, would make an excellent subject . . . it was certainly the happiest thought I ever had.'

The fruits of this 'happiest thought' were not immediate. Barraud had portrayed Nipper with his ear cocked to an 'Edison Commercial' Phonograph, an early dictaphone that used wax cylinders (although, according to James Playstead Wood's *Story of Advertising*, the object of Nipper's interest was really Barraud's brother's coffin!). Having copyrighted his 'dog looking at and listening to a Phonograph' as a work of art early in 1899, Barraud offered the painting to the Edison Bell Company who marketed the phonograph in Britain. It was rejected on the grounds that 'Dogs don't listen to phonographs'.

On 31 May 1899, Barraud went to the newly-formed London offices of The Gramophone Company (forebears of the giant EMI), where he left a photograph of his painting of the dog listening to a phonograph. Two days later, the General Manager of The Gramophone Company, wrote to Barraud asking him to call on him. Impressed with the painting, the company offered him £100 for the picture and copyright, on condition that he replace the phonograph with one of their disc gramophones. Barraud agreed, revised the picture in October 1899, and transferred the copyright on 29 January 1900.

Nipper's portrait first appeared on The Gramophone Company's record labels in the UK in 1909. The following July, the company registered the painting with its title 'His Master's Voice', as their official trademark. By this time, Nipper was already well established in the US as the emblem on the 'Victor' record label.

Today, EMI Records Limited continues to use the Nipper trademark (reproduced here by permission) on selected recordings; a stylised form of the original painting is used by HMV record shops throughout the UK and Europe.

owner's monogram may be used. As part of a national registration scheme, mainly for security, horses in Britain are also freezemarked with one letter and three numbers.

God's marks 16th-century term for the marks of the plague, or according to *The Oxford English Dictionary:* 'marks betokening impending death'.

Hallmark a set of four marks, comprising a sponsor's mark, standard mark, assay office mark, and date letter, stamped on an article of silver, gold, or platinum after it has been tested or 'assayed' by chemical analysis at Goldsmiths' Hall in the City of London – hence the term *hall*mark – or at other assay offices in the UK. Without the marks, no piece made in the UK may be described as silver, gold, or platinum, and legally sold in the UK. The control exercised by hallmarking is said to be the oldest and longest-surviving form of consumer protection. By extension, 'hallmark' is often used figuratively as any mark of genuineness or excellence.

Articles of silver, gold, and platinum are never 100 per cent pure, other 'base' metals being alloyed with them to make them harder and more usable. The concept of marking them as a guarantee of purity or *fineness* originated in France, where standards were set for the Paris goldsmiths in 1260.

In England, marking of gold and silver began officially in 1300, when a statute of Edward I decreed that no goldsmith – a term applied to smiths of both gold and silver – was to sell a piece until it had been

Leopard's head, 1300

Britannia

Lion passant

Lion rampant

Standard mark for platinum

London

Birmingham

Sheffield

Edinburgh

First date letter, 1478

Date letter for 1993

Maker's mark: Paul de Lamerie, London, 1736

assayed, to ensure that it did not contain more base metal than permitted, and marked. The process was rigorously controlled. Any piece 'not up to the mark' was destroyed; counterfeiting the hallmark incurred the death penalty.

The amount of pure **gold** in a piece is measured in carats. Derived from Arabic *qirat*, a carat is literally the 'bean' of the carob or locust tree. In ancient times, the bean was used as a weight for gold. By the Middle Ages 'carat' was being used only in name as a proportional measure of one twenty-fourth part. Thus 18-carat gold is 18/24 or 75 per cent pure. The **first standard in 1300**, set at 19.20 carats, was denoted by a leopard's head. Taken from the royal arms, this symbol was for a time known legally as the **King's Mark**. It was later replaced by other symbols, of which the most notable was a **lion passant***. Since 1975, UK assay offices have marked gold wares with a crown, followed by the relevant proportion of gold in parts per thousand.

The **first standard of purity for silver**, the sterling standard, was fixed at 92.5 per cent, the same as the coinage in 1300. As with gold, if a piece conformed to the standard, it was stamped with the leopard's head, and later with the lion passant. Apart from a brief period (1697–1720), when the standard was denoted by the figure of Britannia*, the lion passant has been the sterling or **standard mark** for English silver ever since. In Scotland the standard mark is a lion rampant; a thistle* has also been used from time to time.

Platinum was introduced into Europe from South America around 1750. The assay and marking of articles of this precious metal was not made compulsory until the Hallmarking Act of 1973. The standard mark – 950 parts per thousand – is an orb and cross. The first piece so marked at a ceremony in Goldsmiths' Hall on 2 January 1975, was appropriately a platinum medal awarded by the Institute of Metals to Professor Robert Hutton, a former chairman of the Assay Office Committee of the Goldsmiths' Company.

The **assay office mark** denotes where the piece was assayed. Shown here are the marks of the four offices in London, Birmingham, Sheffield, and Edinburgh. Former assay offices at Bristol, Chester, Exeter, Glasgow, Newcastle, Norwich, and York, derived their marks from their civic arms. Glasgow's mark, for instance, was 'an oak* tree, the trunk impaled with a fish*, on the top of the tree a bird and to the left of the tree a handbell'. There is also an assay office in Dublin, and marks struck there before 1 April 1923 are recognised as British hallmarks. The Dublin mark is a figure of Hibernia with one hand resting on a shield, in the other an olive* branch.

Used almost continuously since 1478, is the **date letter** – a letter of the alphabet* changed annually to indicate the year the piece was assayed. When the end of the alphabet is reached, the cycle begins again in a different letter style within a different shaped shield. Originally, the date for changing the letter was 19 May, the feast of St Dunstan, the patron saint of goldsmiths. Later, to commemorate Charles II's birthday in 1660, the changeover date was altered to 29 May. Since 1975, all UK Assay Offices have a common date letter, which is changed on 1 January. The letter for 1993 is T, for 1994 U, and so on.

The **sponsor's mark** identifies the manufacturer or sponsor of the article by his initials. Formerly called the maker's mark, it has been compulsory since a statute of 1363. Until 1739, it was a symbol adapted from the sign outside the smith's shop or a pun on his name, or the first two letters of his surname.

A fifth mark is sometimes found. From December 1784 until April 1890 a tax was levied on gold and silverware, and a **duty mark** depicting the Sovereign's head was struck to show it had been paid.

Occasionally, special marks are introduced. For the Accession in 1953, for example, an optional **Coronation Mark** bearing the crowned profile of Queen Elizabeth II was introduced for articles made between 1952 and 1954. A profile of the Queen was also used for the Silver Jubilee in 1977. In 1966, a torch mark was struck on Irish gold and silver to commemorate the 50th anniversary of the October Rising.

Both the UK and Ireland have the most exacting and comprehensive systems in the world. Among other countries with hallmarking laws are Austria, France, the Netherlands, Portugal, and Spain. Elsewhere, such as in Belgium and Denmark, a form of hallmarking is voluntary.

On 1 April 1975 the British Government ratified the International Convention of Hallmarking, under which articles assayed in one country and marked with a **Convention Hallmark** are accepted in another country without further testing or marking. Participating countries besides the UK are Austria, Denmark, Finland, Ireland, Norway, Portugal, Sweden, and Switzerland. A complete Convention Hallmark comprises a sponsor's mark, a common control mark (indicating the metal by its shape, and its fineness in parts per thousand), a fineness mark, and an assay office mark. For instance, on articles for export the two assay offices in Portugal (in Lisbon and Oporto) stamp a swallow* on gold, a sea-horse on silver, a parrot's head on platinum.

Housemark in marketing, a term for the overall trademark device used to identify a company's goods or services, as opposed to a brand, brand name or trademark* devised to identify one particular product or service. A housemark – also called **umbrella mark**, **family mark**, or more commonly today, **corporate logo** – consists typically of the company's name presented as a logo, fanciful letter device, or initials in a cypher* or monogram*. A prime example of a housemark is the ICI 'roundel'*, which is displayed on hundreds of the group's products worldwide, and on letterheads, staff uniforms, buildings and vehicles.

King's Mark term formerly applied to the broad arrowhead stamped or branded on Government stores and other 'royal' property used by the

ICI, one of the world's leading science-based groups with 'products addressing the essentials of life', describes its housemark as 'the single unifying force which brings together and links all the different parts'. The mark originated in 1923 as the logo of Nobel Industries Ltd, so-named after the Swedish chemist Alfred Bernhard Nobel (1833–96),

who invented dynamite in 1867.

Characteristically, the wavy lines are thought to represent the shock waves of an explosion. In December 1926, Nobel Industries amalgamated with three other companies to form Imperial Chemical Industries Limited. As the most attractive housemark of the four companies, Nobel's was adapted to become the ICI 'roundel'. Known until the 1950s as the 'Circle and Wavy Lines Device', the mark was updated in 1969, and revamped in 1987 by the London-based image consultants Wolff Olins. The waves were softened, the letters enlarged, and the blue and white colours reversed to make the roundel stronger.

Duty mark: Victoria

Coronation Mark, 1953

Complete hallmark (example)

Common control marks for Gold (18 carat, 14 carat, 9 carat), Silver (Sterling), and Platinum

King's Mark

Board of Ordnance – the department concerned with the supply of military equipment. Its origin has been explained in various ways, most commonly as deriving from the heraldic pheon* in the arms of Henry Sidney, Earl of Romney, who was Master General of the Ordnance from 1693 to 1702. Under an Act of 1698, use of the mark is described as being 'for the better preventing of the Imbezzlement of His Majesties Stores of War'. Other sources, however, ascribe the mark to a much earlier period. The naval captain and author Frederick Marryat dates its origins back to the 14th century. In his 1830 novel *The King's Own*, he writes that the broad-headed arrow was a mark 'assumed at the time of the Edwards (when it was considered the most powerful weapon of attack) as distinguishing the property of the King; and this mark has been continued down to the present day. Every article supplied to His Majesty's service from the arsenals and dockyards is thickly studded with this mark and to be found in possession of any property so marked is a capital offence, as it designates this property to the King's Own.'

By the end of the 18th century, the King's Mark was also being used on prison uniforms, 'as well to humiliate the wearers as to facilitate Discovery in the case of escapes'. Although such use of the mark ceased in the 1920s, it survives today as an instant identifier for cartoon convicts.

In the earliest hallmarks* on English gold and silver, the King's Mark refers to a leopard's head.

Marks on the move

Tramps, beggars, and, in the US, hoboes once had their own stock of marks which they chalked or scratched on gateposts and doors as warnings or recommendations to their fellow wanderers – sometimes known euphemistically in Britain as 'knights of the road' or 'milestone inspectors'. Shown here are some of the many marks noted by observers over the past 50 years in Britain, France, and North America.

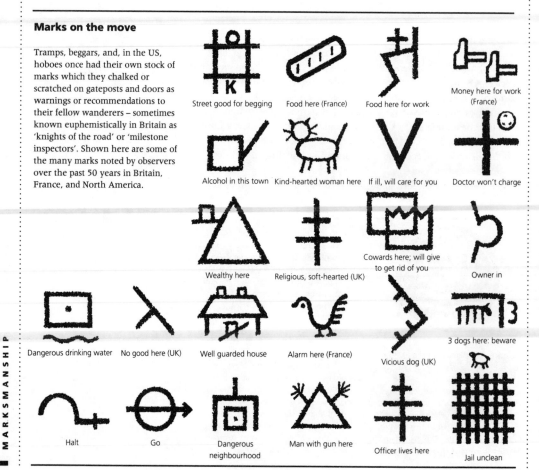

Street good for begging

Food here (France)

Food here for work

Money here for work (France)

Alcohol in this town

Kind-hearted woman here

If ill, will care for you

Doctor won't charge

Wealthy here

Religious, soft-hearted (UK)

Cowards here; will give to get rid of you

Owner in

Dangerous drinking water

No good here (UK)

Well guarded house

Alarm here (France)

Vicious dog (UK)

3 dogs here: beware

Halt

Go

Dangerous neighbourhood

Man with gun here

Officer lives here

Jail unclean

Kitemark the familiar name of the British Standard Mark, so-called because it resembles a toy kite. The device, formed as a monogram of the letters BS, is the certification trademark* of the British Standards Institution.

The Institution has its roots in the Engineering Standards Committee which was formed in April 1901. The committee's first recommendations resulted in a rationalisation of standards used to produce structural steel sections. Within a year, the sizes of sections had dropped from 175 to 113, while the 75 sizes of tramway rails were reduced to just five. This standardisation brought savings in steel production costs estimated at about £1 million a year. With such benefits to be gained, manufacturers called for more standards. By 1903 foundations were laid for the world's first national standards organisation – a voluntary body formed and maintained by industry, and approved and supported by the Government. To indicate to buyers that goods were 'up to standard' the British Standard Mark was introduced. It was first registered as a trademark for tramway rails in 1903. Standards for steam engines and railway lines, telegraph and telephone material, and electrical cable quickly followed.

Registration of the mark in Britain was accepted for all classes of product in 1922. The first licence for its use by a manufacturer to show that his product conformed to the British Standard was issued to the General Electric Company for light fittings in 1926.

In 1918, the Committee had been renamed British Engineering Standards Association. In 1931, the name was changed again to the current British Standards Institution (BSI). The Kitemark, BSI's principal mark, has since appeared on thousands of domestic and industrial products. Some of these, such as car seat belts and motorcyclists' helmets, must by law bear the Kitemark.

Among the other 'hallmarks' of quality introduced by the Institution over the years is the Safety Mark (like the Kitemark, reproduced here by permission), which denotes that a product complies with a British Standard specifically concerned with safety.

Merchants' marks personal marks widely used from the early 13th till the late 16th century in trade and commerce by merchants throughout Europe. The forerunner of today's trademark*, a merchant's identifier also stood for his integrity, and served as a guarantee that the goods he traded in – often from a number of sources – were of a uniform quality.

F. A. Girling, who identifies a wide variety in *English Merchants' Marks*, writes that such marks, which originated around the Baltic and along the lower Rhine, were derived from the Runic* alphabet. Typically the marks – many of them based on monograms* formed from the individual merchant's initials, or a visual pun on his name – consisted of a vertical stem with the main elements at the top and base and with additional arms and circles crossing or flanking the centre. Variants of the cross* were especially common, as were marks with the reversed '4', a symbol in use in other areas, such as watermarks* – though its significance is obscure. Initially simple, but becoming increasingly elaborate, the marks would be drawn, painted or scratched on the goods themselves, or on their canvas-covered bales, or branded on the casks. The marks also identified membership of a company or guild, which maintained records of both local and foreign marks – in some cases protected by law. When goods were sent by sea – often dispatched in two or more vessels for safety reasons – the marks were also inscribed

Kitemark

Safety Mark

Quality control

I was asked on to breakfast-time television to discuss the problems of condoms being sold without a 'Kite' mark (which shows that something has reached the recommended British standard). It was news to me that there was a relevant British standard, but nevertheless I sat through reels of film showing how the things are tested – usually by filling them to vast size with quantities of water or blowing them up till they gave way. The programme was live and I was acutely aware of cameras watching my face to detect the slightest twitch, as the monstrous things burst at the appropriate pressure.

Edwina Currie *Life Lines*

Merchant's mark, 14th century

Bartholomew Toote, 1470

on the bills of lading and in the ships' registers. Within the Hanseatic League – a Baltic-based trading association with posts throughout Europe by the late 15th century – marks on items were regarded as proof of legal ownership. As early as 1332, three Spanish merchants were able, by identifying their marks, to establish rightful claim to packages of wax salvaged in Flanders from a shipwreck. An English statute of 1353 provided that a merchant could 'obtain restitution for lost goods by proving ownership of the mark they bore'.

Towards the end of the 16th century, the use of the mark declined as travelling merchants were supplanted by fixed houses of trade, and their identifying symbols and marks replaced by shop signboards. The great majority of merchants' marks have long since vanished, though others may still be found both inside and outside merchants' properties, or on a merchant's tomb. Occasionally, when a merchant was granted arms, he incorporated his mark as a charge on his shield.

Mintmark in numismatics, any small symbol or letter on a coin to identify where it was struck. Mintmarks are found either in the *exergue* – that part of the coin separated from the main design by a line and usually occupied by the date – or at the beginning of the inscription, when the mark may also be called an **initial mark**. Commonly this was the initial letter of the name of the town or city where the mint was located. In the US for example, the New Orleans mint used the letter O for most of the years between 1838 and 1909, the Denver mint used the letter D between 1906 and 1964. At the principal US mint in Philadelphia no mintmarks were used, apart from some Jefferson nickels on which the letter P appears over the name of Jefferson's home at Monticello, Virginia. Some countries follow the system instituted in 1540 by Francis I of France, by which the letter A was assigned to the principal mint, and subsequent letters to subsidiary mints. Some supposed mintmarks are the personal marks of individual designers or engravers, or the mintmasters who issued the coins. In England in the Middle Ages, symbols used as mintmarks were often the personal badges of the monarch. Shown here are the voided cross* of Henry VI, the boar's head of Richard III, and the dragon* of Henry VII.

Royal mintmarks

Moll Thompson's mark to quote from an early edition of *Brewer's Dictionary* : 'as in "take away this bottle, it has Moll Thompson's mark on it" '. Moll Thompson is of course M.T.

Plimsoll mark the line on the side of a ship's hull indicating the amount of cargo it may safely carry, so-called after the Victorian MP and reformer Samuel Plimsoll (1824–98). Plimsoll campaigned to protect merchant sailors from unscrupulous shipowners who, being well-insured, were not overly concerned if their unseaworthy 'coffin-ships' sank from overloading. Plimsoll's tireless efforts, which earned him the name 'the Sailors' Friend', finally secured the passing of the Merchant Shipping Act in 1876. In addition to providing for strict Board of Trade inspection of all ocean-going vessels, the Act also made compulsory a load-line on the hull of such vessels to indicate the maximum amount of cargo with which they may legally and safely be loaded. Load-lines were subsequently established in many other countries. The first International Load Line Convention was adopted in 1930 by 54 maritime nations, with lines also being stipulated for ships in coastal and inland waters. In 1966, an international treaty set new load limits.

The Michelin man

As a rule, anthropomorphic trademarks tend to date and grow old even faster than their real-life counterparts. However, there are always exceptions, and one such mark that has survived the ravages of time, and indeed looks set to continue in the best of health well into the next century, is the amiable symbol for Michelin tyres, alias Monsieur Bibendum.

Shortly after André and Edouard Michelin produced the world's first pneumatic tyres for motor cars in 1895, they adopted the telling slogan *Le Pneu Michelin boit l'obstacle!* ('Michelin Tyres swallow obstacles').

Bibendum's story begins at the 1898 Lyons Exhibition where the manager of the Michelin stand had built a stack of tyres of varying sizes. To Edouard Michelin the stack suggested an armless man. Some weeks later, glancing through some examples of advertisements brought in by a popular commercial artist named O'Galop, André came across a sketch for a German brewer in which a portly gentleman with a beer mug was announcing *Nunc est Bibendum!!* ('Now is the time to drink!!'). Recalling the stack of tyres, André wondered if something along the same lines might not be possible with a man of tyres.

No sooner said, than done. O'Galop replaced the human drinker with a man of tyres, and the beer mug by a champagne glass brimming with nails and broken glass, and the toast was combined with the existing slogan. The Michelin man first appeared on a poster standing at a banqueting table between two deflated competitors. Raising his glass, he toasted 'Nunc est Bibendum – Your good health; Michelin tyres swallow obstacles'. Inevitably, the sobriquet 'Monsieur Bibendum' followed soon after.

Since his birth, Bibendum, or 'Old Rubber Ribs' as he is sometimes known, has been proclaiming the excellence of Michelin tyres in numerous guises and situations. O'Galop, for instance, went on to depict him as a wrestler pushing road hazards aside. Another advertisement, published in 1905 for the opening of Michelin's first London sales office has him as 'Sir Bibendum', complete with helmet and lance, and a shield emblazoned with the champagne glass brimming with broken glass and a tyre withstanding a long sharp nail.

Adopted in 1876, 'Plimsoll's mark' consists of a circle 12 in (30.5 cm) in diameter, horizontally bisected by a line 18 in (45.7 cm) long. It is accompanied by letters denoting the maritime authority under which the ship is registered – LR for example denotes Lloyd's Register, and AB the American Bureau of Shipping.

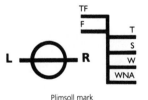

Plimsoll mark

Because ships float higher in saltwater than in fresh, and higher in cold water than in warm – due to density – there are different lines for different areas of the world and seasonal conditions. In saltwater, the safe loading limits are shown by the line marked IS for Indian Summer, S for summer, and W for winter. For winter in the North Atlantic where the worst weather is expected, the load-line is indicated by the letters WNA. In tropical saltwater, the letter T is used. In freshwaters, such as the North American Great Lakes, the letter F denotes the proper immersion mark, and for tropical freshwaters, such as the Amazon River, the letters TF.

As an incidental footnote to this, also named after Samuel Plimsoll are plimsoles, the rubber-soled canvas 'gymshoes' or 'sneakers', whose rubber rim around the shoe resembles a Plimsoll mark.

Postmark an official mark struck or impressed by hand or machine on an item of mail to identify the place of origin and date of posting, and to prevent re-use of the stamp. Philatelists usually define this last as a **cancellation**, or in the US, when designed especially to 'obliterate' a stamp, as a **killer**. A cancellation applied to a stamp before sale or use is called a **precancel**. A postmark struck on the back of an item to indicate arrival or transit is a **backstamp**.

The **first postal markings of any kind** date back around 5000 years to ancient Egypt, where letters of the court received red and blue markings with the exhortation 'In the name of the living king, speed!' In Europe, the earliest examples occurred at the beginning of the 14th century in Venice, where mail was marked in manuscript: *Cito, citissime, volantissime* – quickly, very quickly, very fleetingly.

At about the same time, the **earliest handstruck postmarks** identifying origin of posting were used in Milan. The marks bore the city's coat of arms and the inscription *Sub pena furcarum* – a warning to carriers not to hinder or tamper with the mail, 'under penalty of the forks', an instrument of torture. By 1425, the postmark carried the more precise threat: *Sub pena mille furcarum* – under penalty of a thousand forks. A later mark, which incorporated daggers and a star, is thought to represent the medieval limb-breaking rack.

The earliest marks identifying a letter's origin in England were applied to items sent in 1681 from the Chichester area to London. The impression, known as the 'hot-cross bun' mark, is said to resemble the basic town plan of Chichester. In North America the first mark bearing a placename was a two-line inscription for NEW YORK in 1756.

The **earliest postal datestamp** was the Bishop mark*, so-called after the British Postmaster General Henry Bishop, who invented it in 1661. The **first timestamp** was devised by William Dockwra for his private postal service, the London Penny Post, which was established in 1680. It consisted of a small heart-shaped stamp indicating the hour of dispatch. Dockwra also invented the **first mark recording prepayment of postage**. In the example shown here, L denotes the head office in Lyme Street.

Dockwra postmark, 1680

The **first cancellation** was used to obliterate the world's **first adhesive stamps** introduced in Britain by Rowland Hill on 6 May 1840. The device, based on the Tudor Rose* but inaccurately named 'Maltese Cross'*, was originally stamped in red ink, though in offices around the country other colours were also used, including blue, green, magenta, orange, ruby, vermilion, violet, and at Ormskirk in Scotland even pink. When the Swiss canton of Zürich adopted adhesive stamps in March 1843, they superimposed a Greek cross on the Maltese. This design, called the Zürich rosette, was also adopted by Geneva. Over the next 20 years, postal administrations around the world introduced a variety of cancellation marks, such as an oval grill in Buenos Aires, and a barred diamond in Toronto. To make doubly sure the ink could not be washed off and the stamp re-used, one Spanish postal official proposed corrosive ink, or – even more drastic – impregnating the paper with gunpowder so that the stamp would explode when struck with the canceller!

Maltese Cross cancellation, 1840

The term, incidentally, for collecting envelopes with postmarks is philometry.

Zürich rosette, 1843

Printers' marks devices used by the early printers to identify their work, initially at the end of the text. Such marks, which date from the

MARKSMANSHIP

15th century when printers were also their own publishers, were from the 17th century gradually supplanted by independent publishers' 'housemarks'* and 'imprints'.

The **earliest known mark** is the 'twin shields' device of Johannes Gutenberg's collaborators Johann Fust and Peter Schoeffer in their *Biblia Latina* of 1462. Their *Psalterium* of 1457 also bears the device, though this is believed to have been added by hand at a later date. The first English printer, William Caxton (*c.* 1422-91), based his mark on his initials. According to George D. Painter in his biography of Caxton, the marks between the initials can read as 47 or 74; the former refers to 1447, the year he was granted the freedom of the Mercers' Company, the latter to 1474, when he issued his first book – the first to be printed in English – his own version of a French romance *The Recuyell of the Historyes of Troye*.

As with many other marks of 'trade' during this period, Christian symbols such as the orb and cross* were commonplace. The example shown belonged to Dionysius Bertochus, who worked in Venice in the late 15th century. Some 400 years later, the Bertochus mark won a new lease of life when Adolphus Green of the National Biscuit Company – now generally known as Nabisco – suggested it for the company's housemark. Adopted in 1900, the mark has since been periodically reworked and updated.

Also popular were punning devices: Andrew Myllar of Edinburgh, for example, used a windmill, while the 16th-century London printer John Day, who printed the first exclamation mark* in England, identified his work with a symbol of the rising sun and the legend 'Arise, for it is Day'.

One of the best known marks was the dolphin* and anchor* adopted by the 15th-century printer and scholar Aldus Manutius for the press he founded in Venice in the 1490s, together with the popular Renaissance motto *Festina Lente* – Make Haste Slowly – the dolphin being an emblem of both diligence and swiftness. Referring to Manutius' mark in his classic *Moby Dick*, Herman Melville offers a rather different interpretation: 'As for the book-binder's whale winding like a vine-stalk round the stock of a descending anchor – as stamped and gilded on the

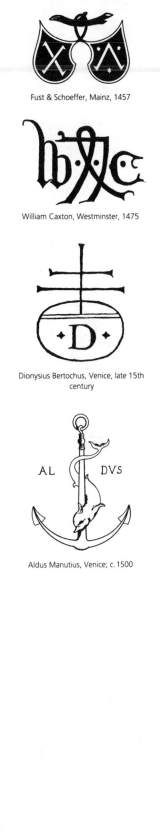

Fust & Schoeffer, Mainz, 1457

William Caxton, Westminster, 1475

Dionysius Bertochus, Venice, late 15th century

Aldus Manutius, Venice; c. 1500

No symbol is more synonymous with paperbacks than that of the penguin. It originated in 1935, when London publisher Allen Lane was preparing to launch a paperback reprint house aimed principally at the discerning but frugal bookbuying public. In line with these objectives, Lane searched for a 'dignified but flippant' name which could be easily depicted in black and white. In the penguin, he found both.

The first ten titles under the Penguin name and symbol (published 30 July 1935 at 6d *2.5p* each) were an immediate success. The original symbol, however, was not quite so well received. 'The notion behind it was to portray a light-hearted dancing version of the familiar bird', wrote William Emrys Williams in *The Penguin Story*, 'but to the more discriminating eye it always seemed to be a Penguin in the throes of appendicitis. Various amateur efforts were made during this time to improve the look of the symbol and, particularly, to iron out the expression of anguish, but the creature remained an eyesore to sensitive observation.' It was to be another 14 years before the company adopted the version still in use today.

Private eye

The world's first and most celebrated private detective agency, Pinkerton's National Detective Agency, was founded by Scottish-born Allan Pinkerton (1819–84) in Chicago in 1850. To symbolise his company's vigilance, Pinkerton adopted the trademark of a large wide-open eye together with the slogan 'we never sleep'. While Pinkerton's was soon nicknamed 'the eye' in underworld slang, its investigators 'for private hire' became known as 'private eyes'. This expression first appeared in fiction in 1938, in a Raymond Chandler story in *Dime Detective*. Chandler used it again the following year in *The Big Sleep*: 'Evening Cronjager. Meet Philip Marlowe, a private eye who's in a jam'.

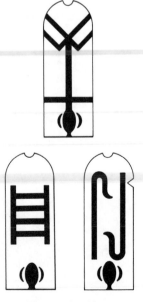

English swan-marks, 16th century

backs and title-pages of many books both old and new – that is a very picturesque but purely fabulous creature, imitated, I take it, from the like figures on antique vases. Though universally denominated a dolphin, I nevertheless call this book-binder's fish an attempt at a whale; because it was so intended when the device was first introduced. . . . in those days, and even down to a comparatively late period, dolphins were popularly supposed to be a species of the Leviathan.'

Scratch mark originally a mark or line scratched on gravel or turf as a starting point for a race, whence the various meanings of 'starting from scratch'. The idea survives in athletics – in the starter's orders 'on your marks' or 'take your marks'; and in horseracing, 'to scratch a horse' means it will not be coming up to scratch as it has been withdrawn. In the early days of boxing, too, opponents had to come up to the scratch mark and with their left foot 'toe the line' between them before the fight could begin. Additionally, according to *Brewer*, under the London Prize Ring Rules of 1839, a round ended when one of the fighters was knocked down. After a 30-second interval, the fallen fighter was given eight seconds to get back unaided to the starting mark. If he failed to make it 'up to the mark' or 'up to scratch', he was declared beaten.

By a similar process, the word **deadline** – now a time limit by which a task must be completed – derives from a boundary line marked some distance from the inner stockade of a Confederate military prison camp during the American Civil War (1861–65), 'over which no man could pass and live'.

Service mark a word, name, symbol, device, or any combination of these used to identify the services (such as advertising, banking, communication, etc.) of one person or organisation and distinguish them from those of another. In some countries, such marks have long been eligible for registration, for which the owner gains a legal monopoly. In the UK, the protection conferred on registered trademarks was not extended to service marks until an amendment to the Act of Parliament governing trademarks in 1984. As with trademarks*, registered service marks are denoted by the international symbol ®. Service marks, which have not been registered, are now sometimes denoted by the symbol ᔆᴹ, which was introduced from the US in the late 1980s.

Swan-mark a mark of ownership cut on a swan's beak. The swan* has been a royal bird in England since at least the 12th century. No one else was permitted to own a swan, although from the 15th century, rights were occasionally granted to favoured individuals or corporations such as the Livery Companies of the City of London. By the reign of Elizabeth I there were 900 licensed flocks or 'games' of swans, each with their own distinguishing nicks cut on the upper mandible. Today, only two city companies maintain the right to own and mark swans on the Thames: the Dyers, who were granted the privilege in 1473, and the Worshipful Company of Vintners who received theirs at around the same time. Both companies maintain Swan Wardens, and each July, they and their assistants – called swan-uppers, in reference to their taking up the birds from the water – accompany the Royal Swanherd upriver to round up the swans. The marks of the adults are examined, and the new season's cygnets of each family are marked accordingly: one nick for the Dyers' birds and two for the Vintners'. The Queen's swans are not marked; any unmarked adults and their cygnets belong automatically to the Crown. Formerly, the annual 'swan-up' used to take more than a fortnight; with today's swan population reduced to around 600, it is usually completed in less than half the time.

Touchmark sometime term for a maker's mark on antique pewterware. Like silver and gold, pewter in the Middle Ages was marked throughout Europe to show the quality of the metal and the workmanship, and the maker. A crowned X stood for best quality, as did a winged angel, the Crown – sometimes in combination with a hammer – and the Tudor Rose*. The Rose and Crown device also appeared as a symbol of quality in Holland, Germany, Austria, Hungary, France, Scandinavia, and America. Encouraged by the guilds, European pewterers first began officially to stamp their 'touch' or mark on their wares in the early Middle Ages. In 1382, pewterers in Paris were forbidden to sell their work without a mark. The practice spread to other pewter centres, notably to London where the Worshipful Company of Pewterers made marking compulsory in 1503. Typically, the marks consisted of the maker's initials. In addition, every craftsman admitted to the guild was also required to record his 'master-touch' on a touchplate – a pewter plate kept at Pewterers' Hall. When the Hall was destroyed in the Great Fire of 1666, so too were the touchplates. After the rebuilding of the Hall, this system of registration was resumed, and the resulting plates – containing 1090 marks, up until 1875, the last year a pewterer stamped his touch – reveal a wide variety of symbols and other pictorial devices, among them exotic animals like the camel*, elephant*, unicorn*, phoenix* and griffin*. Occasionally, the touchmark was a punning reference to the maker's name, such as the fly* used by the London pewterer Timothy Fly (1712–37). Touchplates were also introduced in other centres, notably York and Edinburgh.

'Quality mark', 17th century

Maker's mark: Timothy Fly, London pewterer (1712–37)

Pewter, an alloy of lead and tin, shines like silver when newly made, and in an attempt to exploit the resemblance, some pewterers in the 17th and 18th centuries also stamped their work with imitation hallmarks* – often four small shields in a row combining their initials with a lion passant* or some other mark. Scottish pewterers used the thistle*; Irish pewterers the harp or the figure of Hibernia. Eventually, after repeated objections from the Goldsmiths' Company, the practice was banned.

On early American pewter the rose and crown, and the lion rampant*, were favourite devices. After the War of Independence, pewterers replaced these royal symbols with the American eagle* or liberty cap, sometimes combined with stars, often in allusion to the current number of States in the Union.

Most recently, in 1970, a 'quality' mark appeared on pewter made by members of the newly-formed Association of British Pewter Craftsmen, to be used in addition to makers' own personal marks.

Trademark literally, any sign used by a trader to identify and distinguish his goods from the same or similar goods of a competitor. It can be a **wordmark** – a real or invented word or name, such as Rolls-Royce* (originated 1906) or Xerox (1946, from xerography, dry copying, coined from Greek *xeros*, 'dry', and *graphein*, 'to write'), or a **device mark** – a symbol, number, or distinctive shape: the 'golden arches' (1968) of McDonald's, for instance, or Michelin's Bibendum* (1898). A trademark may also be a composite of any of these: the most famous

A 'saintly' trademark

'There was to come a time when the mere mention of the Saint was sufficient to fill the most unimaginative malefactor with uneasy fears, when a man returning home late one night to find the sign of the Saint – a childish sketch of a little man with straight-line body and limbs, and an absurd halo over his round blank head – chalked upon his door, would be sent instinctively spinning round with his back to the nearest wall and his hand flying to his hip pocket, and an icy tingle of dread prickling up his spine.' So wrote Leslie Charteris in 1930 in *Enter the Saint*, his second book about the 'Robin Hood of modern crime' Simon Templar, alias 'the Saint'. The author's home-drawn haloed stickman, which he first registered as a trademark in 1935, became, and remained for many years, the best-known logo in fiction.

Early 'trademarks'

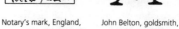

Jost Tauchen (1400–76), bronze founder, Germany

Notary's mark, England, 14th century

John Belton, goldsmith, England, c. 1525

T. Domingo, swordsmith, Toledo, Spain, 16th century

Michael van Orley, tapestry weaver, Flanders, Belgium, mid-17th century

Maximilian Wenger, armourer, Saxony, mid-17th century

Antoni Stradivari (1644–1737), violin maker, Cremona, Italy

example being Coca-Cola, whose name (invented in Atlanta, Georgia, in 1886) in flowing copperplate script above a sweeping 'wave' (derived from the shape of the bottle) has achieved a unique status worldwide.

The use of marks to distinguish goods or indicate their source of origin dates back to antiquity. Some of the oldest, incised on stones on the tombs of the first Egyptian kings around 3200 BC, are believed to denote either the masons who cut and prepared the blocks, or the quarry where the stone originated. Potters of ancient Greece scratched their names in letters or symbols on their work, or sometimes merely impressed their thumbprints in the wet clay. Identifying marks found on the bricks, tiles and other baked-clay items of ancient Rome, have been attributed to individual makers: wordmarks like CATIM (for *Cati manu*, from the hand of Cato), or punning device marks such as the head of a wolf (Latin, *lupus*) used by Marcus Rutilus Lupus, a maker of oil lamps.

To identify and acknowledge their workmanship (and, equally important, to avoid being held responsible for someone else's work), masons in medieval Europe signed the blocks of stone they worked on with a variety of geometric shapes or linear representations of their names. The value of such authentication was furthered by the guilds, who required members' work to bear both the guild symbol and a maker's mark. Marks were also imposed from outside: the earliest recorded reference to a trademark in English law appears in a statute of 1266 in the reign of Henry III for bakers to impress their bread with their

Tiny Big Blue

In April 1990, IBM, founded in 1911 as International Business Machines Corporation and now known affectionately as 'Big Blue' because of its size and corporate colour, became the proud, albeit temporary, owner of the **world's smallest logo**. To demonstrate a breakthrough in miniaturisation at IBM's Almaden Research Center in San Jose, California, two physicists etched the corporation's initials into a nickel crystal. According to *The Guinness Book of Records*, the resulting symbol was measured at 660 billionths of an inch. Using an instrument called a scanning tunnelling microscope, it took Donald Eigler and Erhard Schweizer 22 hours to drag 35 xenon atoms across the nickel surface, which had been chilled to near absolute zero. The symbol flew apart when the temperature rose above −228.89°C (−380°F).

own mark or seal. Subsequent laws include a London ordinance of 1373, which required bottlemakers to identify their vessels with their marks. By the end of the Middle Ages, such distinguishing devices were in use throughout Europe (compare hallmark, merchant's mark, printer's mark).

Over the next four centuries, both the use and variety of trademarks increased. By the late 19th century, when the rapid expansion of trade at home and abroad had brought many new manufacturers and their products into the marketplace, designs ranged from simple abstract devices and names printed in distinctive typefaces, to ornate labels incorporating a mass of informative text, and/or a facsimile signature (that of Arthur Guinness has appeared on bottles of 'Guinness's Extra Stout' in some form or another since 1759). Worthy testimony to the excellence of the product, signatures were often combined with engraved portraits of some well-respected personage or the product's inventor such as King Camp Gillette (safety razor, 1895), whose face adorned millions of packets of razor blades until as late as the 1960s.

Increased competition, however, greatly increased an age-old problem not only of deliberate plagiarism but also of unintended similarity in marks. Although trademarks had for centuries been afforded some protection in common law, entitlement to one had to be proved by

Million dollar marks

Illustrated below are the personal monograms and symbols of a dozen highly-prized artists. Can you identify them? Answers on p.158.

Answers on p.158.

The personal touch

'But who could make the final judgment between the original and the copy? A small cadre of experts, using modern laboratory techniques – and, of course, I myself. My private cipher is painted into every copy I make.'

'May I know what it is?'

'You may not. It's a personal mark which only I can identify.'

Morris West *Masterclass*

establishing usage over a number of years. This was easier said than done, and disputes sometimes entailed lengthy battles in court. These difficulties prompted new protection laws and the setting up of formal registration systems on both sides of the Atlantic.

In the UK, the Trade Marks Registration Act of 13 August 1875 provided for the trader both the opportunity to obtain a monopoly in his mark, and the right to sue for infringement simply on the basis of a certificate of registration. In addition, it established a register open to public inspection, so that traders could check whether a mark they were using or proposing to use was likely to conflict with someone else's registered mark. For the customer, official registration served as assurance that the mark was genuine and, by extension, could be trusted.

The Trade Marks Registry opened at the Patent Office off Chancery Lane in London on 1 January 1876. The **first mark to be registered** was the label with a red triangle for pale ale brewed by Bass & Co. The company, founded in 1777 by William Bass, had already been using the device since 1855. The Bass official, who is said to have braved a cold New Year's Eve on the Patent Office steps to guarantee first place in the queue when the doors opened at 10 o'clock the next morning, also secured the second registration for a label with a red diamond for the brewery's 'Burton Ale', and the third for a label with a brown diamond for its 'Porter and Extra Stout'. All three marks are still registered. Incidentally, the Bass archives hold more than 1900 attempts to imitate the red triangle, and in recent years the company has capitalised on this imitation with the legend: 'They copied our triangle because they couldn't match our beer'. The celebrated label also has the distinction of being the first official trademark to appear in a major work of art: the French impressionist Edouard Manet included two bottles with the prominent red triangle in his *Bar at the Folies Bergères* (1882).

While the Bass mark is generally acknowledged as the world's **oldest existing registered trademark**, it was not the first. Predating legislation in Britain by some five years was an Act in the US of 8 July 1870. The first applicant for registration was the Averill Chemical Paint Company of New York for a 'trade-mark for liquid paint' (the design included an eagle holding a paint-pot in its beak, and a streamer inscribed with the words 'Economical, Beautiful, Durable'). The 1870 Act, however, was declared unconstitutional and void, and official registration did not begin again in the US until after the introduction of a new Act on 3 March 1881. Since 1905 trademarks have been registered with the US Patent Office (established 1802). This federal agency, renamed the Patent and Trademark Office (PTO) shortly after the one millionth registration was recorded in 1974, now deals annually with around 30000 new registrations of trademarks, service marks*, certification marks*, and collective marks (those used by cooperatives, unions, etc.).

Over the years, the laws governing marks have been greatly revised and amended throughout the world. The most recent notable amendment in the UK was in 1986, when registration was extended to **service marks**.

In many countries today, marks registered in that country indicate that fact by the international symbol ®. To display the ® beside an unregistered mark is illegal; however, certain terms such as 'Trademark' may be used to indicate that the company intends to register the mark, or that it considers the mark its property under common law; more commonly displayed in this respect is the symbol ™, which was

Anthropomorphic marks
Nipper, Little Oscar, the Jolly Green Giant, Betty Crocker and others survive because character trademarks have the ability to evoke emotional responses, to stick in our memories, in a way that no abstract corporate logo can. The value of these characters is that they instill confidence in products and invoke in the mind of the consumer those all-important thoughts of trust, integrity and honesty. Faith in corporations may be shaky, but our belief in these symbols persists.

John Mendenhall *Character Trademarks*

invented in the US. Since the late 1980s, ™ has also been used in the UK.

While not compulsory in some countries (such as the UK), registration does ensure more immediate protection in the event of a dispute. In *Living By Design*, Alan Fletcher cites an example of what may happen to an unregistered mark: 'Unable to maintain the exclusivity of the word "Cola", the Coca-Cola Company undertook a worldwide programme to shorten their name to the colloquial "Coke". Instructions were given to register this name, and a company director in South America, who was a little slow off the mark, arrived at the appropriate registration office only to find an unscrupulous employee had got there first. They had to pay him a half a million pounds to buy back the name!'

Watermark a translucent design impressed into paper during manufacture. In its earliest form, the mark was made by attaching a design of fine wire to the sieve in the mould where the paper was made. Pressure of the wire against the pulp mixture pushed out water to leave a lighter image where the finished paper was fractionally thinner. In today's mass-produced paper, the mark is generally produced by the dandy-roll, a roller on a papermaking machine with a wire design which is impressed on to the pulp from above. Such marks created from paper thinning are called **negative watermarks**. Making a depression on the dandy-roll produces a **positive watermark**, which is slightly thicker than the surrounding paper.

The **oldest watermarks**, dating back to the late 13th century, are found on paper produced in Italy, about 150 years after the art of papermaking was introduced into Europe from the Near East. Shown here is an example of an early 14th-century mark from Fabriano, Italy, and one from Sele Mill, the first white papermill in Britain, which was established near Hertford in 1494.

Initially, watermarks consisted of simple designs, many of which were based on crosses, circles, letters, and numerals, including the reversed '4' often found in merchants' marks. Over the years designs became ever more diverse and elaborate with devices depicting the human face, parts of the body, animals, flowers, fruits, trees, ships, anchors, knots, tools, castles, towers, heraldic emblems, and mystic symbols.

The **earliest recorded watermark in the US** was the single word 'company' which was formed in paper, manufactured in 1690 by William Rittenhouse in his mill on the aptly-named Paper Mill Run, in Germantown, Pennsylvania.

It is not known if watermarks were originally created to identify the papermaker and his mill, or the sizes of his moulds and the paper made in them. In time they came to identify both. Before about 1850 the size of a sheet of paper was commonly identified by its watermark. The smallest size, for example, watermarked with a jug or pot, was named **Pot** or **Pott**; the next size known as **Foolscap** derives from a watermark of a jester's head with cap and bells. Although popular tradition has it that Oliver Cromwell ordered the royal arms watermark in the paper used by Parliament to be replaced by a fool's cap during the early 1650s, examples of the mark in England date back to before the time of Shakespeare. Other paper-size names derived from their marks include **Post**, from a post-horn, **Crown**, and **Elephant**. Sadly, such names have now been replaced, in Europe at least, by the dull but practical 'A'

Fabriano, Italy, 1301

Sele Mill, Hertford, 1495

Rostoff, 1555
'fool's cap'

Answers to the artists' marks on p.155:

1 Leonardo da Vinci, Italian 1452–1519
2 Albrecht Dürer, German 1471–1528
3 Antonio Allegri da Corregio, Italian 1494–1534
4 Buonarroti Michelangelo, Italian 1475–1564
5 Anton van Dyck, Dutch 1599–1641
6 Giovanni Battista Tiepolo, Italian 1696–1770
7 Joseph Mallord William Turner, English 1775–1851
8 Gabriel Charles Dante Rossetti, English 1828–82
9 Sir John Everett Millais, English 1829–96
10 Henri Marie Raymonde de Toulouse-Lautrec, French 1864–1901
11 James Jacques Joseph Tissot, French 1836–1902
12 James Abbott MacNeill Whistler, American 1834–1903

(from H. H. Caplan's *Classified Directory of Artists' Signatures, Symbols & Monograms*, and other sources)

Woolmark

Woolblendmark

and 'B' series of International Paper Sizes, of which A4 is probably the best known.

In addition to their use in all kinds of blank paper – often as trademarks and names of paper manufacturers, watermarks in the past were also created specifically on some printed items as security against counterfeiting. The world's first adhesive postage stamps issued in Britain on 6 May 1840 each bore a watermark of a small crown. Watermarking British stamps ceased in 1967. Similarly, marks were produced in paper for banknotes. The first such watermark, a looped border, scroll and a panel with 'Bank of England' at the bottom, was produced by a Berkshire papermaker in 1697 for the bank's handwritten notes, which, until fixed denominations were introduced in 1725, were of odd amounts that included shillings and pence, according to the customer's requirements. More recently, the bank's 'Series D' notes, introduced in 1971, carried remarkably detailed watermark portraits close to their printed portraits of the Duke of Wellington (on the £5 note), Florence Nightingale (£10) and Shakespeare (£20). The highest denomination of that series (£50), which depicts Christopher Wren, is watermarked with a portrait of the Queen. For convenience, future British notes will bear watermarks solely of the Sovereign.

Banknotes of many other currencies are also watermarked. The French 100 franc note, for example, is watermarked with a portrait of the 19th-century painter Eugène Delacroix, the Danish 20 kroner note with an artist's palette and brushes.

Woolmark probably the world's best known certification trademark*. Designed in 1964 by Francesco Sarolgia, an Italian advertising art director, to symbolise a skein of wool, the symbol was chosen by an international jury from 86 designs. Owned by the International Wool Secretariat (IWS) and registered as a trademark in more than 120 countries, the Woolmark was introduced to protect the standards and integrity of wool products at a time when the trade was facing stiff competition from a number of other natural and new man-made fibres.

Used under licence in 69 countries by more than 14 000 companies, whose 500 million customers associate it with 'quality, assurance and naturalness', the Woolmark is applied only to products made from pure new wool. These include knitted and tailored garments, blankets and carpets, which conform to strict quality specifications and performance standards prescribed and controlled by the IWS.

In 1971, the IWS introduced the **Woolblendmark** (registered in more than 70 countries) to identify quality goods with a minimum new wool content of 60 per cent, or in the case of wool/cotton blends a minimum wool content of 55 per cent.

Mobile marques and mascots

Since the early days of motoring, manufacturers have devised distinctive and often highly elaborate badges and mascots* to adorn the bonnets and radiators of their cars, not merely to identify them but also to symbolise their qualities. Here are the stories behind some of the names and marques currently to be seen on highways and byways almost anywhere in the world.

Alfa Romeo links the names of Nicola Romeo, who made his money in earth-moving equipment in Milan, and Anonima Lombardo Fabbrica Automobili or ALFA, the company he took over in 1915. The red cross on a white field and crowned serpent devouring a human figure derive from the coat of arms of the Visconti family, the dukes of Milan. The serpent is said to represent a marauding dragon* in the Milan area in the early 5th century AD, which was slain by Umberto, the traditional founder of the Visconti family. The cross dates from the time of the first Crusade (1095–99) in which an army from Lombardy was involved. For many years the badge was surrounded by a laurel* wreath. This was added in 1926 to commemorate the company's Grand Prix victory in the 1925 World Championship.

Aston Martin combines founder Lionel Martin's name with the Aston Clinton Hill Climb in Buckinghamshire, in which Martin's cars frequently won renown after World War I. The winged badge, designed in 1932 by the racing driver and journalist S. C. H. 'Sammy' Davis, was inspired by the scarab or dung-beetle – the Egyptian symbol of the renewal of life – and the wings of hawks in Egyptian art. Initially wholly black, the badge is now green with gilded wing ribs.

Audi was founded in 1909 by August Horch, shortly after he was forced to leave Horch Werke, the company he had established 10 years earlier. When that company objected to his calling the new venture August Horch Automobilwerke, he Latinised his surname to Audi, of which the nearest English equivalent is Hark! In 1932, the rivals came together when they amalgamated with two other German car companies, DKW and Wanderer, to become the consortium Auto-Union. Owned by Volkswagen* since 1964, Audi retains as its marque a version of the four-ring symbol created in 1932 to represent the amalgamation of the four companies.

BMW stands for Bayerische Motoren Werke, which was formed in 1916 from the merger of Rapp Flugmotorenwerke and Otto-Werke, two small aero-engine manufacturers. The first design for a BMW emblem, in 1917, represented a rotating aircraft propeller. By 1920, the propeller image had been reworked and highly stylised into the solid quarters of the Bavarian state colours of blue and white. The current badge, almost unchanged from those early days, first appeared on BMW's cars and motorcycles in 1963.

Cadillac whose first model was built in 1902, is named in honour of the French explorer Antoine de la Mothe Cadillac, who in 1701 founded the town of Ville d'Etroite, now better known as the world's car manufacturing capital, Detroit (Michigan, US). The company's badge derives from the ancient arms of the Mothe family. The wide band in the first and fourth quarterings is the 'fess'* or 'military girdle of honour', which is said to have been granted for valour in the Crusades. The two groups of birds (three for the Trinity) are merlettes, heraldic versions of the martin; depicted in black against a gold background, they denote 'wisdom, riches, and cleverness of mind'. According to Cadillac, the tinctures silver and red in the second and third quarterings represent purity, charity, virtue and plenty, and 'marked prowess and boldness in action' respectively.

Citroën founded by André Citroën in Paris in 1913 as the Citroën Gear Company. To work more smoothly and quietly, the teeth on the gear wheels he produced were of a double-helical or chevron* design. When

Citroën converted his factory to manufacturing Europe's first mass-produced car – the first, a Torpedo, coming off the line in May 1919 – he adapted the chevron pattern of the original gears for his badge. It has been the company's emblem ever since in one form or another, though somewhat scaled down in size now from that used in the 1930s when it was positioned over the whole radiator. In 1922, Citroën engineered widespread recognition of the chevron by donating 150 000 panels emblazoned with it for use in overhauling and improving signposting throughout France. Three years later, on 4 July 1925, the company scored another notable marketing success with a vertical sign of the name and emblem on the Eiffel Tower. Illuminated by 250 000 lamps in six colours, the sign was – according to *The Guinness Book of Records* – the most conspicuous ever erected, being visible 24 miles (38 km) away. The sign was dismantled in 1936.

Ferrari founded by Enzo Ferrari in 1929, produces one of the world's most renowned status symbols. No less renowned is the company's *cavallino rampante* – the prancing horse* emblem. This was initially sported on the fuselage of the fighter flown by the Italian air ace Francesco Baracca, who was shot down in 1918. Ferrari adopted the emblem by invitation of Barraca's mother shortly after his victory in the first Savio Circuit race at Ravenna in 1923. As a background for the horse, he added the canary yellow of Modena, the closest city to Maranello where the cars are made; the green, white and red at the top of the badge are Italy's national colours.

Jaguar evolved from the Swallow Sidecar Company, formed in Blackpool by William Lyons on his 21st birthday, 4 September 1922, to manufacture sidecars for motorcycles. Its emblem was a swallow* in flight. Within five years, the company was also making car bodies for the Austin Seven, and for Swift, Standard, and Wolseley. In 1931, the Swallow Sidecar and Coachbuilding Company produced its first original car, the 'SS', which was represented by the initials in a hexagonal badge. Seeking a new name and image for its 1935 models from a list of around 500 possibles, 'jaguar' – with its connotations of speed, power, and beauty – emerged a clear winner. The 'SS Jaguar' first appeared in September that year, with a radiator badge based on the popular 'wings' theme. Some years later this was supplanted by a jaguar head. After the war, the company dropped the SS initials – then too closely associated with Himmler's *Schützstaffel* – and adopted the title Jaguar Cars Ltd.

The first mascot – a standing jaguar in chrome plated brass – was not a success. It was replaced in 1938 by a 7 in (17.8 cm) leaping jaguar, sculpted by the company's public relations manager E. W. 'Bill' Rankin and offered as an optional extra for two guineas (£2.10). A stylised jaguar head with winged emblem was fitted as standard on the radiator grill from 1950 to 1956 when a smaller leaping jaguar was introduced. This was withdrawn in the mid-1960s, mainly because of safety regulations in North America.

Lancia founded in Turin in 1906 by two former test drivers for Fiat, Vincenzo Lancia and Claudio Fogolin. Its emblem, a standard on a lance – wordplay on Lancia's name and *lancia*, Italian, 'lance' – superimposed on a four-spoked steering wheel within a shield, was designed by the Italian motoring pioneer Count Biscaretti di Ruffia in 1910. It first appeared that same year on the Lancia 'Gamma' in a slightly more elaborate form than today's emblem.

Mercedes-Benz formed in 1926 as Daimler-Benz AG, united the names and symbols of the two pioneers of the motor industry: Karl Benz, who built the world's first successful petrol-engined car – a three-wheeler – in 1886, and Gottlieb Daimler, who, that same year, built the first four-wheeler. After Daimler died in 1900, his two sons took over the company. Casting around for a distinctive trademark, they recalled a postcard their father had once sent his wife on which he had drawn a star which he hoped would one day rise over the Daimler factory and bring prosperity. Both a three-pointed and four-pointed star were registered in 1909, but it was the three-pointed star – said to represent supremacy on land, water, and in the air – which was adopted. For his trademark, Benz had chosen a gearwheel in 1903; six years later he replaced it with a laurel wreath. To symbolise the 1926 merger, this was combined with Daimler's star. The current plain ring and star emblem became a standard fitment in 1937.

No less distinctive is the name by which all the company's vehicles are now most familiarly known. In 1899, an Austrian businessman, diplomat and motor-racing enthusiast, Emil Jellinek, had won the Nice Speed Trials under the pseudonym Monsieur Mercedes, after his daughter's name Mercédès (derived ultimately from the Spanish for 'mercy'). The following year, Jellinek secured the rights to sell the new Daimler 'Simplex' in Austria and France under the same name, which soon became so well-known and liked that the company adopted it for all subsequent models. Incidentally, by 1903 Jellinek himself was so enamoured of the 'Mercedes' cachet that he officially renamed the family Jellinek-Mercedes.

MG for many years synonymous with sports cars, stood originally for Morris Garages, the retail outlet of the growing Morris factory at Cowley near Oxford. Cecil Kimber, the Garages' general manager, began modifying Morris Oxfords in 1924 under the name M. G. Super Sports. In 1928, he produced the M. G. Midget. Based initially on the Morris Minor, it was Britain's first popular affordable sports car. The badge, which Kimber devised and registered in 1928, is said to derive from an octagonal bolt head. It appeared on bonnet catches and door handles; the octagon was also engraved on the wheel hubs, the gear-lever knob, and dashboard controls.

Mitsubishi one of the largest companies in the world, originated in 1870 as a local shipping business, founded by Yataro Iwasaki. It was established under the name Mitsubishi in 1886. The trademark of three equilaterally placed diamonds derives ultimately from Iwasaki's family crest or mon*. First used for Mitsubishi Motors in 1917, the mark has evolved over the years into the distinctive three diamond shape, usually in the most popular Japanese colour of red. Each of the diamonds, the company claims, embodies a Mitsubishi principle: 'corporate responsibility to society, integrity, and international understanding through trade'.

Nissan the world's fifth largest car manufacturer, was established in 1933 jointly by two companies, Nihon Sangyo and Tobate Imono, to manufacture and sell the Datsun car. Initially called Jidosha Seize, the company was renamed Nissan in June 1934, when Nihon Sangyo ('Ni' means Japan, and 'San' industry) became the sole owner. However, the Datsun name continued to be used in the West as late as 1982, when it was phased out in favour of Nissan. In the logo, the red circle symbolises the rising sun, and the blue rectangle represents the sky. The concept behind the logo, Nissan claims, is the proverb 'sincerity brings success'.

Peugeot dates back to 1810, when Jean-Pierre Peugeot converted the family's corn mill in eastern France's Montbeliard region into a cold roll metal mill, making tools and springs. By mid-century the company's output also included umbrella frames, coffee grinders, hoops for ladies' crinoline, and springs for pince-nez spectacles. In the 1880s Jean-Pierre's grandson Armand turned his attention to more mobile products – the first being a bicycle with wooden wheels. The first Peugeot car was built in 1890, and the following year production began in earnest, reaching, by 1900, almost a car a day. Today, all Peugeot advertising carries the slogan 'the lion goes from strength to strength', an allusion to the emblem which first appeared in 1858 to symbolise the strength of the company's steel products, particularly the teeth and cutting efficiency of its famous saws. The emblem has been periodically updated; the current stylised lion rampant* was introduced in 1978. Two other factors link Peugeot with the lion: Montbeliard is in the province of Franche-Comté which has a lion in its arms, and the factories are grouped near the fortress town of Belfort – where the monumental Lion of Belfort commemorates an unsuccessful German siege of the city in 1871. That lion, incidentally, was sculpted by Auguste Bartholdi, perhaps better known for the 'Statue of Liberty enlightening the world' at the entrance to New York Harbour.

Porsche is named after the German designer Dr Ferdinand Porsche, whose many innovations include a solar energy system to drive a car using electric motors in the wheel hubs (patented 1897), and in the mid-1930s the initial design of the world's best-selling car, the Volkswagen Beetle. Although Dr Porsche set up his own design office in 1931, it was not until 1948 that his son Ferry developed the first of the cars using the name Porsche. Production began in Stuttgart in 1950. The prancing horse* in the company's badge comes from the arms of Stuttgart, which was founded in the Middle Ages on the site of a stud farm (originally *Stuten Garten*, 'Garden of the Mares'); the stag's antlers and red and black stripes derive from the arms of the old kingdom of

Wuerttemberg of which Stuttgart was the capital. The combined 'coat of arms' and inscription have been used on Porsche cars since 1952.

Renault was founded in the late 1890s. Although the company's catalogues, repair and maintenance manuals, and some other printed documents, bore a variety of emblems, including a cogged wheel enclosing a frontal view of the first car, the vehicles themselves carried no badge until 1922, when a circular motif with the Renault name sandwiched between horizontal bars was introduced. The motif represented a metal grill which covered a hole in the curved bonnet to allow the passage of sound from the klaxon. When the grill was redesigned to a diamond shape or *losange* in 1924, the badge was reworked accordingly. A new *losange* in yellow, black, and white, was devised by the sculptor and graphic designer Victor Vasarély in 1973. The current badge and corporate logo shown here was introduced in 1992 to reflect the radical transformation of the company in recent years.

Rolls-Royce 'the symbol of Britishness' was born out of a meeting at the Midland Hotel, Manchester, in May 1904 between the Honourable Charles Rolls, an accomplished speed driver, who had started his own business in 1902, selling continental cars to the aristocracy, and Henry Royce, a designer and manufacturer of electric motors and cranes who, being dissatisfied with motor cars then on the market, had set about designing his own. The two formally joined forces in 1906 under the title Rolls-Royce Ltd. The first of the famous 'Silver Ghost' models was built later that year. The company's badge, soon to become one of the world's most prestigious, also appeared in 1906. One story, probably apocryphal, goes that Royce designed the 'RR' monogram one evening in 1905 on a restaurant tablecloth, then had to purchase the cloth so that he could take the design away with him. The badge, originally red, was changed to black in 1930 to make it more compatible with new colour schemes (not, as commonly thought, to mark the death of Royce in 1933).

Rolls-Royce cars also bear the **world's most famous mascot**. Titled the 'Spirit of Ecstasy', this carved figure of a fairy with her outstretched arms, fluttering draperies, and eyes fixed keenly on the road ahead, was designed by Charles Sykes in 1911 to convey the car's spirit of silent speed, grace and beauty, and to combat a 'rash' of 'frivolous and vulgar' ornaments, such as black cats, gollywogs and policemen, that owners were fitting to the cars' radiator water caps. 'The Flying Lady', as she was soon nicknamed, was also the first metal motor car mascot made in Britain – initially of white metal, then commonly bronze, and later chromium plate. A number of versions of this 'obligatory' extra were produced, including a kneeling version in 1934.

Rover dates back to 1884, when Coventry cycle makers Starley & Sutton adopted the name for their special tricycle design, which they considered the ideal vehicle for 'roving' around the countryside. The name proved so popular, it was adopted as the brand name for all products under the newly-titled Rover Cycle Company, with the word Rover stamped on various shield-shaped badges on the front of cycles. The earliest Rover cars, built in 1904, included the company name only on the hub caps. Rover's Viking theme, with its obvious symbolic association, began in 1922 with a Viking warrior mascot. Offered first as an optional extra for fitment to the radiator cap, the mascot later included a spear or battleaxe as well as a shield. In the first 'Longship' badge, introduced in 1929, the prow and billowing sails of the ship were outlined by a shield with acanthus leaves arranged in the form of waves. As the designs of the cars changed over the years, the badge was frequently reworked, becoming more representational with detailed planking, oars and blue water. The current stylised badge was introduced in 1990.

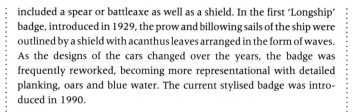

Saab combines two Swedish companies, SAAB – the initials of Svenska Aeroplan Aktiebolaget (Swedish Aeroplane Company) – founded in 1937, and the commercial vehicle company Scania-Vabis. The Vagnfabriksaktiebolaget i Sodertalje (Wagon Factory Company in Sodertalje), or VABIS for short, was established in 1891 to build railway rolling-stock. In 1911, it merged with Maskinfabriksaktiebolaget Scania of Malmö, who had begun producing cars in 1901 with the emblem of the mythical griffin*. The griffin derives from the arms of Scania, the Latin name of the southern Swedish province of Skåne, of which Malmö is the capital. The first logo for Saab, which began car production in the late 1940s, depicted one of their early twin-engined propeller aircraft head-on. Following the merger with Scania-Vabis in 1969, the logo was changed to the Saab initials in white on a blue background. The new logo of the griffin within two circles, was designed by Carl Fredrik Reuterswärd in 1984 to symbolise the group as a whole.

Skoda named after Emil Ritter von Skoda, who founded his own forge in Pilsen, Bohemia, in the late 1860s. By the end of the century, the company was manufacturing armaments, locomotives, and general engineering products; by the early 1920s, production included aircraft engines and tractors. The first Skoda cars were produced in 1925, following a merger with Laurin & Klement, a prominent Bohemian cycle business which had diversified into cars in 1905. Skoda is now separate from the original company. Its logo of a highly stylised winged arrow was designed to express its ideals – the arrow represents technological advance, the wing 'the creative human spirit', and the eye vigilance.

Subaru the auto division of the Japanese combine Fuji Heavy Industries. The stars represent the six brightest stars of the Pleiades (*Subaru* in Japanese), the open cluster known also as the 'Seven Sisters', the daughters of the Greek Titan Atlas, who were transformed into stars. The badge was introduced when car production began in 1958.

Toyota founded in Japan in 1937 by Kiichiro Toyoda, with the proceeds from the sale of his father's loom patent rights to a British company. Initially called Toyoda, the company was renamed Toyota as a result of a competition for a new logo. Besides looking and sounding better than 'toyoda', the winning design comprised eight characters – an auspicious number in Japan. This design was not adopted when Toyota began expansion into Western markets in the 1960s, and the company was without a pictorial emblem until 1989 when the 'ellipses' were introduced: they comprise a vertical and horizontal ellipse, which together form a 'T', enclosed by a third unifying ellipse for the company's 'spirit of creativity in design'. The overall background space is said to represent the company's technological expansion and future opportunities.

Vauxhall takes its name from an area on the south bank of the Thames, where, by an influential marriage, a Norman mercenary, one Fulk le Breant, acquired a house in the early 13th century. In time, the house became known as Fulk's Hall, and ultimately as Vauxhall. When Alexander Wilson founded an engineering firm in the area in 1857 to produce engines for Thames tugs and steamers, he adopted le Breant's griffin* device for his company emblem. In 1903, the company – by then renamed the Vauxhall Iron Works Company – built its first car. Two years later, the company moved to Luton, where, coincidentally, some seven centuries earlier, Fulk le Breant had been granted the Manor of Luton for services to King John.

Volkswagen means 'People's Car'. Conceived in 1934 by the government of the German Reich as the perfect small car, it was designed by Professor Ferdinand Porsche. When Hitler laid the foundation stone of the Volkswagen factory near Fallersleben, about 50 miles (80 km) east of Hanover, on 26 May 1938, he announced that the car would be known as the KdF-Wagen – *Kraft durch Freude Wagen* – literally, 'Strength through Joy Car'. At the same time, construction also began on a new town for the workforce, which was provisionally called 'The Town of the Strength through Joy Car'. When the company was resurrected in 1945 by the British Military Government, the town was officially named Wolfsburg after the nearby castle of Wolfsburg, whose arms also inspired the car's first emblem of a wolf* atop a castle. The emblem adorned the steering wheel centre and the gearstick. Later, with the car in production in so many other countries, the Wolfsburg badge was replaced by the VW roundel, which had first appeared in drawings in 1937.

Incidentally, after the War both the British and Americans were invited to take a hand in redeveloping and marketing the Volkswagen. Both declined. Lord Rootes, heading the British Motor Industry commission to Wolfsburg, decided it did not meet 'the fundamental requirements of a motor car'. Speaking for the American side, a director reported back to Henry Ford II: 'I don't think that what we are being offered here is worth a damn!' How wrong they were. The 'Beetle', as it was nicknamed, became the best-selling car of all time, and the VW roundel one of the world's most familiar marques.

Volvo means literally 'I roll' in Latin. In 1924, Assar Gabrielson, sales manager of the Swedish ball-bearing manufacturer SKF, teamed up with a former SKF designer Gustaf Larson to build cars. Impressed by the initial designs, SKF provided factory premises, credit for 1000 vehicles, and the name AB Volvo, which the company had registered as a trademark some years earlier and then discarded. When the first Volvo – nicknamed 'Jakob' – came off the production line in Gothenburg in April 1927, it bore on the radiator the now familiar diagonal cross-brace with an arrowed circle. The latter, a conventional map symbol for iron, alludes to SKF and Sweden's iron and steel industry which provided the raw materials for the new car. Since 1975, the use of this device (which is also the biological symbol for male, and in astrology and astronomy the symbol for Mars*) has been restricted solely to product identification with the cross-brace.

Doves and dragons
Animal and plant symbolism

Birds and beasts have played a leading role in the symbolism of every age and culture. The ancient Egyptians, for instance, depicted their gods with the heads of animals whose qualities they were thought to possess. Birds, too, were commonly used to symbolise freedom, the soul and its transcendence from the body, or the spiritual from the earthly. Because of their soaring flight and far-sighted vision, birds were also frequently associated with divinity, power, victory; in mythologies worldwide they are the messengers of the gods (a concept which survives in the expression 'a little bird told me'). Since medieval times, animals have been adopted in heraldic arms and badges to embody qualities and virtues possessed by one person, family, or community. Fabulous creatures, such as the unicorn and griffin, were compounded from natural beasts and used symbolically to great effect. Conspicuously less fantastic, but no less important in our stock of traditional symbols, are those derived from the plant world.

Once again, many of the 'visual metaphors' in this chapter are associated with Christianity, either directly or indirectly. A number of symbols from other cultures and civilisations are also included. So, if you have ever wondered why the face of a lion* in brass or cast-iron appears on doorknockers, why weathervanes are frequently in the shape of a cock*, why orange blossom* plays a part at weddings, or why the winner in Grand Prix motor racing is awarded a wreath of laurel* leaves, read on . . .

Creatures great and small
A selection of land and sea creatures commonly used as symbols.

Adder like all snakes* a symbol of cunning and evil. As one of the four aspects of the Devil, according to St Augustine, the adder is sin, especially envy; it is said to have envied Adam and Eve's happiness in the Garden of Eden. During the Gulf War, in the spring of 1991, British troops in the Saudi desert adopted shoulder flashes showing a black adder as their emblem, in allusion to the BBC TV comedy show *Blackadder*.

Ant diligence, frugality, industry, thrift. Proverbs 6 advises, 'Go to the ant, thou sluggard; consider her ways and be wise'. In Christian lore the ant, believed to distinguish wheat, which it ate, from barley, which it shunned, symbolised the wise man who distinguishes true from false doctrine.

Ape the personification of vice in general, lust in particular; also cunning, luxury, malice, sloth, and because of its lumbering movement, drunkenness. In the Middle Ages, the Devil was often depicted in the form of an ape; with an apple* in its mouth it signified the Fall of Man; in chains, it symbolised sin defeated.

Ass meekness, humility, patience; sometimes used to typify the poor. In Christian art, it is often interchangeable with the donkey; it carried Mary to Bethlehem, is present at the Nativity, and on the family's

US Democratic Party symbol (unofficial)

subsequent flight into Egypt. Christ chose to ride one for his triumphal entry into Jerusalem, an honour commemorated by the dark cross in the fur on its back. The ass is also obstinacy, stupidity, and foolishness, hence the expression 'to make an ass of oneself'. In medieval Europe, adulterous women, prostitutes, criminals, even bankrupts, were degraded by being mounted backwards on an ass.

In the US, the donkey represents the Democratic Party. Andrew Jackson (7th President, 1829–37) first used it as a political symbol in 1828, after opponents called him a 'jackass' during his election campaign. Though never adopted officially, the animal became established as the party symbol in the 1880s, through cartoons by Thomas Nast in *Harper's Weekly*.

'Bear and Ragged Staff': badge of the earls of Warwick; the staff represents the tree trunk with which an early earl was reputed to have killed a giant. The device survives as a crest and charge in the arms of Warwickshire County Council

Bear bad temper, uncouthness, evil, cruelty, greed, lust, the Devil, also strength. In the Book of Daniel (7:5), the bear represents the Kingdom of Persia and corruption. In contrast, as bear cubs were in medieval legend born without form and literally 'licked into shape' by their mother, the bear became a symbol of Christianity which converts the pagan. A popular device in central European heraldry, used instead of the lion, as boldness, courage, majesty, often appearing, for example, on the arms of towns in Germany; also as a supporter of arms, sometimes with a collar and chain. On the State Seal of California, a grizzly bear symbolises determination.

Beaver diligence, industry, also chastity: when hunted in former times for its testicles (popularly supposed to have a medicinal value), it was believed to bite them off in order to escape capture. An early symbol of Canada, because of the beaver fur trade; by royal assent, it gained official status in 1975 as 'a symbol of the sovereignty of Canada'.

Boar brutality, cruelty, also the personification of lust. Widely used in heraldry as courage and fierceness, notably the white boar Richard III adopted for his badge (it is said that he ordered 13 000 white boar badges for his coronation in 1483), for which his enemies nicknamed him the 'boar' or 'hog'. Following Richard's defeat at the Battle of Bosworth, 22 August 1485, inns displaying the sign of a white boar tactfully changed to a Blue Boar, the crest of his enemy, the Earl of Oxford. The Boar's Head, once a popular pub sign, symbolises vitality.

Bull the **commonest symbol of sexual potency**. Also brute force. In ancient Egypt, and elsewhere, a symbol of power, fertility, strength; in some cultures, the bull was thought to cause earthquakes by tossing the earth on its horns; in Greece, an attribute of the sky god Zeus. In the zodiac*, the bull, Taurus, is a sun symbol, spring, resurgence of life. A winged bull or ox* is the emblem of St Luke*. A common English pub sign, due to the animal's agricultural importance, or because bull-baiting took place there until it was banned in 1835.

Camel because it kneels to receive its burden, represents humility in Christian art; thus sometimes a symbol of Christ, who humbled himself to bear the sins of the world. As it could endure long periods in the desert without water, it was used to symbolise temperance. In contrast, because a camel on heat was believed to go mad with lust and copulate all day, it was sometimes a symbol of nymphomania. On the coinage of ancient Rome the camel was the personification of Arabia.

John Bull

. . . the collective nickname for Englishmen, and the personification of their spirit, first appeared in *Law is a Bottomless Pit* (1712) and subsequent satirical pamphlets by Dr John Arbuthnot (1667-1735). 'One would think', commented the American writer Washington Irving on this 'bullish' character (traditionally depicted as a bluff country gentleman in top boots, jacket and sometimes a Union Jack waistcoat), 'in personifying itself, a nation would . . . picture something grand, heroic, and imposing, but it is characteristic of the peculiar humour of the English, and of their love for what is blunt, comic, and familiar, that they have embodied their national oddities in the figure of a sturdy, corpulent old fellow . . .' (Incidentally, Arbuthnot, a Scot, also personified the Dutch as Nicholas Frog, frogs being known then as Dutch nightingales; and the French as Lewis Baboon, after Louis XIV and wordplay on Bourbon.)

Another 'personification' of the English or British spirit is the bulldog (so-called because it was formerly used in bull-baiting), a symbol of tenacity, and obstinate courage; hence the epithet 'the Bulldog Breed', perhaps best typified by Winston Churchill in World War II. Significantly, though Churchill's 'star sign' in Western astrology* was Sagittarius, in the Oriental system of horoscopes* he was born (30 November 1874) in the Year of the Dog.

Carp in Chinese symbolism, perseverance, because of the obstacles it overcomes to reach its spawning grounds. Due to this fighting spirit, it became an emblem of the Japanese Samurai for courage, endurance.

A black cat crossing your path signifies that the animal is going somewhere.

Groucho Marx

Purrfect home

When there was room on the ledge outside of the pots and boxes for a cat, the cat was there – in sunny weather – stretched at full length, asleep and blissful. . . . Then that house was complete, and its contentment and peace were made manifest to the world by this symbol, whose testimony is infallible. A home without a cat – and a well-fed, well-petted, and properly revered cat – may be a perfect home, perhaps, but how can it prove title?

Mark Twain *Pudd'nhead Wilson*

Cat deceit, darkness, lust, laziness, malevolence. In medieval superstition, the favourite animal form assumed by Satan, who catches human souls as a cat catches mice. She-cats, considered promiscuous, represented lascivious women. Cats have nine lives, and supernatural powers; black cats, especially, were associated with the black arts; when a witch was burnt at the stake, her cat was also burnt. Despite such negative associations, in some countries, England included, a black cat is considered lucky (perhaps due to the idea that it retained some of the magical power of witches), especially if it crosses your path; elsewhere, such as in the US, a black cat may be an omen of bad luck. Because the cat is so independent and resistant to restraint, it was a symbol of liberty in ancient Rome: the goddess of Liberty was depicted with a cat lying at her feet; also regarded as the guardian spirit of a household.

Belief in the power of cats dates back at least to the ancient Egyptians, who deified them; Bast, the goddess of love, fertility, feminine sensuality, was portrayed as a cat or cat-headed woman; the dilation and contraction of its pupils, considered symbolic of the moon's waxing and waning, made it also a symbol of the moon. When a pet cat died its owners shaved off their eyebrows as a sign of mourning. When an Egyptian was mummified, the body was sometimes entombed with favoured possessions, including cats: to ensure these did not go hungry in the afterlife embalmed mice were also added; whoever killed a cat, even accidentally, was punished by death. In Islamic lore, the cat, born in Noah's Ark from the lioness's sneeze, saved Mohammed from a serpent's cunning: because he stroked the cat's back it never falls on its back (the dark stripes on the foreheads of many cats are said to be the trace of the prophet's fingers). In China, association of the sign for cat, *mao*, with the number 80 made the cat a symbol of long life. In Oriental horoscopes*, the Cat is also known as the Hare or the Rabbit.

Crocodile deceit, hypocrisy: it was reputed to sob (hence 'crocodile tears') to arouse pity and make its victim approach near enough to be caught. In classical mythology it typified silence, since it was thought to be tongueless.

Dog probably the oldest of domestic animals, man's best friend personifies fidelity, courage; vigilance; an emblem of the Christian saints Bernard, Roch, and Dominic: black and white dogs were sometimes used as symbols of the Dominicans (*Domini canes*, 'dogs of the Lord') who wore black-and-white habits. On medieval tombs and monuments, crusaders are often portrayed with their feet resting on a dog to signify that they followed the Lord's banner as the faithful dog follows its master. On the other hand, the dog is dirty habits, and evil. In Islamic lore, angels will not enter a house where there is a dog; black dogs especially are regarded as symbols of the devil or the carnal soul. Charon, the Greek ferryman of the underworld, is occasionally depicted as a dog, as were many gods and demons of death: Anubis, the Egyptian god of the dead, for example, is usually portrayed with a jackal's head.

Dolphin love, diligence, speed, man's friend at sea. In ancient Greece, the dolphin, the king of sea creatures, was the symbol of maritime power; in art, the Greek sea-god Poseidon, or his Roman counterpart Neptune, is often depicted in a chariot drawn by dolphins. The combination of a dolphin twined round the shank of an anchor (as, for example, in the trademark of the Venetian printer Aldus Manutius*), signified 'hasten slowly', or prudence. In Christian art, the dolphin is the most frequently used 'fish'; on an anchor, or pierced by a trident, it represents Christ on the cross; reputed to rescue sailors in distress and carry them to safety on its back it became a symbol of salvation through Christ, and is often shown bearing souls across the waters to the world beyond. It also symbolises Resurrection: to early Christians it was the 'great fish' which swallowed Jonah and disgorged him unharmed three days later (Jonah 1:17). The dolphin is the commonest marine animal in heraldry; it appeared most notably from 1349 in the arms of the Dauphin (French 'dolphin'), the title borne till 1830 by the French king's eldest son.

Heraldic dolphin, 'embowed'

Donkey see ass

Egg procreation, new life; the re-creation of spring (in legend the world was hatched from an egg in spring); also infinity, because its shape has no beginning and no end. In ancient times, the egg was a symbol of fertility and rebirth, particularly at the festival held at the beginning of the vernal equinox in honour of the Anglo-Saxon goddess of dawn and spring, Eostre (from whose name our word Easter is said to derive). In the Middle Ages, Christians absorbed the egg's association with rebirth to symbolise the Resurrection (among many beliefs linking it with Easter, the egg represented the stone that was rolled aside from the entrance to Christ's tomb); they also adopted the pagan custom of colouring and eating eggs at the festival, dyeing them red as a symbol of Christ's blood.

Elephant the largest land animal represents memory, wisdom, longevity, loyalty, patience, power, hence also widely adopted as a good luck charm. In China, the elephant is strength, prudence, energy, and in Buddhism* a symbol of the Buddha's patience and wisdom (in legend, a white elephant appeared to his mother, Queen Maya, in a dream to announce the birth of a world-ruler).

In the medieval church, the elephant was a popular symbol of chastity, and of Christ, the enemy of the serpent which it tramples underfoot. When Alexander the Great (356–323 BC) attempted to conquer India, he encountered armed soldiers in howdahs, towering canopied structures, on the backs of elephants; belief that the elephant had a castle on its back gave rise to the ecclesiastic and heraldic device of the Elephant and Castle to symbolise the impregnable Church supported by faith.

US Republican Party symbol

The elephant is the official symbol of the US Republican Party. It first appeared in 1874 in a cartoon by Thomas Nast in *Harper's Weekly*. The cartoon showed the elephant (representing the Republican vote) trampling on inflation and chaos; nearby is the ostrich with its head in the sand.

Ermine purity; in legend it would rather die than let its white fur become soiled; also chastity, innocence. Ermine is one of the two principal furs* in heraldry; Church and State robes and cloaks are often lined or trimmed with it to signify royalty or nobility.

The traditional symbol of abundance, the 'horn of plenty' or Cornucopia, is said to derive from a horn on the head of the goat which suckled Jupiter (in other legends it is a ram's horn).

Badge of Richard II (ruled 1377–99)

Fish see p.103

Fox hypocrisy, cunning, guile, trickery; lying on its back open-mouthed feigning death to trap its prey, it is the Devil snaring the unwary.

Goat lechery, lust, also the Devil who assumes the guise of a he-goat (see horseshoe); in legend, the goat disappears momentarily from life each day to have his beard combed by the Devil. At the Last Judgment, Christ, the shepherd, will separate the goats (unbelievers), from the sheep (believers). The goat also represents vitality, fertility; like the ram, it is commonly an animal of sacrifice. In the Bible, the high priest symbolically laid the sins of the world on a goat's head, then banished it to the wilderness (hence 'scapegoat').

Hare timidity, fertility, lust; in Christian art the Virgin Mary is sometimes depicted with a white hare at her feet to represent victory over the temptations of the flesh. A potent symbol of procreation and the renewal of life, the hare was the emblem of the Saxon goddess of spring, Eostre. In the Middle Ages, this symbolism was absorbed into the Christian festival of Easter; in some European countries, the Easter hare, or more commonly now the Easter rabbit or bunny lays Easter eggs*.

Hart in Christian art, the male of the red deer is the emblem of solitude, piety, purity of life. Reputedly the sworn enemy of the serpent (which it could lure from its lair with its breath and trample to death), the hart symbolises Christ who seeks out the Devil to destroy him; also the soul thirsting for Christ's word, in allusion to Psalm 42: 'As the hart panteth after the water brooks, so panteth my soul after thee, O God'. The hart's female counterpart is the hind; in Dryden's *The Hind and the Panther*, the panther, with its spots 'of error', symbolises the Church of England, and the milk-white hind the Roman Catholic Church, innocent and 'infallible'.

A white hart was the favourite badge of Richard II; when he ordered inns to display a sign in 1393, many adopted his badge; it is still a popular pub sign today.

Hind see hart

Horse grace, speed, also virility and lust (particularly the stallion). In Christian art, the horse is an emblem of courage and generosity; in the catacombs it symbolised the swiftness of life. In Revelation (6: 2–8), the four horses of the Apocalypse are white (pestilence), bright red (war), black (famine), and pale (death). A white horse was the standard of the ancient Saxons; it was also the device of the House of Hanover; during the reign of the first two Hanoverian kings of England, George I (1714–27) and George II (1727–60), the 'White Horse' supplanted the Stuart 'Royal Oak' on many pub signs.

Lamb see p.102

Lion the king of the beasts, has been one of the most common animal symbols of courage, agility, fortitude, power and majesty for thousands of years; in ancient Egyptian art, for example, the pharaoh was commonly represented as a lion (compare sphinx). In allusion to

One of the most enigmatic examples of animal symbolism in advertising is the 'lion and bees' device which the Scottish businessman Abram Lyle chose for his newly-invented 'Golden Syrup' in 1883. It derives from the biblical story (Judges 14), of Samson's killing a lion as he journeyed to the land of the Philistines in search of a bride. Returning the same way a few days later, Samson noticed that a swarm of bees had formed a honeycomb in the lion's rotting carcass, and from this devised a riddle which he posed to 30 young men at his wedding feast: 'Out of the eater came forth meat and out of the strong came forth sweetness.' If the men failed to solve the riddle during the seven days of the feast, they were to present Samson with 30 lengths of linen and 30 sets of clothing. If, on the other hand, they answered correctly, he was to pay them the same forfeit. In the event, the young men discovered the answer to be 'What is sweeter than honey? What is stronger than a lion?'

Just why Lyle chose the biblical reference and the lion and the bees as his trademark is not known. Possibly he thought that the syrup's consistency and sweetness had something in common with honey, or that it provided strength. As Diana Richards writes in her mini-history of the device: 'Abram Lyle's riddle remains a good deal more mysterious than Samson's'.

Revelation (5:5), Christ is the 'Lion of the tribe of Judah'; one of the Living Creatures in the Book of Revelation, the winged lion became the symbol of St Mark* (and thus, since the 12th century, the emblem of Venice, the city under his protection). In Christian art, a lion fighting a dragon* signifies good battling with evil; conversely, holding a man or a lamb* in his claws, he represents the powers of evil. Popularised by the medieval bestiaries, the belief that lion cubs are born dead and stay that way until their father breathes life into them after three days made the lion a symbol of resurrection; in addition, because he slept with his eyes open, he became vigilance, and symbolically therefore an ideal guardian on church doors, tombs, monuments, and bridges. Similarly, the lion or his head was also commonly portrayed on door stops and knockers.

As the most popular beast in European heraldry, the lion appears in a wide variety of attitudes* on the arms of many families, municipalities, and nations; since the time of Richard I (1157–99), nicknamed 'Coeur de Lion' or 'Lionheart' for his courage, three lions have been the emblem of English monarchs; on the other hand this symbol of British sovereignty could also be tyranny: for instance, the reverse of the State Seal of Pennsylvania, adopted in 1787, shows the female figure of Liberty trampling on the lion, with the words 'Both can't survive'.

For its many characteristics, the lion is one of the most common devices on European trade and service marks, from the power of French car manufacturers Peugeot* (with their slogan 'The Lion goes from strength to strength'), to the vigilance of the British Egg Industry Council, who in April 1990, after a 20-year-absence, revived the Little Lion symbol to serve as a guarantee to consumers that eggs marketed under this symbol comply with current standards of hygiene.

Ox patience, strength, and an ancient symbol of wealth, partly because of its value as a medium of exchange before the first coins. The ox also

British Egg Industry Council's Little Lion

signifies sacrifice; as a sacrificial animal of the Jews, it was often used in Renaissance art to represent the Jewish nation; in early Christian art and literature, the ox was occasionally an alternative to the lamb as a symbol of Christ's sacrifice. A winged ox is the symbol of St Luke*.

Rabbit like the hare*, abundance of life, fertility, hence the Easter rabbit or bunny (a diminutive of the word bun, ultimately of Celtic origin for the rabbit's scut). Since early times, this fertility has been linked with good fortune and prosperity; thus the superstition that carrying a rabbit's foot, the part which came into closest contact with the earth, the source of life, endowed the bearer with luck.

Ram in many cultures since earliest times, virility, sexual potency. In Egypt, Amen, the king of the gods, who represented the creation and generation of life, was depicted as a ram, or a ram-headed man. Commonly a sacrificial animal: in ancient Greece and Rome, where it was sacred to Zeus and Jupiter, it appears as a decoration on sacrificial altars (it was believed that baptism in the ram's blood imbued the baptised with the animal's vital force). In Christianity, the ram caught in a thorny bush for Abraham to sacrifice instead of his son Isaac (Genesis 22:13), has been taken to symbolise Christ crowned with thorns and sacrificed for mankind.

Rat decay, destruction, plague, and death; in contrast, rats also symbolise wisdom and judgment, supposedly because they selected the best food (and deserted the sinking ship). In ancient Rome a white rat signified good fortune; in China, to be born in the year of the Rat is to be born under the sign of charm. British soldiers of the 7th Armoured Division, who fought Rommel's Afrika Korps in the North Africa campaign in World War II, adopted the desert rat (jerboa) for their badge, and nickname, because of its 'scurrying and biting tactics', and ability to survive the harshest conditions. The emblem was again prominent during 'Operation Desert Storm' in the Gulf War in 1991. (After the war ended in March, the smallest member of the 7th Armoured Brigade to return to base in Germany was a desert rat named Patrick, a present from the Saudi royal family.)

Scorpion evil, death; in medieval symbolism, because of the treachery of its sting, the scorpion became a symbol of Judas.

Snake one of the most complex and universal symbols, the snake or serpent shares much of the dragon's* symbolism. In Western culture, the snake is principally cunning, evil, death, destruction, sin and the Devil; it is also wisdom, healing, renewal, regeneration. In Eden the serpent, 'more subtle than any beast of the field' seduced Eve (Genesis 3:1), and brought about the Fall of Man. When the Israelites, on their journey through the desert to the Promised Land, rebelled against Moses, 'God sent fiery serpents among the people; their bite brought death' (Numbers 21:4–6). After the Israelites repented, God directed Moses to make a brazen serpent and raise it high, so that 'if anyone is bitten and looks on it, he shall live'. According to the Roman historian Tertullian, early Christians called Christ the Good Serpent; in art, the brazen serpent coiled around a cross or pole recalls Christ's words 'The Son of Man must be lifted up as Moses lifted up the serpent in the desert'; thus it is also a symbol of healing, and salvation.

To carry a rabbit's foot is a sign that you are a good shot with a gun – or have a friend who is.

Groucho Marx

Emblem of the 'Desert Rats' (7th Armoured Brigade, British Army)

The traditional association with healing, and by extension with renewal and regeneration, derives partly from the ancient belief that the snake, who sheds its skin to renew its youth, held the secret to eternal life. A serpent coiled round a knotty staff or rod is the emblem and symbol of Asklepios, the Greek god of healing (Roman god of medicine Aesculapius), who had the power to resurrect the dead. The Caduceus (from Greek 'herald's wand') has two snakes; in mythology, Hermes, the herald of the gods (Roman Mercury), received a winged staff to bring harmony from strife: when he tested its power by setting it between two fighting snakes they immediately entwined themselves round the staff in peace.

Both the 'rod of Aesculapius' and the Caduceus are used to symbolise the medical profession; also extensively in medical heraldry, for instance, on the arms and insignia of the Royal Army Medical Corps, the American Medical Association, the World Health Organisation; the device of the Imperial Cancer Research Fund has a Caduceus between the arms of the Royal College of Physicians and the Royal College of Surgeons.

Rod of Aesculapius

Mercury's Caduceus

Spider wiliness, evil and the Devil, who spins a web to trap sinners; also the symbol of the miser, who bleeds the poor as the spider bleeds a fly; the cobweb is a symbol of human frailty. On the other hand, killing a spider is a bad omen.

Whale the Devil, magnitude; in medieval art and drama, its open mouth represented the open gates of hell and its belly hell. As sailors in legend sometimes mistook the whale's bulk for an island, anchored their ships to its side, and were subsequently dragged down to a watery grave, it became a symbol of the Devil's cunning. In Herman Melville's *Moby Dick*, or *The White Whale*, it is a symbol of the Devil, or God, or both. The whale also represents rebirth, resurrection; as the 'great fish' which swallowed Jonah, and disgorged him after three days and nights, it symbolises Christ's time in the tomb (compare dolphin).

Wolf cruelty, ferocity, avarice, greed, lust; also the emblem of Francis of Assisi who befriended and reformed the plundering wolf of Gubbi.

Flights of fancy
Birds, bees, and other winged symbols from the natural world.

Albatross symbolises long, sustained and apparently effortless flight, also a burden or guilt. In legend, this largest of sea-birds embodied the soul of a drowned sailor; it was so strong that it could rescue sailors from the sea and carry them to safety; to kill one was to court disaster. Coleridge's *Rime of the Ancient Mariner* (1798), in which a sailor deliberately shoots an albatross (his shipmates hang the dead bird round his neck as a mark of his guilt), is based on this superstition.

Bat blindness, an attribute of night, and as the Devil's bird, associated with black magic and witchcraft. In contrast, the bat also signifies vision, hope, good luck. In Chinese symbolism, as a homophone of *fu*, happiness, it is happiness; five bats symbolise the five blessings: health, wealth, long life, love of virtue, natural death.

Bee diligence, industry, prudence, and since it was believed never to

Pretty soon a spider went crawling up my shoulder, and I flipped it off and it lit in the candle; and before I could budge it was all shrivelled up. I didn't need anybody to tell me that that was an awful bad sign and would fetch me some bad luck, so I was scared and shook most of the clothes off of me. I got up and turned around in my tracks three times and crossed my breast every time.

Mark Twain *The Adventures of Huckleberry Finn*

N&P

National & Provincial Building Society logo

sleep, vigilance. Also, by virtue of its habits, purity. As the bee stores its honey, it signifies economy and thrift, hence is an occasional symbol of banks (similarly, the beehive). Heraldically, the bee appears in many coats of arms: seven bees on a globe in the arms of Manchester, for instance, represent the fruits of the city's industry throughout the world. Napoleon I adopted bees for his badge; Napoleon III used bees as a symbol of the 'working classes'.

Blackbird Satan and sin, because of its black plumage; and for its alluring song, the temptations of the flesh.

Butterfly resurrection, since it evolves from life as a caterpillar through death in the chrysalis to life again. In Chinese symbolism, the butterfly is immortality; in Japan, it signifies inconstancy and a fickle lover.

Ancient pedigree ⅄

Scholars engaged in genealogy in 14th-century England commonly used an arrow-like symbol to link generations when tracing lines of descent. As the symbol resembled the track made by a crane in mud or sand it became known in the court language of Old French as *pied-de-grue* (literally 'foot of crane'). Gradually, this term was applied to the line itself, and distorted into a number of other forms such as *pee de grewe, peti degree, pytagru, pedygru*, before settling down to its modern spelling of 'pedigree'.

Cock courage, vigilance, also arrogance and conceit, hence 'cocky'. Because it heralds the rising Sun, the cock was dedicated to Apollo, the god of the Sun. Associated with Peter's denial of Christ ('the cock shall not crow till thou hast denied me thrice', John 13:38), it is thus an emblem of the Passion; and, because he 'wept bitterly', a symbol of repentance. Mounted on church towers, or as weathervanes, the cock is vigilance, turning in all directions to watch for evil; according to the *Modern Catholic Dictionary*, it also symbolises 'the capacity of the Gospels to meet every wind of human argument'. Because of its fighting spirit, the cock was an ensign of the warrior Goths; adopted on flags during the French Revolution as both vigilance and supremacy, it later became the national emblem. As a visual pun, the great showman Charles B. Cochran placed a crowing cock on the bonnet of his Rolls-Royce*, and generally used the device elswhere as a mark of ownership.

Crane loyalty, and vigilance: according to legend, cranes gather nightly in a circle to protect their king, each keeping awake by standing on one leg with the other raised holding a stone in its claw: should it fall asleep, the stone would drop and awaken it. In China, the crane is longevity.

Universal symbol of peace

Dove universal symbol of innocence and peace, widely used by peace organisations. In Greek myth, the dove with an olive* branch is the emblem of Athene as the renewal of life. The dove bearing a freshly plucked olive leaf to Noah in the Ark (Genesis 8:11), is deliverance, the messenger of God's forgiveness. It is also a symbol of Israel, and purity: one of the few birds under Mosaic law permitted as an offering in the Temple, it was prescribed for purification after the birth of a child. It is the traditional Christian symbol of the Holy Spirit*. Legend has it that the Devil and witches can transform themselves into any bird or animal shape apart from the dove or the lamb*. In Chinese symbolism the dove is longevity, orderliness.

On the fence

In the US, politicians who favour peace, compromise, negotiation, are labelled 'doves' (as opposed to 'hawks' who support war). On the other hand, someone undecided on the question is now dubbed a 'dawk'; the word (combining dove and hawk) was coined by *Time* magazine in the late 1960s to describe politicians who approved of the Vietnam War but for political reasons opposed it.

Eagle the king of the birds is, after the lion*, the commonest animal symbol: divinity, courage, faith, keenness, victory, majesty, and power, especially imperial power. The eagle was sacred to the Graeco-Roman gods Zeus and Jupiter, and as victory, the special emblem of Roman emperors, carried on the standard of the Roman legions. It appears in the heraldry of many nations, including the US where it was first chosen as the principal device on the Great Seal* adopted in 1782. The favoured form of emperors is a double-headed eagle.

In Christianity, the eagle is the symbol and emblem of St John* because of its soaring flight with gaze fixed on 'the sun of glory', and of Christ's Ascension; with a serpent in its beak, it signified Christ's triumph over Satan. It is also resurrection: in legend the eagle rejuvenated itself every 10 years by flying to the Sun, then plunging back to Earth and into the sea three times, thus it is often depicted on baptismal fonts to represent new life; the lectern on which the Bible is placed, is traditionally designed as an eagle with outstretched wings to symbolise divine inspiration and spiritual power.

Emu symbol of Australia; this indigenous bird appears with the kangaroo as a supporter on the national arms granted in 1912; commonly adopted as a badge, or as the trademark or name for many Australian products, for example 'Emu wool'.

Falcon in Christian symbolism the wild bird of prey represents evil thought or action; a falcon tamed symbolises the pagan converted. In ancient Egypt, the 'King of Birds' was one of the first animals to be worshipped; it was believed to be the personification of the sky-god Horus, who is depicted as a falcon or falcon-headed (see sphinx).

Fly feebleness, insignificance, but also corruption, disease, sin; the Devil is the 'Lord of the Flies'.

Goose conceit, folly, stupidity; one fanciful story from the Middle Ages tells of the elders of a town under siege who rashly showed contempt for their opponents by hanging this ancient symbol of ignorance and stupidity from a tower; this insult so incensed the besieging forces that they burned the town to ashes, including of course the goose (hence, it is said, the expression, 'to cook someone's goose'). The animal may also be vigilance: in legend the cackling of sacred geese in the Capitol saved Rome in 390 BC from a secret invasion by the Gauls; to commemorate the event, the Romans carried a golden goose in procession to the Capitol each year.

Ladybird the commonest British species, the seven spot ladybird (or ladyfly, ladycow, and in the US ladybug), is named in honour of 'Our Lady', the Virgin Mary. The red colour represents her cloak (usually depicted as red in medieval art); the seven black spots represent Mary's seven joys* and seven sorrows*.

Owl traditionally the symbol of wisdom because it was sacred to Athene, the goddess of peace, learning, the arts, thus logically of wisdom (and occasionally today of booksellers); also the emblem of Athens, the city named after her. As the personification of night, and sight in darkness, the owl is often used as the trade symbol of opticians.

Peacock in Graeco-Roman myth, sacred to Zeus' wife Hera; when Hermes slew the hundred-eyed giant Argus, Hera revived him as a peacock and set his eyes in his tail. In Christianity, these 'eyes' were sometimes used to symbolise the 'all seeing' Church; as the bird renews its plumage, it signifies immortality; also Resurrection, from the belief that its flesh does not decay, even if buried for three days; additionally, because of its habit of strutting and showing off its tail it is pride and vanity (in heraldry, a peacock shown full-faced with a display of

Eagles don't breed doves.

Dutch proverb

Of all the birds the eagle alone has seemed to wise men the type of royalty, a bird neither beautiful nor musical nor good for food, but murderous, greedy, hateful to all, the curse of all, and with its great powers of doing harm only surpassed by its desire to do it.

Desiderius Erasmus (Dutch scholar, 1466?–1536)

Liberal Democrats

In September 1990, to symbolise their party as 'alive, soaring and free-spirited', British Liberal Democrats adopted a gold 'bird of liberty' (their previous, diamond-shaped logo resembled the 'baby on board' symbol on car rear windows).

The critic's symbol should be the tumble-bug; he deposits his egg in somebody else's dung, otherwise he could not hatch it.

Mark Twain's notebook

'In her piety'

'Vulning herself'

Pelican power

To his good friends thus wide I
ope my arms,
And like the kind life-rendering
pelican,
Refresh them with my blood.

Shakespeare *Hamlet* Act IV scene 5

feathers is blazoned *a peacock in its pride*. In some countries, the peacock is a bird of ill omen, its feathers a symbol of the Evil Eye, and a warning of a traitor's presence.

Pelican self-sacrifice, parental love, charity: according to the medieval bestiaries, the hen smothers her young with love, three days later the male returns to the nest and pierces his side to revive them with his blood. In a variant account the roles are reversed: the father kills them in anger, the mother returns three days later to pierce her breast and revive them; thus also a symbol of resurrection, and, since the 13th century, of Christ (in *The Divine Comedy*, Dante refers to Christ as 'our Pelican'). In art, a pelican is sometimes shown nesting on the top of the Cross.

The heraldic pelican is depicted more like an eagle* or a swan*; standing on the nest nourishing her young with blood, she is described as being 'in her piety'; with raised wings pecking at her bleeding breast, she is wounding or 'vulning herself'. Both forms appear in the arms of Corpus Christi College: at Oxford vulning herself (1516), at Cambridge in her piety (1570).

Raven Satan and sin, because of its plumage, and its supposed habit of pecking out the eyes of the dead; also an omen of bad luck; in Jewish legend the raven was originally white; when Noah sent it from the Ark to see if the Flood had receded and it failed to bring back good news, its feathers turned black. In Greek legend, the raven was associated with Apollo the god of prophecy (because it can talk); he turned it black for informing him of the infidelity of Coronis, whom he loved. In Japanese mythology, a raven and a kite flew down from the gods to guide Jimmu through the mountains to Yamato, where he established the first imperial dynasty. Sacred to Odin, the Scandinavian god of war, the raven was the emblem on the standard of the Danes (who believed that if the bird hung his wings it was an omen of defeat; if he stood erect victory). Traditionally, ravens deserting their roosts are an omen of famine or some other disaster; concerned about the effect on public morale if the ravens deserted the Tower of London during the Blitz in 1940, Winston Churchill arranged special rations for them.

In religious art the bird may symbolise hope: the prophet Elijah is sometimes represented by ravens who, commanded by God, carried bread to him in the desert.

Robin trust; when Christ was on his way to Calvary, a robin picked a thorn out of his crown and blood from the wound stained its breast red. In a variant account it scorched its feathers while carrying water to the suffering souls in the flames of purgatory. The robin is one of the most common Christmas symbols. As the result of a survey conducted by the International Council for Bird Preservation in *The Times* in 1960, it is also Britain's national bird. This choice, incidentally, was not to everyone's taste; in a letter to *The Times* in October 1960, Robert Graves protested that the bird's red breast is 'a mark of his murderous disposition, not as the monks later claimed, of his devout presence at the Crucifixion'.

Stork new life, the coming of spring, good fortune; parental and filial piety. In English, the name originates from a Greek word meaning strong natural affection; its Hebrew name *hasidah* means 'pious'; these attributes of duty and devotion stem from the ancient belief that the stork feeds its parents when they are too old or weak to care for themselves (in ancient Rome, the *Lex Ciconaria* or 'Stork's Law' obliged children to look after their parents in old age). In Christian symbolism, the stork is also chastity, purity, prudence, vigilance. According to a Swedish legend, the stork is named after a bird which flew round Christ on the Cross crying *styrka! styrka!* or 'strengthen! strengthen!' (see swallow). As the enemy and destroyer of reptiles, especially snakes, the heraldic stork is usually depicted with one in its beak.

The tradition in northern Europe that the stork delivers new-born babies to their mothers is thought to derive from the belief that the souls of unborn children lived in its habitat of ponds, swamps, or marshes. Even today, the stork with a cradle hanging from its beak is often a decorative symbol at christenings.

Swallow the coming of spring, new life, resurrection, from its supposed habit of hibernating in mud in winter and returning to life in spring. In Scandinavian legend, it is the bird of consolation: a swallow hovered over the Cross, crying *svala! svala!* (console! console!), hence its name; it also appears in scenes of the Annunciation and Nativity.

A heraldic swallow, called a martlet, is depicted without feet, since by medieval tradition the bird lives only in the air and never touches ground. Naturalistic swallows also occur in heraldry, notably six swallows in the arms of the Arundel family, as a pun on the bird's French name *hirondelle*.

Swan grace, perfection, purity and innocence; also once a symbol of deceit because its snow-white plumage conceals black flesh. As legend has it that the swan only sings just before it dies (hence 'swan song'), it also represents the end of life. In Christian symbolism it represents the Virgin Mary. The pub sign, 'Swan with Two Necks' is commonly explained as a corruption of 'swan with two nicks', a reference to the Vintners' swan-mark*.

Fabulous beasts
A selection of the most commonly portrayed creatures of the imagination.

Centaur adultery, bestial degradation: in Greek myth, a member of a tribe in the mountains of Thessaly with a man's head and torso and a horse's body; also used to portray man torn between good and evil. In the Zodiac*, the archer Sagittarius is represented by a centaur carrying or shooting with a bow and arrow.

Centaur

Chimera according to Homer, a fire-eating monster with a lion's head, goat's body, and serpent's tail, slain by Bellerophon riding Pegasus*. In heraldry, Chimera may be depicted with the head and breasts of a woman, a dragon's tail and sometimes wings; thus now figuratively, a wild fancy, something totally unnatural.

Chimera (from a painting by Raphael in the Vatican)

Cockatrice one of the deadliest of the medieval fabulous beasts, similar to the wyvern*, but with the head, comb, wattles and feet of a cock. Hatched either by a snake* or toad from a cock's egg laid on a dungheap and weaned on filth, it was reputedly so poisonous that it could kill by its glance (the only way to destroy it was to shock it to death with its reflection in a mirror). As 'king of the serpents', because of the crest

Cockatrice, or Basilisk

continued p.180

Emblems of the American states

Many nations have floral and faunal emblems; so, too, have provinces, states, and other territorial divisions within nations such as Australia, Canada, and the US. The emblems have usually been chosen, officially or unofficially, because they are typical of the region, or because they have a legendary or historical significance. In the US, for instance, the state bird of Utah, a gull (*larus californicus*), was adopted after flocks of gulls saved the state in 1848 from a plague of crickets that was destroying the crops; according to a contemporary witness, 'all day long they gorged themselves, and when full, disgorged and feasted again, the white gulls upon the black crickets, like hosts of heaven and hell contending, until the pests were vanquished and the people were saved'. A number of states have adopted additional emblems. Hawaii, for instance, has the pig-snouted triggerfish (*humuhumunukunukuapuaa*), and Tennessee, the ladybug and the firefly.

Listed below are the bird, flower, and tree emblems of the US. The official emblems of the states and territories of Australia are listed on p.190, and of the provinces of Canada on p.195.

	Bird	Flower	Tree
Alabama	Yellowhammer	Camellia	Pine
Alaska	Willow ptarmigan	Forget-me-not	Sitka spruce
Arizona	Cactus wren	Saguaro cactus flower	Paloverde
Arkansas	Mockingbird	Apple blossom	Pine
California	California valley quail	Golden poppy	California redwood
Colorado	Lark bunting	Rocky mountain columbine	Blue spruce
Connecticut	Robin	Mountain laurel	White oak
Delaware	Blue hen chicken	Peach blossom	American holly
District of Columbia	Wood thrush	American beauty rose	Scarlet oak
Florida	Mockingbird	Orange blossom	Sabal palmetto palm
Georgia	Brown thrasher	Cherokee rose	Live oak
Hawaii	Nene (Hawaiian goose)	Pua aloalo (Hibiscus)	Kukui (candlenut)
Idaho	Mountain bluebird	Syringa	White pine
Illinois	Cardinal	Violet	Bur oak
Indiana	Cardinal	Peony	Tulip poplar
Iowa	Eastern goldfinch	Wild rose	Oak
Kansas	Western meadowlark	Sunflower	Cottonwood
Kentucky	Kentucky cardinal	Goldenrod	Kentucky coffeetree
Louisiana	Brown pelican	Magnolia	Bald cypress
Maine	Chickadee	White pine cone	White pine

	Bird	Flower	Tree
		and tassel	
Maryland	Baltimore oriole	Black-eyed susan	White oak
Massachusetts	Chickadee	Mayflower	American elm
Michigan	Robin	Apple blossom	White pine
Minnesota	Common loon	Pink and white lady's slipper	Red or Norway pine
Mississippi	Mockingbird	Magnolia	Magnolia
Missouri	Bluebird	Hawthorn	Flowering dogwood
Montana	Western meadowlark	Bitteroot	Ponderosa pine
Nebraska	Western meadowlark	Goldenrod	Cottonwood
Nevada	Mountain bluebird	Sagebrush	Single-leaf piñon
New Hampshire	Purple finch	Purple lilac	White birch
New Jersey	Eastern goldfinch	Purple violet	Northern red oak
New Mexico	Roadrunner	Yucca	Piñon (nut pine)
New York	Bluebird	Rose	Sugar maple
North Carolina	Cardinal	Dogwood	Pine
North Dakota	Western meadowlark	Wild prairie rose	American elm
Ohio	Cardinal	Scarlet carnation	Buckeye
Oklahoma	Scissor-tailed flycatcher	Mistletoe	Redbud
Oregon	Meadowlark	Oregon grape	Douglas fir
Pennsylvania	Ruffed grouse	Mountain laurel	Eastern hemlock
Rhode Island	Rhode Island Red	Violet	Red maple
South Carolina	Carolina wren	Yellow jessamine	Palmetto
South Dakota	Ring-necked pheasant	Pasqueflower	Black hills spruce
Tennessee	Mockingbird	Iris	Tulip poplar
Texas	Mockingbird	Bluebonnet	Pecan
Utah	California seagull	Sego lily	Blue spruce
Vermont	Hermit thrush	Red clover	Sugar maple
Virginia	Cardinal	American dogwood	American dogwood
Washington	Willow goldfinch	Western rhododendron	Western hemlock
West Virginia	Cardinal	Rhododendron	Sugar maple
Wisconsin	Robin	Wood violet	Sugar maple

which crowns its head, the creature is also called a basilisk (Greek *basiliskos*, 'little king'). In Christian symbolism, one of the four aspects of the Devil (Psalm 91 in the 1581 Douay translation: 'thou shalt tread upon the adder and the basilisk and trample under foot the lion and the dragon'). In heraldry, as a cock with a dragon's tail, legs and wings, it was occasionally adopted to repel enemies. Figuratively, it signifies treachery or anything deadly.

Dragon one of the most complex and widely ambivalent animal symbols: in the West, predominantly destructive, evil; in the East, creative and benevolent. The English word derives from the Greek *drakon*, 'serpent'; in Latin, *draco*, means both 'dragon' and 'snake'. In Christian culture particularly, this fabulous winged beast with its fiery poisonous breath, scaly body, lion's claws, bat-like wings and forked tongue and tail, symbolises death, darkness, and the Devil as the serpent who tempts man into sin: in art, the Archangel Michael with the dragon underfoot, or St George slaying the dragon, represents the triumph of good over evil; similarly a dragon chained is evil conquered, as is its knotted tail, from the belief that like the scorpion the dragon's power lay in its tail.

Despite these connotations, kings and emperors adopted the dragon as their symbol. The concept of the dragon was introduced into Britain by the Romans, who bore the beast on their standards; the ancient Britons made the dragon their symbol of war against their Saxon invaders; among the Celts it symbolised the power to inspire terror, invincibility, and thus sovereignty. The national symbol of Wales is the red dragon of the 7th-century Welsh hero Cadwallader (the Welsh flag bears a red dragon passant on a field of green and white); Henry VII adopted the red dragon to show his descendency from Cadwallader. The City of London's arms are supported by two dragons, from the belief that a dragon once lived in the River Thames as guardian of the city.

In the East, the 'winged serpent' is celestial, supernatural power, the guardian of treasure, fertility and strength; in China, it is the highest spiritual power, life, light; the symbol of the Chinese Imperial family was a golden dragon. In Oriental horoscopes*, the Dragon is the luckiest sign. In 1988, the last year of the Dragon, Chinese parents defied the law of only one child per family by aiming for a Dragon son.

Griffin or gryphon; with an eagle's head and wings, and a lion's body, this mythical beast combines the qualities of the king of the beasts and the king of the birds, thus strength and vigilance, and in medieval Christian symbolism Christ's dual nature, human and divine; in Dante's *Divine Comedy* (Purgatory, canto 29), the griffin pulls the chariot of the Church. Reputedly able to discover and hoard gold, it came to symbolise both knowledge and usury. As the guardian of treasure, and of the sun, the griffin was sacred to Apollo and the sun, whose chariot it pulled across the sky. In heraldry, the winged griffin is female (the male of the species has no wings). The favourite beast of Edward III, the griffin is one of the Royal Beasts of England. The splendidly stylised example shown here is the service mark of the Midland Bank.

Pegasus in classical mythology, the winged horse* of the Muses, born from the neck of Medusa when Perseus cut off her head, stands for eloquence, poetic inspiration and contemplation; thus in European heraldry, it appears occasionally in the arms of 'intellectuals'. During

Red Dragon of Wales

And there was war in heaven . . . and the great dragon was cast out, that old serpent called the Devil, and Satan.

Revelation 12:7

Midland Bank logo

Badge of the British Airborne Forces

World War II, Pegasus, with Bellerophon on his back (see Chimera), was adopted as the insignia of British airborne troops; more commonly today it symbolises air transport or speed.

Phoenix ancient symbol of immortality; resurrection, the Sun. This mythical bird with feathers of red and gold symbolic of the rising Sun lived in the Arabian wilderness; when, after 500 years, the phoenix felt death approaching she built herself a funeral pyre of wild cinnamon, sang a dirge (reputedly so sad that other creatures who heard it fell dead), then igniting the pyre by fanning it with her wings in the Sun's heat, she died in the flames. Three days later a new phoenix arose from the ashes to live another 500 years. Not surprisingly, early Christians depicted the phoenix in the catacombs as a symbol of Resurrection.

In heraldry, the phoenix is always depicted rising from flames; both Elizabeth I and Mary Queen of Scots took the phoenix for their badge. Alchemists in the Middle Ages used it to symbolise their vocation; it was later a frequent device in signs connected with chemistry and pharmacology. In art and literature, the phoenix is often a symbol of rebirth of a person or project, or of rebuilding after destruction, particularly by fire (see firemark).

Phoenix

Salamander usually depicted as a small lizard or wingless dragon, or sometimes as a dog- or man-like figure surrounded by flames. The most poisonous living creature, whose bite was fatal, it was reputed to live and breed in fire which it could quench with its frigid body, thus it became a symbol of the battle against desire (of hot sinful flesh). As it was believed to be sexless, the salamander also represented chastity: in Christian art it signifies enduring faith and righteousness. Francis I of France adopted the salamander for his badge, together with the motto 'I nourish [the good] and extinguish [the bad]'. In British heraldry, it signifies unquenchable bravery and courage. The salamander was adopted by early insurance companies as a symbol of fire or immunity to fire (see firemark).

Salamander

Sphinx dignity, royalty, wisdom, power, strength. In ancient Egypt, there were three main types: the body of a lion, with a human's head (androsphinx); with a falcon's head (hieracosphinx), and with a ram's head (criosphinx). The oldest and largest sphinx is the Great Sphinx at Giza, which guards the entrance to the Pyramids. Dating from the 26th century BC, the colossal limestone monument, 66 ft (20 m) high, 240 ft (73 m) long, depicts the face of the pharaoh Khafre, also believed to represent the god 'Horus the Dweller in the Horizon', watching for his father Ra, the rising Sun.

Egyptian androsphinx

In Greek mythology, the sphinx was a lion-bodied and eagle-winged female sea-monster who posed a riddle to those who passed her:

'What goes on four feet, on two, and on three,

But the more feet it goes on the weaker it be?'

The sphinx devoured everyone who could not solve it; when Oedipus answered correctly as man (who crawls on all fours as a baby, walks upright when grown, and with a stick in old age), the sphinx hurled herself from her cliff. According to C. G. Jung, the legend represents the Great Mother Goddess destroyed by the stronger masculine force. In the Renaissance, the sphinx could be a symbol of enigmatic wisdom, ignorance, or evil. As a symbol of Egypt, the sphinx appears in Britain on monuments of those whose life's work is associated with the

The Sphinx
... not a hideous compound animal, as it is when carved by an English stone mason for a park gate, but a sacred symbol of the union of the strongest physical with the highest intellectual power on earth.

Harriet Martineau *Eastern Life, Past and Present* (1848)

country, and on the badges and crests of British army regiments which have fought in Egypt.

Unicorn (Latin *unus*, 'one', and *cornu*, 'horn'), fabled creature in the folklore and heraldry of many cultures; in China, for instance, it signifies fertility and longevity. In the West, and particularly in heraldry, the unicorn is an elegant but fierce horselike beast with a goatish beard, antelope's legs, lion's tail, and from its forehead, a pointed horn so sharp it could pierce whatever it touched. In Christian art associated with the dove* and the lamb*; according to legend it could only be captured by a virgin sitting alone in the forest: sensing her purity the unicorn would come to her, lay its head in her lap and fall asleep. Thus it became a symbol of purity in general and feminine chastity in particular, also an allegory of Christ, and his Incarnation in the Virgin Mary. As Christ 'raised up an horn of salvation for us' (Luke 1:69), the unicorn's horn became a symbol of the Cross. Similarly, because this horn was believed to purify anything it touched (powdered 'unicorn' horn was included in medieval medical prescriptions and sold by apothecaries as an antidote to poison as late as the 17th century) the animal symbolises Christ's power over sin. The unicorn could also be wrath, and according to one 13th century writer 'the figure of Death, which continually followeth man and desireth to seize him'. In Leonardo da Vinci's bestiary, the unicorn was a symbol of lust.

It began to appear in heraldry around the 15th century; today it may be seen most notably as a supporter in the Royal Arms of the United Kingdom; two unicorns were adopted as the regular supporters of the Royal Arms of Scotland; when James VI of Scotland became James I of England in 1603, he replaced the Welsh dragon* with the Scottish unicorn.

Wyvern or wivern: fabled winged dragon-like beast with two eagle's legs and a barbed scaly tail coiled into a knot represents war, envy, pestilence, plague, Satan; also vigilance. The wyvern was a symbol of the ancient kingdom of Wessex, and the personal emblem of King Harold (in the Bayeux Tapestry, which tells the story of the Battle of Hastings and Harold's death in 1066, the wyvern appears twice).

China's symbolic animals

Slowly gaining ground in the West today as an alternative to the 'starsigns' of the Zodiac* are Chinese horoscopes. In reality, a highly complex system of divination at least 3000 years old and still highly regarded by many in the Far East (where other nations, among them Japan, Tibet, and Vietnam, use a similar system), the horoscopes have become popularised here mainly because of media coverage of the colourful Chinese New Year celebrations, and the 'personality readings' associated with the 'symbolic animals' of the Chinese calendar.

Legend has it that these derive from an invitation Buddha once issued to all the animals in his kingdom to celebrate the New Year with him. When only 12 turned up, Buddha decided to name a year after each of them, and decreed that any human born within a particular animal's year would share some of that animal's characteristics, good and bad. As with any form of divination, there is of course much more to Chinese astrology (for a true horoscope to be cast, many factors have to be taken into consideration, and would-be students are recommended to turn to Derek Walters' authoritative *Chinese Astrology*), but oddly, even at its

Unicorn

Wyvern

Marriage proverbs

The Dragon meets the Rabbit, and good luck is shattered. The Horse fears the Ox. When the Tiger meets the Snake, there is always a battle.

(quoted in Derek Walters' *Chinese Astrology*)

most basic level, the system hits the mark surprisingly often. Here, culled from a variety of sources, are some of the typical human characteristics associated with each of the 12 animal signs, and their most compatible companions (often, but not necessarily, the same in love and marriage):

Rat, the sign of charm; the first animal in the Chinese calendar is typically adventurous, impulsive, literate, intelligent, charming, witty, keen, sharp-minded, persuasive, unsentimental, tenacious, passionate, with a zest for life and eagerness to experience. On the negative side: aggressive, impulsive, poor savers who live off their wits, greedy, rapacious, bad-tempered, pushy and opportunistic. For the Rat, the Dragon, Monkey, or Pig, tends to be the most compatible partner.

Ox, also known as the Buffalo, the twin signs of equilibrium and endurance. Oxen are said to be the most conservative in their thinking, and methodical, dependable; also single-minded, resolute, strong, stubborn, demanding, domineering, ambitious, determined, phlegmatic, inflexible, powerful and imaginative, but tending to instability (both Hitler and Napoleon were Oxen). Although they do not pair naturally or easily, except with a Rooster, Oxen are said to make loyal lovers and good parents.

Tiger, the sign of courage. Tigers are active, courageous, daring, enthusiastic, inventive, and generous, but often independent, rebellious, foolhardy, impatient, uncompromising, fiercely competitive, reckless, and unpredictable, especially in relationships, and liable to self-doubt. The Tiger tends to partner best with the Dog, Pig, Horse, and Dragon.

Hare, also known as the Rabbit, or in popular Western usage, the Cat: the sign of virtue. One of the most feminine signs, Hares are perceptive, orderly, methodical, graceful, sensuous, sensitive, humorous, inventive, cool, diplomatic, well-balanced, good savers; they like and respect privacy, form long and enduring partnerships, are understanding and patient with children. Hares are also cautious, uncompromising; and ready to run from danger or trouble. A Hare's best companion, besides another Hare, is the Snake, Horse, or Dog.

Dragon, the sign of luck. The king of the animal world and the only mythological creature in the system, the Dragon is the luckiest, most auspicious sign of the Chinese horoscope; also a very masculine sign. Larger than life, charismatic, dramatic, energetic, strong-willed, protective, overconfident, Dragons are also hungry, unreliable, superior, impulsive, uncompromising, self-orientated, headstrong, intolerant, perfectionist, easily downcast, and prone to ill temper. A Dragon's most compatible companion is a Rat, Monkey, or Rooster.

Snake, the sign of wisdom. Generally regarded as the most spiritual or mystically inclined sign; active, aggressive, ambitious, charismatic, humorous, intuitive, good with money. Those born in the year of the Snake have an instinctive appreciation for beauty; they are often associated with healing. On the negative side, the Snake may be jealous and possessive, and capable of treachery. According to a Chinese marriage proverb: 'Supreme happiness comes when the Snake meets the Hare'. Other good companions: the Dragon, Horse, or Pig.

鼠
牛
虎
兔
龍
蛇

馬

羊

猴

雞

狗

豬

Horse, the twin signs of elegance and ardour. Considered the most practical and logical of all signs, and also the most political, the Horse is strong-willed, hard-working, generous, personable, gregarious, reliable, and vigorous, but also selfish and intolerant. Although deeply romantic and predominantly faithful, the Horse may be weak in love, and prone to boredom. Horses partner best with the Sheep, Snake, Hare, Dog, or Dragon.

Sheep, may also be called the Goat, the sign of art. The Chinese consider Sheep to be the instigators of peace and harmony. Sometimes deeply religious, the Sheep is typically sure-footed, fastidious, conservative, selfless, charming, witty, but also possibly complacent, stubborn, capricious, contentious, and liable to wander. The most compatible partner for anyone born in the year of the Sheep is the Horse.

Monkey, the sign of fantasy. The most adaptable sign; inquisitive, sharp, quick-witted, agile, good memory and sense of humour, hard-working for success, mentally resilient, cool-headed, efficient, organised, and prudent with money. The Monkey hungers for knowledge and travel, and is often good with languages. Negative characteristics: lazy and restless, self-centred, highly emotional, secretive, underhanded. The Monkey goes best with the Dragon, Pig, Rat, or another Monkey.

Rooster, also known as the Cock, the sign of candour. The most military-inclined, the Rooster is outspoken, strong-minded, highly principled, moral, shrewd, tenacious, brave and courageous (sometimes recklessly so), open, honest, practical, and despite a tendency to daydream, efficient, practical, and organised. The Rooster is also blunt, arrogant, bossy, and overbearing. The Dragon, Horse, or Ox, seems to be the most successful companion for anyone born under this sign.

Dog, the sign of idealism. The Chinese consider the Dog the sign most likely to affect change in the world. Typically, in common with their natural counterparts, Dogs are loyal, reliable, faithful, selfless, compassionate, protective, and stubborn in adversity. They are also gullible, and prone to worry. The Dog is most compatible with the Tiger, Pig, Hare, or Horse.

Pig, also known as the Boar, the sign of honesty; the 12th and final animal of the 12-year cycle is easy-going, sociable, kind, generous, honest, open-hearted, intelligent, understanding, efficient and hard-working. Thought to enjoy the best health, Pigs are also peacemaking and home- and family-loving and, surprisingly, tidy. On the negative side, they are naive, gullible, vain, and possibly spiteful. A Pig's best companion is likely to be another Pig, or a Rat, Tiger, or Dog.

Chinese years 1900–2000

As the Chinese calendar is based on lunar months, the Chinese New Year, which heralds the influence of another animal in the 12-year cycle, falls on a different date each year (but always between 20 January and 20 February; thus, for example, anyone born between 17 February 1988 and 5 February 1989 is under the sign of the Dragon). To find the year of a particular animal, or the sign you were born under, check the following chart:

The year of the Donkey and the month of the Horse is Never.

Chinese proverb

184

1900	Jan 31	Feb 18 1901	Rat
1901	Feb 19	Feb 7 1902	Ox
1902	Feb 8	Jan 28 1903	Tiger
1903	Jan 29	Feb 15 1904	Hare
1904	Feb 16	Feb 3 1905	Dragon
1905	Feb 4	Jan 24 1906	Snake
1906	Jan 25	Feb 12 1907	Horse
1907	Feb 13	Feb 1 1908	Sheep
1908	Feb 2	Jan 21 1909	Monkey
1909	Jan 22	Feb 9 1910	Rooster
1910	Feb 10	Jan 29 1911	Dog
1911	Jan 30	Feb 17 1912	Pig
1912	Feb 18	Feb 5 1913	Rat
1913	Feb 6	Feb 25 1914	Ox
1914	Jan 26	Feb 13 1915	Tiger
1915	Feb 14	Feb 2 1916	Hare
1916	Feb 3	Jan 22 1917	Dragon
1917	Jan 23	Feb 10 1918	Snake
1918	Feb 11	Jan 31 1919	Horse
1919	Feb 1	Feb 19 1920	Sheep
1920	Feb 20	Feb 7 1921	Monkey
1921	Feb 8	Jan 27 1922	Rooster
1922	Jan 28	Feb 15 1923	Dog
1923	Feb 16	Feb 4 1924	Pig
1924	Feb 5	Jan 23 1925	Rat
1925	Jan 24	Feb 12 1926	Ox
1926	Feb 13	Feb 1 1927	Tiger
1927	Feb 2	Jan 22 1928	Hare
1928	Jan 23	Feb 9 1929	Dragon
1929	Feb 10	Jan 29 1930	Snake
1930	Jan 30	Feb 16 1931	Horse
1931	Feb 17	Feb 5 1932	Sheep
1932	Feb 6	Jan 25 1933	Monkey
1933	Jan 26	Feb 13 1934	Rooster
1934	Feb 14	Feb 3 1935	Dog
1935	Feb 4	Jan 23 1936	Pig
1936	Jan 24	Feb 10 1937	Rat
1937	Feb 11	Jan 30 1938	Ox
1938	Jan 31	Feb 18 1939	Tiger
1939	Feb 19	Feb 7 1940	Hare
1940	Feb 8	Jan 26 1941	Dragon
1941	Jan 27	Feb 14 1942	Snake
1942	Feb 15	Feb 4 1943	Horse
1943	Feb 5	Jan 24 1944	Sheep
1944	Jan 25	Feb 12 1945	Monkey
1945	Feb 13	Feb 1 1946	Rooster
1946	Feb 2	Jan 21 1947	Dog
1947	Jan 22	Feb 9 1948	Pig
1948	Feb 10	Jan 28 1949	Rat
1949	Jan 29	Feb 16 1950	Ox
1950	Feb 17	Feb 5 1951	Tiger
1951	Feb 6	Feb 26 1952	Hare
1952	Feb 27	Feb 13 1953	Dragon
1953	Feb 14	Feb 2 1954	Snake
1954	Feb 3	Jan 23 1955	Horse

1955	Jan 24	Feb 11 1956	Sheep
1956	Feb 12	Jan 30 1957	Monkey
1957	Jan 31	Feb 17 1958	Rooster
1958	Feb 18	Feb 7 1959	Dog
1959	Feb 8	Jan 27 1960	Pig
1960	Jan 28	Feb 14 1961	Rat
1961	Feb 15	Feb 4 1962	Ox
1962	Feb 5	Jan 24 1963	Tiger
1963	Jan 25	Feb 12 1964	Hare
1964	Feb 13	Feb 1 1965	Dragon
1965	Feb 2	Jan 20 1966	Snake
1966	Jan 21	Feb 8 1967	Horse
1967	Feb 9	Jan 29 1968	Sheep
1968	Jan 30	Feb 16 1969	Monkey
1969	Feb 17	Feb 5 1970	Rooster
1970	Feb 6	Jan 26 1971	Dog
1971	Jan 27	Feb 14 1972	Pig
1972	Jan 15	Feb 2 1973	Rat
1973	Feb 3	Jan 22 1974	Ox
1974	Jan 23	Feb 10 1975	Tiger
1975	Feb 11	Jan 30 1976	Hare
1976	Jan 31	Feb 17 1977	Dragon
1977	Feb 18	Feb 6 1978	Snake
1978	Feb 7	Jan 27 1979	Horse
1979	Jan 28	Feb 15 1980	Sheep
1980	Feb 16	Feb 4 1981	Monkey
1981	Feb 5	Jan 24 1982	Rooster
1982	Jan 25	Feb 12 1983	Dog
1983	Feb 13	Feb 1 1984	Pig
1984	Feb 2	Feb 19 1985	Rat
1985	Feb 20	Feb 8 1986	Ox
1986	Feb 9	Jan 28 1987	Tiger
1987	Jan 29	Feb 16 1988	Hare
1988	Feb 17	Feb 5 1989	Dragon
1989	Feb 6	Jan 26 1990	Snake
1990	Jan 27	Feb 14 1991	Horse
1991	Feb 15	Feb 3 1992	Sheep
1992	Feb 4	Jan 22 1993	Monkey
1993	Jan 23	Feb 9 1994	Rooster
1994	Feb 10	Jan 30 1995	Dog
1995	Jan 31	Feb 18 1996	Pig
1996	Feb 19	Feb 6 1997	Rat
1997	Feb 7	Jan 27 1998	Ox
1998	Jan 28	Feb 15 1999	Tiger
1999	Feb 16	Feb 4 2000	Hare

From field and forest

Some of the many symbolic flowers, herbs, trees and shrubs from the past and present.

Acacia immortality: because its leaves resemble tongues of flame, reputedly the bush which 'burned with fire . . . and was not consumed', in which the angel of God appeared to Moses (Exodus 3:2); also the sacred Hebrew wood of the Tabernacle; legend has it that Christ's crown of thorns was made of acacia in mockery of this. In Mediterranean countries, acacia blossom symbolises friendship, platonic love.

Almond divine favour: in the Bible (Numbers 17:1–8), 'the rod of Aaron for the house of Levi was budded, and brought forth buds, and bloomed blossoms, and yielded almonds'. Also vigilance, from its Hebrew name *skeked*, 'to waken', 'to watch'. The Virgin Mary is sometimes portrayed within an almond-shaped aureole*. In France, the almond symbolises a happy marriage. In the eastern Mediterranean, its blossom, among the first to appear, is a symbol of spring.

Anemone Greek symbol of sorrow, death, from the legend of Adonis, who was killed by a boar: where his blood stained the earth Venus, who loved the youth, made anemones grow. In Christian lore, anemones sprang up on Calvary at the Crucifixion: the red spots on the flower's petals signify Christ's blood. In the Church's early days the anemone's triple leaf was used to symbolise the Trinity (see shamrock).

Apple ambivalent as temptation, the Fall of Man, and salvation. Since the Middle Ages, considered the forbidden fruit of the Tree of Knowledge in Eden, of which God said: 'Ye shall not eat of it, neither shall ye touch it'. Incidentally, the story in Genesis does not name the fruit which tempted Eve (in art the fig, pear, and quince, are also used); the traditional apple association derives mainly from the fruit's Latin name *malum*, which also means 'an evil'. As a symbol of Christ, 'the new Adam', the fruit is redemption from sin, and thus salvation. The apple means also 'health', 'vitality', hence the old saying: 'an apple a day keeps the doctor away'. In Scandinavian mythology, the gods rejuvenated themselves with apples from the gardens of their legendary home Asgard. Apple blossom symbolises eternal youth, also fertility (see orange), and in China, peace and beauty.

Ash commonly in mythology, the Cosmic or World tree of life; in Norse myth, the ash was sacred to the chief god Odin; it is also Yggdrasil, the source of life and immortality, whose branches, trunk, and roots unite the realms of heaven, earth, and underworld. According to one North American Indian legend, the first humans were 'born' in an ash tree.

Aspen lamentation, shame: when this poplar-like tree heard that Christ's cross was to be made from its wood, its leaves trembled in horror; alternatively, while other trees bowed their tops during the Crucifixion, the aspen remained upright; for this arrogance its leaves were condemned to shiver forever.

Carnation in Christian lore the carnation burst into bloom the day Christ was born. It signifies love, betrothal and marriage, hence a popular floral emblem at weddings. The pink carnation represents the tears of the Virgin Mary, thus motherhood; the white carnation is pure love, the red passionate love, and the yellow disdain, rejection.

Cedar incorruptibility; strength; the Old Testament prophet Ezekiel used the cedar as a symbol of the Messiah. Emblem of the Lebanon since Biblical times, and since independence in 1943 the principal device on the national flag.

'One of the deepest mysteries to me is our logo—the symbol of lust and knowledge, bitten into, all crossed with the colours of the rainbow in the wrong order. You couldn't dream of a more appropriate logo: lust, knowledge, hope and anarchy', wrote Jean-Louis Gassee, a former Vice-President of Apple Computer (quoted in *So Far—The First Ten Years of a Vision*).

But why *Apple* Computer? Nobody is really quite sure. Legend has it that the company was conceived by Steve Jobs and Stephen Wozniak in the garage of Jobs' parents' home in Cupertino, California on April Fool's Day 1976. And as Jobs was eating an apple at the time. . . . Another story, perhaps equally apocryphal, links the name of the company's new generation of 'Macintosh' personal computers in 1984 with the particular variety of apple called Mcintosh (after John Mcintosh, who discovered it in Ontario in 1796). The company's logo (best depicted in its 'deliberately expensive' six-colour glory) with its visual pun on the word 'byte', was designed in 1977 by Regis McKenna, 'a Silicon Valley PR guru'.

Finding a four-leaf clover is a sign that you have been down on your hands and knees.

Groucho Marx

Trefoil

Deathly evergreens
*Sad cypress, vervain, yew,
compose the wreath;
And every baleful green
denoting death.*

John Dryden *Aeneid*

Fleur-de-lys

Chrysanthemum the emblem of the Emperor of Japan (see p.134), also the national flower, and a symbol of long life, happiness, wealth. In the Japanese floral calendar, the flower of September; in China, where it originated, the flower of October and the emblem of autumn.

Clover with three leaves, also called trefoil*, symbolises the Trinity (see anemone, shamrock); belief in the rarer four-leaf clover as a good-luck token may stem from the legend that Eve carried one from Eden to remind her of her lost paradise; a five-leaf clover, on the other hand, may bring bad luck. The Chinese emblem of summer.

Columbine from Latin *columba*, 'dove', because it resembles doves in flight: thus until the 16th century a symbol of the Holy Spirit; as each stalk bears seven blooms it may also represent the Seven Gifts* of the Spirit according to a prophecy in Isaiah (11:2).

Cypress sadness, mourning, and in ancient Greece the symbol of death, because of the leaves' dark hue. Formerly depicted on pagan and Christian tombs and burial places, it is also commonly grown in cemeteries for its reputed power to preserve the body from corruption.

Daffodil the floral emblem of Wales; its origin as the alternative to the leek* as the national emblem is uncertain, though St David's Day falls on 1 March, just as daffodils begin to bloom. Because of its narcotic properties, it was also, in ancient times, 'the flower of deceit'.

Fig fertility, because of its many seeds. In Buddhism*, the fig tree is the sacred Bo-Tree under which Buddha attained enlightenment.

Fleur-de-lys (literally 'lily-flower') is the principal floral charge in heraldry (see p.132), and the traditional emblem of the kings of France.

Hawthorn blossom represents hope, because it heralds the coming of spring. In Greek myth, it was sacred to the god of marriage Hymen: his symbol, a bridal torch, was hawthorn; at weddings, Athenian girls crowned themselves with its blossom. As a charm against evil spirits, the Romans placed hawthorn leaves on the cradles of new-born babies. Henry VII adopted it as a device after Richard III's crown was recovered from a hawthorn bush at the Battle of Bosworth in 1485.

Holly 'the holy tree', associated with both Christmas and the Crucifixion. Sacred to Saturn in ancient Rome, it was used as a symbol of health and happiness in the Saturnalia festival (17–23 December); early Roman Christians likewise adopted the holly for decoration at Christmas; the traditional advent wreath is made of it. In art, the holly may be depicted as the tree of the Cross: its spiked leaves are symbolic of Christ's crown of thorns, its red berries his blood.

Iris named after the Greek goddess of the rainbow, shares much of the symbolism of the lily*; as the 'sword lily' (because of its sword-shaped leaves), it is an emblem of the Virgin Mary and her sorrow. The iris is often disputed as the inspiration for the heraldic fleur-de-lys*.

Ivy as an evergreen, signifies immortality, eternal life; because of its tendency to cling, it is also a symbol of attachment, friendship.

The year in flowers

In some cultures, each of the 12 months of the year is symbolised by a particular flower. Here are three traditional 'floral calendars'.

	Chinese	Japanese	Western
January	plum blossom	pine	snowdrop
February	peach blossom	plum blossom	primrose
March	tree peony	peach blossom	violet
April	cherry blossom	wisteria	daisy
May	magnolia	iris	hawthorn
June	pomegranate blossom	peony	honeysuckle
July	lotus	morning glory	water lily
August	pear blossom	lotus	poppy
September	mallow	chrysanthemum	morning glory
October	chrysanthemum	autumn nanakusa	hop plant
November	gardenia	maple	chrysanthemum
December	poppy	bamboo	holly

Laurel as an evergreen, it signifies immortality, but also triumph, victory, and success (particularly literary). Emblematic of Apollo, the Greek god of poetry and music; at the games held in his honour, which included both arts and athletics, a crown of laurel or sweet bay (Latin name *laurus nobilis)*, was awarded to the victors. The Romans extended this tradition to military victors; Julius Caesar adopted a laurel crown for all formal occasions (it has been suggested this was more to hide his premature baldness than to remind Romans of his immortal status). On English coinage, Charles II, George I, George II, and for a time Elizabeth II, were depicted crowned with laurel. As a symbol of excellence, a laurel wreath was often included on early car badges, such as those of Alfa Romeo*, Fiat, Mercedes-Benz*.

Leek emblem of Wales (see daffodil); according to legend, David, the patron saint of Wales, instructed his countrymen in the 6th century to wear leeks in their caps to distinguish them from their Saxon enemies. In Shakespeare's *Henry V*, the Welsh captain Fluellen reminds the King: 'Welshmen did good service in a garden where leeks did grow, wearing leeks in their Monmouth caps, which your majesty know, to this hour is an honourable badge of the service, and I do believe your majesty takes no scorn to wear the leek upon St Tavy's Day' (St David's Day, 1 March).

Lily (Latin *lilium candidum*) purity, majesty, virginity. In classical mythology, this symbol of purity sprang from the milk of Zeus' wife Hera; similarly, in Christian lore, the lily sprang from the repentant tears of Eve as she left Paradise. In early Christian art, the flowering rod of Christ's 'father' St Joseph, usually has lilies sprouting from it in honour of his purity, while Mary's other suitors are depicted holding barren rods. An emblem of the Virgin Mary, hence the alternative name

By appointment

The epithet 'poet laureate' for the poet of the Royal Household alludes to the ancient belief that the laurel inspired poetry. Although Ben Jonson was the first court poet (appointed 1617), the title was not awarded officially until Jonson's now-forgotten successor Sir William Davenant was appointed in 1638. Other poets laureate include John Dryden, 1668; Colley Cibber, 1730; Robert Southey, 1813; Wordsworth, 1843; Tennyson, 1850; Robert Bridges, 1913; Cecil Day Lewis, 1968; John Betjeman, 1972; and since 1984, Ted Hughes. The term Nobel Laureate, for a Nobel prizewinner, is also used.

Emblem of St David and Wales

Madonna lily, also a symbol of the Trinity, and the three Virtues: Faith, Hope, and Charity. In heraldry, the fleur-de-lys is thought to be a highly stylised lily (see p.132). The lily means also perfection, hence 'to gild the lily' is to attempt to improve what is already perfect, or as Shakespeare describes it in *King John*, 'to gild refined gold, to paint the lily . . . is wasteful and ridiculous excess'.

Lotus as rising from the mud, almost universally a symbol of purity and the perfection of beauty. The floral emblem of India and of Egypt, where in ancient times it represented creation, resurrection, the renewal of life. It is sacred to Buddha, who is frequently depicted seated on a lotus. The flower of July in China; as it buds, flowers, and seeds at the same time it also represents the past, the present, and the future.

Marigold reputedly named in honour of the Virgin Mary. Popular in wedding bouquets (another name is 'summer bride'), as a symbol of constancy, lasting love. In southeastern Europe, if a man cast a roving eye, his lover sowed marigolds in the earth round his footprint to draw him back to fidelity. In China, the marigold is longevity 'the flower of 10 000 years'; in Hinduism*, the flower of Krishna.

Mistletoe fertility, life, protection; believed by primitive man to embody a living spirit; in Roman myth it was the magical 'Golden Bough' the Trojan hero Aeneas plucked to enter the underworld. The Druids venerated it, calling it 'All-heal' for its supposed curative powers; if it grew on an oak*, it was especially potent. According to the 1st-century Roman historian Pliny, 'mistletoe will promote conception in females if they make it a practice of carrying it about them'. Anciently, the plant of peace in Scandinavia, it was hung outside homes as a sign of welcome to strangers. The peculiarly English custom of kissing under mistletoe at Christmas is thought to be a survival of the Saturnalia, the ancient Roman winter solstice festival, a time of licentiousness when kissing between strangers was permitted (in her *Illustrated Encyclopaedia of*

Under the mistletoe
Old Wardle had just suspended, with his own hands, a huge branch of mistletoe, and this same branch of mistletoe instantaneously gave rise to a scene of general and most delightful struggling and confusion; in the midst of which, Mr Pickwick . . . took the old lady by the hand, led her beneath the mystic branch, and saluted her in all courtesy and decorum.

Charles Dickens *Pickwick Papers*

Emblems of Australia

	Floral	Bird	Faunal
Australian Capital Territory	Royal bluebell	–	–
New South Wales	Waratah	Kookaburra	Platypus
Queensland	Cooktown orchid	–	Koala
South Australia	Sturt's desert pea	Piping shrike	or Hairy-nosed wombat
Tasmania	Tasmanian blue gum	–	–
Victoria	Pink heath	Helmeted honeyeater	Leadbeater's possum
Western Australia	Kangaroo paw	Black swan	Numbat or banded anteater
Northern Territory	Sturt's desert rose	Wedge-tailed eagle	Red kangaroo

Traditional Symbols, J.C. Cooper suggests that, as it is neither tree nor shrub, that is, neither one thing nor the other, it symbolised 'freedom from limitation, so that anyone under the mistletoe is free from restrictions'). It was the first plant to be adopted as a state symbol in America, by Oklahoma in 1893.

Myrtle everlasting love, marriage; and in Hebrew lore, a symbol of peace. Myrtle was sacred to Venus, the goddess of love: hence a Roman bridegroom decked himself with it on his wedding day. Myrtle is commonly included in wedding bouquets; in some countries it is traditional for the bride to plant a sprig from the bouquet in her new garden for her daughter when she comes to marry: a sprig from Queen Victoria's bouquet, planted at Osborne, Isle of Wight, in 1840, provided the myrtle in Lady Diana Spencer's bouquet when she married Prince Charles in 1981.

Narcissus self-love, vanity: in Greek myth, the flower sprang up where Narcissus, a beautiful youth, fell in love with his reflection in a pool and drowned trying to embrace it.

Oak the 'king of the forest' symbolises endurance, strength; also glory: in ancient Rome, a wreath of oak leaves was the highest honour awarded to a military victor. To the Druids the oak was the most sacred tree; in Christian symbolism, it means resolute faith and virtue. In Sir Walter Scott's *Ivanhoe*, the device of an uprooted oak on the Saxon knight's shield represented the fate he shared with all Saxons after the Norman Conquest.

Olive peace, plenty, fertility, victory. In Greek myth, the olive was created by the goddess Athene in a contest for the honour to name the city of Athens (Poseidon, her opponent in the contest, created the horse). Subsequently, a crown of wild olives became the highest award conferred on a Greek citizen, and in the Olympic Games held to honour the goddess, the highest prize. The tree's fruitfulness made it a symbol of fertility; at weddings the bride and groom wore or carried a garland of olives (see orange). Olive branches were also displayed by the vanquished as a sign that they wanted to sue for peace, hence the expression 'to show' or 'hold out the olive branch'. In the Bible (Genesis 8:11), the olive leaf the dove* carried back to Noah in the ark was a sign that 'the waters were abated from off the earth', and thus symbolised God's forgiveness. Early Christians sometimes used a crown of olives as an emblem of martyrdom.

Orange as one of the most prolific trees, an ancient symbol of fertility, thus long associated with love and marriage (in legend, for instance, it was the 'golden apple' Juno gave Jupiter on their wedding day). The custom of wearing the white blossom (purity, innocence, chastity) at weddings was introduced into England from France around 1820. The tree is also used instead of the apple or fig tree in scenes depicting Man's Fall in Eden.

Palm from Latin *palma*, 'palm of the hand', from the spread-hand appearance of its fronds, is the principal symbol of victory, triumph. In ancient Rome, victorious athletes, gladiators, soldiers, were awarded a palm branch. The early Church in Rome adopted the palm as a symbol for martyrs to represent their triumph over death. To celebrate Palm Sunday, the last Sunday of Lent, which commemorates Christ's entry into Jerusalem when the multitude strewed the way with palm branches, churchgoers are given strips of palm leaf shaped into a cross; these are blessed and kept at home till the following Ash Wednesday as a sign of Christ's presence; where palms are not available, other branches are used: in Russia, for example, the alternative is pussy willow (see yew). Early English pilgrims who journeyed to the Holy Land (and returned with a palm branch as proof), were allowed to wear a small silver palm branch, and were called palmers.

Pansy thought, meditation: from the similarity between pansy and the Old French *pansée*, meaning 'thought'.

Passion flower from *flos passionis* (Latinised by Linnaeus to *passiflora*), so-named by 16th-century Spanish missionaries to South America who interpreted the flower's parts as emblems of the Passion*: the five sepals and five petals as the faithful disciples (excluding Peter, who denied Christ; and Judas); the leaf as the spear; the five stamens, the wounds; the tendrils, the cords or whips; the column of the ovary, the pillar of the cross; the three styles with rounded heads, the nails; the corona, the crown of thorns; the calyx, the nimbus; the white tint, purity; and the blue, heaven.

Peach with one leaf attached, an ancient symbol of the heart and tongue; thus adopted by Renaissance artists to represent truth, which springs from the union of heart and tongue. The peach is sometimes depicted in paintings of the Virgin and Child instead of the apple* as the fruit of salvation. In China, it symbolises longevity, immortality, because peaches in the 'celestial orchard' are said to ripen only once every 3000 years.

Pomegranate because of its many seeds, fertility. In Greek and Roman mythology it was an emblem of Pluto's wife Proserpine, who returned from the underworld each spring to renew the earth. In Christian art, immortality and resurrection; its seeds enclosed in a tough case symbolised the unity of the Church, or the Monarchy.

Poppy remembrance, silence, sleep. In Greek myth, an emblem of Hypnos, the god of sleep, and Morpheus, the god of dreams, because of its sleep-inducing properties. Appropriately, two poppies appear in the arms of the Association of Anaesthetists of Great Britain and Ireland. Each November, red artificial poppies are sold by the British Legion for Remembrance Day, the annual commemoration of all who died in two world wars, and other conflicts since 1945 (in recent years, a white poppy has been favoured as an alternative symbol by those who feel the red glorifies war). The symbolism was inspired by a poem written on 3 May 1915 during the second Battle of Ypres by Major John McCrae, a surgeon in the Canadian Field Artillery:

> In Flanders fields the poppies blow
> Between the crosses, row on row,
> That mark our place . . .

McCrae's poem, first published in *Punch*, 8 December 1915, was recited as part of the official Armistice Day programme on 11 November 1918.

The first 'Poppy Day', two years later, aimed at alleviating the hardships of servicemen, raised £106 000.

Rose the **most common floral symbol**. According to legend, the 'queen of flowers' grew without thorns in Eden, but sprouted them after the Fall as a reminder. In ancient Greece and Rome the rose was the emblem of the goddesses of love Aphrodite and Venus, and a symbol of beauty, desire. For the Arabs the rose is a symbol of masculine beauty. In Christian lore, the red rose signifies martyrdom, and charity; the white rose means innocence, purity, virginity; the Virgin Mary is the Mystical Rose, the Rose of Heaven, or because she was without sin the 'rose without thorns'.

Emblem of England: Tudor Rose

The rose is the traditional emblem of England, and the most famous English royal badge (see p.132). Following the 'Wars of the Roses' (1455–87), the badges of the two sides disputing the English Crown, the red rose of the House of Lancaster and the white of the House of York, were united to form what is called the Tudor Rose. More recently, the red rose has been adopted by European political parties as an emblem of socialism, notably in 1986 by the British Labour Party.

The rose is also the emblem of silence and secrecy; in Graeco-Roman mythology, the god of silence, Harpocrates, once stumbled upon Venus in the act of love; to bribe him to silence, Venus' son Cupid gave him a white rose. Thus in ancient times, a rose was hung, or carved in wood or sculpted in plaster on the ceilings of banqueting halls and council chambers, and from the early 16th century over confessionals, to signify that anything said *sub rosa*, 'under the rose', was considered confidential. Similarly, *sub vino sub rosa est*, for anything said under the influence of wine.

Rosemary so-called from its Latin name *rosmarinus*, 'dew of the sea', because it is said to flourish near the sea, is a symbol of remembrance from the belief in ancient Greece that this evergreen shrub strengthened the memory (thus students often stuck a sprig in their hair). Traditionally, mourners at a funeral placed rosemary on the coffin to signify that the deceased would not be forgotten; even today the herb is sometimes planted near a grave. In the language of flowers, rosemary represents fidelity: in the 17th century brides wove rosemary into their garlands, and at the wedding feast, to ensure long-lasting love, a sprig was dropped into the newly-weds' wine. As the Elizabethan poet Robert Herrick summed up this dual association with weddings and funerals:

> Grow for two ends – it matters not at all,
> Be't for my bridall, or my buriall.

'There's rosemary, that's for remembrance; pray love, remember; and there is pansies, that's for thoughts.'

William Shakespeare: Ophelia to Laertes, *Hamlet*

Shamrock from Irish *seamróg*, 'little clover'. The emblem and symbol of Ireland; and of St Patrick*, who used the three leaflets growing from one stem to explain the doctrine of the Trinity to the Irish in the 5th century (see clover). The shamrock is traditionally worn on St Patrick's Day, 17 March.

Emblem of Ireland

Emblem of Scotland

Thistle sin, sorrow, because of the curse God laid on Adam (Genesis 3:17): 'cursed is the ground for thy sake; in sorrow shalt thou eat of it all the days of thy life; thorns also and thistles shall it bring forth to thee'. In Roman mythology, Ceres, the god of agriculture and of the fruits of the earth, carried a torch of the plant.

The thistle is the emblem and symbol of Scotland; according to legend, when invading Danes in the 8th century crept barefoot under cover of darkness to attack the Scots, one stepped on a thistle: roused by his cries, the Scots inflicted heavy defeat. The thistle was adopted as the insignia of Scotland in the reign of James III; and into the British arms in 1702 (together with the motto *Nemo me impune lacessit*, 'Nobody provokes me with impunity'). The emblem is also the central motif of the badge of the Most Ancient and Noble Order of the Thistle, an order of chivalry ranking second only to the Garter.

Vine a universal symbol of the Christian faith, recalling Christ's words 'I am the True Vine' (John 15); the disciples are the branches; the vine or grapes, and ears or sheaves of corn or wheat, symbolise the wine and bread of the Eucharist, Christ's blood and body. In Jewish symbolism, the vine represents the Israelites as the chosen people; together with the fig tree, it is peace and plenty.

Violet shyness, modesty, because it grows in the shadows or shelter of larger plants. In the language of flowers, the white violet, thought to spring from the graves of virgins, signifies innocence; the blue faithful love. In a sonnet on the colour blue, Keats describes the flower as the 'queen of secrecy'. In Christian art, it is Christ's humility; St Bernard referred to the Virgin Mary as the 'violet of humility'.

Wheat in Christian art since early times symbolises the bread of the Eucharist, from Christ's words at the Last Supper: 'this is my body'. The wheatsheaf is a common symbol of agriculture and of the earth's fruitfulness, and a popular charge in heraldry (called garb, from French *gerbe*, 'sheaf'); it figures on the arms of the Bakers Company, and was formerly a sign for bakers. In *Pub Signs*, Paul Corballis notes that the wheatsheaf on pub signs may originally have signified that baking was done on the premises, thus combining the 'two staffs of life in one business'.

Willow sadness, mourning; in Psalm 137, in sign of mourning, the Israelites in captivity 'hanged their harps upon the willows'; the weeping willow as a symbol of grief and death appears on paintings of the Crucifixion. Because it flourishes no matter how many branches are cut, the willow became a symbol of Christ's Gospel which remains intact however widely distributed; in some places willow branches take the place of the palm in Palm Sunday celebrations.

Yew this evergreen indigenous to Britain was commonly planted in churchyards as a symbol of death and resurrection; in medieval times, when yew branches were an alternative to the palm, the final Sunday of Lent was known as Yew Sunday (compare willow); also sadness, mourning.

Say it with flowers

As well as the traditional floral symbolism already mentioned, many flowers have been used in courtship and romance to express feelings that, for one reason or another, might not be spoken or written down. In some cultures, the flowers were part of a complex language. A notable example is Selam, the floral language which developed in the harems of Turkey. It was introduced into Europe by the Swedish king,

Emblems of Canada

Provinces and territories marked with an asterisk have also adopted their own tartans.

	Gems/other	Bird	Floral emblems
Bird			
Alberta*	Wild rose	Great horned owl	Petrified wood
British Columbia*	Pacific dogwood	–	Jade
Manitoba*	Prairie crocus	–	–
New Brunswick*	Purple violet	Black-capped chickadee	–
Newfoundland	Pitcher plant	–	Labradorite
Nova Scotia*	Mayflower	–	Agate
Ontario	White trillium	–	Amethyst
Prince Edward Island*	Lady's slipper	Blue jay	–
Quebec	Madonna lily	–	–
Saskatchewan*	Prairie lily	Sharp-tailed grouse	Wheatsheaf
Northwest Territories*	Mountain avens	–	Native gold
Yukon Territory*	Fireweed	Common raven	Lazulite

Charles XII (1682–1718), who learned it at the Ottoman court during exile in Turkey. A few years later, the language reached England, after the writer Lady Mary Wortley Montagu (1689–1762), visiting Turkey with her husband, discovered how to express in a carefully composed bouquet a range of feelings from passion and friendship to reproach and disdain.

Most of the subtleties of this language have long since disappeared. This is probably just as well. According to Claire Powell in *The Meaning of Flowers*, it was rarely as simple as handing someone a flower and hoping the message would be understood. The exact meaning depended on a number of factors: whether the flower was presented upright or inverted, whether its leaves or thorns were removed, or whether it was presented with the left or the right hand. Even the inclination of the hand in the act of presentation conveyed a meaning: to the right it implied an affirmative response, to the left a negative. Where the recipient placed the flower was also important: in her hair, it communicated caution, on her heart, love.

Not surprisingly, a number of comprehensive 'floral vocabularies' were published over the years to guide the uninitiated. In *The Guinness Book of Marriage*, Valerie Porter quotes one such vocabulary, which appeared in 1845 in an American farming magazine! Listed below is a selection from it.

acacia (yellow) concealed love
acacia (rose) elegance
acanthus the arts
agnus castus coldness without love
agrimony thankfulness
almond blossom hope

aloe bitterness
amaranth immortality
amaryllis beautiful but timid
ambrosia returned affection
anemone frailty
angelica inspiration
apple blossom good and great

Flower power

Love's language may be talked with these;
To work out choicest sentences
No blossoms can be meeter;
And, such being used in Eastern bowers,
Young maids may wonder if the flowers
Or meanings be the sweeter.

Elizabeth Barrett Browning
(1806–61)

arum ferocity and deceit
ash grandeur
aspen tree sensibility
asphodel my regrets follow you
aster beauty in retirement
auricula (scarlet) pride
bachelor's button hope in
misery
balm social intercourse
balsam impatience
barberry sourness
basil hatred
bay leaf I change but in dying
beech prosperity
bindweed humility
birch gracefulness
black poplar courage
blackthorn difficulty
bluebell constancy
borage bluntness
box stoicism
broom neatness
buckbean calm repose
burdock importunity
buttercup ingratitude
calycanthus benevolence
candytuft indifference
canterbury bell gratitude
carnation disdain
cedar tree strength
chamomile energy
cherry blossom spiritual beauty
chestnut render me justice
china aster variety
china pink aversion
chrysanthemum cheerfulness
clematis mental beauty
coltsfoot maternal care
columbine half folly
coriander concealed worth
cowslip native grace
crocus youthful gladness
cypress mourning
daffodil delusive hope
dahlia dignity and elegance
daisy innocence
dandelion oracle
dewplant serenade
dogwood durability
eglantine poetry
elder compassion
elm dignity
evergreen poverty
everlasting unceasing
remembrance
fennel strength
fern sincerity
fir time
flax acknowledged kindness
forget-me-not true love
foxglove I am ambitious for
your sake
fuchsia confiding love

geranium
ivy-leaved bridal favour
lemon a tranquil mind
nutmeg I shall meet you
oak true friendship
rose preference
scarlet consolation
silver recall
gillyflower lasting beauty
glory flower glorious beauty
goldenrod encouragement
harebell grief
hawthorn hope
hazel reconciliation
heartsease pansy think of me
heliotrope devotion
hellebore calumny
hollyhock fruitfulness
hops injustice
horse chestnut luxuriancy
houseleek vivacity
hyacinth game, play
hydrangea heartlessness
iceplant your looks freeze me
iris a message for you
ivy friendship
jasmine (white) amiability
jasmine (yellow) elegant
gracefulness
jonquil desire
judas tree unbelief
juniper protection
laburnum pensive beauty
lady's slipper capricious beauty
larch boldness
larkspur fickleness
laurel glory
lavender acknowledgement
lemon bloom discretion
lettuce cold-hearted
lilac first emotions of love
lily (white) purity, modesty
lily-of-the-valley return of
happiness
linden tree matrimony
lobelia malevolence
locust-tree affection beyond
the grave
London pride frivolity
lotus estranged love
love-in-a-mist perplexity
love-in-a-puzzle embarrassment
love-lies-bleeding hopeless,
not heartless
lupin sorrow, dejection
magnolia love of nature
maize plenty
mallow sweet disposition
mandrake rarity
maple reserve
marigold inquietude
meadow saffron my best days
are past

meadowsweet uselessness
mignonette excellence and loveliness
mimosa sensitiveness
mint virtue
mistletoe I surmount all obstacles
moonwort forgetfulness
moss (tuft of) maternal love
motherwort secret love
mouse-ear forget me not
mulberry tree wisdom
mushroom suspicion
myrtle love in absence
narcissus egotism
nasturtium patriotism
nettle slander
nightblooming cereus transient beauty
nightshade dark thoughts
nosegay gallantry
oak hospitality
oats music
oleander beware
olive branch peace
orange tree generosity
orchid a belle
ox-eye daisy obstacle
palm victory
parsley entertainment
passionflower religious superstition
peach blossom I am your captive
pennyroyal flee away
peony ostentation
periwinkle sweet remembrance
peruvian heliotrope infatuation
petunia thou art less proud than they deem thee
phlox we are united
pimpernel assignation
pine pity
pineapple you are perfect
pink purity of affection
plane tree genius
plum tree keep your promises
polyanthus confidence
pomegranate foolishness
poppy consolation of sleep
prickly pear satire
primrose early youth
primrose (evening) I am more constant than thou
privet prohibition
ragged robin dandy
rose
    Austrian very lovely
    bridal simplicity and beauty
    burgundy simplicity and beauty

damask bashful love
monthly beauty ever new
moss pleasure without alloy
musk capricious beauty
white silent sadness
yellow infidelity
rosebud a young girl
rosemary remembrance
rue purification
rush docility
saffron excess is dangerous
sage domestic virtues
St John's Wort animosity
scabious unfortunate attachment
serpentine cactus horror
snapdragon presumption
snowball thoughts of heaven
southernwood jesting
spiderwort transient happiness
star of Bethlehem the light of our path
strawberry perfect excellence
striped pink refusal
sumach splendour
sunflower false riches
sweetbrier poetry
sweet-pea departure
sweet william a smile
syringa memory
tamarisk crime
tansy resistance
teasel misanthropy
thistle I will never forget thee
thornapple deceitful charms
thyme activity
trumpet-flower separation
tulip declaration of love
valerian accommodating disposition
venus's fly-trap deceit
venus's looking-glass flattery
verbena sensibility
vine intoxication
violet
    blue modesty
    white candour
    yellow rural happiness
virgin's bower filial love
wake-robin ardour
wallflower fidelity in misfortune
waterlily purity of heart
weeping willow forsaken
wheat riches
wintercherry deception
witch hazel a spell
wood sorrel joy
woodbine fraternal joy
wormwood absence
yarrow thou alone canst cure
yew sorrow
zinnia absence

A rose is a rose is a rose?

One morning, as he was cutting roses in his garden, Florentino Ariza could not resist the temptation of taking one to her on his next visit. It was a difficult problem in the language of flowers because she was a recent widow. A red rose, symbol of flaming passion, might offend her mourning. Yellow roses, which in another language were the flowers of good fortune, were an expression of jealousy in the common vocabulary. . . . After much thought he risked a white rose, which he liked less than the others because it was insipid and mute: it did not say anything. At the last minute, in case Fermina Daza was suspicious enough to attribute some meaning to it, he removed the thorns.

Gabriel García Márquez *Love in the Time of Cholera*

Chapter 9

Squaring the circle
Signs for all seasons

As every mathematician knows, to square the circle, i.e. to draw a square exactly equal in area to any given circle is, of course, impossible; similarly, to include in a work of this nature all the signs and symbols even in current usage. This final chapter, however, looks at some of the many aspects not mentioned elsewhere. Beginning with alchemy, and ending with the the zodiac, the selection takes in signs and symbols associated with subjects as diverse as music and birthstones, pubs and weather forecasts.

Alchemy

The word is thought to derive from Arabic *al kimia*, 'the art of the land of Khem', the Arabic name for Egypt, and from Greek *khemeia*, 'the art of transmutation'. In the Middle Ages, alchemy was both a science and a philosophy. It was concerned principally with finding a way to transmute or transform base metals, such as lead or mercury, into gold and silver – the noble, or perfect metals (so-called because the air had no effect on them). Alchemists also laboured ceaselessly for the 'philosopher's stone', a magical substance which would transform all

FIRE	WATER	AIR	EARTH
COPPER	LEAD	MERCURY	BRASS
ARSENIC	PHOSPHORUS	SULPHUR	SALTPETRE
GINGER	VINEGAR	BRIMSTONE	SALT

Alchemical symbols

metals into gold (needless to say, the problem of which materials and which processes would effect this transformation was never solved).

Some of the alchemical symbols for materials are illustrated elsewhere (see astronomy); shown here is a selection of the others, beginning with the four elements or 'essences' of air, earth, fire, water, of which everything else was believed to be composed (alcohol, for example, was 'burnt' or 'fire water'; it was represented by the combined symbols of fire and water). Incidentally, this belief in the four principal elements, established in the 4th century BC by the Greek philosopher Aristotle, survived at least until the 17th century; the ancients also believed in a fifth, highest and purest essence. This 'quintessence' was thought to be the substance of the heavenly bodies.

Alchemists used different symbols for the elements and other substances; they varied from age to age and country to country.

Astronomy

Some of the symbols employed in modern astronomy (from Greek *astronomia*, literally 'star arrangement') date back at least to the astrology and alchemy of the Middle Ages, though in some cases their origins are much older. In addition to their use on star charts and maps, they also represented the metals and days of the week associated with the Sun, Moon, and the other classical planets Mercury, Venus, Mars, Jupiter, and Saturn. The symbols, which were standardised in the late 15th century, are listed here in their traditional order, together with those allotted to more recent discoveries.

Sun The disc symbol dates back to Egyptian hieroglyphs. It was also the alchemical symbol for **gold**, and for **Sunday** (Latin *dies solis*, 'the day of the Sun'), which the Romans dedicated to the Sun.

Moon The crescent moon derives from an Egyptian hieroglyph. To medieval alchemists and astrologers, it was the symbol for **silver**, and **Monday** (Anglo-Saxon *monandaeg* meaning 'day of the Moon', a translation of the Latin *dies lunae*, hence the French *lundi*).

Mercury The Greeks called this planet Hermes, after their god of commerce and invention, who also served as messenger and herald for the other gods. Hermes' Roman counterpart was Mercury. The planetary symbol represents the gods' Caduceus* or 'herald's wand', with two serpents entwined around it. Alchemists used the same symbol for **quicksilver** (their name for the element mercury) and **Wednesday** (in Latin *dies Mercurii*, 'Mercury's day', hence the French *mercredi*, Spanish *miercoles*, Italian *mercoledì*). In biology, the symbol signifies any hermaphroditic organism, such as an earthworm, which has both male and female reproductive organs.

Venus The Romans named the second planet from the Sun after their goddess of love and beauty. The original symbol (the crossbar was added in the early 16th century to make it less pagan) is thought to represent, appropriately for the goddess, either a necklace or a mirror. It was the alchemical symbol for **copper** (mirrors were once made of polished copper), and for **Friday** (named after Frigg or Freya, the Norse equivalent of Venus to whom the Romans dedicated this day; in Latin *dies Veneris*, 'the day of Venus', hence the French *vendredi*). The use of Venus' symbol in botany and zoology to denote **female** (and now

The Z's, an ancient sign at grocers shops, look very enigmatical; but I am told they allude to the word zinziber, or ginger, and intimated the sale of that article.

W. Roberts *Looker-on* (1792)

commonly **woman**) was originated by the Swedish biologist Carl Linnaeus in the mid-18th century.

Earth The orb and cross, and the cross within the circle (both Christian symbols) came about in the late 16th century, after the Earth was accepted as being a planet.

Mars Because of its fiery aspect, a symbol of bloodshed, the Romans named the planet closest to Earth after their god of war; the planetary symbol represents his spear and shield. It was the symbol for **Tuesday** (named after the Teutonic god Tiu, who was identified with Mars; in Latin, the day was called *dies Martis*, 'day of Mars', hence the French *mardi*) and for **iron**, the metal most associated with the god. Since the mid-18th century, the symbol for Mars has also been used in biology to signify **male** (see Venus).

Jupiter The symbol for the largest planet, named after the ruler of the gods in Roman mythology, derives from the Greek letter *zeta*, **Z**, the initial of Zeus, the Greek equivalent of Jupiter; a cross was added to it in the early 15th century to make it more Christian. It was the symbol for **tin**, and for **Thursday** (from 'Thor's day', a translation of the Latin *dies Jovis*, 'Jove's' or 'Jupiter's day'; hence the French *jeudi*. Both Jove and Thor were gods of thunder; at one time Thursday was otherwise known as Thunderday, hence the German *'Donnerstag'*). In biology, it is the symbol for a perennial herb or plant.

Saturn To the ancient Greeks, Saturn was the most remote planet. The Greek philosopher Aristotle named it Kronos after the mythological ruler of the Titans and the son of Uranus; the Romans named it Saturn after the deity they identified with Kronos, their god of seedtime and harvest. Saturn's symbol of a scythe or sickle is clearly visible in some versions of the planetary symbol. The ancient astrologers and alchemists also used the symbol for **Saturday** (from *dies Saturni*, the day the Romans dedicated to Saturn), and **lead**.

Uranus The seventh planet, discovered in 1781 by the English astronomer William Herschel, is named after the Greek god of Heaven (the son and husband of Ge, the goddess of Earth). The symbol shown means 'Herschel's planet'; it replaced the original symbol, which was thought too similar to that of Mars.

Neptune The trident is the symbol of the Roman god of the sea (Greek Poseidon), after whom the eighth planet is named. Neptune, discovered by two German astronomers, Johann Galle and Heinrich D'Arrest, in 1846. An alternative symbol, a monogram of L and V, was invented by French astronomers to celebrate their colleague Urbain Le Verrier, who had calculated the existence and position of Neptune shortly before it was officially discovered.

Pluto The symbol for the ninth and furthermost planet has a double significance: both as a monogram of the first two letters of Pluto, the Roman god of the underworld, and the initials of the American astronomer Percival Lowell, who had argued its existence many years earlier, and at whose observatory it was discovered on 18 February 1930. Lowell, incidentally, had called his unknown planet 'Planet X', the name now commonly used for any planet in our Solar System still undiscovered.

In the years since William Procter from England and James Gamble from Ireland first joined forces in Cincinatti, Ohio, in 1837 to make soap, their company, Procter & Gamble (P&G), has become one of the world's leading consumer goods conglomerates. Its corporate trademark originated around 1851, when a wharf hand daubed a cross on a wooden box of Star candles, an early P&G product. The cross developed into an encircled star, and then to represent the original American colonies, 13 stars. Among merchants and riverboat stevedores, the mark became a valuable identifier of P&G cargo. By 1882, when the company registered the symbol with the US Patent Office as its trademark, it had evolved into a 'man-in-the-moon', a popular decorative device of the times. This in turn was further refined over the years. In 1991, two new corporate marks, a 'P&G' logo, and a 'Procter & Gamble' wordmark, were

1882

1992

introduced worldwide for use on company stationery, business cards, and other items. In keeping with the more modern look of the new marks, the 'Moon and Stars' was also modified slightly.

Chemistry

The modern idea of an element as a substance which cannot be reduced into simpler substances was first defined in 1661 by the Irish physicist and chemist Robert Boyle (1627–91) in *The Skeptical Chymist*. The first person to use letters as symbols for the elements was the Scottish chemist Thomas Thomson in an article on Mineralogy in the *Supplement* (1801) to the 3rd edition of the *Encyclopædia Britannica*. Credit, however, for the modern international system of element symbols goes to the Swedish chemist Baron Jöns Jakob Berzelius (1779–1848). In 1818, Berzelius (who also discovered Ce in 1803, Se in 1817, and Th in 1828) proposed using letters of the alphabet based on the Latin names of the elements; hence, for example, Au for *aurum* 'gold'. An element symbol is used in a formula or description of a chemical compound, followed by a subscript figure giving the number of atoms it contains in that compound. H, for example, means one atom of hydrogen, and H_2 one molecule of hydrogen consisting of two atoms; thus the chemical formula for water, H_2O, is a symbolic representation of its composition and signifies one molecule of water consisting of two atoms of hydrogen and one of oxygen.

Listed here in alphabetical order of symbol (with derivations where not immediately apparent), are the elements with their names and atomic numbers. The most recent discoveries, as yet unnamed or not finally named, are in *italics*.

Ac	Actinium	89
Ag	Silver (Latin, *argentum*)	47

Al	Aluminium	13
Am	Americium	95
Ar	Argon	18

'We had a secretary working here once who managed to steal a lot of our most valuable turquoise out of the vault. The labels read "turquoise" then, which made it easy, but now they don't.'

'What do they say?'
She smiled and pointed to a row of boxes. I looked at the labels and read $CuAl_6(PO_4)_4(OH)_8.4-5(H_2O)$ on each of them.

Enough to put anyone off for life', I said.

'Exactly. That's the point. Mr Franklin could read formulas as easily as words, and I've got used to them myself now.'

Dick Francis *Straight*

Symbolic support

When the US Republican Senator from Arizona Barry Goldwater was running for the presidency in 1964, campaign supporters designed a special bumpersticker. It read simply, AuH_2O.

Little Willie is no more,
For what Little Willie thought
*   was H_2O*
Was H_2SO_4.

Child's mnemonic for chemical formulae (H_2SO_4 is sulphuric acid)

Symbol	Element	Number
As	Arsenic	33
At	Astatine	85
Au	Gold (Latin, *aurum*)	79
B	Boron	5
Ba	Barium	56
Be	Beryllium	4
Bi	Bismuth	83
Bk	Berkelium	97
Br	Bromine	35
C	Carbon	6
Ca	Calcium	20
Cd	Cadmium	48
Ce	Cerium	58
Cf	Californium	98
Cl	Chlorine	17
Cm	Curium	96
Co	Cobalt	27
Cr	Chromium	24
Cs	Caesium	55
Cu	Copper (Latin, *cuprum*)	29
Dy	Dysprosium	66
Er	Erbium	68
Es	Einsteinium	99
Eu	Europium	63
F	Fluorine	9
Fe	Iron (Latin, *ferrum*)	26
Fm	Fermium	100
Fr	Francium	87
Ga	Gallium	31
Gd	Gadolinium	64
Ge	Germanium	32
H	Hydrogen	1
Ha	Hahnium	105
He	Helium	2
Hf	Hafnium	72
Hg	Mercury (Greek, *hydrargyros*)	80
Ho	Holmium	67
I	Iodine	53
In	Indium	49
Ir	Iridium	77
K	Potassium (Latin, *kalium*)	19
Kr	Krypton	36
La	Lanthanum	57
Li	Lithium	3
Lr	Lawrencium	103
Lu	Lutetium	71
Md	Mendelevium	101
Mg	Magnesium	12
Mn	Manganese	25
Mo	Molybdenum	42
N	Nitrogen	7
Na	Sodium (Latin, *natrium*)	11
Nb	Niobium	41
Nd	Neodymium	60
Ne	Neon	10
Ni	Nickel	28
No	Nobelium	102
Np	Neptunium	93
O	Oxygen	8
Os	Osmium	76
P	Phosphorous	15
Pa	Protactinium	91
Pb	Lead (Latin, *plumbum*)	82
Pd	Palladium	46
Pm	Promethium	61
Po	Polonium	84
Pr	Praesodymium	59
Pt	Platinum	78
Pu	Plutonium	94
Ra	Radium	88
Rf	Rutherfordium	104
Rb	Rubidium	37
Re	Rhenium	75
Rh	Rhodium	45
Rn	Radon	86
Ru	Ruthenium	44
S	Sulphur	16
Sb	Antimony (Latin, *stibium*)	51
Sc	Scandium	21
Se	Selenium	34

Si	Silicon	14		Une	(unnilnonium)	109
Sm	Samarium	62		Unh	(unnilhexium)	106
Sn	Tin (Latin, *stannum*)	50		Uno	(not yet named)	108
				Uns	(not yet named)	107
Sr	Strontium	38		Uun	(unununium)	110
Ta	Tantalum	73		V	Vanadium	23
Tb	Terbium	65		W	Tungsten (German, *Wolfram*)	74
Tc	Technetium	43				
Te	Tellurium	52		Xe	Xenon	54
Th	Thorium	90		Y	Yttrium	39
Ti	Titanium	22		Yb	Ytterbium	70
Tl	Thallium	81		Zn	Zinc	30
Tm	Thulium	69		Zr	Zirconium	40
U	Uranium	92				

Colours

Since earliest times, colours have been used to great effect in every form of visual and literal symbolism. Their meanings, and the associations they trigger differ widely from culture to culture. Here are the seven principal colours and some of their numerous symbolic uses ancient and modern.

Black night, death, penitence, putrefaction, sin, evil and destructive forces, eternal silence, the void. Because it absorbs or obliterates all other colours, it is also despair or denial, and as the opposite of white, represents negative forces. In Chinese philosophy, it is yin. In the Christian church, black signifies grief and mourning, also sorrow and sympathy. In medieval art, it represents penitence. Formerly one of the five colours prescribed in 1200 by the 176th pope, Innocent III (1198–1216), to mark the seasons of the Christian calendar, it was used at masses for the dead, and at services on Good Friday on vestments, altar hangings, and other liturgical objects in the ceremonies. In recent years, with the Church's taking cultural differences into consideration (in Japan, for instance, black signifies joy), the use of black in ceremonies has been discontinued.

Numerous terms are associated with black as the colour of death; the black flag of anarchy, or of piracy (compare Jolly Roger), for instance, or the black cap (otherwise known as Judgment Cap), the square of black material formerly worn by a judge in an English court when pronouncing the death sentence. The bubonic plague, which killed around 25 million people in 1348 in Europe alone, is commonly known as the Black Death because the disease literally turned the body black with putrefaction. The occult science practised by witches and wizards and others who professed to have dealings with the Prince of Darkness, the Devil, is black magic, or the black arts (black, here, means diabolical, though some derive it from nigromancy, a corruption of necromancy, divination by corpses).

In heraldic language, black is *sable*, from the animal. It is denoted on uncoloured drawings by the abbreviation s or sa, or represented in engravings by crossed horizontal and vertical lines, and in printing as a solid.

Goodness is another quality that always goes with blackness. Very good people indeed, you will notice, dress altogether in black, even to gloves and neckties, and they will probably take to black shirts before long. Medium goods indulge in light trousers on weekdays, and some of them even go so far as to wear fancy waistcoats. On the other hand, people who care nothing for a future state go about in light suits; and there have been known wretches so abandoned as to wear a white hat. Such people, however, are never spoken of in genteel society, and perhaps I ought not to have referred to them here.

Jerome K Jerome *Idle Thoughts of an Idle Fellow*

Black death

The custom of wearing black for mourning and at funerals has its origins in superstition. People believed that black apparel could serve as a disguise so that the spirit of the deceased might not recognise and perhaps haunt them; similarly, veiling one's face was thought to confuse any demon lingering with intent to snare another life.

Black as the colour of death and mourning is by no means universal. Some aboriginal races painted their faces white to fool the dead that the mourners were not living beings to be envied but ghosts themselves. Gypsies used to wear red at funerals to symbolise physical life and energy. In Burma, the colour of mourning is yellow, in Turkey violet; in Ethiopia, a greyish-brown was worn in allusion to the colour of the earth to which the dead return, and in the South Seas, islanders wore white and black stripes as an expression of how hope and sorrow, light and darkness, life and death, are never far apart. In Armenia, blue expresses the hope that the deceased has gone to heaven. White, the prevailing colour in China, represents happiness and prosperity in the next world. Mourners in ancient Rome sometimes wore white; so, too, did the English king Henry VIII after he had his second wife, Anne Boleyn, beheaded in 1536. She, incidentally, had worn yellow just four months earlier in mourning for her predecessor, Catherine of Aragon (some say in elation).

In *How Did It Begin?* Brasch cites an example of cultural difference in some parts of China, where the mourning colour was purple. 'When one US manufacturer of chewing gum changed its wrappers from green to purple, its export sales to China dropped alarmingly. It was subsequently discovered that the Chinese believed that the gum was meant to be chewed at funerals only!'

The custom of wearing a black band around the left sleeve as a sign of mourning in some English-speaking countries is a relic of the days of medieval chivalry, when a knight's lady would tie a scarf around his arm to bind him symbolically to serve her. In time, the scarf became a token of a man's loyalty to the departed, with whom he was linked even beyond the grave.

Blue as the colour of the clear sky above and the sea below, represents both height and depth; also aspiration, devotion, justice, perfection, contemplation, peace. The ancient Egyptians used blue to represent truth; it is an attribute of Zeus/Jupiter and Hera/Juno, the Greek and Roman god and goddess of heaven, who were thought to inhabit the heavens above the skies. Blue symbolises merit and supremacy. A broad dark blue ribbon is the badge of the Order of the Garter, the highest order of knighthood bestowed by the British Crown, which was established by Edward III in 1348. Consequently, 'blue ribbon' (US 'blue riband') expresses outstanding achievements in other spheres; the English horserace the Derby, for instance, is 'the blue ribbon of the turf'; the Blue Ribbon of the Atlantic is held by the passenger liner making the fastest crossing both ways (awarded to the *Queen Mary* 1935–52, from 1952 to the *United States*). Similarly, 'cordon bleu' (literally 'blue ribbon') now synonymous with the best chefs and cuisine, was once the emblem of the highest order of knighthood in France, the ancient order of *St Esprit* (Holy Ghost).

Additionally, blue is associated with royalty (hence, royal blue) and nobility; the epithet 'blue blood' for those of high or noble birth derives from the belief that the veins of the pure-blooded Spanish aristocracy were more blue than those of mixed ancestry. Similarly, 'true blue' implies exceptional integrity and fidelity, probably from the idea of such qualities being characteristic of blue blood. The now disparaging 'blue stocking' for a female intellectual, dates back to the early 15th century, when a society of learned men and women in Venice distinguished themselves by their blue stockings. Intellectual Parisiennes in the 1590s followed the custom. The term was introduced to English in the early 1750s, when Benjamin Stillingfleet, an impoverished gentleman, attended the soirées of the writer and society leader Mrs Elizabeth Montague (whom Dr Johnson dubbed 'Queen of the Blues') in blue worsted stockings instead of the fashionable black silk.

Blue is also doubt, and depression. Such expressions as 'to feel blue', or the more archaic 'have the blue devils', are linked with indigo dyers who were especially susceptible to melancholy (though whether this was due to the dyeing process or the effect of the colour itself is not known). 'Blues', the predominantly melancholic music of slow tempo and flattened thirds and sevenths, originated in the American South in the late 19th century; the earliest published blues is 'The Jelly Roll Blues', by the pianist Jelly Roll Morton in 1905.

In the UK, blue is the traditional colour of the Conservative Party, though why exactly is not known. Certainly, it was a favourite of the former Conservative Prime Minister Margaret Thatcher; as a parliamentary colleague once remarked: 'When she wears blue, the nation is in for a good thrashing'.

In the Christian church, blue is piety, sincerity, prudence; originally a liturgical colour, but now discontinued, it is still used occasionally in Spain for the Mass and certain other religious services. As well as constancy and fidelity, it is specifically associated with the Virgin Mary, the Queen of Heaven, and many white vestments are ornamented in blue for use on her feast days. In the verse 'something old, something new, something borrowed, something blue', traditionally associated with weddings, blue refers to fidelity and the protection of Mary. In the angelic hierarchy, cherubim, who are regarded as being engaged in devout contemplation, are represented as blue. In the Bible, blue, as the colour of a cloudless sky, symbolised revelation (Exodus 24:10); according to the book of Numbers (15:38) the Israelites were commanded to have a ribbon of blue fringe on the edge of their garments to remind them of God. In *Dynamic Dissonance*, Louis Danz records blue as the most expressive colour for the Arabians, 'the color of the very material heavens which hold the stars in place . . . in the mystery of which dwells the very finite infinite'.

The heraldic term for blue is azure (from Arabic *lazura*, for 'lapis-lazuli'). It is sometimes denoted by the abbreviation az, or represented in engraving and printing by horizontal lines.

Green the colour of spring, freshness, new growth, fertility, nature, freedom, joy, hope (because it betokens the coming of spring and the renewal of life), resurrection. Green is often used in the sense of permanence, or even immortality, as, for instance, when we speak of keeping a person's memory green. Compounded of blue and yellow, green is the mystic colour, the link between nature and the supernatural. Green signifies abundance, prosperity, stability; many nations have, or have had, green currency; the paper money first issued by the Government of the United States in 1862 during the Civil War, was called greenback because the back was printed in green. On the other hand, the colour also signified lack of money: in some European countries bankrupts in former times were forced to wear a green bonnet. At sea, a green flag signifies a wreck. On land, the colour is now commonly used to mean 'go ahead', 'proceed'; in railway signalling, the

I began my career in a lower bunkbed, using soft coloured pencils and a Big Red Indian Chief tablet, which I kept on the slats of the top bunk. I stored the stories in the springs. The coloured pencils were for different moods, such as brown for sadness, red for happiness, and blue for when they were outdoors. Mostly I wrote in red.

Garrison Keillor *Lake Wobegon Days*

Hex protection

In southeastern Pennsylvania, members of the Amish and Mennonite communities paint circular 'hex' signs on the sides of their barns, and on the doors and window shutters of their farmhouses. The word hex is thought to derive from the German *sechs*, meaning 'six', for many of the signs are of six-pointed stars. It may also be connected with the German *Hexe*, 'witch'.

The highly colourful signs are not merely decorative, but have a practical purpose. Sometimes known as 'painted prayers', they are used to protect the people and their animals from the evil eye, and from disease and lightning. Additionally, the various signs are said to promote fertility, cropgrowth, sunshine and rain. There are also signs for love and romance, for long life, and for faith, hope, and charity.

Hex signs include a number of traditional symbols, from raindrops, whirling geometric patterns, doves and 'distlefinks' (Pennsylvania Dutch for thistlefinch), to lilies, tulips, hearts, shamrocks, oak leaves and acorns. Often, the symbols are painted within a golden circle to symbolise eternity and everlasting life; blue is commonly used 'for the promise of heaven'.

Shown here is a selection of the many signs in recent or current use.

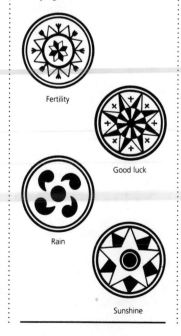

Fertility

Good luck

Rain

Sunshine

modern green for 'line clear', yellow or amber for 'caution', and red for 'stop' was standardised in Britain in 1893, and in the US about twenty years later. Prior to this, green had been used for caution, as expressed in the mnemonic: 'White is right, red is wrong; Green means gently go along.'

Green is decay, and mould. Osiris, the Egyptian god of vegetation and of corpses, was depicted as green. In folklore, it is the colour of pixies, thus mischievousness. It is envy, jealousy; in Shakespeare's *Othello*, Iago describes jealousy as 'the green-eyed monster'. As youth, green is unripeness, immaturity, inexperience, naïvety, the novice; in *Antony and Cleopatra*, Cleopatra refers to 'My salad days, when I was green in judgement'.

In the Christian church, green is the liturgical colour for the period after Epiphany and Trinity Sunday, and for days which are neither feasts nor fasts. Green is the sacred colour of Islam. Ireland is the 'Emerald Isle'; the 'wearing of the Green', an allusion to a popular Irish song, denotes Irish sympathies. The colour is commonly used on national flags to symbolise agriculture or forests. In recent years, its association with healthy plant-life has made it the perfect colour for ecological parties and organisations; such parties are now referred to as Green; their followers, the Greens, hold the 'green vote'.

In heraldic terms, green is *vert* (abbreviation vt); in engraving and monochrome printing, it is represented by diagonal lines 'in bend', from top left to bottom right.

Purple authority, dignity, glory, honour, majesty, royalty, power. As a combination of red and blue, it is the union of love and truth. Due to the fact that purple was the most costly dye, it was once the colour equivalent of the metal gold. Among the ancient Greeks and Romans, purple robes were worn by emperors, kings, military commanders, and magistrates. Hence, it became synonymous with the throne and power. In *Decline and Fall of the Roman Empire*, the historian Edward Gibbon uses the term 'Imperial purple' or 'the purple' to signify the Roman sovereignty. The expression 'born to the purple', used in connection with those born into the ruling class, derives from the tradition of Byzantine emperors that their children be born in a room decorated with the royal purple. When a Roman Catholic priest is created cardinal, he is said to be 'raised to the purple' (even though his hat and robes are red). The literary term 'purple prose' or 'purple patch' describes writing which is excessively rich, ornate, or overworked; the term was first used by the Roman poet Horace in *Ars Poetica* around 20 BC. Purple may also signify lust, decadence, and secrecy.

In the Christian church, purple symbolises absolution, repentance, mourning and sorrow; it is worn on Advent Sundays, during Lent, for ceremonies associated with the Passion, and on Ember Days, special days of fasting and abstinence. In heraldry, purple, known as purpure, is indicated in engravings and monochrome printing by diagonal lines 'in bend sinister', from top right to bottom left.

Red the most aggressive colour, symbolises blood, anger, fire, passion, wounds, war, slaughter, danger, threat, revolution, strength, anarchy, martyrdom, courage, and health and virility (as, for instance, in red-blooded). Red is the colour of life. According to J.E. Cirlot in his *Dictionary of Symbols*, prehistoric man smeared any object he wished to bring to life with blood. To the Romans, the colour signified divinity;

they often painted the faces of their gods red. When a Roman general was received in triumph his face was painted red, in honour of their god of war, Mars. Similarly, they named the planet closest to Earth, regarded as Earth's 'twin', after Mars, because of its fiery red colour. Even earlier, the Babylonians had called the planet Nergal, after their god of death.

As the symbol of bloodshed, red has been used for military purposes for centuries. In the British Navy, a red flag, the 'flag of defiance', was in use as early as the 17th century as the signal to 'engage the enemy'. Red has been the colour of anarchy for at least two centuries. Followers of the Italian nationalist leader Giuseppe Garibaldi (1807–82) were nicknamed 'redshirts' for the red shirts they wore as a symbol of their challenge to the established order. According to the English vexillologist William Crampton, the original Red Flag was hoisted in Paris during the French Revolution to announce the declaration of martial law; the mob promptly took it for themselves, brandishing it to show that their power was superior to that of the law. It was adopted by the Communists in the 1871 Paris Commune, in Russia during the rising of 1905, the October Revolution in 1917, and in other countries where communism found support (hence the term 'Reds'). The red flag is the symbol of international socialism, and left-wing politics in general. The socialist song 'The Red Flag' was written by Irishman James Connell during a 15-minute train journey between London's Charing Cross and New Cross. Published in the socialist newspaper *Justice* on 21 December 1889, it was first performed in public in Liverpool and Glasgow a few days later. The British Labour Party took the song as their anthem at their annual conferences in the early 1920s. Since 1986, when the party adopted a new and less aggressive image, the song has been downplayed; even so, its connotations have never been far from the surface .

Labour's new image includes a red rose, which is commonly regarded as a symbol of human love. The concept of red as the colour of love, derives from fire, which suggests heat, and passion; heart symbols, for instance on playing cards, greetings cards (such as those sent on St Valentine's Day, 14 February) and on slogans such as 'I ♥ NY', are always red (a variation of the last has been adopted by environmental organisations, for instance 'I ♥ Lead-free', with the heart coloured green).

In medieval Christian art, red was the colour of both charity and love, particularly divine love. Seraphim, the highest of the nine choirs of angels in the celestial hierarchy, and nearest to the throne of God, 'having their being in the divine heat and fervour of adoration' are usually depicted in red. It is the liturgical colour for Passion or Palm Sunday, and for Holy Cross or Holy Rood Day (14 September), which celebrates the appearance of the Cross to Constantine; at Whitsuntide, the colour recalls the Holy Spirit who came down from heaven like tongues of fire. It also commemorates martyrs, who shed blood for their faith. A 'red letter day', now a memorable or especially happy day, derives from the former custom of marking saints' or other important holy days in church calendars and almanacs in red ink. The expression 'in the red', meaning 'in debt' derives from the banking practice of recording overdrawn accounts in red ink. The term 'red tape', synonymous with bureaucracy, alludes to the red ribbon used since the 17th century to tie together official legal or government documents.

Red is symbolic of anger, hence the expression 'to see red'; red hair is commonly regarded as a sign of a hot temper. The colour is used on

Life class

Red has been praised for its nobility of the colour of life. But the true colour of life is not red. Red is the colour of violence, or of life broken open, edited, published.

Alice Meynell *The Colour of Life*

Red is the colour of England; I cannot bear the sight of it.

Napoleon Bonaparte

Redheads

Morgan le Fay hated him with her whole heart, and she never would have softened toward him. And yet his crime was committed more in thoughtlessness than deliberate depravity. He had said she had red hair. Well, she had; but that was no way to speak of it. When red-headed people are above a certain social grade, their hair is auburn.

Mark Twain *A Connecticut Yankee in King Arthur's Court*

I don't know why, but whenever I dream of a nurse she always has red hair. Red hair makes a man want to recover his health quickly, so that he can get on his feet and the nurse off hers.

Groucho Marx, letter to his son Arthur, summer 1940

signage worldwide to warn of danger, or as a stop signal; a red alert is an instruction to be prepared for an emergency, the last state of readiness for imminent danger. In international football, and since the 1992/93 season at all levels in English football, showing a player a red card indicates dismissal from the field for misconduct. By extension, the red card has come to mean disfavour and censure in other areas; for instance, 'We needed someone famous to throw into jail. It will show all Christmas drink drivers a red card', said the chairman of the Campaign Against Drinking and Driving, after the England international and captain of the Arsenal football team Tony Adams was sentenced to four months in prison in December 1990.

Red is shame and disgrace. Mark Twain once wrote that 'man is the only creature that blushes, or needs to'. In Puritan New England in the 17th and 18th centuries, women accused of adultery were marked with the scarlet letter 'A'; a scarlet woman is a prostitute, a distant allusion to St John's vision (Revelation 17:1–6) of a woman in scarlet 'upon a scarlet coloured beast, full of names of blasphemy ... drunken with the blood of the martyrs'; upon her forehead was written 'The Mother of Harlots and Abominations of the Earth'. The area in towns where brothels are centred is commonly known as the red light district, from the red light sometimes displayed outside. On a lighter note, the Irish poet W. B. Yeats noted that 'Red is the colour of magic in almost every country. The caps of fairies are well-nigh always red'.

In heraldic language, red is *gules*, (abbreviation gu); in engravings and monochrome printing, it is represented by vertical lines.

Not quite red, not quite white, is **pink**, the colour of flesh, sensuality, and according to the food industry one of the most appetising colours. During World War II, homosexuals in Nazi-occupied countries were forced to identify themselves by wearing a pink triangular cloth badge. Pink, and in some places the pink triangle, has since been adopted by movements such as Gay Pride.

White purity, chastity, peace, virginity, light, wisdom, and because it conceals nothing, innocence and truth. White magic is magic used for the purposes of good, often healing, or against evil or black magic. White is the colour most associated with sacredness and religious devotion. The sacred horses of Greek, Roman, Celtic and Germanic cultures were white. In parts of south-eastern Asia, white elephants are regarded as sacred (mainly because of their rarity). The expression 'white elephant' which is used to refer to a large and possibly impressive but useless and expensive possession, originates with a king of Siam. To rid himself of an unwanted courtier, the king presented him with a white elephant. The cost of maintaining the animal in the manner due to its sacred status ruined the courtier. The lily (*lilium candidum*) is a symbol of purity and of the Virgin Mary, hence its popular name 'Madonna lily'. A white rose is also virginity. In ancient Rome, the vestal virgins, the priestesses who tended the sacred fire in the temple of Vesta, the goddess of the hearth, were dressed in white. The priest of Osiris in ancient Egypt, the Greek priests of Zeus, and the Druids performed their ceremonies in white as do the ministers of many religions today. In the Christian church, white vestments are worn at the consecration of bishops and churches. In the Middle Ages, it was customary during Lent to cover the altar, lectern, and pulpit, with white cloth to signify a period of abstinence by chastity in colour. Pope Pius V (reigned 1566–72) prescribed that ordinary papal attire be white, for both truth and

Passionate pink

Pink is the colour of romance, and a friend tells me that the girl with a pink dress at the party is the one who is selected for each dance.

Alfred Carl Hottes *Garden Facts and Fancies*

Pink acts like benzedrine on most males' jaded chivalry.

William E. Richardson, quoted in *The New York Times*, 30 August 1953

chastity. In the Bible and other religious literature, there are numerous sacred metaphorical uses; in Ecclesiastes (9:8), for example, white garments are expressive of joy; in Isaiah (1:18) white suggests cleansing of sin. It is the colour of baptism and first communion, of Christmas, Easter, Ascension, Corpus Christi, and the feasts of saints who were not martyrs. In the Eastern Church, white is used at all services from Easter to Ascensiontide, even funerals.

A white flag signifies surrender, truce, and by extension peace, goodwill. The custom is thought to have originated in ancient times, when, to announce their peaceful intentions and thus ensure immunity from harm, messengers carried a white scroll or a symbolic representation of it aloft in a cleft stick.

On the other hand, white is also blankness and absolute silence. Combined with red, it may signify death; even today there is a superstition among some nursing staff that red and white flowers brought onto the ward is bad luck, red being symbolic of blood, and white of the shroud. In some countries, such as China and Japan, white is the colour of mourning. Ghosts, who have no substance, are commonly depicted in white. The colour, or rather lack of it, is also symbolic of cowardice. The expression lily-livered derives from the ancient belief that a coward's liver was bloodless. In time of war, and particularly during World War I, men who were not in uniform, and thus thought to be avoiding military duty, were sometimes given or sent a white feather. The symbolism here originates with cock-fighting; the feathers of thoroughbred gamecocks, the best fighters, were red and black; a single white feather in a cock's tail betrayed an impure strain, thus a bird likely to be lacking in courage. Thus 'to show the white feather' came to imply cowardice, both among cocks and men.

In heraldry, silver is depicted as white. Called *argent* (arg), it is represented in engraving and printing by a plain or white field.

Yellow the colour of the Sun, and summer; in alchemy, gold was considered to be congealed light. Because of its solar association (light, heat, power), and as the colour closest to gold, the most revered metal, yellow is often symbolic of glory, and divine power. In Greek mythology, yellow is an attribute of Apollo, the sun god, and the sacred colour of Zeus, the ruler of Heaven and Earth. In China, it signified imperial dignity. During the Ch'ing Dynasty, the last ruling dynasty of China (1644–1911) only the emperor was permitted to wear it. In India, a bride stains her hands yellow to signify the happiness and unity she expects.

By contrast, yellow is the colour of cowardice, jealousy, treachery, deceit. In France, it is the colour of a cuckold; in some parts of medieval Europe until the 16th century, yellow was daubed on the doors of felons and traitors; in art, both Cain and Judas Iscariot are commonly depicted with yellow beards. In some Christian countries, Jews were made to dress in yellow, because they betrayed Jesus; during World War II, in countries under Nazi occupation, Jews had to identify themselves by wearing a yellow star, 'the 'badge of shame'. Heretics condemned by the Spanish Inquisition to be burned at the stake were dressed in yellow as a symbol of their treachery to God. Cowards have a yellow streak, or are yellow-bellied or yellow-livered, this last from the ancient belief that a coward's liver, being bloodless, was yellow (see white).

Yellow is the colour of sickness. Formerly displayed on board ship as a signal of capital punishment, a yellow flag or 'Yellow Jack' was later

All looks yellow to the jaundiced eye.

Alexander Pope *An Essay on Criticism* 1711

Cross purposes

Advocates of alphabet reform have often proposed the 24th letter X as the likeliest candidate for extinction, but even if they had their way, this 'embodiment of symmetry' would still survive as one of the most versatile graphic symbols. In the ancient Phoenician alphabet, the symbol signifying the t-sound (also written as +, which evolved into the Greek and Roman T and t) was called taw, their word for mark or sign. Listed here are just a few of the many ways in which X makes its mark.

In Roman numeration, it is 10 (thus XX is 20, XXX 30, and so on); on its side or *couché*, X means 1000, and surmounted by a horizontal bar 10 000. In mathematics, it denotes multiplication, and when indicating dimensions in measurements, it represents the word 'by', as for instance in 2 x 2. In algebra, x denotes an unknown or variable quantity. X, y, and z, were introduced by the French philosopher and mathematician René Descartes in 1637 to provide symbols of unknowns to correspond to the symbols a, b, c, of knowns. X is now commonly used to denote any unknown or unnamed factor, thing, or persons, for example, 'Mr X', or 'brand X'. In astronomy, the name 'Planet X' is used for any planet as yet undiscovered in the Solar System beyond the orbit of Pluto, the furthest known and named planet. When Professor Wilhelm Konrad von Röntgen accidentally discovered new and penetrating rays at Würzburg, Bavaria in 1895, he christened them X-rays 'for the sake of brevity', but more specifically because he was unable to determine their exact

nature. On the other hand, the idiom 'As sure as eggs is eggs', which came into popular usage in the 17th century, means that something is certain; it is a corruption of the mathematical phrase 'as sure as X is X'.

In biology, an X chromosome is one of an identical pair in a woman's cells (X chromosomes are associated with female characteristics); a man has one X and one Y chromosome; it is also used to represent 'mated with' or 'cross-fertilised with'. In chemistry, it was formerly the symbol for the element Xenon (now designated Xe). In cartography and geology, X marks the spot, the location or position of a point. It is also the power of magnification, for instance 'a 50x telescope'.

X stands for words such as extra, experimental (in the US Air Force it designates experimental aircraft); in chess, X means 'captures', and in finance 'ex' or 'without', as for example 'ex dividend', which in stock market trading indicates that the next dividend is to be excluded in that sale.

X is commonly 'the error mark', used to mark or cross out mistakes in writing. Similarly, 'to x', the shortest verb in English, means to cancel or obliterate with a series of x's. In proofreading, x indicates a mechanical defect in type.

In films for public exhibition, X is the most censorious rating. Introduced by the British Board of Film Censors in 1951 for films which *The Times* (14 July 1950) referred to as 'wholly adult in conception and treatment', X replaced H (for horror) to include sex and horror, and films designated

used as a signal of infectious disease aboard, or of quarantine. In the International Code of Signals, a yellow flag stands for the letter Q; when entering territorial waters from abroad a ship flies the Q flag to mean 'My ship is healthy and I request free pratique' (clearance to proceed into port after compliance with quarantine or health regulations). As the International Safety Colour, yellow is commonly used on signage (though it is said to disturb horses); rescue helicopters, and in some countries fire engines, formerly red, are now yellow. Along with brown, yellow is thought to be the safest colour on the road. (According to an accident-by-colour survey conducted by the UK Department of Transport in 1991, black or white cars will more likely be involved in accidents than cars of other colours; the next most accident-prone

X were prohibited to persons under 16. The **first 'X' certificate** was awarded to a French film *La Vie Commence Demain* (Life Begins Tomorrow), which opened in London on 9 January 1951 (the film was given X status because of a sequence dealing with artificial insemination. By the end of the 1960s, 'x-rated' films had surpassed the number of A (adults and accompanied children only) and U (universal exhibition) films combined. The age was raised to 18 in 1970; in 1980 X was replaced by the symbol 18, meaning not permitted to be shown publicly to persons under 18. In the US, the classification, called 'x-rated' ('used only for out-and-out porn', according to *The Guardian*, 15 October 1983) was introduced by the Motion Picture Association of America in November 1968 (for persons over 16 only). The **first film to be x-rated in the US** was Brian de Palma's *Greetings*, which opened in New York on 15 December 1968. The term 'x-rated' is now commonly used to describe anything considered shocking, for example 'x-rated language'. Obscene expletives, for instance, are occasionally denoted in print by a series of X's.

Commonly used in flags and heraldry, X is the cross known as saltire (see St Andrew's Cross, St Patrick's Cross). Derived from Latin *saltare*, 'to leap'; the word originally meant a cross-shaped stile erected to prevent cattle straying, but which people could jump over. One of the simplest charges in heraldry, a saltire was said to be granted only to soldiers who had successfully besieged a town.

Among its many sacred connotations, X sometimes stands for the name Christ (from the first letter of the Greek XPICTOC *khristos*). The commonest use these days is in the word Xmas. According to *The Oxford English Dictionary*, Xmas is first found in print in 1755, though an earlier form, X'temmas, had appeared as early as 1551.

On beer barrels, X once indicated beer on which the tax (possibly in multiples of 10 pence or shillings) had been paid, and that the beer was of a recognised strength. Since the 17th century, brewers have used X's unofficially to indicate beers of a stronger or superior quality, for instance XX for medium strength, and XXX for a more potent brew. The advertising for a certain Australian beer cleverly combines this concept of strength with the x, as sometimes used to represent a swearword, to tell us that 'Australians wouldn't give a XXXX for anything else'.

Finally, and most popularly, X is love and affection. 'Yours for ever. Then twenty-one X's', writes a character in Dylan Thomas' *Under Milk Wood*. The use of X as the symbol for a kiss dates back to the Middle Ages, when most people were illiterate. Unable to write their own names, but having to validate a document, they inscribed X; then, as an affirmation of faith and sincerity, they kissed their 'christ cross' as it was formerly known in this context, in the same way as they kissed the Bible when taking an oath. In time, the cross and the kiss became synonymous. Also in faith, we cast our votes with x, a personal mark which conveniently guarantees anonymity!

Making your mark

Skulpit held the pen, and made little flourishes with it in the air, but still hesitated.

'And if you'll be said by me,' continued Handy, 'you'll not write your name to it all, but just put your mark like the others . . . we all know you can do it if you like, but maybe you wouldn't like to seem uppish, you know.'

'Well, the mark would be best,' said Skulpit. 'One name and the rest marks wouldn't look well, would it?'

'The worst in the world,' said Handy . . . and stooping over the petition, the learned clerk made a huge cross on the place left for his signature.

Anthony Trollope *The Warden*

colours are red, blue, grey, gold, and silver.) In traffic signals, yellow implies caution, and in international football, players are 'cautioned' with a yellow card.

The term 'yellow press' or 'yellow journalism', journalism that distorts or sensationalises the truth to boost circulation, derives ultimately from an early experiment in colour printing designed to attract readers, in particular a cartoon in an edition of the US *New York World* in 1895 in which 'The Yellow Kid', a child in a yellow dress, was the central character. Also in the late 19th century, some newspapers alarmed their readers with talk of 'the Yellow Peril', the presumed threat to the rest of the world of the rising populations of China and Japan. In modern China, incidentally, yellow literature and yellow films are synonymous with pornography; on the other hand, according to the *Book of Chinese Symbols*, a 'yellow-blossom woman' is one who is still a virgin.

In heraldry, yellow substitutes for gold, called *or*; it is represented in engraving and monochrome printing by small dots.

Gems

Precious stones have always been highly prized not merely for their value but also as being symbolic of a particular quality, or for the supernatural and medicinal powers they were believed to possess, especially when carried or worn in jewellery. The **diamond** was believed to endow the wearer with strength in battle, and to protect against ghosts, madness, the evil eye, and plague (Queen Elizabeth I wore one in her bosom to guard against infection). The **sapphire**, considered the most spiritual of all stones, was, because of its blueness, a symbol of heavenly bliss; in the Bible, the Throne of Heaven is made of sapphires. The ancient Persians believed that the colour of the sky came from a giant sapphire on which the Earth rested. In addition, the sapphire was a symbol of faithfulness, and protected the wearer against betrayal. The **emerald**, sacred to Venus, was believed to shatter in the presence of marital infidelity; placed under the tongue it endowed the wearer with the gift of prophecy. The Egyptians treasured the **garnet** as a symbol of life; according to legend, Noah's Ark was lit with one. **Jade** is the Chinese symbol of good fortune; as the unified powers of yin

Anniversary gifts

The concept of commemorating a couple's wedding day with a significant gift is thought to have originated in medieval Germany. If a woman lived with her husband for 25 years, her friends gave her a ring of silver. Similarly, after another 25 years she was presented with a ring of gold. In time, other anniversaries came to be marked. The following list includes the gifts traditionally designated, and in *italics* their modern substitutes, as suggested by some British and American publications.

First cotton; *clock*

Second paper; *china*

Third leather; *crystal, glass*

Fourth fruit, flowers; *electrical appliance*

Fifth wood; *silverware*

Sixth iron, sugar; *wood*

Seventh copper, wool; *desk set, pens*

Eighth bronze, pottery; *lace, linen*

Ninth pottery, willow; *leather*

Tenth tin; *aluminium*

Eleventh steel; *fashion jewellery*

Twelfth fine linen, silk; *pearls*

Thirteenth lace; *fur, textiles*

Fourteenth ivory; *gold jewellery*

Fifteenth crystal; *watch*

Sixteenth none traditional; *silver plate*

Seventeenth none traditional; *furniture*

Eighteenth none traditional; *porcelain*

Nineteenth none traditional; *bronze*

Twentieth china; *platinum*

Twenty-fifth silver; *same*

Thirtieth pearl; *diamond*

Thirty-fifth coral; *jade*

Fortieth ruby; *same*

Forty-fifth sapphire; *same*

Fiftieth gold; *same*

Fifty-fifth emerald; *same*

Sixtieth diamond; *same*

Seventieth platinum; *diamond*

and yang, it is the purest and most divine of natural materials. The Romans associated the purple **amethyst** (from Greek, 'not drunken') with Bacchus, their god of wine; it was worn as a charm against intoxication (similarly, their drinking cups were sometimes made of it). **Pearls** were regarded as the tears of angels shed for the sins of mankind; in the Koran, the trees of Paradise are hung with pearls. In ancient Rome, pearls were an emblem of nobility; Julius Caesar banned women below a certain rank from wearing them. The **bloodstone**, a symbol of peace, was said to have been created by drops of blood from Christ's wounds on the Cross falling upon a green stone. Because of the rainbow effect in an **opal**, the Romans regarded it as a symbol of hope. The **ruby**, once used as an antidote to poison, was thought to promote love, happiness and peace. The **topaz** was said to ward off epilepsy; and the **turquoise** to prevent injury due to falls, especially from a horse, and to protect against the evil eye (even today, camels and horses in some parts of the Middle East have turquoise beads tied to their manes or tails). Thought to be one of the earliest stones ever mined, turquoise was also believed to ensure the fidelity of those in love, and the rejection of rivals.

In the Middle Ages, astrologers linked many of these stones with the 12 signs of the zodiac, and with the 12 months of the year. The connection is thought to derive from biblical times, and a description in Exodus of the breastplate of judgment worn by Aaron, the high priest of Israel and brother of Moses. The breastplate (*hoshen*) was decorated with 12 stones representing the 12 tribes of Israel (see p.117). Although it was for many years considered good fortune to carry or wear the appropriate stone for each month, by the 18th century the custom had begun in Poland of wearing the stone associated with the month or zodiac sign of one's birth. There are, of course, no hard and fast rules on this, though it has to be said that some superstitious people consider it profoundly unlucky to wear a birthstone of the month or zodiac sign other than one's own, particularly opal. Jade and crystal, however, are believed to bring good luck to all who wear or carry them.

From time to time, jewellers have revised the list of stones associated with the 12 months to take availability and cost into account, especially when synthetic stones have occasionally replaced rarer but less durable ones. The last major revision was officially established in the US by the National Association of Jewelers at a convention in Kansas City in 1912, and approved by the Jewelry Industry Council in 1950. As an indication of how widely thought on gem symbolism differs, the stones associated with the 12 signs of the zodiac are also listed, together with their meanings according to J.C. Cooper's *Illustrated Encyclopaedia of Traditional Symbols*.

Stones of the month

January *garnet*: constancy

February *amethyst*: sincerity

March *aquamarine* or *bloodstone*: courage

April *diamond*: innocence

May *emerald*: success in love

June *alexandrite*, *moonstone*, or *pearl*: health and longevity

July *ruby*: contentment

August *peridot* or *sardonyx*: marital happiness, friendship

September *sapphire*: clear thinking

October *opal* or *tourmaline*: hope

November *topaz*: fidelity

December *lapis lazuli*, *turquoise*, or *zircon*: prosperity

Stones of the zodiac

Aries *bloodstone*: courage, endurance, longevity, wealth; *diamond*: fearlessness, fortitude, purity, strength

Taurus *sapphire*: divine favour, happiness, peace; *turquoise*: courage, success

Gemini *agate*: vigour, strength, success

Cancer *emerald*: constancy, domestic happiness; *moonstone*: inspiration, love; *pearl*: purity, tears

Leo *tourmaline*: friendship, inspiration; *sardonyx*: brightness, courage

Virgo *cornelian*: concord, health; *jade*: excellence, purity

Libra *lapis lazuli*: courage, divine favour, success; *opal*: foresight, friendship

Scorpio *beryl*: hope, married love, youth; *carbuncle*: bloodshed, prosperity, success

Sagittarius *topaz*: divine favour, faithfulness, strength, wisdom

Capricorn *black onyx*: inspiration, strength; *ruby*: invulnerability, longevity

---

Fortune and misfortune

A wide variety of animate and inanimate objects are associated with luck and fortune, or lack of it. Some, such as the clover, or the black cat, are mentioned elsewhere. One of the most popular lucky symbols today is the **horseshoe**. Wherever horses are shod, this has long been regarded as protection against witches and evil spirits, and by extension as a bringer of luck. Because of its resemblance to the crescent shape of the new moon, an ancient sign of increase, the horseshoe is also a fertility symbol. In addition, sailors believed a horseshoe would avert storms and shipwreck. Lord Nelson, for instance, had one nailed to the mainmast of HMS *Victory*.

Various legends account for the horseshoe as protection against evil. The best known in Christian tradition relates to Dunstan, the patron saint of blacksmiths and goldsmiths. He was working at his forge when the Devil appeared and demanded a shoe for his 'single hoof'. Recognising his visitor, the saint dutifully complied by pinning him to the wall and performing the operation so painfully that the Devil begged for mercy. Dunstan only released him after he promised never to enter a place where a horseshoe was hung.

In former times, when the belief in good and evil was much stronger, it was popularly supposed that witches feared horses (which may be why they to chose to ride broomsticks). They were also thought to be repelled by iron. The English diarist John Aubrey tells us in *Remaines* (1687) that 'most houses at the west-end of London have a horseshoe on the threshold' and that 'it is used for a Preservative against the mischiefe or power of Witches . . . an old use derived from the Astrological principle, that Mars [iron] is an enemie to Saturn, under whom the witches are'.

Purists maintain that to be at all effective, horseshoes must be found accidentally, not bought. But they differ in opinion as to the way the prongs or 'horns' of the shoe are to be placed. Some believe that they should point downwards for protection, others say that in this position the luck will run out into the ground. The usual position in England is with the horns up. The shoe is said to be especially lucky if fixed to a door or threshold with its own nails. Even more auspicious is the horseshoe from the hind leg of a grey mare!

The **cross** has already been mentioned extensively for its beneficial powers. According to Carabeau and Donner's *Dictionary of Superstitions*, however, some crosses may bring bad luck, especially any made by accident. Arms crossing in a group of people shaking hands, for instance, or knives, forks and spoons forming a cross on a table. Similarly, tools which form a cross when dropped, crossed branches or straws in one's path, and even a bed forming a cross with ceiling beams may spell trouble. Fortunately, the

---

Moving images

Hanging from the top of the windshield were the penates: a baby's shoe – that's for protection, for the stumbling feet of a baby require the constant caution and aid of God; and a tiny boxing-glove – and that's for power, the power of the fist on the driving forearm, the drive of the piston pushing its connecting rod, the power of person as responsible and proud individual. There hung also on the windshield a little plastic kewpie doll with a cerise and green ostrich-feather headdress and a provocative sarong. And this was for the pleasures of the flesh and of the eye, of the nose, of the ear.

John Steinbeck *The Wayward Bus* [In Roman mythology, the Penates were the household gods]

Mathematics

The earliest recorded use of the symbols for plus (+) and minus (−) is in *Mercantile Arithmetic* by John Widman, which was published in Leipzig in 1489. William Oughtred of Albury, Surrey, first used the multiplication symbol (×) in his *Clavis Mathematica* in 1631. The division symbol (÷) was invented in 1668 by John Pell of Cambridge, who first used it as Professor of Mathematics in Amsterdam. The symbol (=), used to indicate that one thing is equal to another, was invented by Robert Recorde, Fellow of All Souls, Oxford, in his algebra text *The Whetstone of Witte*, published in London in 1557; Recorde chose two parallel straight lines because 'noe 2 thynges can be moore equalle'. The symbol for per cent (%) derives from the formula $x/100$, 'by the hundred', from

authors reassure us, there is an antidote. Uncross arms and shake hands again in the normal way; uncross the tools and cutlery (though some superstitious people insist a second person must do this to cancel the possible consequences); and pick up any straws or branches with your right hand and toss them over your left shoulder. As for the bed, simply move it.

As well as being symbols in their own right, **numbers** have also acquired symbolic significances. When Shakespeare has Falstaff say in *The Merry Wives of Windsor*, 'there is divinity in odd numbers, either in nativity, chance or death', he is echoing an ancient belief that odd numbers, such as 3, 5, and 7 were especially influential. Traditionally, the **unluckiest number** is 13. It was the most unfortunate number for the ancient Hebrews: m, the 13th letter of the alphabet, began and ended their word for death, *mem*. In Norse mythology, 12 gods were invited to a banquet in Valhalla, the great hall of immortality. When Loki, the god of strife and evil, intruded (bringing the number to 13), Baldur, the god of light, was killed. There is a parallel here, in superstition at least, with Christ and the twelve disciples at the Last Supper, which preceded the Crucifixion. In French, the number is referred to as *le point de judas*, from Judas Iscariot being the first to rise from the table, and the first to die (hence the belief, even today, that first person to rise from a table of thirteen will die within the year). In parts of the Christian world, 13 is avoided in a variety of ways. In France, for example, it is rare to find a house of that number (12 is followed by 12½, then 14); in the US the 13th floor in skyscrapers is omitted; so too is room 13 in hotels, and seat 13 in aircraft. The 13th is the unluckiest date in any month on which to begin a sea voyage, especially if it falls on a Friday (the day of the Crucifixion). Certainly fatal for some was the variation 'thirteenpence-halfpenny'. This was the nickname given to the hangman in 17th-century England, 13½d (about 5½p) being the sum he received for executing his duty.

Not everyone, of course, subscribes to triskaidekaphobia (the official name, from Greek 'thirteen fear'). Some people even go out of their way to tempt fate. In *The Guinness Book of Numbers*, Adrian Room cites a society of 13 doctors in Toulouse, France, who meet on the 13th of the month in room 13 of a local hotel, a practice the society has been following, apparently without mishap, since 1854. Similarly, a Thirteen Club was founded in the US in the late 19th century, expressly to counter the superstition by arranging dinners with 13 present. Other people are equally dismissive. 'Recognising the number 13 is a clear sign that you have been to school', quipped Groucho Marx, though he did concede that 13 at table is unlucky, 'when the hostess has only twelve chops'.

On the spot

While the pirate flag, the Jolly Roger, struck terror into the hearts of sailors, another symbol had a similar effect on the pirates themselves. If one of their number was suspected of treachery, his companions would sentence him to death, and would serve him notice of this fact by means of 'the black spot'. This was originally the ace of spades with its single black pip, but frequently a makeshift was used. In Robert Louis Stevenson's *Treasure Island*, a sea-captain is given a piece of paper and promptly dies of an apoplectic fit. Kneeling to examine the body, the story's hero, Jim Hawkins, finds 'on the floor close to his hand . . . a little round of paper, blackened on the one side. I could not doubt that this was the black spot; and taking it up, I found written on the other side, in a very good, clear hand, this short message: "You have till ten tonight".' Later, the pirates 'tip' their leader Long John Silver the black spot – this time on a page torn from the Bible: 'It was a round about the size of a crown piece. One side was blank, for it had been the last leaf; the other contained a verse or two of Revelation . . . the printed side had been blackened with wood ash, which already began to come off and soil my fingers; on the blank side had been written with the same material the one word "Depposed".'

By the late 1920s, this 'black spot' had evolved into 'on the spot', a slang expression in the American underworld meaning 'marked for assassination'. 'If I put someone on the spot, I don't expect them to die of old age', says the ruthless leading character in Edgar Wallace's 1931 play *On the Spot*. Set in Al Capone's Chicago, this melodrama was so accurate in its portrayal of gangsters that when it played in Chicago even the gangsters sent round notes of congratulation. Being 'put on the spot' has since acquired the broader meaning of being placed in a difficult or embarrassing position.

Latin *per centum*; similarly, per mil (‰), 'by the thousand'. The earliest recorded use of the mathematical symbol for infinity (∞) was in 1665 in *De Sectionibus Conicis* by John Wallis; he adapted it from an early Roman numeral for 1000, CIↃ, which is thought to derive from the Greek letter ɸ, 'phi'.

Money

The monetary unit of the UK, the pound (£), derives ultimately from the unit of weight of the same name. In the late 8th century, 240 silver pennies were minted from a pound weight of pure silver. After the Norman Conquest, the pound was divided into 20 shillings, each to the value of 12 pennies. In medieval Latin documents, the pound, shilling, and penny were denoted by the Latin words *libra*, 'pound', from which derives the pound weight symbol (lb), *solidus* (originally a Roman gold coin), and *denarius* (originally a Roman silver coin). In time, the words were abbreviated. *Libra* was indicated by L before the numeral, and occasionally l after it. Later a double horizontal line was added to distinguish the letter; this form is still used, though commonly the symbol now has only one line. *Denarius* became d, and *solidus* s. Until the 18th century, the letter s was much longer, more like the modern small f. This became merely an oblique line or stroke (still called solidus*) to separate shillings and pence, for example as in 7/6d (seven shillings and six pence). After the change in the UK to decimal currency on 15 February 1971, when the pound was divided into 100 pence, s and d were replaced initially by np (new penny), and later by p.

The monetary unit of the US, the dollar, was adopted by the Continental Congress on 6 July 1785, but the first dollars were not coined until 1794, two years after the Mint was established. The dollar

If only God would give me a clear sign! Like making a large deposit in my name at a Swiss bank.

Woody Allen

symbol ($) first appeared around that time. One patriotic theory has the symbol as a combination of the initials US. More likely, the symbol is a variation of the '8' stamped on the old Spanish dollar, as the peso or 'piece of eight' (having the value of eight *reals*) was known. The two vertical lines were added to avoid confusion. The standard form is now with a single vertical line. The symbol for cent (one hundredth part of a dollar) is ¢.

The monetary unit of Japan, the yen, was officially adopted in 1871. The name derives ultimately from Chinese *yuan*, 'round thing' or 'circle'. The horizontal lines on the capital Roman Y for the international symbol ¥, are sometimes explained as representing the two swords of the samurai; alternatively, 'Japan' in Japanese is pronounced Nihon, which also means two lines.

£ and $ are now employed worldwide on currency notes, price labelling, and other commercial documentation, wherever the terms pound or dollar are in use. Internationally, the symbols are usually prefaced by a letter or abbreviation to identify the country, for example, Aus$ for Australian dollar. Most other monetary systems use simple

The weaver's hand had known the touch of hard-won money even before the palm had grown to its full breadth; for twenty years, mysterious money had stood to him as the symbol of earthly good, and the immediate object of toil.

George Eliot *Silas Marner*

Oscar

Few symbols generate such interest and speculation each year as the golden statuettes, or 'Oscars', awarded by the American Academy of Motion Picture Arts and Sciences for outstanding merit in the film industry.

Oscar was created by MGM art director Cedric Gibbons shortly after the Academy was founded in 1927. His design of a man with sword standing on a reel of film, sketched on a tablecloth at the Hollywood Biltmore Hotel, was executed by George Stanley, a Los Angeles sculptor, and manufactured by the Dodge Trophy Co. of Crystal Lake, Illinois. The gold-plated bronze figurine is 10 in (25 cm) tall, and weighs 7 lb (3.2 kg). It has a face value of around $250, but all winners pledge never to sell it except back to the Academy who will pay $10 for it.

The first statuettes, for films released between 1 August 1927 and 31 July 1928, were presented at a ceremony at the Hollywood Roosevelt Hotel on 16 May 1929. The original categories were best picture, actor, actress, directing, cinematography, writing, interior decoration, and (for the first and last time) comedy direction, title writing, artistic quality of production, and engineering effects.

The statuette did not acquire the familiar nickname 'Oscar' until

1931. Claims abound as to its origin. Brewer, for instance, cites the unlikely theory that the name derives indirectly from Oscar Wilde. Referring to his Newdigate Prize for Poetry, he quipped with typical modesty that while many people may win the Newdigate, 'it is seldom that the Newdigate gets an Oscar'. The most plausible legend, however, comes from the Academy itself. When Mrs Margaret Herrick reported for her first day's work as librarian there, she saw the statuette on a desk and remarked that its expression reminded her of her Uncle Oscar. Incidentally, one person who had more opportunity than most to gaze on Oscar was Gibbons himself. He was one of the first recipients (for *The Bridge of San Luis Rey*, 1929), and went on to win a further ten 'Best Art Direction' awards.

Although guaranteed to boost the box office by millions, Oscar is not always regarded with reverence. Helen Hayes, for instance, voted best actress in 1932 for *The Sin of Madelon Claudet*, used hers as a doorstop. Frances Marion, who won twice for screenplays (*The Big House*, 1930; *The Champ*, 1932) described Oscar as 'a perfect symbol of the picture business; a powerful athletic body clutching a gleaming sword, with half of his head, that part which held the brains, completely sliced off'.

I would rather write 10 000 notes than one letter of the alphabet.

Ludwig van Beethoven *Letter*, 28 November 1820

abbreviations of the unit name, sometimes prefaced by a country letter, for example, DM, Deutschmark.

Music

The system of representing music in graphic form is called notation. The **earliest graphic notation in the West** appeared in the 7th century in plainsong, the chief music of Christian worship. The music was notated in signs in the form of dots and squiggles written above the text. The signs, called **neumes** (from Greek *neuma*, 'gesture'), are thought to have been influenced by accentual signs devised by Greek and Roman grammarians to guide declamation. Neumes, which could represent both single notes and groups of notes, served principally to remind the singer of the approximate shape of the melody.

The beginnings of the **modern notation** now used internationally date back to the early 11th century, and an Italian Benedictine monk, Guido d'Arezzo or Aretino (*c.* AD 990–1050). To help singers learn a new melody more quickly than by laborious rote, d'Arezzo invented a system in which the notes of the then hexachord or six-note scale were identified by names derived from the initial syllables of the lines of a 9th-century hymn to St John the Baptist: *UT queant laxis REsonare fibris MIra gestorum FAmuli tuorum, SOLve polluti LAbii reatum, Sancte Iohannes.*

An extra syllable, si (from *Sancte Iohannes* in the last line of the hymn), was later added for the 7th note of the scale (this became te in England in the 16th century). During the 17th century ut was changed to do (possibly from Latin *dominus*, 'Lord'). The syllables now used to represent the notes in the modern octave or eight-note scale (CDEFGABC) are: do (variant, doh), re (ray), mi (me), fa (fah), sol (soh), la (lah), te (ti), do.

D'Arezzo is also credited (*c.*1030) with the concept of the staff or stave – the set of horizontal lines on and between which note symbols are placed so as to indicate pitch. To indicate fa (F) Guido established a bass line in red ink, for la (A), a line scratched with a needle; and for ut (C) a top line in yellow ink. With these lines and the spaces between, above, and below, he was able to indicate positions for the seven notes of the range E to D. To extend the range of sounds, a pitch letter was introduced. This fixed a given pitch on a given line. The letters F, C, and G were the most commonly used. From these ordinary letters developed the abstract clef signs in use today. Written at the beginning of every line of music, the clef (French for key, from Latin *clavis*; German *Schlüssel*, Italian *chiave*) literally provides the key of the level at which the note is fixed and indicates the exact location of a particular note on the staff.

Notation to indicate the exact duration or value of notes and their equivalent intervals of silence (rests) was systematised in 1260 by the German musical theorist Franco of Cologne. He proposed a series of symbols of different shapes to express different durations both of sounds and of silences. The two earliest notes, derived from neumes of the time, were the long (a black square with a tail) and the breve (a black square). Towards the end of the 13th century, two other notes appeared: the large or double long or maxima (a black rectangle with a tail) and for faster-moving passages the semibreve (a black diamond). Over the centuries shorter note values were introduced (a summary of these and their rest equivalents is given below). During the 15th century, the square and lozenge shapes of notes were replaced by ovals, mainly because they were easier to write.

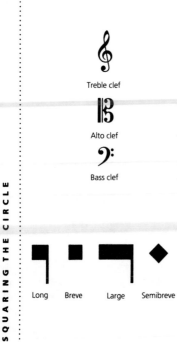

Treble clef

Alto clef

Bass clef

Long Breve Large Semibreve

Flats and sharps

In Western staff notation, each note is assumed to be natural unless altered at the beginning of the piece by a key signature, or on a more temporary basis by one of two 'accidentals': a sharp or a flat. The **sharp** symbol ♯ (French *dièse*, German *Kreuz*, Italian *diesis*) preceding a note indicates that the pitch is to be raised one half step or semitone (US half tone), the smallest interval normally used in Western music; a double sharp ✕ (French *double dièse*, German *Doppelkreuz*, Italian *doppio diesis*) raises the pitch by a tone. In the same way, the **flat** symbol ♭ (French *bémol*, German *Be*, Italian *bemolle*), lowers the pitch by a semitone, and a double flat ♭♭ (French *double bémol*, German *Doppel-Be*, Italian *doppio bemolle*) by a tone. Accidentals affect all subsequent notes of that pitch in the same bar unless preceded by the **natural** symbol ♮ (also US 'cancel'; French *bécarre*, German *Auflösungszeichen* or *Quadrat*, Italian *bequadro*) which restores a note to its natural pitch. After a double accidental, reversion to a single is signified either by the use of a single sharp or flat, or occasionally by a natural followed by a sharp, or a natural followed by a flat.

Accidentals have their origins in suggestions by Guido d'Arezzo for symbols for the two possible pitches of the note B: *rotundum*, round b, also *b molle* or soft b to represent B flat; and *quadratum* or 'square b' to represent B sharp (from which the natural symbol also derives). The notation in Germany of B for B flat and H for B natural derives ultimately from the letter h which 16th-century German printers used to represent 'square b'.

To identify the key a piece is written in (i.e. the particular scale used), and to avoid accidentals before notes that are to be consistently sharpened or flattened, a **key signature** or **staff signature** is placed directly after the initial clef sign. The signature holds good throughout the piece unless countermanded temporarily by the natural sign, or more permanently by a new signature. The earliest use of a signature (one flat) appeared in the 11th century; sharps were not widely used in signatures until the 17th century.

Each key signature can indicate either a major key (represented here by a white or hollow note) or its relative minor key (a black note). On keyboard instruments, the keys F sharp major and D sharp minor (6 sharps) are the equivalent of the keys G flat major and E flat minor

[SHARP]

MAJOR

C   G   D   A   E   B   F sharp   C sharp

a   e   b   f sharp   c sharp   g sharp   d sharp   a sharp

minor

[FLAT]

MAJOR

C   F   B flat   E flat   A flat   D flat   G flat   C flat

a   d   g   c   f   b flat   e flat   a flat

minor

(6 flats). Similarly, the keys C sharp major and A sharp minor (7 sharps) are the equivalent of D flat major and B flat minor (5 flats). Although either one of these may be used to the same effect, composers find it more convenient to write in a key with five flats.

Notes and rests

Staff notation enables composers to indicate how long each note should be held. The shape of a note shows its time value. The German and US nomenclature is based on proportional lengths, i.e. a fraction of a semibreve or whole note; the French, Italian, and some other European note names recall their Latin origins. To express silences of exact lengths, a series of rests corresponding in length to each of the notes was introduced. The modern note symbols and their equivalent rests are as follows:

breve (US double whole note, French *carrée*, *brève* or *double-ronde*, German *Doppeltaktnote*, Italian *breve*); the sole surviving relic of early 13th-century neume notation, where as *punctum* it was written as a black square; until the creation of the semibreve later in the century, the breve was the **shortest note** expressible, hence its name (from Latin *brevis*, 'short'); now with a value of eight beats, it is the **longest note**. It is rarely found today except in church music.

semibreve literally 'half-short' (US whole note, French *ronde*, German *Ganze Taktnote*, Italian *semibreve*) first appeared in the late 13th century as a black lozenge. In his treatise *Musica Deo sacra* (1668), Thomas Tomkins describes the length of the semibreve as being equal to two heartbeats. The only note value of early medieval notation to survive in regular use, it is now the longest with a duration of four beats. The equivalent rest symbol is also used to denote a one-bar rest whatever the metre.

minim (US half note, French *blanche*, German *Halbe*; Italian *minima* or *bianca*); first appeared in French music in the early 14th century. Half semibreve length, normally two beats. The rest symbols for the minim and semibreve, which originated in the late 14th century, are remembered by the mnemonic 'semibreve suspends, minim mounts'.

crotchet (US quarter note, French *noire*, German *Viertel*, Italian *semiminima* or *nera*). Its English name derives from its appearance in the 14th century as a minim with a crook. With a value of one beat, i.e. a quarter of a semibreve or half a minim (hence it may still be called a semiminim), the crotchet is employed as the 'standard pulse' in Western music; as such, it is found as the denominator in the most frequently used time signatures: e.g. 4/4 or 3/4 (waltz time).

quaver (US eighth note, French *croche*, German *Achtel*, Italian *croma*); first appeared in the 15th century with the name *fusa* as a minim with two extensions or flags on the stem. The English name derives ultimately from a 14th-century word meaning to tremble or quiver. Value: one eighth of a semibreve (half a beat).

semiquaver (US sixteenth note, French *double croche*, German *Sechzehntel*, Italian *semicroma*); first appeared with the Latin name *semifusa* in the 15th century. Value: 1/16 semibreve (a quarter beat).

demisemiquaver or occasionally demiquaver (US thirty-second note, French *triple croche*, German *Zweiunddreissigstel*, Italian *biscroma*). Originally called by the Latin name *fusella*, it first appeared in 16th-century instrumental music. Value: 1/32 semibreve (one eighth beat).

hemidemisemiquaver or semidemisemiquaver, i.e. half of half of half a quaver (US sixty-fourth note, French *quadruple croche*, German *Vierundsechzigstel*, Italian *semi-biscroma*; Latin *fusellala*); first appeared in late 17th-century music. With the exception of the now rare five-flag **semihemidemisemiquaver** (US hundred and twenty-eighth note), it is the **shortest note** in modern notation, with a value of 1/64 of a semibreve or 1/16 beat.

Pharmacology

From the 16th to 19th centuries, apothecaries often identified their premises with exterior signs depicting a phoenix*, salamander*, or dragon*. The mortar and pestle was also common. More widespread was a red cross, a symbol of healing from the days of the Crusades. Since this was appropriated by the International Red Cross* (the red cross on white is now protected in international law) chemists' stores in many countries have adopted a blue or green cross on white as their trade sign. Physicians and pharmacists have been using the letter R with a bar across the descending diagonal stroke as the symbol for a medical prescription since the 16th century. The letter is a contraction of the Latin word *recipe*, literally 'take!' The barred diagonal is said to derive from the symbol for the fifth and largest planet (see astronomy), which was named after Jupiter, the supreme Roman god and patron of medicines. The symbol is still widely used on prescriptions and drugstore signboards in the US.

Road and traffic

The first known 'traffic' signs in Britain date back to the Roman Occupation in the 1st century AD. The Romans set up 'milliaries', stone columns about 2 ft (60 cm) high, indicating the distance to the next posting station in Roman miles (1000 paces, computed to have been about 4854 ft (1479 m); the modern mile is 5280 ft/1609 m). The 'London Stone', now embedded in a niche in the wall of the Oversea-Chinese Banking Corporation in Cannon Street, and reputedly the oldest relic in the streets of London, is thought to be the key stone from which the Romans measured all distances to other posts and settlements. The **oldest milliary** *in situ* is on the Stanegate, at Chesterholme, near Bardon Mill, Northumberland; it dates from AD 150.

Signposting began on an official level after the General Turnpike Act of 1773. The Act required the Turnpike Trusts to erect and maintain on all roads under their charge signposts indicating the direction and distance to the next place of importance. From these developed the oak 'fingerposts' still to be seen in some rural areas.

The **earliest cautionary road signs** were prompted by the popularity of the bicycle in the 1880s. The Bicycle Union erected 'danger boards' to warn cyclists of sharp bends and other hazards. Signs depicting the skull and crossbones* were set up on the steepest hills.

The **first uniform signs with standardised symbols** (white on a rectangular black plate) were adopted in France in 1903. They included signs for Level Crossing, Bridge, Steep Hill, and Turn Right and Turn Left.

A scientific diagnosis

Dr William Osler, having been invited to inspect a famous London hospital, was proudly shown about by several physicians and surgeons. Finally the charts were reached, and he looked them over carefully, observing the system of abbreviations: SF for Scarlet Fever, TB for Tuberculosis, D for Diptheria, and so on. All diseases seemed to be pretty well under control except one indicated by the symbol GOK.

'I observe,' said the famous doctor, 'that you have a sweeping epidemic of GOK on your hands. This is a symbol not in common use in American medical circles; just what is GOK?'

'Oh!' one of his hosts lightly replied, 'when we can't diagnose, God Only Knows.'

Walter Neale *Life of Ambrose Bierce*

The symbol of the learner driver in the UK, a red capital L on a white square, was introduced in 1935 by the Minister of Transport, Leslie Hore-Belisha, following the introduction of driving tests on 13 March. Initially used on a voluntary basis, 'L plates' were made compulsory on 1 June 1935. In 1991, the Department of Transport introduced green L plates for newly qualified drivers to display on their vehicles until they are more confident. The plates, which are not compulsory, also serve to invite other motorists to treat them with extra consideration.

If you haven't got your license yet in England your car bears a big red L for learner, but you can't tell the difference in the driving.

James Thurber, letter to E.B. White 1937

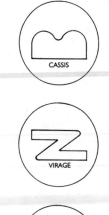

CASSIS

VIRAGE

PASSAGE A NIVEAU

Earliest international road danger signs, adopted 1909. They indicate 'bump', 'sharp bend', and 'railway level crossing'

When the lights turn red in Los Angeles, and it is time to walk across the road, an illuminated sign comes on. It is not the green, arm-swinging man you find at British crossings, nor the simple instruction – WALK – you read in other American cities. Here a rather laboured, hunched-over figure – the torso reminds one, oddly enough, of Ronald Reagan at a press conference – battles into a headwind of car exhaust and indifference. It expresses what everyone thinks about walking in LA: Don't.

Adam Nicolson *Book of Walks*

A year after the 1903 Motor Car Act UK imposed on local authorities the duty of setting up signs for crossroads, dangerous corners and 'precipitous places', a Local Government Board circular attempted to bring some order to the profusion of different designs by recommending that warning signs be surmounted by a hollow red triangle, speed limit signs (a rectangular plate giving the limit in figures, often 10 miles/16 km) by a hollow white ring, and prohibition signs by a solid red disc.

In 1909, at the Convention on International Circulation of Motor Vehicles in Paris, nine European countries adopted a set of signs with **the first internationally standardised symbols**. These included symbols to indicate uneven road, dangerous bend, intersection, and level crossing. The UK was not a signatory to the agreement.

The first classification of roads in the UK was completed in 1921. First class roads were indicated by a black letter 'A' and road number, and second class roads by a white letter 'B' and road number on a black background. New symbols for danger signs were introduced, including a flaming torch representing the 'beacon of learning' for 'School'. In the 1930s, there were further additions to traffic signage, such as a steam engine symbol for open level crossings (1930), and symbols to indicate 'hospital', 'road narrows', 'No entry' (1933), 'hump-back bridge' (1934), and 'STOP - Children crossing' (1936).

In 1949, a range of signs with symbols was adopted by 30 European countries under the Protocol of the UN World Conference on Road and Motor Transport, Geneva. These signs are still in use today. Once again, the UK was not a signatory, and it was not until 1965, after recommen-

Road code

The first edition of the UK *Highway Code* was issued by the Ministry of Transport on 14 April 1931. Priced 1d (0.4p), the modest booklet was 'intended as a supplementary guide to the proper use of the highway and as a code of good manners to be observed by all courteous and considerate persons'. Surprisingly, unlike later editions, the code barely mentioned traffic signs and symbols. It did, however, include a number of rare hand signals (albeit not legally enforceable) to be given by 'police constables' and drivers of motor vehicles, and whip signals for drivers of horse-drawn vehicles. Here are two examples:

'I am going to slow down, or stop, or turn to my left'

'I am going to turn'

dation by the Worboys Committee, that UK road signage was brought into line with the European colour-coded signs containing symbols without text to explain them. Warning signs have an appropriate symbol within a red triangle, prohibitory signs a symbol within a red ring, and for mandatory signs a white symbol on a blue circular sign. In 1986, white on brown direction signs were introduced to signify tourist attractions in England and Wales, with symbols to denote the type of attraction. Scotland has its own tourist attraction signs using a blue thistle* symbol.

Over the years, the US has developed its own road signage system. Increasingly, international symbols are appearing in their signs, but there are still many differences. Traffic regulatory signs are generally square or rectangular; the symbols are black or red on a white background, with red usually indicating 'stop', 'yield', or a prohibition. Warning signs are mainly diamond-shaped, with the symbols in black on a yellow field.

The **first traffic signals** in the UK were invented by J. P. Knight, a railway signalling engineer. With semaphore arms and red and green gas lanterns for night use, the signals were mounted on a cast-iron pillar 22 ft (6.7 m) high in Westminster on 8 December 1868, at the junction of New Palace Yard and Bridge Street off Parliament Square, mainly for MPs wishing to gain access to the Houses of Parliament. Less than a month later, on 2 January 1869, the constable assigned to operate the semaphore was injured when the gas apparatus exploded. The signals were removed in 1872.

The **first electric traffic lights system** was set up by the American Traffic Signal Company at the junction of Euclid Avenue and 105th St in Cleveland, Ohio on 5 August 1914; 15 ft (4.5 m) high, the system had red and green lights, and was used with a warning buzzer.

In 1918, the **first manually operated three-colour signals** (red, green, amber) were installed in New York. The red, green, and amber lights were regulated from a tower in the middle of the street. The first manually operated three-colour signals in the UK were switch-controlled by police in London's West End at the junction of St James's Street and Piccadilly in 1926.

The **world's first automatic traffic lights** were introduced in the UK with a one-day trial in Wolverhampton on 11 February 1928. They were first permanently operated in Leeds, Yorkshire on 16 March 1928; mounted on cast-iron standards 8 ft (2.4 m) high, the 'all-electric policeman', as the lights were nicknamed, were timed to show red for 28 seconds, amber for two seconds, and green for 28 seconds. Similar lights were first operated in Edinburgh, Scotland on 19 March 1928.

The **first vehicle-actuated lights**, controlled by rubber pads set in the road, were installed by the Automatic Electric Company of Liverpool at the junction of Cornhill and Gracechurch Street in the City of London in April 1932.

In the early years of the war, when Hitler was threatening to invade England, the authorities blanked out the names on signposts to confuse German paratroopers. So about a mile from Stratford, there was a large sign that read as follows:

> *YOU ARE APPROACHING*
> *XXXXXXXXX*
> *UPON*
> *XXXX*
> *THE*
> *BIRTHPLACE*
> *OF*
> *WILLIAM SHAKESPEARE*

William Golding *The Hot Gates and Other Occasional Pieces*

It was said that my New York licence plates would arouse interest and perhaps questions, since they were the only outward identifying marks I had. And so they did - perhaps twenty or thirty times in the whole trip.

John Steinbeck *Travels With Charley*

There are stop signs on several intersections near our little house. Like every other stop sign, they read STOP in giant white letters on a red background. However, unlike the stop signs in Grosse Pointe or Chevy Chase, these also say, in a very personal handwriting, ME FROM DOING IT AGAIN . . . PLEASE. It adds a little neighborly touch.

Ben Stein *Hollywood Days, Hollywood Nights*

International distinguishing signs

Signs to signify the country of registration of vehicles, sometimes known as International Vehicle Registration or IVR signs, were introduced in 1926, under an agreement made at the International Convention on the Regulation of Traffic. Increasingly, the signs are used to denote the country of origin on a variety of international products and product documentation. While some are immediately recognisable (the same distinguishing letters, such as GB for United Kingdom, and USA, are often used at international sporting events), others may not be so obvious. Most are included in the United Nations list of established signs, but some are unofficial. At the time of writing, no signs have been officially agreed for some of the newer nations, for example Russia, Ukraine, and Belarus, which emerged from the USSR (formerly signified by SU), although all are likely to gain their own IVR signs in time.

A	Austria	DOM	Dominican Republic	P	Portugal
AL	Albania	DZ	Algeria	PA	Panama
AND	Andorra	E	Spain	PK	Pakistan
AUS	Australia	EAK	Kenya	PE	Peru
B	Belgium	EAT	Tanzania	PL	Poland
BDS	Barbados	EAU	Uganda	PY	Paraguay
BG	Bulgaria	EC	Ecuador	RA	Argentina
BH	Belize	ET	Egypt	RB	Botswana
BR	Brazil	F	France	RC	Taiwan
BRN	Bahrain	FJI	Fiji	RCA	Central African Republic
BRU	Brunei	FL	Liechtenstein	RCH	Chile
BS	Bahamas	FR	Faroe Islands	RH	Haiti
BUR	Burma	GB	United Kingdom	RI	Indonesia
C	Cuba	GBA	Alderney	RIM	Mauritania
CDN	Canada	GBG	Guernsey	RL	Lebanon
CH	Switzerland	GBJ	Jersey	RM	Madagascar
CI	Ivory Coast	GBM	Isle of Man	RMM	Mali
CL	Sri Lanka	GBZ	Gibraltar	RN	Niger
CO	Colombia	GCA	Guatemala	RO	Romania
CR	Costa Rica	GH	Ghana	ROK	Korea
CS	Czechoslovakia	GR	Greece	ROU	Uruguay
CY	Cyprus	GUY	Guyana	RP	Philippines
D	Germany	H	Hungary	RSM	San Marino
DK	Denmark	HK	Hong Kong	RU	Burundi
		HKJ	Jordan	RWA	Rwanda
		I	Italy	S	Sweden
		IL	Israel	SD	Swaziland
		IND	India	SF	Finland
		IR	Iran	SGP	Singapore
		IRL	Ireland	SME	Surinam
		IRQ	Iraq	SN	Senegal
		IS	Iceland	SWA	Namibia
		J	Japan	SY	Seychelles
		JA	Jamaica	SYR	Syria
		K	Kampuchea	T	Thailand
		KWT	Kuwait	TG	Togo
		L	Luxembourg	TN	Tunisia
		LAR	Libya	TR	Turkey
		LB	Liberia	TT	Trinidad & Tobago
		LT	Lithuania	V	Vatican
		M	Malta	VN	Vietnam
		MA	Morocco	WAG	Gambia
		MAL	Malaysia	WAL	Sierra Leone
		MC	Monaco	WAN	Nigeria
		MEX	Mexico	WG	Grenada
		MS	Mauritius	WS	Western Samoa
		MW	Malawi	WV	St Vincent
		N	Norway	YU	Yugoslavia
		NE	Netherlands Antilles	YV	Venezuela
		NIC	Nicaragua	Z	Zambia
		NIG	Niger	ZA	South Africa
		NL	Netherlands	ZRE	Zaire
		NZ	New Zealand	ZW	Zimbabwe

Some ale-houses upon the road
I saw,
And some with bushes showing
they wine did draw.

Poor Robin's Perambulations 1678

Trading signs

Traders have been exhibiting signs outside their premises to identify themselves and their goods for thousands of years. The ancient Egyptians and Greeks are said to have employed a variety of signs for this purpose. The Romans seem to have been prolific users of signboards, either fixed to the wall or hanging; more than 900 were excavated from the ruins of the Roman town of Herculaneum, which was buried in the eruption of Vesuvius in AD 79. The most famous sign of the times was the bunch or bush of ivy which was mounted outside a Roman *taberna* (from which our word tavern derives) to indicate that a new wine had been delivered and was available for consumption. The bush relates to the Bacchanalia, a festival celebrated every three years till 186 BC in honour of their god of wine Bacchus, whose emblem was a bunch of ivy or vine leaves. Ivy was also sacred to the Greek god of wine Dionysus. As well as being a symbol of immortality, the evergreen signified revelry. When the Romans occupied Britain after AD 43, they introduced both their *tabernae* and the emblem. (The proverb 'a good wine needs no bush' stems from the reasoning that there is no need to advertise a good wine with a bush, because word about it will get round soon enough; this saying is sometimes applied to other quality goods, the implication being of course that such goods will speak for themselves.) Reference to the bush may be found in pub names and signs throughout England. Another early pub sign introduced by the Romans, is the Chequers; displayed outside a *taberna*, it proclaimed that games such as chess and draughts could be played within.

There are more than 70 000 pubs in England. That almost all of them display a brightly coloured and highly individual pictorial sign may be due in part to Richard II. In 1393, he decreed that 'Whosoever shall brew ale in the town with the intention of selling it must hang out a sign; otherwise he shall forfeit his ale'. This law was not so much for the benefit of customers, as to inform the 'ale-conner', an examiner appointed by the local courts, of the location of each inn so that he could test the quality of each brew and ensure it was 'good for men's bodies'. Following this decree, many inns took Richard's heraldic badge of a white hart as their sign. Others adopted their signs from coats of arms (with permission, of course), or in reference to historic events, or local activities and trades. Nautical and religious connections were also frequently implied in signs. In an age when few people could read or write, such visual identifiers were invaluable. An inn became known by its sign, which in time became its official name. Modern pubs with names like the Angel, Beehive, Bishop's Head, Boar's Head, Cross Keys,

We came to a huge, heavy new building and stopped to stare at it, impressed, because etched in the stone was the name ONE WUI PLAZA.

'The Chinese are really booming!' said Patsy. 'One Wui Plaza is finished and Confucius Plaza is going up. Write that down.'

I was writing that down when I happened to notice, above the name of the building, the zigzag symbol used to denote electricity.

'Let me ask you something,' I said. 'Is Western Union an international company?'

Helene Hanff *Apple of My Eye*

Pub extravaganza

The **largest pub sign** was erected in 1655 outside the White Hart Inn at Scole, a few miles from Diss in Norfolk. At a cost of more than £1000 (no small sum in those days), it was probably also the most expensive pub sign ever. Of the type known as a 'beam' or 'gallows' sign, it spanned the road to Norwich; the exact measurements are not known, the sign having disappeared more than 200 years ago. It must have been impressive by any standards. The Norwich doctor and author Sir Thomas Browne described it in 1663: 'I came to Scoale where there is a very handsome inn and the noblest signpost in England about and upon which was carved a great many stories as of Charon and Cerberus, Actaeon and Diana and

many others; the sign itself is a White Hart, which hangs down carved in a stately wreath'. In addition to those Browne mentions, the 25 lifesize figures included supporting lions and angels, Jonah emerging from the whale's mouth, Neptune on a dolphin, the cardinal virtues of Justice, Prudence, Temperance, and Fortitude, and an astronomer seated on a device which 'by some chymical preparations is so affected that in fine weather he faces that quarter from which it is about to come'. For good measure, and patronage no doubt, this massive structure was further decorated with the coats of arms of the Norwich merchant (and the inn's landlord) James Peck, his wife, and 12 other members of Norfolk nobility.

1900

1948

1971

The world's most successful visual pun in advertising belongs to the Netherlands-based oil giant Shell. The company originated with a curio dealer, Marcus Samuel, who established a thriving business in London's Houndsditch in the late 19th century in the import and sale of, among other things, sea-shells. These were highly prized by the Victorians as ornaments, particularly for shell-studded boxes. When Samuel's son, also Marcus, inherited the business, he expanded into the import and export of other commodities, including Russian oil, which he shipped in vast quantities to the Far East. As well as naming his company Shell, in honour of his father's business, Samuel also called his first tanker *Murex*, after a spiny shell found in the east.

The first symbol of The 'Shell' Transport and Trading Company appeared in 1900, as a mussel. Four years later, it was supplanted by the more attractive shell of the edible scallop (*pecten maximus*). A modified scallop was retained when Shell merged in 1907 with 'The Royal Dutch Petroleum Company for the Working of Oil Wells in the Netherlands Indies'. The corporate colours, red and yellow, first appeared in 1915, when Shell began trading in California. Adopted in allusion to the national colours of Spain, which had once governed California, the red and yellow were first used on the logo in 1948. The current logo, created by the American designer Raymond Loewy, first appeared in 1971.

Elephant and Castle, Feathers, Globe, King's Arms, Lamb and Flag, Nag's Head, Pig and Whistle, Red Lion, Rose and Crown, and so on, are all inheritors of this tradition.

Over the centuries, laws were passed to regulate the profusion of increasingly large and sometimes dangerous hanging signs, particularly those outside inns. Nevertheless, accidents still occurred. In 1712, for example, an oversized sign in Fleet Street collapsed and dragged down the front wall of the pub with it, killing two women, a cobbler and the king's jeweller. This and other sign-related accidents finally prompted the Shop Sign Act of 1792, which banned the use of large signboards. Most pub signs today are roughly uniform in size, usually measuring about 4 ft (1.2 m) by 3 ft (1 m).

Many other traders advertised themselves with a three-dimensional symbol above the door. Usually, the signs were directly linked with the goods or services on offer. Thus the glover indicated his premises by means of a glove, the hatter by a hat, the optician by spectacle frames (sometimes enclosing large painted eyes), and the locksmith by a lock and key. The reasoning behind some other signs is less obvious. A black wooden doll dressed in white formerly identified a 'rag and bone' or secondhand clothes shop. The 'dolly shop', as it became known, also served as an illegal pawn-shop. Legitimate pawnbrokers identified themselves with **three golden balls**. This once familiar sign is said to derive ultimately from the coat of arms of the Medici family, who ruled Florence in the 15th and 16th centuries. According to legend, the family adopted the balls as their emblem after Averardo de Medici, a commander under Charlemagne, slew a giant who wielded a three-balled mace. The device was introduced to Britain in the early 14th century,

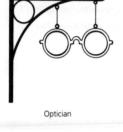

Optician

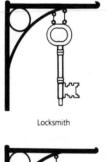

Locksmith

Baker

Pawnbroker

when bankers, goldsmiths, and money-lenders from Lombardy in northern Italy set up quarters in London in place of Jewish financiers who had been expelled from England in 1290. These Lombards also established a monopoly in pawnbroking; their premises became known as 'Lombards', and goods in pawn as 'lombard goods'. One explanation of the positioning of the balls is that whoever pawned an item had two chances to one of redeeming it.

Incidentally, some banks in Lombard Street (the City's banking centre, so-named after those early merchants) still display hanging signs in medieval fashion. The most famous are the prancing black horse of Lloyds Bank, and the black spread eagle of Barclays Bank.

Another old sign still in evidence is the **barber's pole**. This pole, painted with red and white spiral stripes, dates back to the days when the local barber was also the surgeon. Until the dissolution of the Company of Barber Surgeons in 1745, a barber's duties included phlebotomy or venesection, a once common remedy for numerous ailments, in which a vein was cut open to draw blood. To make the vein swell and so encourage the 'bloodletting', patients were given a pole to grip. When not in use, the barber hung the pole outside his premises with the blood-stained bandage used for tying up the arm twisted around it, possibly to dry. In time the pole was replaced by a symbolic one. The gilt knob still to be seen at the end of some barber's poles represents the brass basin the barber used both for lathering the customer before shaving, and for collecting his blood during venesection.

Weather

Symbols used internationally on weather maps and charts are regulated by the World Meteorological Organisation (WMO) in Geneva. When plotted on weather maps, they provide essential information for forecasting.

Wind speed is measured in knots: 1 knot = 1.15 mph (1.85 km/h), and indicated by feathers on arrows; half feathers represent 5 knots, full feathers 10 knots, and a solid pennant 50 knots. The arrows fly in the direction from which the wind is blowing.

Symbol	Speed in knots	mph (km/h)
◎	1/calm	1 (1.85)
	2	2.3 (3.7)
	5	5.75 (9.25)
	10	11.5 (18.5)
	15	17.25 (27.75)
	20	23.0 (37.0)
	25	28.75 (46.25)
	30	34.5 (55.5)
	35	40.5 (64.75)
	40	46.0 (74.0)
	45	51.75 (83.25)
	50	57.5 (92.5)
	55	63.25 (101.75)
	60	69.0 (111.0)
	65	74.75 (120.25)
	90	103.5 (166.5)
	100	115.0 (185.0)
	105	120.75 (194.25)

Swinging signs creaked in the wind, the street's whole length. The candy-striped pole which indicates nobility proud and ancient along the palace-bordered canals of Venice indicated merely the humble barber-shop along the main street of Dawson's Landing. On a chief corner stood a lofty unpainted pole wreathed from top to bottom with tin pots and pans and cups, the chief tinmonger's noisy notice to the world (when the wind blew) that his shop was on hand for business at that corner.

Mark Twain *Pudd'nhead Wilson*

Wind strength or force can also be expressed according to the Beaufort Scale (named after the British admiral Sir Francis Beaufort, who devised it in 1805).

Beaufort Number	Description	Wind force (km/h)	(mph)	(knots)
0	Calm		less than 1	
1	Light air	1–5	1–3	1–2
2	Light breeze	6–11	4–7	3–6
3	Gentle breeze	12–19	8–12	7–10
4	Moderate breeze	20–29	13–18	11–16
5	Fresh breeze	30–39	19–24	17–21
6	Strong breeze	40–50	25–31	22–27
7	Near gale	51–61	32–38	28–33
8	Gale	62–74	39–46	34–40
9	Strong gale	75–87	47–54	41–47
10	Storm	88–101	55–63	48–55
11	Violent storm	102–117	64–73	56–63
12	Hurricane	118+	74+	64+

The following symbols indicate the state of the sky or **cloud cover**, which is measured in oktas literally 'eighths', and expressed in terms of the number of eighths of the sky covered or obscured by clouds:

○	clear sky
◐	1 okta, 1/8th or less covered
◑	2 oktas, 2/8ths covered
◑	3 oktas, 3/8ths covered
◐	4 oktas, 4/8ths covered
◑	5 oktas, 5/8ths covered
◑	6 oktas, 6/8ths covered
◐	7 oktas, 7/8ths covered or more
●	8 oktas; sky completely covered
⊗	sky obscured; e.g. by fog

Some of the symbols used to indicate weather conditions being experienced in a particular region:

•	rain
,	drizzle
▽	shower
✳	snow
⊹	drifting snow
▲	hail
⧖	ice pellets
∞	haze
≡	fog
⊓↗	thunderstorm
⚡	lightning
⚡	hurricane
⛛	dust whirls
∥	tornado
↯	tropical storm

Isobars connect points of equal atmospheric **pressure**. Pressure is recorded in millibars (mb): 1 millibar = 100 newtons per m² or 0.75mm of mercury.

L   area of low pressure
H   area of high pressure

A **front** is the interface between air masses of differing temperatures. Fronts are represented by the following symbols:

cold front: a cold air mass pushing into a warm air mass

warm front: a warm air mass pushing into a cold air mass

occluded front: a cold front has overtaken a warm front

stationary front: the interface between two air masses of similar temperature

Zodiac

In **astronomy** (from Greek *astronomia*, literally 'star arrangement') the zodiac is a belt, extending eight degrees (8°) to either side of the ecliptic, the apparent annual path of the Sun through the heavens. The belt, which also contains the orbits of the Moon and major planets apart from Pluto, was divided around 150 BC by the Greek astronomer Hipparchus into 12 zones of 30°, each named for the principal constellation or group of stars within it. Because the outlines of many of these star groups resembled animals, the Greeks called them collectively the *zoidiakos kyklos*, or 'circle of animal figures' or 'signs' (ultimately from *zoion*, 'animal', from which the English word 'zoo' derives).

Western **astrology** (from Greek *astrologia*, literally 'starspeaking') is the study of positions and aspects of these **signs of the zodiac** in relation to the Sun, Moon, planets and other stars, for the purpose of assessing and, by drawing up horoscopes, predicting their supposed influence on our daily lives. As the Earth revolves around the Sun, the Sun appears to move each month from one constellation into the next, and a new sign comes into power. On a popular level, modern astrology is most concerned with Birth Signs. A Birth Sign is the zodiacal sign you were 'born under', i.e. the sign the Sun appeared, from the Earth's point of view, to be occupying during the month of your birth. Since the zones were fixed more than 2000 years ago, the constellations have been shifting position by about one degree every 70 years. Because of this 'precession', the astrological signs no longer correspond with the astronomical constellations they were originally named after (thus for example, the sign of Aries is now among the stars of Pisces; it will not return to its starting-point for approximately 24 000 years).

Early astrologers classed the signs in groups of the four elements: fire, water, air, and earth. Fiery signs are ardent, keen, energetic, enthusiastic; watery signs are emotional, sensitive, unstable; airy signs are articulate, intellectual, the thinkers of the zodiac; earthy signs are practical, cautious, stable, strong. The signs were also grouped by qualities: cardinal signs are dominant, instigators (excellent at starting things, but not so good at finishing them); fixed signs are preservers, sustainers (who do see things through to the end); mutable signs are adaptable, changeable. In addition, the signs are regarded alternately as masculine (positive, assertive) and feminine (negative, passive).

There was a flurry of premature snow in the air and the stars looked cold. Staring up at them, he saw that they were his stars as always – symbols of ambition, struggle and glory.

F. Scott Fitzgerald *The Crack-up*

Astronomy is to look in the sky and see stars, while astrology is to look up and see lions and virgins and other spooky creatures.

Anon

Listed here are the 12 signs in their traditional order, with their astrological dates, some of their mythological origins, and the signs' symbols. Most of these symbols (sometimes known as sigils) date from medieval times. Also included is a tongue-in-cheek selection of the so-called positive and negative characteristics to which, according to some astrologers, each sign may be prone.

Aries 21 March–19 April: fire/cardinal/masculine/ruled by Mars. The name of the first sign derives from the Latin *aries*, 'ram', which the second constellation was thought to resemble. In Greek mythology, Aries was the winged ram that carried the royal children Phrixus and Helle from the fury of their stepmother Ino. Helle fell into the sea that links the Aegean with the Sea of Marmara, and separates Europe from Asia Minor (named the Hellespont after her). After Phrixus reached safety, he sacrificed the ram to Zeus, who placed it in the heavens. Aries' fleece was the Golden Fleece sought and recovered by Jason and the Argonauts. The symbol clearly represents the horns of the ram; some astrologers, however, claim it is a drawing of the human eyebrows and nose, which, with the rest of the face and the head, Aries is said to influence. The sign of the pioneer or warrior. Typical Arians are brave, energetic, outgoing, creative, self-reliant, idealistic, enthusiastic, freedom-loving, active, intense, resourceful, impulsive, courageous and loyal; on the downside they are also proud, impatient, destructive, overbearing, dictatorial, jealous, coarse, short-tempered, argumentative, selfish and self-centred.

Taurus 20 April–20 May: earth/fixed/feminine/ruled by Venus. The name of the second sign derives from the Greek *tauros*, 'bull', for the third constellation. In mythology, Zeus disguised himself as a snow-white bull when he abducted Europa, Princess of Phoenicia, to Crete, where she became the mother of King Minos. The symbol represents the head and horns of the bull. It is also suggested that this is a vestigial drawing of the larynx in the throat, which Taurus is said to influence (along with the neck). Taureans are sensuous, warm, stable, loyal, reliable, patient, generous, determined, constructive, strong-willed, conservative, practical, intractable, relentless; equally, they may be overbearing, jealous, repetitive, selfish, stubborn, possessive, prejudiced and quick tempered.

Gemini 21 May–21 June: air/mutable/masculine/ruled by Mercury. The third sign is named (from Latin *geminus*, 'twin') after the fourth constellation, which the ancient Sumerians and the Babylonians called 'the great twins'; the Greeks named the two brightest stars after Zeus' twin sons Kastor and Polydeukes (later Latinised into Castor and Pollux). When Kastor was killed, his brother asked to give up his immortality. Zeus/Jupiter rewarded the twins' devotion to each other by placing them in the heavens. The symbol is said to represent them holding hands. The twins have also been related to other pairs such as Romulus and Remus. Gemini influences the shoulders, arms, and lungs. Because of this sign's dual personality, it has been described as the butterfly of the zodiac. Typically, Geminis are generous, versatile, idealistic, communicative, inventive, lively, cheerful, self-confident, inquisitive; they may also be childish and immature, restless, impatient, unstable, superficial, indecisive, lacking in concentration, and contradictory.

Cancer 22 June–22 July: water/cardinal/feminine/ruled by the Moon. The fourth sign is named after the fifth constellation, which appears when the Sun has reached its highest northern limit, then begins to return sideways to the south. In mythology, the crab (Latin, *cancer*) nipped Herakles/Hercules' foot as he was battling with the multi-headed snake, the Hydra. In retaliation, Hercules crushed the Crab. Hercules' enemy Hera/Juno rewarded the creature by placing it in the heavens. In early astrology, both the sign and constellation were often depicted in the image of a crayfish or lobster. Its symbol, said to represent the Crab's claws or pincers, has also been explained as two spermatozoa twisted together, to signify the male and female seed. The sign influences the chest and stomach. Cancerians are sensitive, imaginative, romantic, sociable, shrewd, domesticated, intuitive, artistic, loyal, but also cautious and shy, selfish, over-emotional, opinionated, acquisitive, moody, superficial, and tenacious.

Leo 23 July–22 August: fire/fixed/masculine/ruled by the Sun. The fifth sign (Latin *leo*, 'lion') is named after the sixth constellation, which was so-called by the ancient Sumerians more than 5000 years ago. In Greek myth, Leo represents the lion of the Nemean forest which Herakles strangled as one of his 12 labours. The original symbol was said to be a corruption of the Greek letter *lambda*, the initial of the constellation's Greek name *Leon*; the modern version evolved from a late medieval form, which is thought to represent either the Lion's mane or its tail. Leo influences the heart, lungs, and liver. Those born under the sign are typically brave, strong, generous, self-reliant, enthusiastic, warm-hearted, sensitive, self-expressive, creative, dignified, inspirational, exuberant, flamboyant, hospitable; also selfish, vain, intolerant, impetuous, pompous, conceited, blunt, demanding, predatory, imperious, dogmatic, self-satisfied, ostentatious, militant.

Virgo 23 August–22 September: earth/mutable/feminine/ruled by the planet Mercury. The sixth sign is named Virgo (from Latin for 'virgin') after the seventh, and second largest, constellation. In many mythologies, Virgo is represented either as the goddess of love, or a fertility goddess such as the Greek Persephone, or the corn goddess Demeter; the constellation's line pattern represents the figure of a virgin holding a sheaf of wheat. The modern symbol derives either from a monogram of the first three Greek letters of *Parthenos*, 'virgin', or from the merged initials MV for *Maria Virgo* (Virgin Mary). The sign influences the stomach and intestines. Virgos love order and harmony; they are gentle, modest, earthy, hard-working, practical, discriminating, quiet, exacting, nervous, shrewd, methodical, dignified, clever, intelligent, nervous, graceful, mentally alert; also aloof, bookish, fussy, perfectionist, carping, hypercritical, shrewish, backbiting.

Libra 23 September–23 October: air/cardinal/masculine/ruled by the planet Venus. Named after the eighth constellation, the seventh sign, known as the Balance or Scales, is the only one which does not represent an animate being. The ancient Greeks regarded it as the claws of the constellation Scorpius; the 2nd-century AD mathematician Ptolemy described it as 'the claws'. The sign's Latin name Libra may have originated in early Christian times, when the autumnal equinox, which marks days and nights of equal length, was in Libra before precession carried it into the neighbouring constellation of Virgo. Another suggestion is that the cluster of stars was once considered to be the scales of justice held by Virgo; the symbol is thought to represent these scales. One of the Egyptian hieroglyphs for the sign suggests that the symbol derives from a picture of the Sun setting over the Earth. Libra is represented by a woman (sometimes identified with Astraea, the Roman goddess of justice, who weighs the deeds of men), holding scales, or by the scales alone. The sign influences the backbone and kidneys. Librans are gentle, artistic, sensitive, peaceful, charming, romantic, delicate, harmonious, loyal, sympathetic, understanding, elegant, idealistic, orderly, comparative, peaceful, changeable, helpful, perceptive, affectionate; because they weigh matters equally, they may be indecisive, also impractical, lazy, untidy, frivolous, vain, easily persuaded.

Scorpio 24 October–21 November: water/fixed/feminine/ruled originally by Mars, but now considered to be ruled by Pluto, the ninth and farthest planet from the Sun. The name for the eighth sign (in astronomy Scorpius), derives from the Latin for scorpion, the creature it clearly resembles. According to Greek myth, when the giant hunter Orion angered the virgin goddess of the Moon and the hunt, Artemis (identified with the Roman goddess Diana), she roused the scorpion to sting Orion in the foot and kill him; hence, so it is said, Orion sets in the sky as Scorpius rises. Roman astronomers later separated the cluster of stars that were considered to form the scorpions' claws from the rest of the constellation and made them into Libra. The symbol represents the scorpion's legs and sting; it is also said to symbolise the male genitals over which the sign has influence, also the kidneys. Other astrologers claim it to be a vestigial drawing of the severed tail of a serpent; the earliest known symbol, an Egyptian demotic symbol, represents the sign as an erect serpent, with the arrow on the tail as the sting. Scorpio is said to be the most intense sign; those born under it are shrewd, sincere, magnetic, emotional, penetrating, determined, secretive, dignified, disciplined, self-confident, kind, masterful, sensitive, critical, tenacious, forceful, passionate, competitive, extremist, natural fighters; equally, they may also be single-minded, cruel, rebellious, sceptical, suspicious, secretive, sulky, sarcastic, jealous, selfish, violent, indulgent, domineering, arrogant, ruthless, vindictive, manipulative.

Sagittarius 22 November–21 December: fire/mutable/masculine/ruled by the planet Jupiter. The association of the ninth sign and tenth constellation with a mounted archer (Latin *sagittarius*), was made by the Babylonians as early as the 11th century BC. In Greek myth, the constellation was linked with the centaur* Chiron, whom Herakles killed with a poisoned arrow. Zeus placed Chiron in the heavens, where he now aims his arrow at the scorpion; the symbol represents an arrow being shot from a bow. The sign is said to influence the liver, thighs, and hips. Typical Sagittarians are open, cheerful, honest, dignified, optimistic, independent, enthusiastic, philosophic, idealistic, generous, open-minded, loyal, magnanimous, frank; they have great potential, but are also impulsive, indolent, self-indulgent, conceited, dogmatic, outspoken, restless, and 'subject to wandering'.

Capricorn 22 December–19 January: earth/cardinal/feminine/ruled by the planet Saturn. The name of the 11th constellation (Capricornus) and 10th sign derives from the Latin *caper*, 'goat', and *cornu*, 'horn'.

Capricorn is also known as the Sea Goat, and since Babylonian times the goat has often been represented with a fish tail. This image is conveniently explained by the Greek legend of Pan. To escape the hundred-headed monster Typhon, Pan attempted to change into a goat; but as he jumped into the Nile before the transformation was complete, the half above the water took on the shape of a goat, while his lower half, the tail, changed into a fish. The sign influences the knees, bones, skin, and teeth. The symbol is said to stand for the first two Greek letters (*tau, rho*) of *tragos*, the word for 'goat'; alternatively, it represents the goat's horn and twisted tail. Capricorn is said to be the sign of the achiever; people born under it are ambitious, determined, practical, industrious, prudent, perservering, diplomatic, cautious, methodical, dependable, trustworthy, efficient, just, honest, undemonstrative, conservative, responsive, patient; they may also be pessimistic, secretive, fearful, miserly, unsympathetic, stern, rigid, suspicious, selfish, materialistic, brooding, egotistical, gloomy.

Aquarius 20 January–18 February: air/fixed/masculine/originally thought to be ruled by Saturn, the sign is now said to be under the rule of the planet Uranus. The 11th sign is named the water-carrier (from Latin *aqua*, 'water') after the 12th constellation; to the Sumerians, it was one of the most sacred constellations, representing their sky-god An pouring the waters of immortality on the earth. The Graeco-Egyptian mathematician Ptolemy (*c.* 90–*c.* 168) called it 'the water-pourer', and since earliest times the image has been that of a man carrying an urn, from which water pours towards the mouth of the neighbouring constellation, the 'southern fish' Piscis Austrinus. Ancient civilisations associated Aquarius with their annual rainy seasons; the symbol of zigzag lines, thought to be of Egyptian origin, is said to represent the flow of water, probably of the Nile. The sign is thought to rule the calves, ankles and blood. Aquarians are warm, friendly, outgoing, serious, intelligent, progressive, persistent, confident, curious, creative, unconventional, open-minded, fond of science and literature, discreet, optimistic, independent; also solitary, perverse, lazy, opportunist, unsympathetic, irresponsible, and sometimes difficult to get to know deeply.

Pisces 19 February–20 March: water/mutable/feminine/ruled by Neptune, though prior to that planet's discovery, by Jupiter. The 12th and last sign is named Pisces (Latin, 'fishes') after what is now considered to be the first constellation of the zodiac. The image relates to the Greek myth of Aphrodite and Eros, who changed into fish when they jumped into the river to escape the monster Typhon (see Capricorn). The symbol is said to be a drawing of the fish united by a 'silver cord' which joins their two mouths together; usually the fish are depicted facing in opposite directions to symbolise the conflict in the human being between spirit and soul. The sign rules the feet and lymph glands. Typically optimistic, emotional, generous, loving, imaginative, intuitive, sentimental, sympathetic, easy-going but highly sensitive to the emotional needs of others, poetic, suggestible, Pisceans are also insecure, dreamy, self-pitying, self-indulgent, stubborn, inconstant, lazy, restless, impractical, fickle and hypochondriac.

Symbolic associations

A glossary of words associated with signs and symbols

The derivations and definitions of the following words are taken from *The Oxford English Dictionary* (OED) and others. Many of the words, to do with writing of one form or another, have the affix 'graph' or 'graphy', from Greek *graphos*, writing, drawing; or 'gram', from Greek *gramma*, letter, both from *graphein*, to write, also to draw. Some terms that are specifically defined elsewhere are not entered here.

abecedary derived from the first four Roman letters; a list of alphabetic symbols in their traditional fixed order, often for teaching purposes. Abecedarian means arranged alphabetically, or someone who teaches or studies the alphabet. In an odd reversal, the word once also applied to a member of a 16th-century German Anabaptist sect who refused to learn to read.

acrophony from Greek, literally 'top sound'; using what was originally a picture symbol of an object to represent the initial sound of the name of that object, e.g. the sign of a wavy line for water to represent n, the initial sound in the Egyptian word for water (nu), or the sign for mouth (ro) to stand for the sound of r. Also the process for naming a letter: by a word whose initial sound is the same as that which the letter represents. The names of the Greek letters are acrophonic, e.g. *beta, kappa*, etc, but apart from *omega* (great o), *omicron* (little o), *epsilon* (bare e), and *upsilon* (slender u), they have no meaning. Similarly acrophonic are some of the names in the English alphabet; two notable exceptions are aitch, and double-u.

allegory from Greek, literally 'other speak'; a story or visual image in which the characters and events are symbols of something else, i.e. convey one literal or visible meaning on the surface, with another abstract or spiritual meaning hidden beneath.

allusion an indirect or incidental reference to someone or something in art, literature, history, mythology etc. Derived ultimately from Latin *ludere*, 'to play', the verb 'allude' came to be used in the sense of play

with a word, i.e. pun. Thus in John Foxe's *Book of Martyrs* (1563), Christ 'alluding to his [St Peter's] name, called him a rock' (Latin, *petra*). Allusions are common in heraldry (see canting arms) and in trademarks, e.g. the three-pointed Mercedes-Benz* badge is said to allude, among other things, to a steering wheel; the international Woolmark* to a skein of wool.

alphabet from the Latin *alphabetum*, coined in the late 2nd century AD by the Roman theologian Tertullian from *alpha* and *beta*, the names of the first two symbols of the Greek writing system, to describe that particular system. In time, it was used in connection with the written letters of other languages, then with other sets of basic symbols or characters representing sounds, words, or things (e.g. the Semaphore* alphabet or the manual alphabets used by the deaf*). By extension, it has come to mean the elementary principles of anything. The study or science of alphabets is **alphabetology**.

amulet ultimately from Latin *amoliri*, 'to avert', any charm believed to possess protective powers against evil spirits, injury, disease, or bad luck in general; usually worn round the wrist or neck.

analphabetic archaic term for someone who is 'unlettered' i.e. 'illiterate'; also descriptive of a language written not with an alphabet, but by means of pictograms (Sumerian*, Chinese*), hieroglyphs (ancient Egyptian*), ideograms (Chinese*), or a syllabary (Cherokee*).

armory archaic term for heraldry; hence **armorial bearings**: the arms (i.e. the devices on a shield, and formerly on a surcoat), helmet, crest, supporters, mantling, insignia, etc., in a full **achievement of arms** (see Chapter 6).

attribute an object or emblem associated with and serving to identify a person; commonly used in religious art and stained glass to identify saints. In allusion to her torture, St Catherine's attribute is a spiked wheel. (See Chapter 5 for a

selection of saints and their attributes.)

badge originally a device worn as a distinguishing mark by servants, retainers, or followers attached to a royal or noble family (see cognisance). Now used as an identifying token of employment, membership of a society, school, university, organisation, etc., or to indicate rank (e.g. in the police or armed forces). Shakespeare uses the word metaphorically: for example, Falstaff describes a pale liver as 'the badge of pusillanimity and cowardice'; to Shylock in *The Merchant of Venice*, 'sufferance is the badge of all our tribe'. To Mr Pritchard in Steinbeck's *The Wayward Bus*, his wife's fur coat 'was the badge of their position. It placed them as successful, conservative, and sound people'. In the US, lapel badges in enamel, metal, plastic, etc, are 'buttons', so-called because the first were manufactured on button-making machinery, and referred to as pinback buttons (by a process patented in 1893 by the Whitehead and Hoag Company of Newark, New Jersey).

blazon from Old French *blason*, 'shield'; a verbal or written description of heraldic bearings, usually in traditional language. John Guillim in *A Display of Heraldrie* (1610) offers this definition: 'to blazon is to expresse what the shapes, kinds, and colour of things born in Armes are, together with their apt significations'. Hence **blazonry**: the art of drawing or deciphering coats of arms.

boustrophedon a style of writing, so-called from the Greek 'as the ox turns' (i.e. when drawing a plough up and down a field). As Lawrence Durrell describes it in *Justine:* 'The members of the inner Cabal corresponded with one another, using the curious old form of writing, known as the *boustrophedon*; that is to say a writing which is read from right to left and from left to . right in alternate lines'. First applied to ancient Greek, and later to some other systems.

brachygraphy from Greek, literally 'short writing'; the term applied to certain old systems of shorthand*.

calligraphy beautiful handwriting, penmanship (from Greek *kallos*, 'beauty'); as opposed to **cacography** (from Greek *kakos*, 'bad') bad handwriting.

character from Greek *kharakter*, a tool for stamping, marking (from *kharassein*, 'to cut grooves'), or the impression it left on metal or stone; thus a distinctive mark or symbol, particularly in a writing system such as Chinese*. Also a letter, numeral, punctuation, or similar mark cast in printing type; by extension, a style of printing or writing. A **charactery** is a system of symbols used to express thought and meaning.

charm from Latin *carmen*, 'song', 'incantation', originally chanted or recited to conjure up occult forces; now applied to any ornament or trinket (such as on a charm bracelet) that protects against evil, bad luck, etc.

cherology also **chirology**, from Greek *cheir*, 'hand', literally hand speech; the art of communicating by signs or gestures made with the hands or fingers. A form of hand signs, termed **cheironomy**, was used to guide performers in the earliest form of music 'notation'* in ancient Egypt, Greece, Israel, China, India, Rome and other early civilisations. Described as 'writing on the air', cheironomy survives today in the teaching of the Coptic* liturgy in Egypt.

chirography handwriting, penmanship.

cipher or **cypher** from Arabic *çifr*, 'empty' or 'void', a translation of the Sanskrit word for empty; the symbol written in Hindu and Arabic numeration for zero or nought (0), which by itself denotes nothing, but which increases or decreases the value of other numerals according to its position. (Considered one of the greatest inventions of civilisation after the wheel and the alphabet, the zero was invented (?*c*. 600 BC) by Hindu mathematicians; it was introduced into Europe by the Italian mathematician Leonardo Fibonacci in 1202.) By the mid-16th century, the word cipher was being applied to all other Arabic numerals. More commonly today, it describes a coded system of writing intelligible only to those possessing the key; the transference of meaning resulted from the use of numerals for letters in older systems of cryptography. Cipher is also applied to interwoven

letters, especially initials (see monogram).

coat of arms heraldic bearings, generally accepted as including the helmet and crest (see Chapter 6). The term derives from the custom in the Middle Ages of embroidering a knight's distinguishing device, badge or family insignia on the linen surcoat he wore over his armour. The derogatory term 'turncoat', now someone who changes his party, principles or loyalty, was originally one who literally turned his coat inside out to hide his badge.

cognisance archaic term for the badge or mark by which a person or company is known.

colophon now a publisher's identifying emblem or logotype on the title-page and often on the spine of a book, e.g. the Guinness device with three slanting strokes (an allusion to books on a shelf). It also refers to the inscription on a title-page or on the back of it, giving details such as the publisher's name, date and place of publication, information which, in the early days of printing, was placed at the end of the book. The word derives from Greek *kolophon*, 'summit', or 'finishing stroke', possibly after the warriors of Colophon near Ephesus (now in western Turkey). According to legend, whenever the Colophonians gave their support in a battle, they always waited till the last minute to attack and 'finish off' the other side (hence the now archaic 'to add the colophon', to put the finishing touch to any enterprise).

cryptography from Greek *kryptos*, 'hidden'; the art of writing or deciphering code invented for secret communication by arbitrary characters, by using letters or characters in other than their usual sense, or by other means; hence cryptogram, cryptograph: anything written in cipher, or in such a form or order that is intelligible only to those possessing the key to decipher it. In Edgar Allan Poe's *The Gold Bug* (1843), William Legrand finds a piece of parchment containing the following arrangement of numerals, punctuation and reference marks: 53‡‡†305))6*;4826)4‡.)4‡); 806*; 48†8¶60))85;I‡(;:‡*8†83(88)5*†;46 (;88*96*?;8)*‡(;485);5*†2:*‡(;4956*2 (5*—4)8¶8*;4069285);)6†8)4‡‡;I (‡9;4808I;8:8‡I;48†85;4)485†528806*8I (‡9;48;(88;4(‡?34;48)4‡;I6I;:I88;‡?; (Legrand deciphers the code, which

gives the location of buried treasure, by beginning with the assumption that since 8 occurs more than any other symbol and e is the commonest letter in English, and 'the' the commonest word, then the combination ';48' represents 'the'.)

cryptology the scientific study of codes.

cuneiform wedge-shaped, from Latin *cuneus*, 'wedge'; coined by Thomas Hyde (1636–1703) Regius Professor of Hebrew at Oxford University to describe the ancient writing in which wedge-shaped characters were impressed by a stylus in soft clay.

curiology picture writing; archaic word for hieroglyphic writing, in which objects were represented by pictograms*.

cursive rounded or flowing writing, particularly handwriting (see uncial); in printing, the term is applied to type that imitates handwriting.

dactylology from Greek *dactyl*, 'finger'; the art of communicating with finger signs, as in the one- and two-handed manual* alphabets used by the deaf.

demotic from Greek *demotikós*, 'popular', something that is typical of, or used by, the 'common' or ordinary people; applied particularly to the very cursive script of the ancient Egyptians.

device any graphic design used as an emblem, symbol, trademark; also in heraldry a distinctive mark adopted by a person, family etc. 'A knight of Sparta, my renowned father; And the device he bears upon his shield Is a black Ethiop reaching at the sun.' Shakespeare, *Pericles*.

diacritic any mark added above (ü), beneath (ç), or through (ø) a letter to distinguish it, or to indicate a special phonetic value; e.g. the acute accent (´) above the e in café indicates that it is pronounced ay; with the possible exception of the dot or tittle over the letter i, diacritical marks, even in borrowed words such as café are rare in modern English orthography (see Chapter 2).

digraph a pair of letters representing one sound, e.g. ea and ch in each, or joined as in the Old English æ (see ligature).

235

emblazon to adorn with heraldic devices; to portray arms in their colours, furs etc. (see blazon).

emblem from Latin *emblema*, 'inlaid work', derived from Greek *emballein*, 'to throw in'. Blount's *Glossographia* (1656), defines it as 'any fine work cunningly set in wood or other substance, as we see in chessboards and tables, notwithstanding it is commonly taken for a sweet moral symbol, consisting of picture and words, by which some weighty matter is declared'. Some 14 years earlier, Thomas Fuller noted in *The Holy State and the Profane State*: 'I like that Embleme of Charity . . . a naked child, giving honey to a Bee without wings'. Now sometimes interchangeable with symbol, for an object, or picture of an object with a meaning 'inlaid', i.e. representing something different from itself; for example, the anchor is an emblem of hope, the menorah* of Judaism. In *Robinson Crusoe*, Daniel Defoe uses the word in the sense of personification: 'And my father, an emblem of our blessed Saviour's parable, had even killed the fatted calf for me'. In heraldry, the distinguishing badge of a person, family, nation; in religious art, a symbolic object accompanying a saint (see attribute).

ensign ultimately from Latin *signum*, 'sign'; originally a Roman military standard, which consisted of a symbol or emblem surmounting a pole. Later, a sign or characteristic mark: thus John Bulwer in his *Anthropometamorphosis* (1650) calls the beard 'the ensigne of manhood'. Also, the term for a military or naval standard (see Red Ensign); ensigns were first flown on British ships at the end of the 16th century. Now describes any special form of national, trading, or association flag on ships, in which the reduced flag itself occupies the canton or union (upper corner of the flag near the staff).

epigraph an inscription, usually on a monument, building, statue, tomb etc; hence **epigraphy**, the study of inscriptions carved or scratched on hard surfaces.

exponent in mathematics, any number or symbol written above and to the right of a number, symbol, expression, to indicate how many times it is to be multiplied by itself, e. g. in 10^9 (1 000 000 000, billion) the number 9 is the exponent; also called the index or,

more commonly, power. The index placed below and to the right of a symbol, e.g. as in x_n, is termed a suffix.

fetish from Portuguese *feitiço*, 'sorcery', 'charm'; applied by early Portuguese travellers on the Guinea coast to amulets* worshipped by natives there. Any object thought to possess magic or protective powers. 'Each man had his own little fetish. It was known as the pocket-piece or mascot. In some cases it might be a dice or a playing-card . . . in other cases it might be a locket, then again a medal, while many of us carried little wooden dolls.' E.M. Roberts, *Flying Fighter* (1918).

figurehead the carved bust or full-length figure fixed to a ship's bows originates from the days when ships were dedicated to goddesses (hence ships are referred to as she or her). Believed to embody the ship's soul, the figurehead was regarded with respect; to set sail without one was considered highly unwise.

gesture any head, hand, body movement expressing emotion or giving information; or as Desmond Morris defines it, any action that sends a visual signal to an onlooker (see Chapter 3). Gestures played an important role in oratory in the past; they were also thought to be part of a universal language. 'By gesture, we render our thoughts and our passions intelligible to all Nations. . . . 'Tis as it were the common language of all mankind, which strikes the understanding in at our eyes, as much as speaking does in at our ears'. Michel le Faucher, *The Art of Speaking in Public* (translated by John Henley, 1727).

graffiti from Italian *graffio*, 'claw', 'scratch'; first applied to inscriptions found on the walls of Pompeii when the city was unearthed in 1755 from its burial by volcanic ash from Mount Vesuvius in AD 79.

grapheme a written symbol such as any of the 26 letters of the English alphabet, or combination of letters (e.g. æ), used to represent a single unit of speech or phoneme.

graphology the study of the systems of symbols devised to communicate language in written form; also the art of analysing someone's character and personality, from their handwriting.

heraldry the term originally applied to the science and function of a

herald*, but now to the knowledge and proper descriptions of armorial bearings or arms.

hieroglyph from the Greek *hieroglyphikà grámmata* (from *hierós*, 'holy', *glyphen*, 'to carve', and *grámma*, 'letter'); coined by the Greeks to describe what they believed to be 'sacred carvings' on ancient Egyptian monuments; since the late 19th century, also used to designate other picture-sign scripts, e.g. those of the Mayan and Aztec civilisations. Also applied to a character or symbol with a secret meaning, or any sort of illegible or barely legible writing. 'It [buried treasure] lays there a long time and gets rusty; and by and by somebody finds an old yellow paper that tells how to find the marks—a paper that's got to be ciphered over about a week because it's mostly signs and hy'roglyphics . . . pictures and things, you know, that don't seem to mean anything.' Mark Twain, *Tom Sawyer*.

hierogram a sacred character or symbol; a hieroglyph.

icon from Greek *eikon*, 'image', 'likeness'; since the 19th century, used to describe a sacred image or representation as an object of devotion, e.g. of Christ, or the Virgin Mary, in mosaic or on a painted wooden panel, particularly in the Eastern Orthodox Church. Now also applied to non-religious representations. In sign language, signs that look in some way like the idea they represent are called **iconic**.

ideogram also **ideograph**, from the Greek *idea*, 'form', 'notion'; any stylised symbol or character (e.g. as in Chinese*) representing an idea or object without expressing its name or indicating its pronunciation; a graphic symbol such as $, &, %, or 7. A picture-sign of a circle, standing for the sun, becomes an ideogram when used also to represent day, time, etc. Many international road signs are ideograms.

idiograph from Greek *idios*, 'private'; a mark or signature unique to one person or organisation; a trademark or logotype devised from handwriting.

impresa a personal badge usually comprising a device and complementary motto alluding to some character trait or important event in the individual's life; a popular adornment of royalty and nobility in the 16th and 17th centuries. The word derives from

Italian *impresa*, 'enterprise'. According to *Hall's Dictionary of Subjects and Symbols in Art*, the badge's forerunner was the *impresa amorosa*, 'the personal emblem worn by a jousting knight, whose meaning was understood only by his chosen lady'. Hall cites as a notable example of an impresa that of the French king Louis XII (1462–1515), which coupled the device of a porcupine, with its sharp spines shooting in all directions, with the motto *Cominus et eminus*, 'hand to hand and at a distance', an allusion to the king's power to strike his enemies near and far. (See also salamander.)

ligature from Latin *ligare* 'to bind'; in printing, a piece of type combining two or more letters, e.g. æ, fi or ff (incidentally, the initial Ff or ff still to be found in some English surnames is a relic of the Old English capital F (**Ff**) which resembled two small f's interlocked).

logo see logotype

logogram also **logograph** (from Greek *logos*, 'speech', 'word'), any symbol, sign, character, etc which represents a word: e.g. & for 'and', # for 'number' (US), © for 'copyright'. The use of signs to represent whole words is called **logography**.

logotype from Greek, literally 'word impression'; early 19th-century printing term for a single piece of type bearing two or more characters to aid hand-setting of frequently recurring syllables or words such as 'and'; later also a name and/or address, or trademark* cast on one piece of type, or in a particular typeface. Now commonly abbreviated to **logo**, and virtually synonymous with trademark: any special design used to represent a company or organisation.

majuscule a large capital or uncial letter.

mark from Old English *mearc*, 'boundary'; later, sign of a boundary, then sign in general; used in a very wide sense for both sign and symbol (see Chapter 7, also punctuation). In Raymond Chandler's *The Pencil*, Philip Marlowe receives a parcel by special delivery: 'It contained nothing at all but a freshly sharpened pencil – the mobster's mark of death'.

mascot anything animate or inanimate believed to bring good luck. Derived from the Provençal *mascotto*, a diminutive of *masco*, 'sorcerer', the word was brought into notice in its current sense by Edmond Audran's opera *La Mascotte* (premiered Paris, 29 December 1880) in which a young country-girl is sent to a farmer to end his bad luck. Also, a figurine adorning a car bonnet, e.g. the 'Flying Lady' on a Rolls-Royce*. The use of mascots, or the attachment to or belief in mascots, is **mascotry**.

minuscule a small cursive script originated by monks in the 7th century; now a printing term for a lower-case letter such as e.

monogram from the Greek meaning single line, originally referring solely to a picture drawn in outline only; later a character composed of two or more linked letters, usually the initials of a person's name; now often such a character or device stamped, stitched or printed on possessions (linen, silver, stationery etc.) to personalise them. 'His coat caught an ash-tray and spun it to the floor. His own initials were exposed, E.K. The monogram had been designed by Sweden's leading artist. E.K—the same initials endlessly repeated formed the design of the deep carpet he crossed to the door. E.K. in the waiting rooms; E.K. in the board-room; E.K. in the restaurants; the building was studded with his initials' (the industrialist Erik Krogh in Graham Greene's *England Made Me*. Later Krogh refers to the monogram and says: 'he was surrounded by himself').

motto ultimately from Latin *muttum*, 'a murmur', 'grunt', and possibly originating in a war cry; a word, phrase or sentence usually expressing some worthy sentiment or code of conduct; when accompanying a coat of arms or crest, it often contains a reference to the bearer's name, exploits, or heraldic device (see Chapter 6).

notation a system of symbols used to represent music (e.g. the pitch and duration of the notes), numbers*, or other facts or values. In mathematics, exponential notation, e.g. 10^{12}, saves space in writing large numbers, in this case, 1 000 000 000 000 (a million million, US trillion); in binary notation (used in computers), numbers are expressed by only two digits: 0 and 1. The principal system of dance notation, in which symbols are used to record parts of a dancer's body, direction in space, dynamics, etc., is called labanotation, after its inventor, Hungarian-born choreographer Rudolf Laban (1879–1958), whose *Kinetographie Laban* was published in 1928.

numeral from Latin *numerus*, 'number'; any graphic symbol, e.g. 7, X, α', used to represent a number*.

orthography from Greek *orthos*, 'right', 'straight'; loosely, any method of representing the sounds of language by symbols, i.e. letters, and their sequences in words; the art or study of correct spelling.

paedography from Greek *paidos*, 'boy'; any system invented to help children to read and write, for example, an alphabet such as i.t.a.*

palaeography from Greek *palaios*, 'old'; the study of ancient writing, the change and development of ancient letters and signs.

personification an animate or inanimate object, or concept such as Industry or Victory, given human form or personal attributes. Death for example is personified by a skeleton, or the 'Grim Reaper', a faceless cloaked figure, often carrying a scythe and an hourglass, common emblems of time, mortality. Uncle Sam, usually depicted as a tall thin man with a white goatee beard, dressed in red-and-white-striped trousers, a blue tailcoat, and a tall hat with a band of stars, personifies the US Government, or the US in general (the nickname originated during the War of 1812 from the initials US branded or stamped on government stores at Troy, New York, superintended by Samuel Wilson, who was known as Uncle Sam). Liberty was a popular female personification in the Italian Renaissance, together with Peace, and Plenty. The Statue of Liberty (a gift from France in 1885) at the entrance to New York Harbour, holds a flaming torch, the symbol of 'enlightenment'. The female personification of Great Britain, Britannia (from the Latin name for Britain), first appeared on coins during the reign of the Roman emperor Hadrian (AD 117–138); she reappeared on new copper coinage in 1672, as a seated figure with shield and spear. Holding a trident to symbolise Britain's naval prowess, Britannia survived on the penny until decimalisation in 1971. (See also John Bull.)

petroglyph a carving (Greek *gluphe*) on rock (Latin *petra*) or drawing cut into it, usually prehistoric.

petrogram a drawing or inscription on rock.

phonogram from Greek *phone*, 'sound', 'voice'; a symbol representing a particular spoken sound.

phonography writing according to sound in order to represent the pronunciation; any system of writing or shorthand based on phonetic transcription, and specifically, the system of phonetic shorthand invented by Isaac Pitman* in 1837. 'The heart of our trouble is with our foolish alphabet. It doesn't know how to spell, and can't be taught. In this it is like all other alphabets except one – the phonographic. That is the only competent alphabet in the world.' Mark Twain, *Essays: A Simplified Alphabet*.

phraseogram a single symbol for a whole phrase written without lifting the pen, especially in shorthand*. Phraseograph, a phrase for which there is a phraseogram.

pictogram or **pictograph**, from Latin *pictus*, 'painted'; a picture used as a symbol in early writing, e.g. a crescent for the Moon, wavy lines for water; a sign referring to a particular object, but which to give clearer or quicker information is reproduced in a conventional or typified form; hence **pictography**, a form of writing using pictograms as characters; the art of recording events or expressing ideas by pictures; also a pictorial representation of statistical data, or relationships as by charts, symbols or the like.

rebus literally 'by things' (Latin *res*, 'thing'), from the phrase *non verbis sed rebus* , 'not by words but by things'; representation of a name, word, or phrase by figures, pictures, arrangement of letters etc., which suggest its syllables, e.g. the combination of the phonograms of the picture of a bee and a leaf to represent the word belief; as such, used in some of the earliest writing systems. The word also applies to a badge, distinguishing device, etc., whose components pun on the name of the bearer. Rebuses were popular in medieval times to ornament buildings and possessions, especially with ecclesiastics: the rebus in the chapel in Winchester

Cathedral of Bishop Thomas Langton (d.1501), comprises a long (a symbol in early music notation*) protruding from a tun or barrel. Also used in trademarks, such as that of the Birmingham bakers Starkey, which consists of a star and key.

roundel heraldic term for a circular device; also a painted coloured circle identifying the nationality of aircraft, particularly the RAF's 'bull's eye' design of concentric red, white and blue circles. (See also ICI.)

seal ultimately from Latin *sigillum*, 'seal', a diminutive of *signum*, 'sign'; usually a metal die with a raised or engraved emblem (often heraldic) used to stamp an impression on wax as a symbol of authenticity or authority; also the impression made. The use of such devices dates back to the Sumerians (*c.* 3000 BC). Their seals were made from small cylindrical pieces of stone engraved with pictograms that identified the owner: the impression obtained when rolled over soft clay constituted his legal signature. (See US Great Seal.)

semaphore from Greek *sema*, 'sign', 'signal', and *phoros*, 'bearing', 'bearer' (see Chapter 4).

sematography the use of signs or symbols instead of letters in writing.

sematology the science of signs as expressions of thought; the doctrine or use of 'signs', especially words, in relation to thought and knowledge.

semiology also **semeiology** (from Greek *semeion*, 'sign'): the general science of signs indicating ideas or symbols, and their application in linguistics and other forms of human communicative behaviour, such as sign language. In this sense, also termed **semiotics**. Additionally, as with symptomatology, the branch of medicine concerned with the study of disease symptoms.

serif possibly from Dutch *schreef*, 'stroke'; a small line at the extremities of the main strokes of many letters e.g. as on A, or T, invented by Roman stonecutters because of the difficulty of ending wide strokes without blunt lines. Now the more common of the two basic kinds of printing typefaces, the other being sanserif, i.e. without the finishing strokes.

shorthand the generic term for styles of writing which use signs to represent syllables or words, usually for speed. 'Though I like to get pretty postcards in your patent shorthand, I always have to read the copies in ordinary writing you so thoughtfully send me'. (Mrs Higgins to Professor Higgins in Bernard Shaw's *Pygmalion*.)

sigil from Latin *sigillum*, a diminutive of *signum*, 'mark'; a seal or signet; an astrological or occult sign.

sigillography the study or science of seals.

sign from Latin *signum*, 'mark'. (See p.9.)

signage coined in the US in the mid-1970s to describe public signs collectively, for example road signs on signposts.

signal loosely, any sign conveying information to a distance (see Chapter 4).

signet a small seal; an object used for impressing a small pattern in wax as an official or private seal to authenticate or give authority to a document; often fixed to or part of a finger ring, thus signet ring, a ring with a seal set in it.

sign language any system of hand movements for expressing meanings, as used for instance in various occupations, by North American Indians, or by the deaf (see Chapter 3).

sphenography writing in cuneiform*, i.e. in wedge-shaped or arrow-headed characters.

sphragistics the scientific study or knowledge of seals or signet rings, such as those with distinguishing devices used to seal documents.

stenography from Greek *stenos*, 'narrow'; narrow or close writing used in shorthand writing. Also commonly applied to the process of taking down dictation in shorthand and later transcribing it in typewriting.

syllabary a set of written characters, each representing a syllable (derived ultimately from Greek *sullambánein*, 'gather together', from which derived *sullabé*, a gathering together of letters); an alternative in some languages, e.g. Cherokee, to an alphabet. **Syllabism** is the use of syllabic rather than alphabetic characters in writing.

symbol ultimately from Greek *sumballein*, literally 'to cast together' (see p.9). Two 20th-century symbol labels in common usage relate to sex and status. The OED defines **sex symbol** (first recorded 1911) as 'the epitome of sexual attraction and glamour'. In their biography *Valentino* (1976), Noel Botham and Peter Donnelly describe Rudolph Valentino (1895-1926) as 'the world's first and most enduring sex symbol'. As the *Duke of Bedford's Book of Snobs* notes, certain objects also attract the label: 'The trouble with sports-cars is that they are regarded as sex-symbols. Some people will regard a fast powerful sports-car as the expression and symbol of your virility and sexual prowess. Others will suggest nastily that it is a substitute for them.' From the same book comes the observation: 'Servants may be necessities but . . . they still remain status symbols.' The latter term, descriptive of those possessions or assets 'which determine the status to be imputed to a person', was coined in the US in 1955. Four years later Vance Packard reported in *The Status Seekers*: 'Most of us surround ourselves, wittingly or unwittingly, with status symbols we hope will influence the raters appraising us, and which we hope will help establish some social distance between ourselves and those we consider below us. The vigorous merchandising of goods as status symbols by advertisers is playing a major role in intensifying status consciousness.' The OED quotes this example from an edition of the *Church Times* (October, 1981): 'A fragment of the true Cross – a status symbol if ever there was one'.

symbolism the practice of representing things by means of symbols or of attributing symbolic meaning or significance to objects, events, relationships. The word is also applied to the late 19th-century movement in French art and literature by a group of artists and poets now known as the **Symbolists**, who, in reaction to the realism and naturalism of the period, expressed their ideas and emotions through symbols.

symbology the study or interpretation of symbols or symbolism.

tachygraphy from Greek 'swift writing', the art or use of rapid writing, especially Greek or Roman shorthand, or medieval cursive writing.

talisman an object often marked with special magical signs or words, with magical and protective powers; an amulet, charm.

technography any system which enables a specialised field to perform its function; e.g. chemical notation, or phonetic transcription.

token derives from the same Anglo-Saxon root as 'teach', in its original sense of 'to show'; something tangible which signifies something such as authority or identity, e.g. the orb and sceptre are tokens of 'kingship'; a sign or symbol serving as an indication or representation of some fact, event, or emotion. In *Troilus and Cressida*, Shakespeare refers to the spots caused by the plague as 'death-tokens'; similarly in *Love's Labour's Lost* as 'the Lord's tokens' (compare God's mark). Also used to describe a gift given as a symbol of esteem, respect, or love. In H.G. Wells' semi-autobiographical *Kipps* (1905) the eponymous hero reads about lovers splitting a coin and each keeping half: ' "But what do you break it for?" said Ann. "It's no good if it's broke." "It's a Token", said Kipps. . . . "you keep half and I keep half, and when we're sep'rated you look at your half and I look at mine – see! Then we think of each other".'

totem derived from an Algonquin (North American Indian) word; a figure of an animal, plant or other natural object adopted and venerated by members of a clan or tribe as its emblem. The figure, often carved or painted in wood, symbolises some enduring relationship with the group; also of an individual; thus in James Fenimore Cooper's *The Last of the Mohicans*: 'There was one chief of his party who carried the beaver as his peculiar symbol, or "totem".' Hence also, totem pole, a tall wooden post embellished with totemic symbols in ascending order of importance; made by some Indians of north-western North America and erected outside their homes. Coined by US comedian Fred Allen in the 1940s, and still descriptive of someone of very low rank in an organisation, is the expression 'low man on the totem pole'.

trademark any sign, mark, symbol, name, word or other distinctive device used by an individual or company on its products, advertising, etc. to indicate that it is made by a particular individual or company, and thus the protected property of that individual or company (see Chapter 7). Now also applied to a particular sign, feature, mode of behaviour, by which a person or thing may be recognised. 'There was the letter L cut into her forehead. Quite unmistakable. A detective-constable who was talking to me later told me that it's one of the Whistler's trademarks.' P. D. James, *Devices & Desires*.

transliteration changing the symbols of one script into the equivalent symbols of another script, e.g. representing the Greek φ as f in English. Also known as metagraphy, literally 'change-writing'.

typography from Greek *tupos*, 'mark', 'stamp', 'impression'; the art of printing, also the arrangement, style, and appearance of printed matter.

uncial from Latin *uncia*, 'a twelfth part' (the origin of our words 'inch' and 'ounce'); a style of writing in fairly rounded capitals, especially in Greek and Latin manuscripts of the 4th to 8th centuries AD; easy to form, the style provided the model from which most modern capitals are derived. The Romans used uncials for signs on which the letters were about an inch high. By extension, the word also applies to large, open handwriting. 'The address was . . . of the delicate kind which used to be esteemed feminine before the present uncial period'. George Eliot, *Daniel Deronda*.

vexillology the study of the history and symbolism of flags, from the Latin *vexillum*, 'standard' (see Chapter 6), ultimately from *vehere*, 'to carry'; hence also **vexillologist**, a flag historian, and **vexillophilist**, a flag collector.

Bibliography

A Century of Trade Marks, 1876–1976, The Patent Office, HMSO, London 1976

Achen, Sven Tito, *Symboler Omkring Os*, GAD, Copenhagen 1975

Addison, Josephine, *The Illustrated Plant Lore*, Sidgwick & Jackson, London 1985

Admiralty Manual of Seamanship, HMSO, London 1979

Attwater, Donald, *A Dictionary of Saints*, Penguin, London 1974

Axtell, Roger E., *Gestures: The Do's and Taboos of Body Language Around the World*, John Wiley, New York 1991

Baker, Margaret, *The Folklore of the Sea*, David & Charles, Newton Abbot 1979

Barakat, Robert A., The *Cistercian Sign Language*, Cistercian Publications, Kalamazoo, Michigan 1975

Barber, Richard, & Riches, Anne, *A Dictionary of Fabulous Beasts*, Boydell Press, Ipswich 1971

Barraclough, E.M.C., *Flags of the World*, Warne & Co, London 1969

Biggs, Katharine M., *A Dictionary of British Folk-Tales*, Routledge & Kegan Paul, London 1970

Black, Matthew (editor), *Peake's Commentary on the Bible*, Nelson, Sunbury-on-Thames 1976

Bodmer, Frederick, *The Loom of Language*, (ed. Lancelot Hogben), George Allen & Unwin, London 1944

Brands – An International Review by Interbrand, Mercury Business Books, London 1990

Brasch, R, *How Did It Begin?*, Longmans, London 1965

Brewer's Dictionary of Phrase & Fable, Cassell, London 1894, 1988

Brewer's Twentieth Century Phrase & Fable, Cassell, London 1991

Briggs, Geoffrey, *Civic and Corporate Heraldry*, Heraldry Today, London 1971

Brun, Theodore, *The International Dictionary of Sign Language*, Wolfe Publishing, London 1969

Bulwer, John, *Chirologia*, London 1644

Capitman, Barbara Baer, *American Trademark Designs*, Dover Publications Inc, New York 1976

Caplan, H. H., *The Classified Directory of Artists Signatures Symbols & Monograms*, George Prior, London 1976

Caradeau, Jean Luc, & Donner, Cecile, *Dictionary of Superstitions*, Granada, London 1985

Carey, G. V., *Mind The Stop*, Cambridge University Press, 1958

Carey, G. V., *Punctuation*, Cambridge University Press, 1957

Chajet, Clive, *Image by Design – from Corporate Vision to Business Reality*, Addison-Wesley, NY 1991

Child, Heather, *Christian Symbols, Ancient and Modern*, G. Bell & Sons, London 1971

Child, Heather, *Heraldic Design: A Handbook for Students*, Bell & Hyman, London 1965

Chrisman, Harry E., *1001 Most-Asked Questions about the American West*, Swallow Press, Ohio University Press, 1982

Cole, W. Owen, & Sambhi, Piara Singh, *A Popular Dictionary of Sikhism*, Curzon Press, London 1990

Collinge, N. E. (editor), *An Encyclopaedia of Language*, Routledge, London 1990

Colombo, John Robert, *Colombo's Canadian Quotations*, Hurtig, Edmonton 1974

Cooper, J. C., *An Illustrated Encyclopaedia of Traditional Symbols*, Thames and Hudson, London 1978

Corballis, Paul, *Pub Signs*, Lennard Publishing, Luton 1988

Coulmas, Florian, *The Writing Systems of the World*, Basil Blackwell, London 1989

Crampton, William, *The Complete Guide to Flags*, Kingfisher Books, London 1989

Crystal, David, *The Cambridge Encyclopaedia of Language*, Cambridge University Press, 1987

Dahlby, Frithiof, *Symboler och Tecken*, Stockholm 1964

Darley, Gillian, & Lewis, Philippa, *A Dictionary of Ornament*, Macmillan, London 1986

Davies, W. V., *Egyptian Hieroglyphs*, British Museum Publications, London 1987

Department of Transport, *The History of Traffic Signs*, London 1991

Dickson, Paul, *Words*, Delacorte Press, New York 1982

Diethelm, Walter, *Signet Signal Symbol*, ABC Edition, Zürich 1976

Diringer, David, *A History of the Alphabet*, Gresham Books, London 1983

Diringer, David, *The Alphabet*, Hutchinson, London 1968

Dirsztay, Patricia, *Church Furnishings*, Routledge & Kegan Paul, London 1978

Dreyfuss, Henry, *Symbol Sourcebook*, McGraw Hill, New York 1972

Duggleby, Vincent, *English Paper Money*, Gibbons, London 1984

Dunkling, Leslie, *The Guinness Book of Names*, Guinness Publishing, Enfield 1991

Eberhard, Wolfram, *A Dictionary of Chinese Symbols*, Routledge & Kegan Paul, London 1986

Elliott, R. W. V., *Runes*, Manchester University Press 1963

Emsley, John, *The Elements*, Clarendon Press, Oxford 1989

Fazzioli, Edoardo, *Understanding Chinese Characters*, Collins, London 1987

Ferguson, George, *Signs & Symbols in Christian Art*, Oxford University Press 1966

Franklyn, Julian, *Shield & Crest*, Macgibbon & Kee, London 1960

Friar, Stephen, *A New Dictionary of Heraldry*, Alphabooks, Sherborne 1987

Friend, Hilderic, *Flowers and Flower Lore*, Sonnenschein & Co, London 1884

Gaur, Albertine, *A History of Writing*, British Library, London 1984

Gettings, Fred, *Dictionary of Astrology*, Routledge & Kegan Paul, London 1985

Girling, F. A., *English Merchant Marks*, Oxford University Press, London 1964

Glaister, Geoffrey Ashall, *Glossary of the Book*, George Allen & Unwin, London 1960

Grambs, David, *Literary Companion Dictionary*, Routledge & Kegan Paul, London 1985

Green, Jonathon, *Dictionary of Jargon*, Routledge & Kegan Paul, London 1987

Grigson, Geoffrey, *The Shell Country Alphabet*, Michael Joseph, London 1966

Gyngell, Dudley S. Hawtrey, *Armourers Marks*, Thorsons, London 1959

Hall, James, *Hall's Dictionary of Subjects & Symbols in Art*, John Murray, London 1974

Handbook of Chemistry & Physics, 70th edition, edited by David R. Lide, CRC Press, Boca Raton, Florida

Healey, John F., *The Early Alphabet*, British Museum Publications, London 1990

Heaps, Willard A., *Birthstones and the Lore of Gemstones*, Angus & Robertson, London 1971

Herrera, J. E., *The Art and Meaning of the Pennsylvania Dutch Hex Symbols*, York Pennsylvania Press 1964

Highwater, Jamake, *Fodor's Indian America*, Hodder & Stoughton, London 1976

Hofsinde, Robert, *Indian Sign Language*, William Morrow, New York 1956

Hough, Jean, *Louder Than Words*, Great Ouse Press, Cambridge 1983

Howard, Philip, *The State of the Language*, Hamish Hamilton, London 1984

Inn Signs: Their History and Meaning, The Brewers' Society, London 1969

International Code of Signals, HMSO, London 1969, 1982

Isaacson, Philip M., *The American Eagle*, New York Graphic Society, Boston, Mass. 1975

Jackson, Donald, *The Story of Writing*, Studio Vista, London 1981

Jean, Georges, *Langage de Signes, L'Écriture et Son Double*, Gallimard, Paris 1989

Jobes, Gertrude, *Dictionary of Mythology, Folklore and Symbols*, The Scarecrow Press, New York 1962

Junge, Ewald, *World Coin Encyclopedia*, Barrie & Jenkins, London 1984

Katan, Norma Jean, *Hieroglyphs, The Writing of Ancient Egypt*, British Museum Publications, London 1987

Katzner, Kenneth, *The Languages of the World*, Routledge & Kegan Paul, London 1977

Kemp, Peter (editor), *Oxford Companion to Ships & the Sea*, Oxford University Press, 1976

Kendon, Adam, *Sign Languages of Aboriginal Australia*, Cambridge University Press, 1988

Knight's Modern Seamanship, revised by John V. Noel Jr., Van Nostrand Reinhold Company, New York 1984

Knowlson, T. Sharper, *The Origins of Popular Superstitions and Customs*, Werner Laurie, London 1930

Koch, Rudolf, *Gamle Tegn og Symboler*, Notabene, Copenhagen 1972

Kramer, Samuel Noah, *The Sumerians*, University of Chicago Press, 1963

Lehner, Ernst & Johanna, *Folklore and Symbolism of Flowers, Plants and Trees*, Tudor, New York 1960

Lehner, Ernst, *Symbols, Signs & Signets*, Dover Publications Inc, New York 1950

Lewis, John, *Printed Ephemera*, W. S. Cowell/Faber & Faber, London 1962

Linton, Ralph & Adelin, *The Lore of Birthdays*, Rider & Co., London 1953

Long, Jean, *The Art of Chinese Calligraphy*, Blandford Press, Poole, Dorset 1987

Macdonald-Taylor, Margaret (editor), *A Dictionary of Marks*, The Connoisseur, London 1976

Mendenhall, John, *British Trademarks of the 1920s & 1930s*, Angus & Robertson, London 1989

Mendenhall, John, *Character Trademarks*, Angus & Robertson, London 1991

Metford, J. C. J., *Dictionary of Christian Lore and Legend*, Thames & Hudson, London 1983

Mitchell, Stephen, & Reeds, Brian (editors), *Coins of England and the United Kingdom*, 26th ed., Seaby, London 1990

M'Millan, William, *Scottish Symbols*, Alexander Gardner, Paisley 1905

Morris, D., Collett, P., Marsh, P., & O'Shaughnessy, M., *Gestures*, Jonathan Cape, London 1979

Morris, Desmond, *Manwatching*, Jonathan Cape, London 1977

Morris, Desmond, *The Naked Ape*, Jonathan Cape, London 1967

Murphy, John, & Rowe, Michael, *How to Design Trademarks and Logos*, Phaidon, Oxford 1988

Napoles, Veronica, *Corporate Identity Design*, Van Nostrand Reinhold, New York 1988

New Groves Dictionary of Music & Musicians, Stanley Sadie (editor), Macmillan, London 1980

New Oxford History of Music, Oxford University Press 1974

Nielsen, Karl, *Bomaerker Signaler Symboler og Tegn*, Gyldendal, Copenhagen 1987

Ogg, Oscar, *The 26 Letters*, Harrap, London 1949

Opie, Iona, & Peter, *The Lore and Language of Schoolchildren*, Oxford University Press, 1959

Opie, Iona, & Peter, *The Oxford Nursery Rhyme Book*, Oxford University Press, 1955

Opie, Iona, & Tatem, Moira (editors), *Dictionary of Superstitions*, Oxford University Press, 1989

Page, R. I., *Runes*, British Museum Publications, London 1987

Painter, George D., *William Caxton, A Quincentenary Biography of England's First Printer*, Chatto & Windus, London 1976

Patterson, Richard S., & Richardson Dougall, *The Eagle and the Shield*, US Department of State, Washington 1976

Pei, Mario, *The Story of Language*, George Allen and Unwin, London 1966

Perrin, W. G., *British Flags*, Cambridge University Press 1922

Pine, L. G., *International Heraldry*, David & Charles, Newton Abbot 1970

Potter, C. F., *Funk & Wagnall's Standard Dictionary of Folklore, Mythology & Legend*, N. E. L., London 1972

Powell, Claire, *The Meaning of Flowers*, Jupiter Books, London 1977

Rechendorff, Lis, *Symboler og Tegn – Tro i Fortid*, GAD, Copenhagen 1986

Robertson, Patrick, *The Shell Book of Firsts*, Ebury Press & Michael Joseph, London 1975

Robinson, L. J., *A Dictionary of Graphical Symbols*, F C Avis, London 1972

Rolo, Charles J., *Radio Goes to War*, Putnam's, New York 1942

Room, Adrian, *Dictionary of Astronomical Names*, Routledge, London 1988

Room, Adrian, *Dictionary of Changes in Meaning*, Routledge & Kegan Paul, London 1986

Room, Adrian, *Dictionary of Trade Name Origins*, Routledge & Kegan Paul, London 1982

Room, Adrian, *The Guinness Book of Numbers*, Guinness Publishing, Enfield 1989

Roth, Laszlo, *Display Design*, Prentice-Hall, New Jersey 1983

Rowland, Beryl, *Animals with Human Faces*, George Allen & Unwin, London 1974

Ryan, Joseph P., *Design of Warning Labels and Instructions*, Van Nostrand Reinhold, New York 1991

Seton, Ernest Thompson, *Sign Talk*, Doubleday, Page & Company, New York 1918

Shepherd, Walter, *Shepherd's Glossary of Graphic Signs and Symbols*, J. M. Dent, London 1971

Smeltzer, Donald, *Man and Number*, A. and C. Black, London 1970

Stafford, Maureen, & Ware, Dora, *An Illustrated Dictionary of Ornament*, George Allen & Unwin, London 1974

Stearn, William T., *Botanical Latin*, David & Charles, Newton Abbot 1966

Stiling, Marjorie, *Famous Brand Names, Emblems & Trademarks*, David & Charles, Newton Abbot 1980

Summers, Peter, *How to Read a Coat of Arms*, Alphabooks, Sherborne, Dorset 1986

Tallman, Marjorie, *Dictionary of American Folklore*, Philosophical Library, New York 1959

Terrell, John Upton, *American Indian Almanac*, World Publishing Company, New York 1971

The Third Cuckoo, More classic letters to The Times 1900–1985, chosen by Kenneth Gregory, George Allen & Unwin, London 1985

Urdang, Laurence (editor), *Dictionary of Advertising Terms*, Crain Books, Chicago 1980

Vervliet, H. D. L. (editor), *The Book Through 5000 Years*, Phaidon, London 1972

Vince, John, *Fire-marks*, Shire Publications, Aylesbury, Bucks 1973

von Volborth, Carl Alexander, *The Art of Heraldry*, Blandford Press 1987

von Volborth, Carl Alexander, *Heraldry of the World*, Blandford Press 1973

Walters, Derek, *Chinese Astrology*, Aquarian Press, Wellingborough 1987

White, T. H., *The Book of Beasts*, Jonathan Cape, London 1954

Whittick, Arnold, *Symbols Signs and their Meaning*, Leonard Hill, London 1960

Wildbur, Peter, *International Trademark Design*, Barrie & Jenkins, London 1979

Wilson, Geoffrey, *The Old Telegraphs*, Phillimore & Co, Chichester 1976

Wilson, Timothy, *Flags at Sea*, HMSO, London 1986

Woodcock, Thomas, & Robinson, John Martin, *The Oxford Guide to Heraldry*, Oxford University Press 1988

Yapp, Peter (editor), *The Travellers' Dictionary of Quotations*, Routledge & Kegan Paul, London 1983

Yearout, Floyd (editor), *Heraldry – Sources, Symbols, and Meaning*, Macdonald and Jane's, London 1977

Index

Page numbers in *italics* refer to
illustrations